WESTERN EUROPE'S DEMOCRATIC AGE

Western Europe's Democratic Age

1945–1968

Martin Conway

PRINCETON UNIVERSITY PRESS

PRINCETON & OXFORD

Published by Princeton University Press
41 William Street, Princeton, New Jersey 08540
6 Oxford Street, Woodstock, Oxfordshire OX20 1TR

press.princeton.edu

ISBN 978-0-691-20348-5
ISBN (e-book) 978-0-691-20460-4

British Library Cataloguing-in-Publication Data is available

Editorial: Ben Tate and Josh Drake
Production Editorial: Jenny Wolkowicki
Jacket design: Carmina Alvarez
Production: Jacqueline Poirier
Publicity: Katie Lewis and Alyssa Sanford
Copyeditor: Maia Vaswani

Jacket photo: © Studio Patellani / CORBIS / Corbis via Getty Images

This book has been composed in Miller

Printed on acid-free paper. ∞

Printed in the United States of America

10 9 8 7 6 5 4 3 2 1

CONTENTS

ILLUSTRATIONS

A BOOK ON the modern history of democracy in Europe does, I suspect, require little justification. Over the years I have been researching and writing about democracy in twentieth-century Europe, I have become conscious of how the past has been increasingly invaded by the present. What began as a historical act of reconstruction has become enmeshed in recent years in the fierce debates about democracy that have come to the fore in Europe as a whole, and within its national and local cultures. This book will, I hope, be a contribution to those wider discussions. But it studies democracy primarily through the prism of history. It is not an attempt to explain the present through the past, and it avoids present-minded concepts of the crisis of democracy or its impending demise. Instead, I hope that the book demonstrates how democracy became a deeply embedded element of Western Europe's political and social cultures in the decades after 1945. Democracy was not just a political regime. It became part of Europe's identity, and how post-war generations of Europeans defined who they were, and how they lived their lives. Democracy does of course have to change to adapt to changes in society and in political aspirations; and the latter chapters of this book attempt to explain how dissatisfaction with the existing models of democracy developed in Europe from the 1960s onwards, and have contributed to the present-day sense of crisis.

This is emphatically a European book: in terms of its subject matter, the sources on which it draws, the various locations where it was written, and above all the people who have assisted me along the way. Contemporary European history is a collaborative exercise, and I have long felt myself to be very fortunate in the ways that I have benefited from discussions with colleagues across Europe. During the preparation of this book, I have been especially grateful for the advice, friendship, guidance, and innumerable other forms of assistance I have received from Christian Bailey, Tom Buchanan, Camilo Erlichman, Robert Gerwarth, John-Paul Ghobrial, José Gotovitch, John Horne, Pieter Lagrou, Colin Lucas, Jim McMillan, Jeppe Nevers, Phil Nord, Kiran Patel, Alex Paulin-Booth, Johanna Rainio, Peter Romijn, Alexis Schwarzenbach, and Mary Vincent. In addition, I am indebted to a number of long-standing friends whose support I value greatly; notably, Henrietta Foster, David Grogan, Mario Nehrlich, and Lut Van Daele. Family is of course the network through which we most readily access the recent past. As mischance would have it, almost all of those who surrounded me during my early life died within a short period of time while I was writing this book. They were all in their different ways witnesses to Europe's Democratic Age, and I would like to acknowledge the enduring influence of my parents Joan and Steve Conway, my aunt Joan Meadows, my uncles Vivian and George Conway, my godfather Bill Blake, and my cousin Susan Conway.

I am indebted to my colleagues and students in Balliol College and the History Faculty in Oxford, who have provided many different forms of assistance and, most importantly, have provided me with the stimulus of participating in a scholarly community of teaching and research. I am also one of very many who have been fortunate to benefit from the unfailing professionalism of Isabel Holowaty and her colleagues in the Bodleian Library in Oxford. Much of this book was written in Combe in West Oxfordshire, and I am indebted to a number of neighbours and friends—especially David Cotterill, Elizabeth Davies, Chris McGrath, Christopher Williamson, and Jo Willis-Bund—for their encouragement and company. Other sections of the book were written, and much of the thinking about it was undertaken, in Isenay, a small village in the Nièvre in central France. I am especially grateful for the support and friendship there of Philippe and Anne-Marie Lafaye, and Daniel and Marie-Claire Kieffer, along with many others.

I am most grateful to Ben Tate and his colleagues at Princeton University Press for their professional assistance and support in bringing this book to publication. During the production of the book, I have been particularly indebted to the skills of Maia Vaswani for her expert copyediting of the text.

My greatest debt, as always, is to Nick Conway and Denise Cripps. It is conventional to apologise for the way in which writing a book has distracted an author from family and other responsibilities. But I think that the experience of researching and writing this book, the time we have spent together, and the discussions it has prompted, has had the opposite consequence. This is a book which has benefited immeasurably from them; and in return it is dedicated to them.

ABBREVIATIONS

CCF Congress for Cultural Freedom

CDU Christlich Demokratische Union

CIA Central Intelligence Agency

CLNAI Comitato di Liberazione Nazionale Alta Italia

CNR Conseil national de la Résistance

CVP-PSC Christelijke Volkspartij–Parti Social Chrétien

DC Democrazia Cristiana

DPS displaced persons

ECSC European Coal and Steel Community

EEC European Economic Community

ERP European Recovery Program

ESC Economic and Social Council

FLN Front de libération nationale

FPÖ Freiheitliche Partei Österreichs

GDP Gross Domestic Product

ILO International Labour Organization

KPÖ Kommunistische Partei Österreichs

MRP Mouvement républicain populaire

NATO North Atlantic Treaty Organization

NGO Non-Governmental Organization

NSDAP Nationalsozialistische Deutsche Arbeiterpartei

ÖVP Österreichische Volkspartei

PCE Partido Comunista de España

PCF Parti communiste français

PCI Partito Comunista Italiano

PSB Parti socialiste belge

PSC Parti social chrétien

PSI Partito Socialista Italiano

PSOE Partido Socialista Obrero Español

PSLI Partito Socialista dei Lavoratori Italiani

RPF Rassemblement du peuple français

SAP Sveriges socialdemokratiska arbetareparti

SFIO Section française de l'Internationale ouvrière

SPD Sozialdemokratische Partei Deutschlands

SPÖ Sozialdemokratische Partei Österreichs

UDCA Union de défense des commerçants et artisans

UFF Union et fraternité française

UNESCO United Nations Educational, Scientific,
and Cultural Organization

UNR Union pour la Nouvelle République

WESTERN EUROPE'S DEMOCRATIC AGE

A Democratic Age

SPEAKING AT THE CONFERENCE held by the Congress of Cultural Freedom in West Berlin in June 1960, the highly influential French political
philosopher Raymond Aron (1905–83) reflected on the democratic stabilization that he believed had occurred in Europe, west of the Iron Curtain,
since the Second World War.[1] Compared with the destructive struggles
of ideology, class, and ethnicity that had marked the first half of the twentieth century in Europe, Aron argued that a new form of industrial society
had emerged in the fifteen years since the war, characterized by representative democratic institutions and guarantees of personal freedom.
Stability was not, of course, guaranteed. As he readily admitted, the recent
collapse of the Fourth Republic in France in 1958, and its replacement by
the presidential Fifth Republic headed by Charles de Gaulle, demonstrated
that there was no determinism to the process whereby socio-economic
modernization led to political stability. And yet what Aron termed the
démocraties stabilisées or *pacifiées* that had taken root in Western Europe
since the Second World War were more than the by-product of the political
immobilism imposed on Europe, west and east, by the Cold War. In Aron's
view, they marked the coming of age of a new model of Western European
government and society, which had not so much resolved the divisions of
the past as rendered them obsolete through a combination of economic
prosperity, effective governmental action, and social compromise. Just as
nobody would seriously imagine a renewed Franco-German war, so the

1. Raymond Aron, "Les institutions politiques de l'occident dans le monde du XXe
siècle," in *La démocratie à l'épreuve du XXe siècle*, by Aron, A. Schlesinger, G. Arciniegas,
A. K. Brohi, M. Berger and F. Bondy (Paris, 1960), 11–15.

political conflicts between the extremes of communism and fascism had been transcended by a hegemonic democracy. Given the broad agreement that he believed now existed regarding the essential nature of the political system, Aron argued that debate within the Western democracies had shifted to essentially secondary issues, such as the role the state should assume in economic policy-making, and the relative priorities to accord to goals of equality and liberty.[2]

The location, the event, the date, and the individual are all essential elements for understanding Aron's thesis of the democratic stabilization of Western Europe. Nowhere in Europe were the shadows of the Second World War and of the Cold War more present than in the western half of the divided former capital of Germany. West Berlin had become during the Soviet-imposed blockade of 1948 an exceptional place, where the ruins of the capital of Hitler's Third Reich and the present-day reality of the Cold War partition of Europe—as expressed by Berlin's four zones of Allied military occupation—appeared to be projected, as it were, on to the topography of the city.[3] West Berlin became, in the loaded language of the time, an outpost of freedom, juxtaposed starkly against the Soviet military occupation of eastern Germany and the institutions of the Communist German Democratic Republic established in East Berlin from 1949. During the 1950s, the Cold War tensions had receded somewhat from Berlin, but they would return suddenly and dramatically a year after Aron's speech, when in August 1961 the Soviet and East German authorities abruptly ended free passage between the Soviet-controlled east of the city and the three zones of West Berlin. The Berlin Wall, which divided East and West Berlin in the most stark manner possible, rapidly became both the dominant physical symbol of the Cold War partition of Europe, and, during the tense military and diplomatic stand-off that followed its construction, the most likely stimulus to full-scale conflict between the opposing camps.[4] Appearance did not entirely match reality. Whatever the fears of a military confrontation between the Soviet and American forces based in the city, the closing off of the porous frontier between the Soviet-controlled sector of Berlin and the west of the city removed an anomaly and contributed to the pervasive stabilization that characterized the Cold

2. Raymond Aron, "Institutions politiques de l'occident," 11–42. See also his very similar argument in "La société industrielle et les dialogues politiques de l'occident," in *Colloques de Rheinfelden*, by Aron, G. Kennan, and R. Oppenheimer (Paris, 1960), 9–38.

3. J. Evans, *Life among the Ruins: Cityscape and Sexuality in Cold War Berlin* (Basingstoke, UK, 2011).

4. P. Ahonen, *Death at the Berlin Wall* (Oxford, 2011).

War within Europe during the 1960s.[5] In the context of the time, however, the crisis of 1961 gave new force to the image of Berlin as the preeminent Cold War city: the place where east and west, and more especially the political and cultural systems that they represented, confronted each other with implacable directness.[6]

It was therefore no accident that West Berlin was chosen by the Congress for Cultural Freedom (CCF) as the location of its 1960 conference. The CCF established itself as the quintessential institution of Cold War liberalism.[7] Its inaugural conference had also been held in the city at the post-war peak of the Cold War in June 1950, assembling an eclectic array of prominent western intellectuals in defence of the values of cultural and intellectual freedom and to protest against the oppression of artists, writers, and scientists in Soviet-controlled Central and Eastern Europe. Funded from the outset by the CIA through a variety of front organisations, the CCF was one of the key institutions of an American cultural diplomacy that sought to assert the values of individual liberty as a means of countering the appeal exercised by Communism in the immediate post-war years over many western intellectuals. Yet, though its propagandistic purposes always remained close to the surface, the success of the CCF's initial conference, as well as the broader progression of the Cold War, led to an evolution in the purposes and character of the Congress. The emergency atmosphere of the early years—rallying all like-minded intellectuals in the defence of freedom—gave way to a broader role for the CCF as a forum for an influential phalanx of predominantly liberal American and European intellectuals concerned as much with analysing the nature of contemporary western society as with denouncing the horrors of the totalitarian east. The CCF established its headquarters in Paris and with the help of its American backers funded a number of high-profile intellectual

5. L. Freedman, "Berlin and the Cold War," in *The Berlin Wall Crisis: Perspectives on Cold War Alliances*, ed. J.P.S. Gearson and K. Schake (Basingstoke, UK, 2002), 1–9.

6. P. Steege, *Black Market, Cold War: Everyday Life in Berlin, 1946–1949* (Cambridge, UK, 2007), 8.

7. The CCF has generated a substantial historical literature. See notably P. Grémion, *Intelligence de l'anticommunisme: Le Congrès pour la liberté de la culture à Paris, 1950–1975* (Paris, 1995); P. Coleman, *The Liberal Conspiracy: The Congress for Cultural Freedom and the Struggle for the Mind of Postwar Europe* (New York, 1989); F. S. Saunders, *Who Paid the Piper?: The CIA and the Cultural Cold War* (London, 1999); G. Scott-Smith, "The 'Masterpieces of the Twentieth Century' Festival and the Congress for Cultural Freedom: Origins and Consolidation, 1947–52," *Intelligence and National Security* 15 (2000): 121–43, and "The Congress for Cultural Freedom: Constructing an Intellectual Atlantic Community," in *Defining the Atlantic Community: Culture, Intellectuals and Politics in the Mid-Twentieth Century*, ed. M. Mariano (New York, 2010), 132–45.

magazines as well as organizing cultural festivals and conferences during the 1950s.

The most significant of these was the conference that it held in Milan in 1955. Entitled "The Future of Freedom," this event—in the organisation of which Aron played a leading role—reflected strongly the new orientation of the Congress. Almost dismissive of the challenge presented by the post-Stalinist Soviet Union, it looked rigorously to the future, analysing how technological developments, socio-economic modernization, and the rapid growth in industrial productivity were generating a new form of society in which conflicts of ideology would be replaced by issues of economic policy and social planning. The seductive thesis of "an end of ideology," advanced by the American liberal intellectual Daniel Bell in his book of the same name, published in 1960 and derived in part from his presentation to the Milan conference, caught the intellectual mood of the resurgent liberalism of the later 1950s. The notion of ideologies as self-contained world views based on abstract principles appeared at odds with the realities of the new world generated by the economic growth of the post-war era, which was almost literally concreting over the legacies of Europe's traumatic past. These ideas, somewhat simplified from Bell's formulation of them, became the leitmotif of the CCF's activities and provided an obvious theme for the Congress's next major conference, held in West Berlin in 1960.[8]

This Berlin conference marked the apogee of the Congress's influence. Compared with the similar event the CCF had held in the city ten years earlier, its tone was self-consciously superior, even celebratory. The CCF was now a well-established and prestigious organization, and the conference was attended by 213 participants from across the globe, including an impressive range of European intellectuals.[9] The host city had changed too: while the West Berlin of 1950 had been tangibly dominated by the ruined buildings of its wartime destruction, and by the material hardships

8. D. Bell, *The End of Ideology: On the Exhaustion of Political Ideas in the Fifties* (Glencoe, IL, 1960). See also Bell's retrospective comments (dedicated to the memory of Aron) on the publication of his book and its origins in the Milan conference in D. Bell, "The End of Ideology Revisited," *Government and Opposition* 23 (1988): 134, as well as G. Scott-Smith, "The Congress for Cultural Freedom, the End of Ideology and the 1955 Milan Conference: 'Defining the Parameters of Discourse,'" *Journal of Contemporary History* 37 (2002): 437–55, and T. B. Müller, *Krieger und Gelehrte: Herbert Marcuse und die Denksysteme im Kalten Krieg* (Hamburg, 2010), 567–76.

9. Grémion, *Intelligence de l'anticommunisme*, 379–80. M. Hochgeschwender *Freiheit in der Offensive?: Der Kongress für kulturelle Freiheit und die Deutschen* (Munich, 1998), 528–34, gives a figure of 221 participants from 48 countries.

exacerbated by the blockade imposed by the surrounding Soviet forces, the West Berlin of 1960 was a very different city. The ruins that remained had now become symbolic relics of the city's past, while the modernist architecture of its reconstruction expressed the prosperity and increasing self-confidence of the Federal Republic. West Berlin was no longer a beleaguered outpost but a "showcase of the west," as personified by the city's vivid cultural life and cosmopolitan character.[10] Its mood was personified too by the city's highly visible young mayor, Willy Brandt, whose election in 1957 had symbolized the victory of a self-consciously modernizing tendency within the German Socialist Party, the SPD. Strongly if discreetly supported by the American authorities, Brandt saw himself as a symbol of the new progressive mood in German politics, focused more on the challenges of creating a prosperous future than on loyalty to the Marxist heritage of the SPD. Brandt addressed the CCF conference, expounding his social-democratic politics of social reform, support for liberal freedoms, and marked anti-communism.[11]

Above all, the political context had changed. Given the brutal suppression by Soviet forces of the uprising against Communist rule in Hungary in 1956 and the daily stream of citizens choosing to leave East Germany through the open door of Berlin to move to West Germany, the urgency of countering the appeal of Communism had receded. Instead, Aron's speech gave rise to a wide-ranging debate among the participants about the evolution of western society. Not all agreed with Aron's analysis; and the declaration issued by the Congress in Berlin was notable for the way in which it looked outside of the ideological frontiers of Europe. It paid as much attention to deploring attacks on freedom in Castro's Cuba and apartheid South Africa as it did to the more familiar cause of the persecuted intellectuals in the totalitarian states of the east.[12]

The timing of Aron's speech was therefore also very important. Though he was unaware of it, 1960 marked a point of transition from a European-oriented definition of democratic politics to the more globalized forms of

10. P. Broadbent and S. Hake, eds., *Berlin: Divided City, 1945–1989* (New York, 2010), 113; C. Mesch, *Modern Art at the Berlin Wall: Demarcating Culture in the Cold War Germanys* (London, 2008), 36–48.

11. B. Marshall, *Willy Brandt* (London, 1990), 31–42; S. Krause "*Neue Westpolitik*: The Clandestine Campaign to Westernize the SPD in Cold War Berlin, 1948–1958," *Central European History* 48 (2015): 79–99.

12. Grémion, *Intelligence de l'anticommunisme*, 381–87. The texts of the papers given at the conference in the session based around Aron's speech were republished, in German translation, in Kongress für kulturelle Freiheit, *Die Bewährung der Demokratie im 20. Jahrhundert: Das Seminar von Berlin* (Zurich, 1961).

democracy that emerged over the subsequent decade. Moreover, what seemed at the time to be the almost miraculous process whereby Europe had escaped from cycles of military warfare, economic instability, and political conflict to enter a new era of prosperity and peace was to prove to be merely a brief interlude in Europe's continuing conflicts. If Western Europe was enjoying a democratic peace in 1960, this was a peace achieved at the expense of the denial of those same democratic freedoms to the populations of the post-fascist dictatorships of Spain and Portugal and the Soviet-controlled states of Central and Eastern Europe, as well as those who remained the disenfranchised subjects of Europe's colonial empires. And yet, even as Aron was speaking in Berlin, violent events elsewhere in Algeria, Congo, and many of the colonial territories in between presaged the impending demise of those empires, and with them of the Eurocentric structures of power—military, economic, political, and cultural—that had provided the basis of modern Europe's global ascendancy. Moreover, though the Soviet Union of Khrushchev no longer inspired the same fears within Europe as had that of Stalin ten years earlier, Communism was far from being a spent force. The success of Communist revolutions in China in 1949 and, over the subsequent years, in Indochina, Cuba, and many other areas of the non-European world effectively destroyed any prospect of a global hegemony of western democratic values, and gave a new and unpredictable energy to the political conflicts of the 1960s and 1970s in the post-colonial world.

Even within the walled garden of post-war Western Europe, the muffled conflicts of ethnicity, gender, and social class that had been apparent to those who chose to listen to them in the 1950s would give way within a few short years to the much more contested politics of the later 1960s. From the protest marches on the streets of Paris and many other major European cities (including West Berlin) to the civil-rights campaigns in Northern Ireland and numerous strikes and factory occupations of the 1960s and early 1970s, Western Europe would return all too rapidly to many of its old habits of ideological conflict, state repression, and social and political violence that Aron had regarded as having been vanquished in 1960. The CCF itself was one of the first victims of these changes. The public revelation of its CIA funding in 1966–67 led to a rapid decline in the Congress's public influence, and within a few years to its liquidation. In truth, the Congress had by the end of the 1960s outlived its intellectual heyday. The combination of anti-communism, liberalism, and social-democratic planning that had provided the oxygen of its intellectual development during the 1950s appeared outmoded in the much more polarized intellectual climate of the subsequent decade, in which the emergence of an anti-American

New Left and a much more individualist neoliberalism of the right eroded the consensus that the post-ideological CCF had proclaimed.[13] Aron, too, was obliged to accept that times had changed. In a much less confident book entitled *Plaidoyer pour l'Europe décadente*, which he published in 1977, Aron admitted, in a tone that was part defiant and part reflective, that many of his predictions of 1960 had proved to be misplaced. Though he remained convinced more than ever of the superiority of liberal freedom over the state socialism of the USSR and of Communism's western fellow travellers, he feared that the resurgence of social and political conflict in Western Europe marked a return to the violence that he had witnessed as a young man in Germany. Moreover, he warned that what he regarded as the abandonment by many intellectuals of liberal values might lead to a wider "loss of legitimacy" on the part of the democratic regimes.[14]

Thus, viewed even through the prism of his own hindsight, Aron's comments in 1960 must inevitably appear inadequate, if not wilfully complacent. His perspective was that of a privileged French intellectual, deeply rooted in the anti-communist mentalities and networks of the era, who passed over in silence the manifold inequalities of class, race, and gender that disfigured the democracies of Western Europe. Indeed, his statement that Europe had arrived at some form of political and social consensus rested on a disregard not only for the millions of Western Europeans who continued to vote for Communist parties, but also for the many millions more who, through unemployment, economic migration, and the structural inequalities that limited access to housing, education, and welfare, were experiencing the costs of Western Europe's supposed "miracle years."[15] Europe did not become a democratic society in or after 1945, and Aron's perspective, like that of many subsequent historians, was based far too exclusively on the experiences of a white, educated bourgeoisie who were the principal beneficiaries of post-war economic and social change. In more strictly political terms too, Aron's central assumption that the political regimes of Western Europe were indeed democratic must be relativized. The democratic refounding of Europe in 1945 did bring an unprecedented stability and uniformity to the politics of the western half of the continent. But the democracy it inaugurated was always circumscribed by

---

13. Hochgeschwender, *Freiheit in der Offensive?*, 535–47; Coleman, *Liberal Conspiracy*, 219–34.

14. Raymond Aron, *Plaidoyer pour l'Europe décadente* (Paris, 1977), 13–29. See also p. 297.

15. The concept of the "miracle years" owes much to H. Schissler, ed., *The Miracle Years: A Cultural History of West Germany, 1949–1968* (Princeton, NJ, 2001).

the stability it sought to achieve and the interests it was constructed to serve. By creating a top-down democratic order that eschewed the governmental weakness and parliamentary instability associated with Europe's previous experiments with democracy, the architects of post-1945 European democracy limited opportunities for popular control of rulers and for expressions of dissent at the same time as they enhanced the freedom of action of state officials. The consequence, as its critics in 1968 would declare, was a "formal democracy," founded on the regular rituals of parliamentary elections and negotiation with a range of interest groups, but from which the people, and something of the noise and vibrancy inherent to a pluralist democratic culture, was at times strangely absent.[16]

This does not mean that Aron's comments in 1960 were without value. He was of course not the only figure in the twentieth century to have declared that the conflicts of the past had given way to a new era of harmony.[17] His view, moreover, was shared at the time by many others, from a wide diversity of backgrounds and opinions, who felt that Europe had passed over a watershed of experience after 1945 that rendered many of the errors of past dreams newly visible and invested the democratic process with a new sobriety.[18] Aron, besides, was no apologist for the established order. During his long intellectual career from the 1930s to the 1980s, he acquired a distinguished reputation within France and beyond, both as a public intellectual and as the author of important works of political philosophy and sociology. Above all, he worked hard. He had a deep familiarity with Marx's ideas at a time when many preferred to feign such a knowledge. He was highly cosmopolitan, and had read the work of many German, English, and American intellectuals when many of his fellow Parisian intellectuals remained confined within their exclusively francophone intellectual culture. And, in an age of humanist generalization, he recognized that an understanding of contemporary society demanded a training in economic theory and quantitative sociological methods. His wide-ranging expertise led him to be occasionally trenchant in his criticism of those intellectuals, such as his nemesis and exact contemporary Jean-Paul Sartre, whom he regarded as motivated more by romantic dreams than by careful

16. Re. "formal democracy," see pp. 272–73.

17. The obvious comparison is with Francis Fukuyama's essay, initially published in the immediate aftermath of the revolutions of 1989, *The End of History and the Last Man* (London, 1992). But one might equally well think of the Bolshevik seizure of power in 1917: J. Bergman, *The French Revolutionary Tradition in Russian and Soviet Politics, Political Thought, and Culture* (Oxford, 2019).

18. V. Depkat, *Lebenswenden und Zeitenwenden: Deutsche Politiker und die Erfahrungen des 20. Jahrhunderts* (Munich, 2007).

analysis. But he was similarly forceful in his attitude towards successive French governments, notably in his denunciation of the purposes and conduct of the Algerian War, and of the policies of de Gaulle.

Aron readily acknowledged, too, the flaws of modern democratic structures, commenting on one occasion that "Modern society . . . is a democratic society to be observed without transports of enthusiasm or indignation."[19] Indeed, it was this relativism that, in the view of his most enthusiastic recent disciple, Tony Judt, made him such a distinctive figure. Politics, Aron insisted, required facing up to hard truths; it "is never a conflict between good and evil, but always a choice between the preferable and the detestable."[20] If this led him on occasions, as during the upheavals in Paris in May 1968, to side with the established order, it gave him the courage also to stand up to authority when it made the wrong choices. Above all, he presented himself as a self-consciously moderate pragmatist, in the tradition of de Tocqueville. At a time when many European intellectuals were certain most of all of the rectitude of their views, Aron preferred to be right about his facts. His preoccupation with empirical knowledge and with what Judt termed the "uncomfortable minutiae of political and economic reality" was also redolent of the empirical mentality of the post-war years, when ideological rhetoric was giving way to a cult of the objective (and preferably statistical) fact.[21] But it also gave Aron's work a seriousness and a durability denied to those of many of his contemporaries. His concept of the modern industrial society was, again, very much a product of its time, reflective of the assumptions of an era when all societies, regardless of their cultural heritage or political label, appeared to be converging towards a common model of modernity. But, whatever its undoubted limitations, it marked the emergence of a new spirit of social analysis that sought to investigate the internal fabric of societies. Aron was, by general reputation, a cold writer; and for him that was also a form of praise.[22] He saw himself as a *spectateur engagé*, whose self-conscious distancing from the passions of the moment did not disguise his firm but disabused support for pluralist and democratic values. Like

19. Quoted in T. Judt, *The Burden of Responsibility: Blum, Camus, Aron and the French Twentieth Century* (Chicago, 1998), 163.

20. Quoted in A. Craiutu, "Thinking Politically: Raymond Aron and the Revolution of 1968 in France," in *Promises of 1968: Crisis, Illusion, and Utopia*, ed. V. Tismaneanu (Budapest, 2011), 126–29. Aron's emphasis on realism was particularly apparent in his comments on the French war in Algeria: Raymond Aron, *La tragédie algérienne* (Paris, 1957), i–iii.

21. Judt, *Burden of Responsibility*, 26. See also A. Craiutu, "Raymond Aron and the Tradition of Political Moderation in France," in *French Liberalism from Montesquieu to the Present Day*, ed. R. Geenens and H. Rosenblatt (Cambridge, UK, 2012), 271–90.

22. N. Roussellier, "Raymond Aron," in *Dictionnaire des intellectuels français*, ed. J. Julliard and M. Winock (Paris, 1996), 85–87.

FIGURE 1. Raymond Aron circa 1960. Jean-Louis
Swiners/Gamma-Rapho via Getty Images

many others—perhaps most notably Henry Kissinger—who shared his Jewish background and who had lived through the upheavals of the 1930s and the war years, Aron was always aware that worse regimes than democracy existed; but he was also unconvinced that any better regime was possible.[23]

This book is therefore intended as an attempt to take seriously Aron's thesis of a democratic stabilization of Western Europe by exploring the

23. Re. Aron, see notably Judt, *Burden of Responsibility*, 137–82, and B. Anderson, *Raymond Aron: The Recovery of the Political* (Lanham, MD, 1997), as well as his substantial but personally unrevealing memoirs: Raymond Aron, *Mémoires: Cinquante ans de réflexion politique* (Paris, 1983). Re. Kissinger, see J. Suri, *Henry Kissinger and the American Century* (Cambridge, MA, 2007), esp. 16–51.

nature and development of democracy, as well as its limitations, in Europe between the end of the Second World War and the political and social upheavals of the later 1960s and early 1970s. The stability and uniformity of the regimes of parliamentary democracy that established themselves across the western half of Europe after 1945, from Norway to Sicily, were a remarkable phenomenon, and all the more so given the chaotic instability of political regimes that had been evident in many areas of Europe since the First World War. In that respect, 1945 was the moment when the music stopped, and Western Europe acquired a certain stability, and even predictability. The linked chain of elections, parliaments, and governments established itself with such emphasis after the Second World War that any alternative, especially one that stepped outside the conventions of parliamentary democracy, came to seem to almost all non-Communist political figures of the post-war era heretical, or indeed illegitimate. As a parliamentary commission set up during one of Belgium's many post-war governmental crises commented succinctly in 1945, "outside of democracy, there lie only adventures, miseries, and dangers" (hors de la démocratie parlementaire, il n'est qu'aventures, misères et périls).[24]

This comment, on the part of a committee composed of parliamentarians, was self-interested, but the attitude it expressed was one with which many would have come to concur. Important sources of conflict remained, most notably across the durable fault line between Christian and liberal or socialist conceptions of democracy. But Western European politics did converge during the post-war years on a particular way of doing democracy: national and local elections, conducted under a simple principle of one (male and female) citizen one vote, chose the people's representatives, who, assembled in the parliaments and council chambers of Europe, voted on projects of legislation proposed by governments composed of the elected representatives of one, or generally more, political parties. Alongside this electoral sovereignty, however, the increasingly complex dossiers of social and economic legislation obliged governments to work with, and in some cases to devolve responsibility to, a range of socio-economic interest groups, including trade unions and farmers' and employers' organizations. Democracy, consequently, became less a matter of victory or defeat than a process of continuous negotiation. Civil servants, elected politicians, the representatives of interest groups, and an

24. Chambre des représentants, "Rapport au nom de la commission" [March 1945], cited in M. Conway, *The Sorrows of Belgium: Liberation and Political Reconstruction 1944–47* (Oxford, 2012), 251.

expanding penumbra of expert advisors constituted an increasingly homogeneous if at times rather aloof culture of government, from which the people themselves were largely absent. It was also, however, a world where decisions accorded, more often than not, with the logics of a rational pragmatism, and with the constraints imposed by respect for the rule of law. Compared with the rowdy assemblies of the past, democracy had become more professional and also more serious.

This was also a model of democracy that endured. In the roughly twenty-five-year period from 1945 to the upheavals of the late 1960s and 1970s, the only changes of regime that occurred in Europe were the demise of the Fourth Republic in France in 1958 and the military coup that overthrew the Greek parliamentary regime in 1967, before being reversed in 1974. Neither, however, generated a durable alternative to the political status quo in Europe, which increasingly found its transnational expression in the consolidation and subsequent expansion of the institutions of European cooperation and integration. Notions of a "consensual democracy"—consensual in its principles as well as in its methods of decision-making—became increasingly current by the 1960s, reflecting the widespread sense that Western Europe had arrived at a fixed definition of its political identity.[25] This consensus was, of course, always more limited than it appeared. But the very fact that such a phrase could be used demonstrated how much had changed in Europe since the Second World War: democracy was something on which the people of Western Europe felt themselves to be largely agreed.[26]

The rather sudden transition of mid-twentieth-century Western Europe to this democratic age has seemed so obvious that it has, at least until recently, evaded substantial historical analysis.[27] In part, the reasons for this relative neglect lie in the politics of more recent decades. The twofold reshaping of European politics that followed the regime changes in central and eastern Europe in 1989 and the attacks by Islamic militants on the United States in 2001 and associated acts of violence that occurred in a number of European cities over the following years gave a new intensity to the association of Europe and democracy. This was evident in the

25. N. Elder, A. H. Thomas, and D. Arter, *The Consensual Democracies?: The Government and Politics of the Scandinavian States*, rev. ed. (Oxford, 1988), 9–28.

26. C. Maier, "Democracy since the French Revolution," in *Democracy: The Unfinished Journey 508 BC to AD 1993*, ed. J. Dunn (Oxford, 1993), 145; P. Buton, *Une histoire intellectuelle de la démocratie* (Paris, 2000), 143.

27. M. Conway, "The Rise and Fall of Western Europe's Democratic Age, 1945–1973," *Contemporary European History* 13 (2004): 67–88.

celebration of the "return" of the hitherto Soviet-controlled territories to Europe and to democracy after 1989, as well as in the democratic legitimation that underpinned the projection of European power (albeit under an American logistical and diplomatic aegis) to the former Yugoslavia, Iraq, Afghanistan, Libya, and the other European frontier wars of the early twenty-first century. It has been reinforced too by the internal politics of Europe. The popular disaffection that has enveloped in recent years the project of European unity, the emergence of movements of right-wing populism hostile to a political elite perceived to be too remote from the real concerns of the people, and the politics of austerity provoked by the monetary crisis of the euro have all, in different ways, provoked a diffuse but wide-ranging debate about the shortcomings of Europe's democratic culture. In this way, 1945 has become one of the mythic foundations of the European present: a moment when Europe incontestably made a change for the better, and when the causes of democracy, of Europe, and of social progress were for once aligned.[28]

By linking 1945 with the politics of the present day, this interpretation has acted as an obstacle to historical understandings of the era that followed the Second World War. Far from receding further away—and soon beyond the memory of living Europeans—the establishment of democratic institutions in the states of Western Europe after 1945 has become part of a continuous present. The shortcomings of such an account—most obviously its marked western bias—matter less than the way in which it has tended to deprive Europe's mid-century reconstruction of its distinctiveness as a period of complex historical change. The perception that—in the phraseology of numerous university courses and associated textbooks—"Europe since 1945" forms part of a single historical span, linking the Europe of the twenty-first century with the immediate aftermath of the demise of the Third Reich, imposes a teleological framework and flattens historical perspectives.[29] Above all, it renders too easy the transition from fascism to democracy. The possibility that anything other than parliamentary democracy—communism, a resurgence of fascism, authoritarian dictatorship, or simply political chaos—could have followed the death of Hitler disappears all too rapidly from view.

28. C. Crouch, *Post-Democracy* (Cambridge, UK, 2004), 6–8.

29. Re. the use of the formula "Europe since 1945," or its equivalents, see notably W. Laqueur, *Europe since Hitler* (London, 1970); M. Fulbrook, ed., *Europe since 1945* (Oxford, 2001); and R. Wegs and R. Ladrech, *Europe since 1945*, 4th ed. (New York, 1996). For a valuable corrective to these teleologies, see T. Buchanan, *Europe's Troubled Peace: 1945 to the Present*, 2nd ed. (Chichester, UK, 2012).

This perception of 1945 as a fixed frontier, when a certain history ended and the Europe of the present began, has been reinforced, too, from the other end, by the imposing energy with which European historians have addressed the causes and character of the exterminations, atrocities, mass violence, and civil wars that swept across Europe, partly under Nazi control but also at times entirely beyond it, during the 1930s and early 1940s. The much more sophisticated interpretation that this historical work has generated of what it has become conventional in France to term the *années noires* has had the consequence of contrasting, implicitly or explicitly, the collective violence of the years leading up to 1945 with the more peaceful and democratic character of the era that followed.[30] The more that historians have explored the horrors of the pre-1945 period, the more they risk reducing what happened in Europe subsequently to a contrast between the wartime panoramas of death camps and ruins, and the consumer products of post-war prosperity. And yet, as historians have demonstrated, the continuities of politics, of state policies, and simply of experience across the dividing line of 1945 were substantial. The idea of a "zero hour"—a *Stunde Null*—in Germany or indeed anywhere else in Europe when the military battles of the Second World War came to an end is a myth, but one that has remained with us, dividing the twentieth-century history of Europe into two distinct but also rather unequal halves.[31]

Perhaps unsurprisingly, therefore, historical work undertaken on the years after 1945 has often focused on the way in which the legacies of the war years jutted into the history of the subsequent decades. The idea that the post-war period was precisely that—post-war—has been reflected not only in the uncompromising title of one of the most successful historical accounts of Europe after 1945,[32] but also in the large body of historical literature that in recent years has examined how Europeans, collectively and individually, came to terms with, or evaded, the legacies of the mass killings, civil wars, and forced migrations that had occurred over the previous years.[33] Histories of public memory and commemoration, as well as

30. P. Lagrou, "De l'histoire du temps présent à l'histoire des autres: Comment une discipline critique devint complaisante," *Vingtième siècle* 118 (2013): 101–19.

31. Histories that seek, with differing degrees of success, to transcend this mid-century divide include M. Mazower, *Dark Continent: Europe's Twentieth Century* (London, 1998); E. J. Hobsbawm, *Age of Extremes: The Short Twentieth Century 1914–1991* (London, 1994); and D. Bloxham and R. Gerwarth, eds., *Political Violence in Twentieth-Century Europe* (Cambridge, UK, 2011).

32. T. Judt, *Postwar: A History of Europe since 1945* (London, 2005).

33. Examples of such an approach include R. Bessel and D. Schumann, eds., *Life after Death. Approaches to a Cultural and Social History of Europe during the 1940s and 1950s*

of the more private discourses of suffering, bereavement, and loss, have demonstrated that much of the apparent optimism of the post-war years rested on conspiracies of silence and the construction of highly selective accounts of the war years that occluded the complicity of public authorities and individual citizens in many of the darker actions of the preceding years. Only from the 1960s onwards did Western European societies gradually develop the means, and perhaps the collective confidence, to confront more directly the legacies of this traumatic past.[34]

At the same time, this post-war paradigm has its natural limits. Europe did change, and in fundamental ways, after 1945. People moved, and moved on; and, as a consequence of high rates of post-war fertility and substantial immigration from beyond the post-war borders of Western Europe, the people changed too. Societies also changed in shape and spirit, partly as the consequence of economic growth and partly because of the emergence of new ways of living and of a more individualized culture of consumerism. All of these developments served to distance Europeans from their wartime past, at the same time as integrating them into new generational or gendered identities. The statistical teleologies of ever hastening change, economic growth, and social modernization presented in many histories of post-war Europe do, however, convey only a partial truth, and this is particularly so with regard to the political history of the era. The numbers of fridges or cars owned by Europeans, the number of foreign holidays they took, or even more obviously relevant data such as the percentage of students continuing to higher education or the audiences of television news programmes, can go only so far in explaining the character of post-war democracy. Western Europe did indeed, as a consequence of such changes, become a very different place to live in, especially for those fortunate enough to have the means to participate in the new forms of consumerism; but the frameworks of political life, such as national frontiers, state institutions, parliaments, and parties, tended to lag behind the rather pell-mell pace of these wider social changes.

The challenge in understanding the particular mid-century democracy that took shape after 1945 is therefore to approach it on its own terms, neither as simply defined by the past—even when that past was

---

(Washington, DC, 2003); P. Lagrou, *The Legacy of Nazi Occupation: Patriotic Memory and National Recovery in Western Europe, 1945–1965* (Cambridge, UK, 2000); R. G. Moeller, *War Stories: The Search for a Usable Past in the Federal Republic of Germany* (Berkeley, CA, 2001).

34. For an influential statement of this process, see H. Rousso, *The Vichy Syndrome: History and Memory in France since 1944* (Cambridge, MA, 1991).

as overwhelming as that of the Second World War—nor as simply the political vessel of Western Europe's post-war socio-economic modernization. The inauguration of the new democracy was on the whole muted. The Europe of 1945 had little of the euphoria of 1848, and democracy was viewed, especially by those in positions of authority, with a mentality of caution. Many of those who played an influential role in the construction of democracy after 1945 remained scarred by their personal experiences of the pre-war and wartime years, notably the traumas of military conflict, loss of family members, and displacement and exile. This was especially so of the influential cadre of exiles from Germany and elsewhere in central Europe, who had found wartime refuge in North America, and whose service in the Allied military and civilian bureaucracies often exercised a strong influence over the models of government that they sought to implement on their return to Europe.[35] For figures such as these, the re-establishment of the institutions of democracy—in particular free elections and the inauguration of parliaments—symbolized the recovery of freedom and of self-government. But the governing spirit of these returning exiles, as well of many of those who had lived through the events of the war years within Europe, was one of disabused sobriety. They did not want to return to the past but escape it, by forging a new model of democracy that would provide stable parliamentarism and effective government.

Consequently, the sovereignty of the people was emphasized less than the re-establishment of legitimate governance and the construction of a legal framework. The people would indeed rule, but their rule would be primarily indirect: by electing their representatives, both to parliaments and to the socio-economic organizations that assumed a prominent role in post-war politics, the people would in effect give the initial impetus to a process that would then be carried forward by those best qualified to address the increasingly technical challenges of government. In contrast to the people's democracies established in the east and advocated by the Communist parties of the west, the democracies of the post-war era were designed to be institutions of an orderly and inclusive liberty, symbolized by the centrist orientation of the major political forces—in much of Europe the Christian and Social Democrats—and by the succession of short-lived and rather anonymous governing coalitions in which they participated.

35. On the post-war influence of exiles from Germany and Austria, see notably C. Bailey, *Between Yesterday and Tomorrow: German Visions of Europe, 1936–1950* (New York, 2013), esp. 1–18; U. Greenberg, *The Weimar Century: German Emigrés and the Ideological Foundations of the Cold War* (Princeton, NJ, 2014).

This was a democracy that also remained influenced by the ghosts of its own past. Democracy was not a new form of government in 1945, but one embedded in a complex and highly contested past. Competing national narratives of democracy interlaced with the diverse and often contradictory intellectual heritages of republican, liberal, socialist, and Catholic interpretations of democracy as they had developed across the nineteenth and early twentieth centuries. There was therefore no agreed definition of democracy, and no shared perception of Europe's democratic past. The French Revolution of 1789 and its many successors across Europe during the nineteenth century had polarized Europeans into different ideological camps, while memories of more recent democratic experiences—such as those of the Weimar Republic, the interwar Austrian Republic, the French Third Republic, or the pre-Fascist parliamentary regime in Italy—were dominated by civil strife and their subsequent collapse into authoritarian and fascist rule. Democracy did not therefore have a good reputation among Europeans in 1945; and many of them feared that a return to democratic government would lead all too quickly to a resurgence of the violent social and political mobilizations on left and right that Aron had observed in Germany in the interwar years.[36] Though the war years might have provided an education as to the failings of fascism and communism, the path towards a viable new democracy was far from apparent. The project of building post-war democracy was thus an exercise in cautious improvisation, as Western Europeans moved tentatively forward, seeking above all not to repeat the errors of the past.

This hesitant rebirth of democracy has begun in recent years to find its historians, who have explored the diverse paths by which during the war years and their aftermath European political leaders, administrators, and particular communities of intellectuals came to find a home in democracy. Some could claim a prior commitment to democratic values, or were real converts to the cause; but most were figures who were drawn to democracy, less because of its fundamental legitimacy than because of the failure of other ways of imagining and, more especially, of managing the challenges and tensions of a modern society. Democracy was, in that respect, less a new beginning after 1945 than the place where European politics had ended up.[37]

36. Raymond Aron, *Mémoires*, 72–76.
37. See, notably, S. A. Forner, *German Intellectuals and the Challenge of Democratic Renewal: Culture and Politics after 1945* (Cambridge, UK, 2014); H. Chapman, *France's Long Reconstruction: In Search of the Modern Republic* (Cambridge, MA, 2018); N. B. Strote, *Lions and Lambs: Conflict in Weimar and the Creation of Post-Nazi Germany* (New

Despite this welcome recent interest in the political complexities of the immediate post-1945 era, the wider history of democracy in twentieth-century Europe has struggled to acquire a clear identity. There remains a tendency on the part of historians and others to regard democracy as the default modern historical regime, at least in the western territories of Europe. It is thus not democracy but its opposites that appear to require historical explanation. Studies of anti-democrats—or, perhaps more accurately, of those who had very different understandings of democracy, most notably communists and fascists—have therefore outweighed considerably in their number and scholarly impact studies of democrats in the historiography of the European twentieth century. This has also encouraged a somewhat ahistorical conception of the modern evolution of democracy, whereby democracy is regarded as the political regime to which states revert when the specific conditions that generate anti-democratic alternatives abate. Such an approach has a number of shortcomings, but perhaps one of the most pervasive is the way that it tends to assume too great a similarity, or family resemblance, on the part of different democratic regimes. Other political traditions may come in different ideological and national forms, but democracy, it is assumed, is always essentially similar—one democratic regime differing from another only in terms of how inclusive or otherwise is its conception of democracy. Thus, the democracy of the modern era is foreshortened to a unitary story of its gradual expansion from the debating society of the male notable world of the mid-nineteenth century to the universalism and socio-economic diversity of the late twentieth century.[38]

Such an approach minimizes the importance of the multiple variants of democracy that have contested for ascendancy in Europe across the era of its modern development. Democracy as an ideal—or indeed as a peril to be held at bay—was rooted in many of Europe's political traditions of left and right; and the points of divergence were often more visible, and more tangibly felt, than the similarities. These were not simply struggles for political or electoral ascendancy, but also deeply felt conflicts over ownership of the concept of democracy, which reflected the seriousness with which

---

Haven, CT, 2017); J. Chappel, *Catholic Modern: The Challenge of Totalitarianism and the Remaking of the Church* (Cambridge, MA, 2018).

38. G. Eley, *Forging Democracy: The History of the Left in Europe, 1850–2000* (New York, 2002). See also the perceptive points made in U. Jakobsen, "Inventions and Developments of Democracy: The Approach of Conceptual History," *European Political Science* 9 (2010): 316–17.

the advocates of these different ideological camps had contemplated and matured "their" definitions of democracy.[39] In addition, however, a *longue durée* history of democracy—which emphasizes its (literally) progressive unfolding over the nineteenth and twentieth centuries—neglects the ruptures, or indeed jump cuts, in its history. Democracy is never ready-made; and it acquires its shape not through grand declarations but through practice within real political contexts.[40] The power of the state, the shape of the society it sought to rule, the influence of historical legacies and of national identities, and the ability of political parties to insert themselves as the intermediaries between individuals and groups of citizens and the process of government were all factors that defined the shape of Europe's modern democratic regimes. There were continuities in that process— more especially the durable connection that developed between certain national identities and democratic values—but there were also important discontinuities. Wars, economic crises, and the development of the structures of a mass society were all forces outside the internal dynamics of democracy that impinged upon its structures, its mentalities, and its very existence.

There is, therefore, a need for a more complex but also a more historically specific account of the contexts in which democracy has developed. With the stimulating exception of Margaret Lavinia Anderson's study of the practice of democracy in the German Empire prior to 1914,[41] the question of what made some democracies work and others fail in modern Europe has remained largely the domain of political scientists. This has resulted in much interesting research, notably in the form of comparative studies of the social and political conditions underpinning the divergent fortunes of democratic regimes in interwar Europe.[42] Foremost among these are the works of Gregor Luebbert and Michael Mann, both of which go well beyond the level of questions of institutional organization

39. This is the theme of the collection of articles edited by Tom Buchanan and myself and published as a special issue in *European History Quarterly* 32 (2002). See also the comments in A. Orzoff, *Battle for the Castle: The Myth of Czechoslovakia in Europe, 1914–1948* (Oxford, 2009), 219–20.

40. See the reflections in K. Owen, *Political Community in Revolutionary Pennsylvania* (Oxford, 2018), 1–18.

41. M. L. Anderson, *Practicing Democracy: Elections and Political Culture in Imperial Germany* (Princeton, NJ, 2000).

42. D. Berg-Schlosser and J. Mitchell, eds., *Conditions of Democracy in Europe 1919–39: Systematic Case Studies* (Basingstoke, UK, 2000); G. Capoccia, *Defending Democracy: Reactions to Extremism in Interwar Europe* (Baltimore, MD, 2007).

in exploring why some democracies endured while others were swept away by the political and economic upheavals of the 1920s and 1930s.[43] Socio-economic structures, the legacies of wars, the disruptive impact of ethnic conflicts, and the transmission belts by which popular grievances were transferred into the policies of parties and parliaments have all come to form prominent elements of the way in which political scientists, but also historians of the extreme right in interwar Europe, have analysed why so few of the parliamentary regimes established after the First World War still existed some twenty years later.[44] Central to such work is a recognition that democracy was not always the author of its own successes, or indeed failures. Democratic regimes are by definition more open to societal influences than their more authoritarian alternatives; and their viability throughout the modern world has depended on their ability both to assert their authority over that society and respond effectively to the expectations of the population.

Little of that methodology and historical specificity has, however, filtered into studies of the period following the Second World War. Too often the victory of democracy after 1945 continues to be explained largely in terms of a dictatorship of its origins: the defeat of Nazism, along with that of the other authoritarian regimes of New Order Europe, combined with the victory of the Allied powers, is assumed to provide a sufficient explanation of what came next.[45] One of the principal ambitions of this book is therefore simply to make the emergence of democracy in post-1945 Western Europe appear more historically complex, and also more open-ended. The limits of what was politically possible in Europe after the defeat of the Third Reich and the division of the continent into territories dominated by Germany's former opponents had certainly narrowed. The violent demise of Hitler's empire, so soon after its forces had overthrown many of the pre-existing state structures in Europe, created an intimidating vacuum of state power and of constitutional structures in many areas of

43. G. Luebbert, *Liberalism, Fascism, or Social Democracy: Social Classes and the Political Origins of Regimes in Interwar Europe* (New York, 1991); M. Mann, *Fascists* (Cambridge, 2004). See also T. B. Müller and A. Tooze, eds., *Normalität und Fragilität: Demokratie nach dem Ersten Weltkrieg* (Hamburg, 2015).

44. J. Osmond, *Rural Protest in the Weimar Republic: The Free Peasantry in the Rhineland and Bavaria* (New York, 1993); K. Passmore, *From Liberalism to Fascism: The Right in a French Province, 1928–1939* (Cambridge, UK, 1997); R. Paxton, *French Peasant Fascism: Henry Dorgères's Greenshirts and the Crises of French Agriculture, 1929–1939* (New York, 1997).

45. See, for a characteristic example of such an approach, S. Berstein, "La seconde guerre mondiale et les fondements d'une démocratie libérale rénovée," in *La démocratie libérale*, ed. Berstein (Paris, 1998), 689–729.

Europe. Consequently, the former wartime Allies were obliged, with differing degrees of enthusiasm, to act as the arbiters of the political future. In the east, this excluded, after the demise of the multi-party regime in Czechoslovakia in February 1948, the option of a pluralist political democracy; while in the west, it led by the end of the 1940s to the establishment of a de facto ban on Communists occupying positions of significant power in national government. Yet, within Europe's limited sovereignty in the immediate postwar years, there remained a considerable margin of manoeuvre in terms of the democracy that emerged. The "long reconstruction" of Europe—to borrow the framework applied to France by Herrick Chapman—was a process rather than an event, which stretched forward to the end of the 1950s, but which also drew on the legacies of forms of state action and socio-economic intervention initially developed in the interwar years.[46]

This medium-term perspective diverts attention away from the moment of democratic transition at the end of the war to the larger questions of why democracy endured in Western Europe after 1945, and more especially why it assumed specific forms. One fruitful, and indeed essential, means of approaching such questions is through the prism of individual national experiences. There have been a number of high-quality studies of individual regimes—most notably those of Jean-Pierre Rioux on the French Fourth Republic, Paul Ginsborg on the Italian Republic, and Mary Hilson on the Scandinavian states[47]—all of which well convey the complexity of post-war politics, in which the path that eventually emerged was only one among a diverse spectrum of possibilities. But these studies also raise the familiar problem in European history of national frames of reference. By taking as their subject the nation-state, they convey almost unconsciously the idea of a multiplicity of *Sonderwegen*—distinct paths— that all flowed into the common sea of Western European democracy that had come into existence by the 1960s. The democratization of post-war Europe was, however, from the outset a phenomenon that transcended nation-state frontiers. The Allied occupation of Europe, the pace of postwar economic growth, and the increased intensity of transnational intellectual and cultural exchanges created a political culture of newly porous

46. Chapman, *France's Long Reconstruction*, esp. 4–16. See, for broadly similar approaches, P. Nord, *France's New Deal: From the Thirties to the Post-war Era* (Princeton, NJ, 2010); Greenberg, *Weimar Century*, 5–11; K. K. Patel, *The New Deal: A Global History* (Princeton, NJ, 2016).

47. J.-P. Rioux, *The Fourth Republic* (Cambridge, UK, 1987); P. Ginsborg, *A History of Contemporary Italy: Society and Politics 1943–1988* (London, 1990); M. Hilson, *The Nordic Model: Scandinavia since 1945* (London, 2008).

national frontiers, in which democracy was as much (Western) European as it was national. Indeed, by melding together concepts of European identity with a certain set of democratic values, the politics of the post-war era became itself a site of "Europeanization."[48]

It is therefore necessary to go beyond the national in explaining how and why democracy became the regime of choice of most Western Europeans in the twenty-five years following the Second World War.[49] This explains why I have chosen to adopt a deliberately rather European approach to the subject matter of this book, leaving to one side some of the forms of national specificity that continued to define democratic structures and experience, while emphasizing the broader factors of state power, intellectual culture, social class, and other components of social identity that framed how democracy was conceived, structured, and experienced across Western Europe. However, this raises unavoidable questions about the external frontiers and internal contours of that Europe. One of the more surprising outcomes of the Second World War was the way in which it gave birth to a smaller Europe. The partition imposed by the Cold War was supplemented by the loss after 1945 of territories, notably to the south and east of the European continent, that had formerly been closely tied to Europe. Instead, a smaller and more bonded Western Europe emerged, reinforced by economic integration, transnational institutions, and a shared understanding of democracy. This Europe excluded until the 1970s the authoritarian dictatorships of Franco in Spain and Salazar in Portugal, even if economic migration, cultural influences, and the tentative emergence of proto-democratic forms of organization long prefigured the institutional transformations that followed the final collapse of the two regimes.[50] Somewhat more ambivalent was the relationship between the core of Western Europe that came into being during the 1950s and the territories to its north. The integration of the Nordic states (including Finland) followed its own dynamic, while Ireland and Britain became semi-detached from mainstream European processes of integration as the consequence of the decision of most British post-war leaders to prioritize their international and transatlantic connections. This was

48. M. Conway and V. Depkat, "Towards a European History of the Discourse of Democracy: Discussing Democracy in Western Europe, 1945–60," in *Europeanization in the Twentieth Century: Historical Approaches*, ed. Conway and K. K. Patel (Basingstoke, UK, 2010), 132–56.

49. I owe the phrase "regime of choice" to Alexander Groth. See his stimulating essay *Democracies against Hitler: Myth, Reality and Prologue* (Aldershot, UK, 1999), 352.

50. J. Grugel and T. Rees, *Franco's Spain* (London, 1997), 74–93.

formally reversed by the entry of the United Kingdom (and Ireland) into the European Communities in 1973, but it came too late to efface the differentness of British democracy—the so-called Westminster model—and more profoundly the temper of British society from that of the other states of Western Europe.

The structure of this book reflects these internal fault lines. Its principal focus is the interlocking structure of Western European states that emerged during the decade following the Second World War, while discussing the other states of Europe—including the United Kingdom—largely in terms of how they impinged on this Western European process. In many respects, Western Europe was an entirely new entity; the consequence of the abrupt amputation of much of central and eastern Europe that was brought about by the Great Power partition in 1945.[51] But it proved to be a resilient reality. Western Europe outgrew its Cold War origins, developed its own institutions and identity, progressively emancipated itself from the constraining structures of American control, and across the final decades of the twentieth century drew into its sphere of influence the newly democratic states of the Mediterranean south and its north-European neighbours, and, most strikingly, succeeded in reabsorbing after 1989 the former state-socialist regimes to the east with the confidence of an act of recolonization.[52]

Democracy was essential to this victory of the West. What had begun as a pragmatic choice became not only the dominant institutional system but also exerted a much wider influence over the terms of intellectual debate, the relations of power within society, and perhaps most profoundly the ways in which Europeans related to one another and thought of themselves. This explains why the book ranges beyond the political. Much of the literature on democracy, especially that written within social-science paradigms, tends to be unduly self-limiting in its conception of democracy as a political system. In contrast, the approach that I have adopted might seem to run the opposite risk of being overly inclusive. I draw somewhat indiscriminately on themes from political, socio-economic, and cultural history in order to present a more holistic account of post-war democracy. In doing so, I have been concerned to explore what Till van Rahden, writing about post-Nazi Germany, has termed "democracy as a way of life."[53]

51. See pp. 147–49.

52. M. Conway, "Democracies," in *Europe's Postwar Periods—1989, 1945, 1918: Writing History Backwards*, ed. Conway, P. Lagrou, and H. Rousso (London, 2019), 124–27.

53. T. van Rahden, "Clumsy Democrats: Moral Passions in the Federal Republic," *German History* 29 (2011): 489. Van Rahden acknowledges his debt to Sidney Hook: S. Hook,

His analysis of how German society, and more especially its elites, gradually came to feel at ease with a form of government and social values that they had not in any substantive sense chosen has a wider relevance for Western Europe. Much of the success of post-war democracy, at least until the 1960s, lay in its success in reconciling its erstwhile social and ideological opponents. The grievances of particular regional and social constituencies, such as middle-class groups and farmers, who had been to the fore in the anti-democratic movements of the interwar years were addressed, while the centrist logic of post-war electoral politics was reinforced by an inclusive process of government in which almost everybody could feel that they had some share of power. Oppositional cultures of left and right consequently lost much of their vitality, as political parties and more especially their electorates discovered the material and other advantages of participating in the democratic political system rather than fulminating against it from the outside.

The need to go beyond the regimes themselves and to explore how they became embedded in the social textures of post-war Europe also implies avoiding an approach based on questions of institutional structure. The approach of historians to political regimes has often been implicitly architectural. Terms such as the "making," "foundations," and "construction" of regimes proliferate, reflecting a recognition that in the twentieth century the durability of regimes often depended on the structures of power by which they could enforce their rule over their sometimes recalcitrant citizens. That was true, too, of the democratic regimes of post-war Europe, which benefited from the increased resources, technology, and professional skills available to modern state authorities to discipline and, when necessary, confront their citizens. The inequality of power between governments and their opponents in post-war Europe was, from the end of the 1940s, more emphatic than at any other period in Europe's modern history, thereby rendering redundant the forms of mass protest and insurgency that had been commonplace in previous eras. Europeans, in that sense, had little choice but to be citizens, however they might seek to circumvent or evade particular forms of state regulation. But in their large majority they also came to perceive advantages in compliance. The governments of post-war Western Europe were the source of various forms of

"Democracy as a Way of Life," in *Tomorrow in the Making*, ed. J. N. Andrews and C. A. Marsden (New York, 1939), 42–44. Hook subsequently attended the CCF conference in Berlin in 1960.

financial assistance, such as welfare payments and economic subsidies, as well as a rapidly expanding range of benefits in kind, including education, housing, infrastructure projects, and employment. In order to fund these ambitious programmes of provision, governments demanded an ever-greater share of private income in the form of taxation. But the quiescence of most citizens lay in their confidence—aided by the increases in living standards generated by economic growth—that government was giving them more than it was costing them.

The benefits of democracy were not, however, equal. Europe remained after the war emphatically a class society, and one in which the resources of the state were used to reinforce these class differences. The expansion in welfare provision, much of it channelled by the state through semi-autonomous institutions, addressed some of the more flagrant causes of poverty and destitution in European societies; but it left largely untouched the entrenched inequalities of wealth, property, and access to education. Indeed, by institutionalizing these inequalities through income-related pensions, subsidies for higher education, and the pervasive economic protection of small businessmen, middle-class professionals, and commercial farmers, the governments of the post-war era often did more to reinforce class differences in European societies than to erode them.[54] This was not accidental. Government after 1945 was above all a middle-class business, which reflected the social recruitment of political elites, and the increasing professionalization of state bureaucracies. It also matched the interests of their electors. The ascendancy of parties of the centre-right in post-war Europe was the consequence of the greater success of these parties in appealing to an increasingly individualistic and, it should be remembered, in its majority, female electorate, who appeared concerned less by questions of ideology than by the family economy and the effective provision of public services. To differing degrees, the democracies of post-war Western Europe rested on a social alliance of middle-class, lower-middle-class, and rural electors, from which the working class was largely excluded. Workers assumed much of the burden of the post-war reconstruction of Europe, but participated only modestly in its benefits. Their wages lagged behind increases in productivity, while the participation of trade unions in a politics of corporatist negotiation with employers and the state brought them only modest benefits.

This social landscape also helps to explain what is often described as the conservatism of the post-war democracies. In party-political terms,

54. See below, pp. 227–31.

this was undoubtedly so: when Aron gave his speech in West Berlin in 1960, the left, astonishingly, formed part of the ruling governmental coalitions in only three European states—Norway, Sweden, and Austria—while elsewhere, and most notably in all of the states of the newly founded European Economic Community, regimes or coalitions of the centre-right dominated.[55] This imbalance owed much to a combination of particular parliamentary circumstances, but it also reflected what appeared to be a broader crisis of the Socialist left at the end of the 1950s: Communism was visibly on the wane, while the non-Communist Socialist parties, outside of Scandinavia, struggled to construct programmes that would appeal to a sufficiently broad coalition of electors. With time, this would change, as a new generation of social-democratic leaders, such as Brandt in Germany, came to the fore. But in other ways, too, the temper of the post-war era appeared conservative. The ascendancy of the nuclear family, the priority that governments and citizens alike accorded to moral propriety, and the capitalist character of the post-war economies moulded a public discourse that asserted the values of the mainstream over those of dissident minorities. Post-war Western Europe may well have been more democratic, but it was not obviously more pluralist.

In so far as it provides a corrective to the easy assumption that projects of democratization always come from the political left, this conservatism provides a useful means of approaching post-war democracy. Indeed, viewed in a longer perspective, one of the most remarkable features of the period after 1945 lay in the historic reconciliation of political forces of the right, most notably political Catholicism, with parliamentary democracy.[56] The evolving project of democracy in Western Europe was not, however, tied to a political colour. Rather, it marked the ascendancy of a constellation of state structures and of political, economic, and social forces that found their centre of gravity in a form of democracy, as well as a discourse about democracy, that for all their evident inadequacies marked an emphatic turning point in modern Europe's political wars. This ascendancy would not endure: by the end of the 1960s, a wide variety of political and social movements would criticize, often virulently, the multiple failings of the post-war democratic model. In doing so, too, they adopted

55. D. Sassoon, *One Hundred Years of Socialism: The West European Left in the Twentieth Century* (London, 1996), 189.

56. I have discussed this process in M. Conway, introduction to *Political Catholicism in Europe 1918–1965*, ed. T. Buchanan and Conway (Oxford, 1996), 28–33, and "The Age of Christian Democracy," in *European Christian Democracy: Historical Legacies and Comparative Perspectives*, ed. T. Kselman and J. Buttigieg (Notre Dame, IN, 2003), 43–67.

a new democratic language, articulating concepts of a more participatory and pluralist democracy that would prove to be influential over the final decades of the twentieth century. Such critiques, however, serve less to question the democratic character of the post-war era, than to demonstrate its contingent character. Democracies, more than other forms of political regime, do not endure indefinitely; they reflect the realities of their time.

CHAPTER ONE

Making Democracy

THE CONSTRUCTION OF A POST-WAR
DEMOCRATIC ORDER IN WESTERN EUROPE

THE DEFEAT OF THE THIRD REICH did not provide the basis for the establishment of democracy as the dominant political regime in Europe. Indeed, the final extirpation of the Nazi regime in the bombed-out ruins of Berlin in the first days of May 1945 seemed to be anything but a victory for European self-government. The fiercely contested conquest of Europe undertaken over the course of the previous two years primarily by three powers (the Soviet Union, the United States, and Britain) from the edges of Europe appeared to mark the demise of Europe's sovereignty. The peoples of Europe might indeed have been liberated—albeit quite a number of them at the expense of their lives—but their political regimes had been among the principal victims of that process of liberation. If one exempts those states that had remained rather uncertainly neutral throughout the conflict (Ireland, Portugal, Spain, Sweden, and Switzerland), almost all of the regimes of Europe, with the exceptions of those of Britain and Finland, had been overthrown, defeated, or occupied over the course of the previous years. Moreover, as the wartime conferences of the Allied powers held in exotic locations such as Casablanca, Cairo, Teheran, and Yalta seemed to indicate, Europe's future would be decided not by the peoples or the governments of Europe but by the imperially minded powers that had brought about their liberation.

There was therefore no straightforward path from war, through liberation, to democracy. Indeed, in the Iberian peninsula, such a transition never began; while in most of those areas of central and eastern Europe liberated (or conquered) by the Red Army, its terminus proved to be not democracy but regimes of state socialism. However, in a large swathe of northern, central, and western Europe, military liberation set in motion a wide-ranging process of constitutional, political, and social change that culminated a few years later in a new democratic order. This outcome was very much less than inevitable, but also something more than chance. Instead, as this chapter will show, Western Europe's post-war transition to democracy arose from the interplay of four dominant forces: the actions of the powers who liberated and, subsequently, occupied Europe; the successful refoundation of national state structures; the consequent demobilization and marginalization of other, more locally based or informal political authorities; and the re-emergence of a structure of political parties that, along with a range of other social associations, became the principal intermediaries between rulers and ruled. Taken together, these factors brought into existence a resilient democratic order, but one which through its limitations betrayed the determining influences on its creation.

At the beginning, however, there was confusion. Some communities had been destroyed by the arbitrary violence of war, while others had been left almost entirely unscathed; some had experienced bitter political or ethnic conflicts that had verged on civil war, but in others the adversities of war had reinforced social solidarity. In many urban centres, shortages of the basic needs of food, heat, and housing had reduced millions to destitution, while others, notably in rural areas away from the front lines, had proved able to maintain a life of relative ease. These differences were not national, but highly localized, coexisting often starkly within or between neighbouring communities.[1] Indeed, the principal consequence of the vast mobile military campaigns waged on land and in the air in Europe during the final years of the Second World War had been to shatter, rather in the manner of the destruction of a set of venerable crockery, any coherent pattern of national government. With the rare exception of Denmark, which emerged from under the cloak of German occupation in May 1945 with its constitutional institutions largely intact,[2] government was notable at the moment of liberation mainly by its absence. The combined impact of Nazi and Allied occupations during the final years of the war destroyed much of the conventional framework of public administration, replacing it with haphazard regimes of military occupation that coexisted, often somewhat awkwardly, with a wide range of self-proclaimed or improvised

---

1. See, for example, P. Morgan, *The Fall of Mussolini: Italy, the Italians and the Second World War* (Oxford, 2007), 131–37.

2. B. Lidegaard, *A Short History of Denmark in the Twentieth Century* (Copenhagen, 2009), 144–97.

committees of liberation, Resistance movements, and groupings of social notables.[3]

The dominant reality almost everywhere was local. Difficulties of communication and the collapse of the hierarchies of bureaucratic administration had liberated many communities effectively to themselves. Across large areas of Italy between 1943 and 1945, in France in the summer of 1944, in the Low Countries in the winter of 1944–45, and across the territories of the defeated Third Reich in the summer of 1945 millions of Europeans experienced an enforced break from their role as citizens of their nation-state.[4] The consequence was certainly not anarchy. Even as Europeans found themselves without a government, they for the most part continued to behave much as if one existed. Habits of obedient citizenship and respect for law were for most Europeans, especially in western and central Europe, difficult to unlearn. But much of the distinctiveness of liberation, and a strong reason why the period has remained subsequently an emotional reference point in European memories, lay in its sense of being an exceptional moment, when the normal frameworks of daily life had ceased to exist. The consequences could be arbitrary, unpredictable, and dangerous. The general settling of accounts—what in Italy became known as the *resa dei conti*—that followed liberation was an unscripted process that took place beyond or alongside more legal patterns of justice.[5] Throughout liberated and Allied-occupied Europe, power was at times exercised through the barrel of a gun, and all of Europe was provided with an unprecedented number of guns, many of which had fallen into ill-trained or ill-intentioned hands. Authority in these circumstances, as in cities such as Marseille or Florence in the summer of 1944, tended to reside in the hands of whoever acted most swiftly in occupying public buildings and issuing decrees to the population.[6] But it could also be empowering, as communities at the level of the factory, the village, or indeed the refugee or prisoner-of-war camp, took matters into their own hands. The inhabitants of a village in the Auvergne decided in the summer of 1944, long before the arrival of any liberation from outside, to set up a sign at the

3. For a general account of the process of liberation, see W. Hitchcock, *Liberation: The Bitter Road to Freedom, Europe 1944–1945* (London, 2009).

4. M. Koreman, *The Expectation of Justice: France 1944–46* (Durham, NC, 1999), 2.

5. J. Foot, *Italy's Divided Memory* (New York, 2009), 168–82; W. Rauscher, *Karl Renner: Ein österreichischer Mythos* (Vienna, 1995), 328–29.

6. G. Unger, *Gaston Defferre* (Paris, 2011), 71–95; S. Neri Serneri, "Resistenza e insurrezione nel secondo conflitto mondiale: Il Comitato Toscano di Liberazione nazionale verso la 'battaglia di Firenze,'" *Rivista storica Italiana* 131 (2019): 51–92.

boundary of their commune announcing "Ici commence la France libre." This was less a partisan statement as to who should rule France than a reassertion of the sovereignty of the local community.[7]

As that sign indicated, the nation was very much present in people's minds at the war's end: as a badge of personal and collective identity, an ethnic label, or a project for the future. What was absent was its modern corollary of effective state power. Unsurprisingly, this created fears that the nation-state itself was broken beyond repair, and that the bonds of political and legal authority that had developed across Europe over roughly the previous hundred years would not be restored.[8] The reality, however, was more complex: the nation migrated from the hierarchical structures of the state to the more local level of community and neighbourhood, creating simultaneously a sense that the nation was a more present reality—as expressed through the patriotic trappings of liberation— and also more distant. The changes that this brought about in the varied political cultures of Europe were subtle, and durable. Most obviously, the absence of effective state authority served as an education in the possibility of self-government. Europeans began to do democracy for themselves. Men and, more especially, women organized the provisioning of their own communities, improvised forms of collective welfare, and set up neighbourhood committees and councils.[9] In some cases, these practices drew on semi-submerged pre-existing forms of direct democracy. Workplace or town-square meetings, the establishment of local militias, and, more strikingly, the "unofficial" purges carried out of those who had transgressed social norms by engaging in collaboration with the occupiers during the war years were all aspects of the politics of the liberation era that reached back to the era of the French Revolution, or indeed to the urban cultures of the early modern era.[10]

In other ways, however, the impact of the liberation period proved to be depoliticizing. The chaos caused by the sustained and rather indiscriminate aerial bombing of the final years of the war was destructive of more

7. H. R. Kedward, introduction to *The Liberation of France: Image and Event*, ed. Kedward and N. Wood (Oxford, 1995), 1. See also H. R. Kedward, *In Search of the Maquis: Rural Resistance in Southern France 1942–1944* (Oxford, 1993), 222–23.

8. G. Della Loggia, *La morte della patria* (Rome, 1996).

9. M. McLaren, "'Out of the Huts Emerged a Settled People': Community-Building in West German Refugee Camps," *German History* 28 (2010): 42–43.

10. M. Conway, "Justice in Post-war Belgium: Popular Pressures and Political Realities," in *The Politics of Retribution in Europe: World War II and Its Aftermath*, ed. I. Deak, J. Gross, and T. Judt (Princeton, NJ, 2000), 133–56; F. Virgili, *Shorn Women: Gender and Punishment in Liberation France* (Oxford, 2002).

than buildings. It destroyed governance and social norms, encouraging an intense and at times amoral individualism evident in the endemic small-scale criminality of the era, but also in an obsessive preoccupation with one's own welfare and—for women especially—that of one's family.[11] Confronted by a daily struggle to obtain food, fuel, and money, many Europeans had little time for, or interest in, notions of community, and still less political engagement. As two British Members of Parliament reported on their visit to Austria in early 1946: "The main daily task of the Viennese is to creep quietly about the city, providing . . . necessities for themselves and their families."[12] The impact of the war had often been atomizing, and this was especially so in the case of the millions of refugees, displaced persons (DPs), and demobilized soldiers who in the summer of 1945 were wandering across central Europe in search of family, food, and shelter.[13] The incremental advance of the Allies, from south, west, and east, into the core territories of the Third Reich, from the original landings in southern Italy in the summer of 1943 to the fall of Berlin almost two years later, had been a welcome deliverance for many, but one that provoked the collapse of much of the fabric of daily life. In his vivid description of Naples during the Allied occupation of 1944, Norman Lewis, for example, portrayed a society where social bonds had simply dissolved: extreme deprivation and the collapse of the Fascist structures of government were exacerbated by the corrosive impact of an army of occupation possessed of vast resources but no real comprehension of Neapolitan society.[14] This was, however, not a state of primitive equality. In a society of chronic shortages and limited legality, power, in its more direct forms, was everything, as individuals sought to exploit and barter whatever limited assets they possessed—such as food, cigarettes, clothing, and their bodies—to make their lives more bearable.[15]

The term "exhaustion" often used by historians to convey the character of the immediate post-war era may therefore contain less a metaphorical truth than a physical one.[16] Many Europeans had been worn down by the

11. R. Blank, "Wartime Daily Life and the Air War on the Home Front," in *Germany and the Second World War*, vol. 11, pt. 1, ed. J. Echternkamp (Oxford, 2008), 458–74.

12. S. W. Jeger and M. Orbach, *Austria 1946* (London, 1946), 20.

13. G. Grass, *Peeling the Onion* (London, 2008), 202–46. See also Steege, *Black Market, Cold War*, 18–63.

14. N. Lewis, *Naples '44* (London, 1978). See also I. Williams, *Allies and Italians under Occupation: Sicily and Southern Italy 1943–45* (Basingstoke, UK, 2013).

15. See the fictionalized accounts presented in C. Malaparte, *The Skin*, new ed. (New York, 2013); A. Hayes, *The Girl on the Via Flaminia* (London, 1949).

16. See, e.g., Mazower, *Dark Continent*, 294; B. Marshall "The Democratization of Local Politics in the British Zone of Germany: Hanover 1945–47," *Journal of Contemporary History* 21 (1986): 446.

sufferings and exigencies of daily life, which in some areas of Occupied Europe provoked surges in political radicalization.[17] As Nazi rule began to fracture, neighbourhoods fought back against German oppression, through actions of direct resistance or the subversion of German orders as well as the creation of networks of clandestine power. After liberation, this led also to a general and essentially uncontrollable release of the social and political tensions that had built up during German occupation, as groups such as industrial workers launched strikes and factory occupations to improve their material conditions, and reverse the unequal social equations of power in their workplaces and daily lives.[18] But, more frequently, the legacies of the war were evident less in movements of mass mobilization than in the narrowing of personal and political horizons. People looked to their own interests and the interests of those close to them, creating what one Belgian Catholic writer termed with some disdain in 1945 a culture of "individualisme alimentaire."[19]

In the same way, the hunger felt at liberation was therefore often more material than political. This was a truth that had to be learned by those many movements that presented themselves as the agents of post-war revolution. Within Axis-occupied Europe, the engagement of many intellectuals in Resistance movements as well as the enforced suspension of more conventional forms of political activism had created a torrent of clandestine manifestos and programmes, each seeking to outdo the others in its exposition of the radical changes that must be enacted after the defeat of Nazism.[20] At the liberation, however, these groups generally struggled to find a mass audience. Newspapers founded with the ambition of acting as the agents of political renewal soon discovered that their readers were

---

17. L. Taylor, *Between Resistance and Collaboration: Popular Protest in Northern France, 1940-45* (Basingstoke, UK, 2000), 3; J. Lewis, *Workers and Politics in Occupied Austria, 1945-55* (Manchester, 2007), 115–20; H. Vaizey "Empowerment or Endurance?: War Wives' Experiences of Independence during and after the Second World War in Germany, 1939–1948," *German History* 29 (2011): 67–77.

18. G. Gribaudi, "Naples 1943: Espaces urbains et insurrection," *Annales. Histoire, sciences sociales* 58 (2003): 1089–96; T. Behan, *The Long-Awaited Moment. The Working Class and the Italian Communist Party in Milan, 1943-1948* (New York, 1997), 126–28, 148–50; R. Hemmerijckx, *Van Verzet tot Koude Oorlog* (Brussels, 2003).

19. "Le mois politique," *La revue nouvelle*, 1 February 1945, 66; S. L. Fogg, *The Politics of Everyday Life in Vichy France: Foreigners, Undesirables and Strangers* (Cambridge, UK, 2009), 1–2, 190. Re. the longer-term legacies of such individualism, see also pp. 252–53.

20. See, for characteristic examples: R. Bédarida, *Les armes de l'esprit: Témoignage chrétien (1941-1944)* (Paris, 1977), esp. 341–45, 358–62; W.P.J. Pompe, *Bevrijding: Bezetting—herstel—vernieuwing* (Amsterdam, 1945); C. Andrieu, *Le programme commun de la Résistance: Des idées dans la guerre* (Paris, 1984), 31–81.

more interested in the price and availability of bread and the sports news than they were in plans for political and social change.[21] Similarly, many of the new political movements established at the liberation to act as spokesmen for Resistance ideas were marginalized by those established political forces that proved more adept at tailoring their messages to immediate agendas of material improvement.

The war had proved to be more of a rupture in people's lives than in their politics. There were real changes in political attitudes: it was in the 1940s that a significant proportion of Europeans became, and remained, supporters of Communist parties and trade unions, at the same time as millions of others disengaged from the politics and mentalities of the authoritarian or radical right. Moreover, for some Europeans—especially a certain younger intelligentsia—the impulse of events provided a heady baptism of political engagement. After the constraints of war and dictatorship, they were set free to advocate their ideas of a new social and political order, rooted within the networks of intellectual affinity and friendship, and their participation in discussion groups and periodicals.[22] This set the political trajectory, often for decades to come, of those whom Sean Forner has termed the "engaged democrats."[23] But, alongside this ferment and innovation, there was also much continuity of views and attitudes. The labels of parties, and indeed their organizational structures, might be new, but values and a socially rooted sense of what constituted legitimate government remained largely intact.[24] There was also a newly cautious character to people's political commitment. The experience of the war years, and indeed that of the 1930s, had been an education for many citizens in the dangers that could arise from political engagement. Individuals and communities were newly conscious of what they had to lose from committing themselves too emphatically, or too visibly, to any cause. There was consequently a perceptible wariness in political attitudes in the aftermath of the war. Voters were understandably distrustful of empty promises, and were more interested in local and material changes than in grandiose projects of institutional change. This produced a pragmatic reorientation in political attitudes: rather than challenging

21. P. Gérard, "La presse à la Libération dans la région de Toulouse," in *La Libération dans le midi de la France*, ed. R. Trempé (Toulouse, 1986), 331–45.

22. N. Bobbio, *A Political Life* (Cambridge, UK, 2002), 37–64; E. Hobsbawm, *Interesting Times: A Twentieth-Century Life* (London, 2002), 127–51.

23. Forner, *German Intellectuals*, 1–43. See also G.-R. Horn, *Western European Liberation Theology: The First Wave (1924–1959)* (Oxford, 2008).

24. M. Conway and P. Romijn, eds., *The War for Legitimacy in Politics and Culture 1936–1946* (Oxford, 2008), esp. 17–20.

the representatives of authority, most people seemed more concerned to negotiate with them to obtain what they needed, notably in terms of housing, employment, and welfare benefits.[25]

It is therefore easy to exaggerate the extent of the new in European political loyalties after 1945. There was an inevitable hyperbole to the rhetoric deployed at the end of the war. Everybody—including those who in more normal times were distinctly more conservative in inclination and language—declared that change on a large scale was necessary and desirable. As no less a figure than Pius XII declared in his widely noted Christmas message of 1944, "this world war, this universal upheaval, must mark the inauguration of a radically new and completely reordered world."[26] Such statements did of course often disguise more careful calculations of material interest; but there was an undeniable wish that the enormous human and material sacrifices of the war years should find their recompense in the achievement of a more peaceful and prosperous order. Contrary to what had happened after 1918, the final military victory must this time be accompanied by changes of regime, of society, and above all of mentalities, which would create, in the characteristic words of the progressive Belgian Catholic philosopher Jacques Leclercq, "une ère nouvelle où la justice et la fraternité humaine pourront atteindre un niveau auquel nos ancêtres ne pouvaient aspirer" (a new era where justice and human solidarity will be able to attain a level to which our ancestors could only aspire).[27] It is this language, and the emotions that gave it its oxygen, that lent 1945 its character as a moment of political innovation and of optimism. Yet, compared with other moments of fundamental change in modern European history—such as 1789, 1848, or 1917–19—there was little explicit appeal to the conventional forms of radical action. Europeans, it seemed, wanted to enter into a new world, but without destroying the old, or engaging in the fratricidal civil wars of the recent past.

There was therefore an air of revolution without revolution to the political rhetoric of liberation. Too much blood had been shed in the recent past for Europeans to be able to embrace the politics of domestic revolution in the way that had, for example, occurred in Spain a mere decade earlier. Rather than barricades and renewed violence, Europeans aspired to a much wider but less concrete process of change, one that would bring about a transition in political and social structures as well as in popular

25. See below, pp. 222–24.

26. Pius XII, "Democracy and Peace," in *Selected Letters and Addresses of Pius XII*, ed. Catholic Truth Society (London, 1949), 302.

27. J. Leclercq, *Allons-nous à une société sans classes?* ([Namur, 1946]), 20.

mentalities.[28] This aspiration—for a revolution of spirits as much as of structures—was well captured by the Italian Socialist leader, Pietro Nenni, when he repeatedly called in 1944 and 1945 for a "vento del Nord" that would sweep down the Italian peninsula from the Resistance heartlands of the north, bringing with it a radical change of political and social culture.[29]

Nenni's hopes, in common with those of many others throughout Europe, would be disappointed. Over the subsequent few years, much did change in Italy: the country became a republic, a new democratic constitution was introduced, women were enfranchised, and national elections were held that led to the durable ascendancy of two parties—the Christian Democrats and the Communists—that were emphatically different from the major political forces of the past. These were radical changes, and more far-reaching than those that occurred in many other areas of Europe. But, in Italy, just as elsewhere in Western Europe, Nenni's hopes that the war would lead to a moment of fundamental political refoundation proved to be misplaced.[30] The vision articulated by Resistance activists in both France and Italy, of a "new" or "true" democracy—what the Italian Socialist Giuseppe Faravelli termed a "democrazia integrale," accompanied by wide-ranging programmes of industrial, agrarian, and educational reform—soon appeared to be little more than a utopian dream. As early as 1946, Faravelli was already bemoaning the notion of a missed revolution. Presented with the opportunity to act decisively, the Italian Socialists had failed to seize the initiative, instead allowing other, less democratic forces with more self-interested agendas to come to the fore.[31]

In truth, this concept of a missed moment of radical change—which would have a long future before it—rested on a superficial understanding of the popular mood. Europe had moved beyond the era of revolutions. New principles, parties, and personalities did indeed come to the fore after the war, but they did so within a framework of continuities of institutional structures and of social power that blunted the energy of political innovation, and caused much of the optimism of liberation to ebb away over the subsequent months. Populations, too, were not slow to appreciate this reality. When Danes came to refer to the summer of 1945 as "the short

28. G. Bernanos, *Tradition of Freedom* (London, 1950), 17–25.

29. E. Santarelli, *Nenni* (Turin, 1988), 261. See also F. F. Rizi, *Benedetto Croce and the Birth of the Italian Republic, 1943–1952* (Toronto, 2019), 168–81.

30. Ginsborg, *History of Contemporary Italy*, 72–120.

31. Chapman, *France's Long Reconstruction*, 3; A. Agosti, *Rodolfo Morandi: Il pensiero e l'azione politica* (Bari, 1971), 418; G. Faravelli, *Per l'autonomia del Partito Socialista: Marxismo ed utopismo* (n.p., 1946), 3–4.

summer of liberation," they conveyed both the hopes generated by liberation from German occupation, and the way in which they had soon recalibrated their expectations to reflect the return of the normal.[32]

Control of the state—or, more precisely, of those institutions that could claim to such a title—was essential to this process of incremental normalization. The question of state power was indisputably the most urgent one at the end of the war, and certainly loomed largest in the minds of those who aspired to be the rulers of the new Europe. The structures and bureaucracies of government had to be remade, and then reinserted into the fabric of local communities and the lives of individuals. This process of state reconquest took longer than military conquest; it was also generally more contested. Whatever their confident rhetoric, the candidate rulers were intensely aware of the precarious nature of their authority. Few could claim a monopoly of legal or political legitimacy, and none possessed the resources—be they military, financial, or bureaucratic—simply to impose their authority on their liberated territories. The variety of exile regimes established in London and elsewhere during the war years had prepared obsessively for the moment of liberation, and the forms of opposition that they anticipated they would encounter.[33] They therefore tried to overawe potential opponents, moving with nervous haste to seize control of the levers of national and local government, issuing legal decrees that granted them wide powers to arrest potential opponents, as well as making promises of generous economic and welfare reforms. Government in such circumstances was a matter of smoke and mirrors, and nobody understood this better than Charles de Gaulle. Striding purposefully to choreographed effect down the Champs-Elysées of newly liberated Paris on 26 August 1944, the self-styled leader of the Gouvernement provisoire de la République française consciously sought to project his image as the rightful head of the French state. This was little more than make-believe. More so than the other putative national leaders, de Gaulle's authority rested on his distinctly dubious claim to be the agent of what he had carefully termed in the decree he issued on 9 August 1944 the "rétablissement de la légalité républicaine."[34] Unsurprisingly, he consciously avoided any

32. Lidegaard, *Short History of Denmark*, 192.

33. M. Conway, "Legacies of Exile: The Exile Governments in London during the Second World War and the Politics of Post-war Europe," in *Europe in Exile: European Exile Communities in Britain 1940–45*, ed. Conway and J. Gotovitch (New York, 2001), 259–61.

34. O. Rudelle, "Le Général de Gaulle et le retour aux sources du constitutionnalisme républicain," in *De Gaulle et la Libération*, ed. Fondation Charles de Gaulle (Brussels, 2004), 11–13.

FIGURE 2. The appearance of authority: de Gaulle walks down the Champs Elysées in Paris in August 1944. Bettmann/Bettmann via Getty Images

reference to the pre-existing Vichy regime, which had a much better claim to be the legal successor of the Third Republic; but he was just as concerned to avoid the whiff of revolution. On arriving in Paris, he rejected the wish of the Resistance forces that he should declare a new republic from the balcony of the Hôtel de Ville. Instead, he acted in the manner of a de facto head of state, taking possession of the principal ministries and inspecting the forces of the state *gendarmerie* before meeting with the Resistance leaders and effectively declaring that their political and military role was at an end.[35]

Rhetoric and theatre, supported where necessary by timely displays of armed force, were therefore essential components of the reassertion of state authority in liberation Europe. But so too was the re-bonding of external and internal structures of government. This was primarily a matter of negotiation. Ahead of liberation, the Allied and exile

35. S. Berstein, "L'arrivée de de Gaulle à Paris," in *De Gaulle et la Libération*, ed. Fondation Charles de Gaulle (Brussels, 2004), 136–38; Chapman, *France's Long Reconstruction*, 24–26.

authorities, internal political movements, social organizations, and Resistance groups had engaged in complex and often wary attempts at coordination. Thus, in France, the Gaullist authorities encouraged the creation of a Conseil national de la Résistance (CNR) within German-occupied France that invested the Resistance with a sense of its official status, while at the same time enabling the Free French authorities in London and subsequently Algiers to draw Resistance groups under their higher political authority.[36] Similarly, in Italy, at the urgent prompting of the Allied authorities, a Committee of National Liberation for Northern Italy (CLNAI) was created in January 1944 composed of the burgeoning Resistance movements in the German-occupied north of the country. The committee accepted the authority of the royal regime in the Allied-occupied south in return for Allied military assistance and a presence in the reconfigured government created in Rome after the city's liberation in June 1944.[37]

Short-term pragmatism, coupled with an instinctive preference for order—any order, so long as it was predictable and not explicitly repressive—was therefore the defining feature of Allied rule in liberated Europe. The Charter of the Atlantic, concluded by Roosevelt and Churchill in August 1941, ahead of American intervention in the war, had made broad promises of the new regime of democratic freedoms that would follow an Allied victory.[38] But these aspirations were rapidly overtaken by more immediate considerations, not the least of which was the need to secure full Soviet participation in the war effort. Moreover, as the Allied advance in southern and western Europe evolved during the summer and autumn of 1944 from initial hopes of a relatively uncontested military promenade to a bitter struggle against the German armies and their allies, so control of territory, resources, and people became their dominant preoccupation.[39] In the lengthy period between the initial Allied landings in Italy and France in 1943 and 1944 and the final collapse of German resistance in May 1945, power in American- or British-liberated areas often lay primarily in the hands of the Allied officials, who operated with a wide range of latitude but with limited resources, and even more

36. C. Andrieu, "Le CNR et les logiques de l'insurrection résistante," in *De Gaulle et la Libération*, ed. Fondation Charles de Gaulle (Brussels, 2004), 75–81; Chapman, *France's Long Reconstruction*, 19–37.

37. D. Ellwood, *Italy 1943–1945* (Leicester, UK, 1985), 160–64.

38. Berstein, "Seconde Guerre mondiale," 694–95.

39. This is well conveyed in official histories of Allied liberation: e.g., F.S.V. Donnison, *Civil Affairs and Military Government in North-Western Europe 1944–1946* (London, 1961).

limited understandings of local realities. The nature of rule, unsurprisingly, was heavily dependent on the character of the military officers who found themselves in positions of authority, as well as the prevailing political dynamics in the liberated territories. Popular attitudes to the Allies were rarely as uniform as the cheering crowds who had lined the streets on their arrival initially suggested. Moreover, attitudes soon changed, once the perception of the Allied armies evolved from that of transient liberators to more permanent occupiers, and more especially once they selected local figures to act as their agents.

This was particularly so in those areas where Allied officials were obliged to act as mediators in the establishment of local and national governance. In Belgium, no agreement between the various representatives of authority had proved possible prior to the liberation in September 1944, creating in effect a multilateral contest for power within the liberated country between the representatives of King Leopold III (who had been deported to the German Reich in June 1944), the former government in exile, the internal institutions of the Belgian state, and a variety of Resistance groups. The British military authorities were obliged over the subsequent autumn and winter to act as the somewhat reluctant arbitrators of conflict. They intervened to support the post-liberation government they had helped to bring into existence, while also seeking to advance those figures within it whom the British regarded as most reliable, as well as opposing the political ambitions of Resistance radicals, and blocking the return of Leopold to his position as monarch by appointing his more malleable brother, Charles, as regent.[40] Allied actions were decisive elsewhere too, most notably in Germany in 1945 where the emphatic nature of the occupation and the absence of any legitimate structures of state authority required them to engage much more closely with issues of public administration. Even here, however, Allied rule generally operated through a screen of local intermediaries, who in turn used their Allied-derived authority to establish themselves as the representatives of a putative German structure of governance.[41] In Germany, as in many areas of liberated Europe, this resulted in what might best be described as a form of semi-democratization. The new rulers of Western Europe arrived speaking English and deploying predominantly Anglo-American concepts of

40. Conway, *Sorrows of Belgium*, 69–70, 94–109, 142–43.
41. C. Erlichman and C. Knowles, "Introduction: Reframing Occupation as a System of Rule," in *Transforming Occupation in the Western Zones of Germany: Politics, Everyday Life and Social Interactions, 1945–55*, ed. Erlichman and Knowles (London, 2018), 5–7; Marshall "Democratization of Local Politics," 413–51.

freedom and justice; but, even as they did so, their actions, rooted within the mentalities of professional soldiers, imposed clear limits on the political freedom enjoyed by the local populations. As numerous Resistance groups and local committees of liberation were rapidly obliged to accept, power derived not from the people but from the hierarchical command structures of the Allied forces.[42]

Moreover, Allied military governance served as a template for those who followed. For those national and local civilian officials who gradually succeeded the uniformed representatives of the Allied armies, democracy came a rather distant second place to governance. The key objective was to reassert the effective authority of central government, through creating a state that possessed, in the anxious words of Pius XII, "the power to command with real and effective authority."[43] This was not an easy ambition to achieve. The improvised power structures of the post-liberation months had to be centralized, or perhaps more accurately verticalized, as the tasks and powers assumed by local bodies, Resistance committees, and social organizations during the era of liberation were reconnected to state institutions and their hierarchies. This process was rarely uncontested, especially when—as was the case in the Trieste area of north-eastern Italy—rival state structures (Italian and Titoist Yugoslav) claimed sovereignty.[44] In that case, but also in numerous other areas, there was a strong undercurrent of localism. People did not challenge the essential legitimacy of the state so much as its right to interfere in issues of local concern, especially when state officials tried to limit the post-liberation role of Resistance groups or bring the purges of wartime collaborators within recognized legal structures. On occasions, notably in Toulouse in the summer of 1944 and in Brussels in November of the same year, these conflicts took on the appearance of an insurrection, prompting the authorities to engage in displays of force out of proportion to a threat that existed largely in their nervous imagination.[45] This overreaction was, however, symptomatic of the mood of the time. There was ample scope for misunderstanding and

42. See the case studies examined in Koreman, *Expectation of Justice*.

43. Pius XII, "Democracy and Peace," 307. See also the preoccupation with state reconstruction evident in P. Badoglio, "Internal Reconstruction," in *Italy in the Second World War: Memories and Documents*, ed. Badoglio (London, 1948), 203–23.

44. S. Mihelj, "Imperial Myths between Nationalism and Communism: Appropriations of Imperial Legacies in the North-Eastern Adriatic during the Early Cold War," *European History Quarterly* 41 (2011): 634–56.

45. P. Laborie, "La libération de Toulouse vue par le pouvoir général: Représentations mentales et enjeux de pouvoir," in *La Libération dans le midi de la France*, ed. R. Trempé (Toulouse, 1986), 149–73; Conway, *Sorrows of Belgium*, 105–8; G. Warner, "Allies,

distrust, as the official representatives of the state came into contact with the improvised titles and uniforms of local groups and organizations.[46] For state officials the greatest fear was not a direct Communist seizure of power, but the emergence of a dual-power structure similar to that which had developed in Russia in 1917, whereby the substance of power gradually slipped out of the hands of the state into an alternative political world, based around political militias and local liberation committees.

That fear was not entirely misplaced. The Communist parties in German-occupied western Europe had prepared intensively for a revolutionary insurrection during what was anticipated to be the chaotic and prolonged collapse of Nazi rule. When this failed to come about—partly as a consequence of the decision by German military forces in large areas of western Europe simply to withdraw rather than to stand and fight—the Communist parties were obliged to improvise a policy of *attentisme*, waiting to see what would come of the attempts of the Allied authorities and their local collaborators to establish a viable structure of rule.[47] But they continued to encourage the development of the local committees and trade-union organizations that they hoped would supplant, or at least co-exist alongside, the formal institutions of the state. Their goal, as the French Communist Party declared in September 1944, was to use these organizations to bring about what they termed with some menace a real and active democracy: "une démocratie réelle et agissante."[48] In this uncertain context, nobody could predict whether the nascent state institutions would succeed in establishing themselves, or whether they would collapse and be replaced by a different power structure—or indeed none at all.

The precedent provided by events in Russia in 1917 was therefore on many minds, especially those of Communist militants. In provincial Russia the powerful centrifugal forces generated by the First World War and the collapse of the authoritarian frameworks of the Tsarist regime had produced a similar situation of multiple sources of power, both local and provincial and formal and informal, that succeeded in inserting themselves between the people and the state. While the elite in the centres of

---

Government and Resistance: The Belgian Political Crisis of November 1944," *Transactions of the Royal Historical Society* fifth series, 28 (1978): 45–60.

46. Kedward, *In Search of the Maquis*, 218–20.

47. J. Gotovitch, *Du rouge au tricolore: Les Communistes belges de 1939 à 1944* (Brussels, 1992), 367–94; P. Buton, *Les lendemains qui déchantent: Le parti communiste français à la Libération* ([Paris], 1993), 11–13, 102–6.

48. Quoted in Buton, *Lendemains qui déchantent*, 166.

power in Moscow and St. Petersburg set about building a new political regime, many ordinary Russians acted according to localism and self-interest, simply disregarding the orders of the state. Thus, far from producing a new era of stable government, "democratization," in the words of Sarah Badcock, "resulted in an acceleration of chaos."[49]

Much of the same potential for a fragmentation of state authority was also present in Europe in the final years of the Second World War. Indeed, the chaotic and often violent micro-politics that developed in the Balkan Mountains and eastern Poland and the western Ukraine in the mid-1940s resembled strongly what had occurred in large areas of Russia during the revolution of 1917 and the subsequent civil war.[50] But Western Europe took a different course. Here, the reassertion of national state power was sufficiently emphatic to intimidate potential rivals, and to draw them into the orbit of the official state authorities. There was also less appetite for outright insubordination or rebellion. Whatever the anxieties of rulers regarding the volatility of the populations, especially in southern French cities at the moment of liberation in 1944, the reality was more modest.[51] In particular, few of the Resistance groups proved able to project their power beyond the immediate circumstances of liberation. The rapid development of Resistance networks in many areas of Occupied Europe during the final years of the war had created a widespread expectation that they would become the progenitors of wide-ranging political and social change. The Resistance in that sense had become the local manifestation of the values of patriotism, egalitarianism, and solidarity generated by struggle against Nazi occupation.[52] But, once they were exposed to the daylight of normality after the liberation, the Resistance groups rapidly lost much of their discipline, coherence, and moral authority. Organizational and personal rivalries, as well as more political divisions, sapped their ability

49. S. Badcock, *Politics and the People in Revolutionary Russia: A Provincial History* (Cambridge, UK, 2007), 238–43.

50. S. Kalyvas, *The Logic of Violence in Civil War* (Cambridge, UK, 2006); T. Snyder, "The Causes of Ukrainian-Polish Ethnic Cleansing 1943," *Past and Present* 179 (2003): 197–234; T. C. Amar, *The Paradox of Ukrainian Lviv: A Borderland City between Stalinists, Nazis, and Nationalists* (Ithaca, NY, 2015), 88–142.

51. J.-M. Guillon, "Administrer une ville ingouvernable: Marseille (1938–1946)," in *Lyon dans la seconde guerre mondiale: Villes et métropoles à l'épreuve du conflit*, ed. I. von Bueltzingsloewen, L. Douzou, J.-D. Durand, H. Joly, and J. Solchany (Rennes, 2016), 61–72.

52. This emerges strongly from Kedward, *In Search of the Maquis*; J.-M. Guillon, "La Résistance au village," in *La Résistance et les Français*, ed. J. Sainclivier and C. Bougeard (Rennes, 1995), 223–43.

to present themselves as plausible agents of national renewal.[53] Parties based on Resistance-derived agendas of political change were established, notably the Partito d'Azione in Italy and the Union démocratique belge in Belgium; but, to the disappointment of their predominantly intellectual leaderships, they failed to acquire the mass support they required to exercise a durable impact on post-war politics.[54]

Much more emphatic in political terms was the return of the old. The war years had destroyed many individual political careers, and made only a few new ones. The result was a change of generation as older figures, discredited by their wartime choices or more simply by their age, left the political stage.[55] In some cases, this enabled new, generally younger, figures from outside the established elites to emerge as powerful local politicians, drawing on the prestige derived from their wartime actions, often within Resistance movements.[56] These, however, were the exceptions. On the whole, the leaders of post-war Europe were not so much new men, as new faces drawn from within those same milieux that, since the advent of mass politics in Western Europe at the beginning of the twentieth century, had provided the large majority of the political personnel. Politics consequently remained largely in the hands of middle-aged and middle-class men, supplemented in some cases by a few women and by figures from more modest origins who were drawn into the political world by their education or their roles within trade unions and welfare organizations.[57]

This stability of personnel formed part of a broader restoration, or reassertion, of pre-existing frameworks of ideology, confession, and social class. With the striking exception of the re-establishment of the two principal pre-war parties (the Socialists and Christian Socials) as the twin dominant forces in Austria, nearly all of the major non-Communist parties across Europe were at pains to present themselves as new in the immediate post-war years. The extent of their newness was, however, distinctly

53. Conway, *Sorrows of Belgium*, 90–92, 224–26.

54. G. de Luna, *Storia del Partito d'Azione 1942–1947* (Rome, 1997); W. Beerten, *Le rêve travailliste en Belgique: Histoire de l'UDB 1944–1947* (Brussels, 1990).

55. See, for example, the marginalization of Benedetto Croce within Italian politics after 1943: Rizi, *Benedetto Croce*.

56. Unger, *Gaston Defferre*; S. Farmer, "The Communist Resistance in the Haute Vienne," *French Historical Studies* 14 (1985): 113–16; R. Long, *Les élections législatives en Côte d'Or depuis 1870* (Paris, 1958), 143–45; P. Tilly, *André Renard: Biographie* (Brussels, 2005).

57. See the local study J. Estèbe, "De l'avant-guerre à la Libération: La stabilité du personnel politique toulousain," in *La Libération dans le midi de la France*, ed. R. Trempé (Toulouse, 1986), 283–95.

relative. In many cases, political labels changed, as with the relaunch of the Dutch Socialist party in February 1946 as the more inclusive Partij van de Arbeid.[58] In other cases, the entire framework of the political parties was new. This was most obviously so in the case of the Christian Democratic parties, which rapidly acquired a prominent presence across a broad belt of largely Catholic territories stretching from the Low Countries to north-eastern Italy. These were in most cases much more than a reconfiguration of the Catholic political movements that had existed since the late nineteenth century. Their leaders consciously sought to break with the confessional priorities of the past, presenting their parties as modern, cross-class movements, operating independently of the Catholic Church, that would combine economic and social reform with a Christian-inspired concern for the development of the individual.[59]

The spirit of ideological innovation evident within these parties was, however, mitigated by the worlds within which they operated. In the case of the Christian Democrats' endeavours to present themselves as a new political movement, and the somewhat more hesitant efforts of Socialist parties, the intellectual momentum for change ran ahead of the more conservative mentalities of their local organizations and, more especially, of their electors.[60] The moulds within which politics were shaped, especially at the level of communities, remained remarkably durable, reflecting the ways in which these political cleavages were rooted in the textures of social life. Politics in liberated Europe therefore had something of the character of a river returning to its former shape and direction of flow after a flood. Whatever the aspirations for change, the return to past practices often obeyed forces stronger than the aspirations of leaders and activists.

Europeans, it seemed, had difficulty thinking in new political languages after the war. Some had changed their politics, or were obliged to recognize the demise of the political movements that they had formerly supported. But many had not changed their underlying political opinions, and preferred familiar slogans and structures to the lure of the new. This was reflected in the post-war elections, which, behind the changes of nomenclature and of candidates, often demonstrated the underlying

58. J. Bank, "De theorie van de vernieuwing en de praktijk van de wederopbouw: Het Nederlandse socialisme in de tweede helft van de jaren veertig," in *In dienst van het gehele volk: De West-Europese sociaal-democratie tussen aanpassing en vernieuwing 1945–1950*, by J. Bank, M. Van Haegendoren, and W. Kok (Amsterdam, 1987), 102–4.

59. See, for example, M. Van den Wijngaert, *Ontstaan en stichting van de CVP-PSC: De lange weg naar het kerstprogramma* (Brussels, 1976). See also pp. 188–91.

60. See p. 165.

continuity of the frontiers of religious confession and of social class. Most strikingly, there was no durable shift of voters to the political left; instead, the consolidation of a new political pole of the centre-right proved to be the principal electoral trend of the later 1940s and the 1950s. With the demise of movements of the extreme right, many of their former electors, it seemed, adopted without any great difficulty the language of a more moderate right, and in particular of Christian Democracy, which combined a certain social conservatism (and anti-communism) with the defence of particular material interests. It was these parties of the centre-right that proved to be the most effective in building broad coalitions of social interest during the post-war years. They exploited not only fears of Communism—both external and internal—but also the way in which many electors, especially in the towns and villages of provincial Europe, identified with a non-dogmatic conservatism that accepted modernization while seeking to mitigate its disruptive consequences.[61]

This ascendancy of a cautious conservatism was most apparent in the former territories of the Third Reich. Nowhere did the political vacuum of 1945 seem more emphatic than in Germany and Austria, and yet this resulted in Germany in the fifteen-year hegemony of the Christian Democrats led by the elderly Konrad Adenauer, and in Austria in the establishment of a durable coalition of the two principal political parties of the interwar years, the Socialists and the Christian Socials of the newly renamed Österreichische Volkspartei (ÖVP). Neither outcome was especially democratic. In Austria, the representatives of the parties, operating under the aegis of the veteran Socialist (and subsequent president of the Republic) Karl Renner, simply seized the opportunity provided by the collapse of the Third Reich in order to re-establish their rule, for which they sought retrospective popular endorsement through the elections held in November 1945.[62] In Germany, no such pre-emptive political coup was possible: the weakness of the post-Nazi political forces was too great and the opposition of the Allies too emphatic to permit the simple recreation of a German government. Instead, during the Allied occupation from 1945 to 1949 the British, American, and French forces gradually drip-fed forms of self-government into German local and regional administration, before capping

61. Long, *Elections législatives*, 171–76; R. Vinen, *Bourgeois Politics in France, 1945–1951* (Cambridge, UK, 1995). See also pp. 229–32.

62. R. Saage, *Der erste Präsident: Karl Renner—eine politische Biografie* (Vienna, 2016), 303–33; M. Herz, "Compendium of Austrian Politics" (2 December 1948), in *Understanding Austria: The Political Reports and Analyses of Martin F. Herz, Political Officer in the US Legation in Vienna, 1945–1948*, ed. R. Wagnleitner (Salzburg, 1984), 551–52.

it off with the final establishment of the Federal Republic in 1949, separate from the Democratic Republic established under Communist leadership in the Soviet zone. This process was not planned in advance, most especially in the way it resulted in the emergence of two rival German states in east and west. But, despite significant differences in the approach adopted by the three western military administrations in their zones of occupation, the principles of the Federal Republic that gradually took shape resembled those adopted elsewhere in Western Europe. This was most apparent through the concern that democracy should be the outcome rather than the method. The German people were kept at a distinctly wary distance from this process of state building. Power was vested by the Allied authorities in the hands of a cadre of predominantly Christian Democratic and Socialist political figures from the Weimar years, who gradually assumed responsibility for municipal, regional, and ultimately federal government.[63]

The managed temper of this democratic transition in West Germany reflected the broader relations of power in post-war Europe. Administrative power, especially that of institutions associated with Allied military and political rule, loomed large, while democratic power was much weaker. Governmental administrations, and not parliaments or political parties, were initially the real locus of authority. In most European states the political energies of liberation were constrained within a dominant politics of national union, in which the major parties subordinated their individual programmes to the shared task of national reconstruction. Though the dominant fault line of politics lay between a renovated but rather limited parliamentary democracy and the wider *Volksdemokratie* or *démocratie populaire* espoused by the Communists and certain of their Resistance allies,[64] this choice rarely became explicit in the politics of the post-liberation era. In large part, this was the consequence of the decision of the Communist parties of Western Europe during the winter of 1944–45 to draw back from launching a direct challenge to the nascent post-war regimes. This was probably wise: the forceful British military intervention on the streets of Athens in December 1944 to support the police of the British-backed state against the Communist-directed EAM Resistance movement served as an unmistakable warning to radical forces

63. R. Boehling, *A Question of Priorities: Democratic Reform and Recovery in Post-war Germany* (New York, 1996); Marshall "Democratization of Local Politics," 413–51; M. Roseman, "Restoration and Stability: The Creation of a Stable Democracy in the Federal Republic of Germany," in *European Democratization since 1800*, ed. J. Garrard, V. Tollz, and R. White (Basingstoke, UK, 2000), 153.

64. Emmanuel d'Astier, quoted in Andrieu, "CNR," 105; KPÖ, "Programmische Leitsätze der Kommunistischen Partei Österreichs, 1946," in *Österreichische Parteiprogramme 1868–1966*, ed. K. Berchtold (Munich, 1967), 318–19.

elsewhere in Europe of the unwillingness of the Allied powers to tolerate challenges to their authority or that of their local allies.[65] But the Communist willingness to accept the limits imposed on their freedom of action by participation in coalitions of national unity, and the abandonment that this implied of many of their hard-won positions of political strength within alternative power structures such as the Resistance groups, had consequences that were more than tactical. It removed any sense of a clear political choice at the end of the war, instead casting a cloak of national union over the divisions of politics and of social class.[66]

The Communist decision was an understandable one. National union, at a time when the defeat of the Third Reich remained to be secured, communities had to be rebuilt, populations fed, and industrial production resumed, was anything but an empty slogan. Loyalty to the Soviet Union in its effort to impose a complete military defeat on Nazi Germany merged with the patriotic spirit of the hour to create an obsessive concern within Communist ranks to subordinate everything—including their political goals—to the urgent needs of the war effort.[67] However, the primacy accorded to national union acted as a roadblock to the relaunching of democratic politics. Political disagreements were muffled by the need for patriotic unity, and freedoms subordinated to the collective discipline required for the war effort. Extended by the unexpectedly lengthy final military campaign against the Third Reich, the framework of national union constrained democracy within the exceptionalism of war, and perhaps most importantly ensured that the reassertion of state power preceded the inauguration of democracy.[68]

{⚔️}

Thus, when by the autumn of 1945 Europe finally began to escape from the most immediate consequences of war, liberation as an event, but also

65. M. Mazower, "Policing the Anti-Communist State in Greece, 1922–1974," in *The Policing of Politics in the Twentieth Century*, ed. Mazower (Providence, RI, 1997), 130–43. See also P. Papastratis, *British Policy towards Greece during the Second World War, 1941–1944* (Cambridge, UK, 1984).

66. Gotovitch, *Du rouge au tricolore*, 395–441. See also the much more hostile presentation of a Communist betrayal of the working class in Behan, *Long-Awaited Moment*.

67. See, for example, the virulent language of the PCF tract *Au travail pour gagner la bataille de la production* (n.p., [1945]). See also the retrospective justification of the policy provided in *Histoire du Parti communiste français: Manuel* (Paris, 1964), 445–51.

68. L.G.A. Schlichting, "De eenheid en de herzuiling," in *Visioen en werkelijkheid: De illegale pers over de toekomst der samenleving* (The Hague, 1963), 47–50.

as a period—and indeed a state of mind—was already at an end. In its place, the dominant ethos was one of normality. The tangible sense that an exceptional period had ended was apparent everywhere in Western Europe over the course of the subsequent winter. The fighting had come to an end in Europe if not in the colonial territories of the European powers, the armies of liberation were leaving Europe or being demobilized, structures of military government were being dismantled, families were being reunited or refounded, and economic production, trade, and employment were slowly restoring a modicum of stability to daily lives. This normality was of course often more a facade than a reality. There could be no recovery of normality for the millions of Europeans who had been bereaved or uprooted, or whose property, businesses (large or more frequently small), families, and lives had been irredeemably destroyed or overturned by the events of the war years. To take just one statistic among many: it was estimated that some thirteen million European children had lost one or both parents in the war, generating an immediate need for structures of care, such as orphanages, as well as a psychological legacy of trauma that endured through the subsequent decades.[69]

When villagers in the Apennines referred back to the war years, they apparently often described it as the *rastrellamento*, an agricultural description of the process of raking through the soil, whereby everything is broken up but, significantly, a new order is created.[70] The metaphor is an appealing one. Everything had indeed been transformed by the events of the war years, and yet the outcome in much of Western Europe was a new normality that was directed firmly towards the future. Europeans, understandably enough, wanted to escape from the war, with all of its trials and dangers, and embrace the security of a private and predictable daily life. As one Resistance woman activist in Toulouse subsequently recalled to an oral history enquiry: "All we hoped for from the Liberation was to live normally again."[71]

This desire for normality should not be taken at face value. For those in authority, it provided a convenient means of legitimizing actions that excluded radical change in the name of restoring a distinctly one-sided form of order. Nevertheless, the re-establishment of normality in 1945–46

69. T. Zahra, *The Lost Children: Reconstructing Europe's Families after World War II* (Cambridge, MA, 2011), 4–6.

70. R. Sarti, *Long Live the Strong: A History of Rural Society in the Apennine Mountains* (Amherst, MA, 1985), 227.

71. H. Diamond, "Women's Aspirations 1943–47: An Oral Enquiry in Toulouse," in *The Liberation of France: Image and Event*, ed. H. R. Kedward and N. Wood (Oxford, 1995), 93.

was more than a trick of the light. Elsewhere, in the bitter civil war raging in the mountains of northern Greece, or in eastern Europe, where enormous processes of ethnic, social, and political change continued to unfurl, much about the nature of the post-war order remained profoundly unclear. In Western Europe, however, that uncertainty—and the consequent sense of open-ended political possibility—proved to be of much shorter duration. Significant issues of domestic policy remained to be resolved; but, by the end of 1945, nation-state structures had been restored everywhere except in Germany, elections were being held or were planned, the rubble of the conflict was being cleared away, and employment, stable currencies, and provision of food and housing were slowly being restored.[72] Restoration, rather than revolution, had, it seemed, become the dominant mentality. This was reflected too in the way that the state became an instrument of normalization rather than of innovation. Those often technocratic-minded figures who had hoped that the liberation would provide the opportunity for the top-down reshaping of European societies were obliged to recognize that state institutions had instead become the instrument of largely conservative interests.[73]

Even the novel concept of a west of Europe was in its own way a reflection of this tentative sense of normality. Western Europe had by the end of 1945 acquired boundaries that were defined in the east by the very different politics generated by Soviet occupation, and in the south by the civil war in Greece, and the large-scale challenges to British and French colonial rule in the Middle East and Algeria. Moreover, despite a noisy propaganda campaign by the French Communist Party and Spanish Republican exiles, Western Europe, it was now clear, also ended at the Pyrenees. The never clearly stated commitment of the Allies to bring about the overthrow of the authoritarian regimes of the Iberian Peninsula wilted rapidly after the defeat of Nazism. The French authorities closed the border with Spain, almost as if to cut off potential contagion from the Franco regime, but there was little appetite for a further military crusade for democracy. The Spanish members of French Resistance groups who tried to transfer their tactics of guerrilla warfare to Spanish soil were repressed with almost complete impunity by Franco's forces, while the governments of Western

72. This pursuit of normality is a prominent theme of the essays contained in Bessel and Schumann, *Life after Death*.

73. F. Bloch-Lainé and J. Bouvier, *La France restaurée, 1944–1954: Dialogue sur les choix d'une modernisation* (Paris, 1986), 43–47; Agosti, *Rodolfo Morandi*, 424–25. The rhetoric of "restoration" had of course a particular resonance in Germany. See Roseman, "Restoration and Stability," 141.

Europe soon discovered the pragmatic advantages of concluding agreements with the Spanish regime.[74]

The political character of the new Western Europe was also becoming clear. By 1946 the coalitions of national union that had been created at the moment of liberation had begun to unravel. In their place, there was a resurgence of fierce partisan rivalries, exacerbated by the material shortages of the era, and by the often rapid succession of local and national elections. These conflicts took various forms, opposing Socialists against parties of the centre-right, and Catholics against secular parties; but increasingly the primary division was between the Communists and the other parties. Throughout Europe, both east and west, collaboration between Communists and non-Communists proved difficult to achieve, and even more difficult to sustain. In Czechoslovakia, which fell within the Soviet sphere of influence, this culminated in the winter of 1947–48 in the collapse of multiparty democracy and its replacement in reality, if not in name, by a single-party state.[75] In the west, however, it led in the spring of 1947 to the semi-enforced departure of the Communists from the coalition governments of France, Italy, and Belgium, and the subsequent marginalization of Communist parties, movements, and militants.[76]

This too was in its own way a return of normality: Communism had long been a much-distrusted presence in European political life. The parting of the ways between Communism and West European democracy that took place in the second half of the 1940s was, however, all the more dramatic because it occurred after an era when the commitment of the Communists to the national cause had been demonstrated in rhetoric and in deed through the prominent role that party militants had played in the struggles for national liberation against Nazi rule. The sacrifices that the Communists, alongside their Soviet allies, had made for the cause of patriotic resistance gave the parties in much of post-war Europe a moral legitimacy as the *parti des fusillés*—the party of the executed—as the members of the French Communist Party, the PCF, characterized themselves at the

74. D. A. Messenger, "Exporting Republicanism: The French Government's Defence of Political Prisoners in Franco's Spain after France's Liberation," in *After Fascism: European Case-Studies in Politics, Society and Identity since 1945*, ed. M. Berg and M. Mesner (Vienna, 2009), 37–57; F. Guirao, *Spain and the Reconstruction of Western Europe, 1945–57: Challenge and Response* (Basingstoke, UK, 1998), 189–92.

75. M. Myant, *Socialism and Democracy in Czechoslovakia 1945–1948* (Cambridge, UK, 1981).

76. A. Boxhoorn, *The Cold War and the Rift in the Governments of National Unity: Belgium, France and Italy in the Spring of 1947* (Amsterdam, 1992).

liberation.[77] This gave them the prestige and levels of popular support that seemed destined to assure them a central role in post-war democracy.

This was, moreover, a responsibility that many Communist leaders appeared eager to assume. The war years had invested Communists' definitions of their political goals with a new seriousness. In particular, the struggles and sacrifices incurred in the Resistance led them to emphasize the national context of their ambitions. Communist programmes of the mid-1940s rejected much of their former internationalist rhetoric in favour of their pursuit of national paths to socialism.[78] The Communists had become the hyper-patriots of the era, and this in turn gave increased importance to their commitment to democracy: the peoples of Europe freed from Nazi occupation would become the masters of their own affairs within their national boundaries. Thus, rather than pursuing the elusive prospect of revolution, the Communist parties of Western Europe focused on the twin causes of national liberation and the construction of a progressive democracy. Indeed, in the fluid political circumstances of the era from 1943 to 1947, the Communists were almost alone in embracing wholeheartedly the language and symbolism of democracy. The project of a people's democracy was expressed with different linguistic and national nuances by all of the Western European Communist parties. In part, their purpose was instrumental: at a time when the Communists were fully engaged in what they regarded as a race towards electoral victory, this language was intended to reassure hesitant voters that their goals were no longer those of the revolutionary template of 1917, or the conspiratorial revolutions attempted by the Communists during the interwar years. Instead, the PCF's goal of a *République démocratique, laïque, et sociale*, or the *democrazia di tipo nuovo* advocated by Togliatti as the leader of the Italian Communist Party, the PCI, was presented as a broad-based progressive regime, in which enhanced social rights would be accompanied by political pluralism.[79] In a prominent interview given (in a sign of the new political realities) to *The Times* in November 1946, the French Communist leader Maurice Thorez referred repeatedly to the "national and democratic character" of the PCF, insisting that "the Communist Party,

77. *Histoire du Parti communiste*, 451.

78. E. Lalmand, *Bâtir une Belgique nouvelle* (Brussels, 1946); Gotovitch, *Du rouge au tricolore*; Z. Suda, *Zealots and Rebels: A History of the Ruling Communist Party of Czechoslovakia* (Stanford, CA, 1980), 193.

79. E. Mortimer, *The Rise of the French Communist Party 1920–1947* (London, 1984), 328–33; R. Ventresca, *From Fascism to Democracy: Culture and Politics in the Italian Election of 1948* (Toronto, 2004), 53–57; P. Major, *The Death of the KPD: Communism and Anti-Communism in West Germany 1945–1956* (Oxford, 1997), 76.

in its action as part of the Government and within the framework of the parliamentary system it has helped to re-establish, will hold strictly to the democratic programme which has won for it the confidence of the masses of the people."[80]

These were, of course, words carefully crafted to appeal to a particular audience at a moment when Thorez was hopeful of becoming the next French prime minister. But they demonstrated, too, the distance that European Communist leaders had travelled since the international leadership of the Comintern had rather abruptly adopted its popular-front strategy in the mid-1930s.[81] Though disrupted by the subsequent voltes-faces in Soviet policy, most notably the Nazi-Soviet pact of 1939, as well as by the changes in leadership brought about by political persecution during the war years, the ambition for some form of juncture between the final goal of a socialist transformation of society and the more inclusive language of freedom, democracy, and social progress remained a consistent element of the mindset of many European Communists. It had found an outlet in the patriotic language of wartime resistance, which was carried over into the espousal of democracy in the post-war years. This did not imply an abandonment of Marxism: in contrast to the conventional parliamentary democracy of capitalist society, the Communist vision of popular democracy proposed a wider, deeper, and more powerful democratization of state, and more especially of society, in which popular participation and control would finally become a reality.[82]

This somewhat nebulous vision of democracy as a flexible vessel, by which European societies would pass beyond the conflicts of capitalism to enter a new socialist world, always sat uneasily with long-established Marxist assumptions about the necessity of a moment of revolutionary rupture.[83] However, until the uncompromising rejection of these ideas at the inaugural meeting of the Comintern held at Szklarska-Poreba in Poland in September 1947, the concept of a people's democracy enjoyed

80. "M. Thorez Explains His Party's Programme," *The Times*, 18 November 1946, 6. See also *Histoire du Parti communiste*, 486–89.

81. D. R. Brower, *The New Jacobins: The French Communist Party and the Popular Front* (Ithaca, NY, 1968).

82. Speech of Marcel Cachin in *Journal officiel de la République française, débats parlementaires, Assemblée nationale*, 14 January 1947, 3; G. Lyon-Caen, "L'avenir de la démocratie classique," *Cahiers internationaux* 26 (1951): 11–26; Buton *Lendemains qui déchantent*, 251–56.

83. The term "nebulous" is used by Joan Barth Urban to describe Togliatti's vision of a democratic path to Socialism in J. B. Urban, *Moscow and the Italian Communist Party: From Togliatti to Berlinguer* (London, 1986), 206–12.

wide support in Communist ranks, even in the USSR.[84] Moreover, whatever its doctrinal shortcomings, the appeal of a people's democracy was for many Western European Communists as much emotional as it was intellectual. For those who had suffered so much in the struggle against Nazism, it appeared finally to offer the means of reconciling their commitments to Communism and the nation, through a progressive democracy.

There was also much in this language that matched the political circumstances of the liberation era. It appeared to offer the opportunity for Communism to escape from its sectarian isolation within European political life, by reaching out to those broader sections of the population—notably women, young voters, and intellectuals—who were believed to sympathize with its goal of bringing about what the French Communist Party termed at its first post-war conference in Paris in June 1945 "l'élargissement de la démocratie".[85] Indeed, it was their fears as to its potential appeal that motivated the fierce hostility to Communist rhetoric of a people's democracy from other political groupings. Rather than welcoming their conversion to democratic values, Socialists, Christian Democrats, and any number of more-conservative-minded groups denounced the dictatorial and revolutionary ambitions that, they claimed, lay behind the duplicitous Communist use of the language of democracy.

In this way, the early years of the Cold War took the form of a rhetorical war over ownership of the concept of democracy. In response to the Communists' language of popular democracy, their opponents adopted the banner of what they regarded as a true democracy—one rooted in supposedly European values of freedom and pluralism—as the defining symbol of their anti-Communist identity. Thus, the regimes established in Western Europe by the end of the 1940s derived much of their coherence, and indeed their identity as democracies, through the exclusion of Communists from national government, as well as the enactment of state policies of discrimination against any grouping, such as trade unions or peace movements, believed to be a front for Communist subversion. The consequence was to create what was in effect an internal frontier within the democratic politics of post-war Europe—between east and west, but

84. Buton, *Lendemains qui déchantent*, 305–14; H. G. Skilling, "'People's Democracy' in Soviet Theory," *Soviet Studies* 3 (1951): 16–33. See also the retrospective critiques of the concept of people's democracy, half sincere and half opportunistic, voiced by the Yugoslav foreign minister Edvard Kardelj at a time when, immediately after its break with Moscow, the Titoist regime was eager to present itself as the voice of a pure Communism: E. Kardelj, *De la démocratie populaire en Yougoslavie* (Paris, 1949).

85. *Histoire du Parti communiste*, 456.

also within states—whereby Communists and non-Communists adopted what they came to regard as starkly antithetical visions of Europe's democratic future. When UNESCO (the United Nations Educational, Scientific, and Cultural Organization) convened a group of experts with the aim of reaching a common definition of democracy, they celebrated the fact that everybody now declared themselves to believe in democracy, but were also obliged to accept that this apparent agreement disguised two polarized discourses about democracy: "Both sides profess good reasons to believe that the conditions essential to democracy in one sense are incompatible in the other."[86] Of course, the emergence of this fault line owed much to wider events, and most especially the repercussions that the deterioration in relations among the victorious Allied powers had on all of the regimes in Europe, west and east. But it also had origins that predated the realpolitik of the nascent Cold War, and that reflected the way anti-Communist reflexes had become over the previous years an important component of political culture.

Almost everything that had happened in Europe since the mid-1930s had served to undermine the tentative common ground for collaboration between Communists and progressive-minded non-Communists generated by the anti-fascist campaigns of the Popular Front era. The collapse of the Popular Fronts in the late 1930s, the reversal in international Communist strategy imposed by the Nazi-Soviet Pact of 1939, and the subsequent de facto repression of the Communist parties in most European states in 1939–40 had created a much more polarized politics. This was changed only superficially by the German invasion of the Soviet Union in June 1941 and the subsequent engagement of the European Communist movement in armed resistance and campaigns of patriotic mobilization. Though Communists and non-Communists were now allied in a common cause, the political and organizational fault lines between them remained for the most part clearly defined. Fears of Communist machinations within the Resistance were felt particularly strongly by those, such as the Socialists, who were conscious of their weakness within this new organizational world.[87] These divisions were also strongly reinforced after liberation by bitter struggles between Socialists and Communists for control of trade unions and local councils, and thereby of factories and local communities. Town halls, committees of liberation, union offices, and welfare

86. R. McKeon and S. Rokkan, eds., *Democracy in a World of Tensions: A Symposium Prepared by UNESCO* (Paris, 1951), 523.

87. M. Pradoux, *Daniel Mayer, un socialiste dans la Résistance* (Paris, 2002), 211–26; Lidegaard *Short History of Denmark*, 185–86.

institutions all formed part of a very direct tussle in the industrial heart-lands of Europe for the vital levers of power and of political legitimacy.[88]

The prospect that the defeat of Nazism would enable a return to the Popular Front politics of the 1930s, or indeed a broader progressive union, therefore proved to be illusory. This was not due to a lack of effort on the part of the Communist leaders. They made repeated offers to the Socialists to form political alliances or, more radically, to fuse their political organizations in a "reunified" socialist movement, by reversing the split between the Communist and Socialist movements that had occurred in nearly all European states after the First World War.[89] Anti-communism proved, however, to be a much more powerful legacy of the war than did philo-communism. For most European Socialists, Communism was an essentially anti-democratic and even totalitarian political movement, which through its commitment to Leninist notions of a dictatorship of the proletariat constituted the opposite of the democratic values that, a little retrospectively, many European Socialists regarded as a core element of their political ideology.[90] This was a lesson learnt from wartime struggles, and which appeared to be confirmed by the events they observed in Soviet-occupied central and eastern Europe in the immediate post-war years. The visible spectacle of heavy-handed Soviet political and military intervention provided an education in instalments in anti-Communism, culminating in the so-called Prague Coup in February 1948, which destroyed the functioning democracy in Czechoslovakia and replaced it with a Communist-led dictatorship.[91] Nor were such actions limited to the east. Many Western Europeans regarded the turbulent protest campaigns and strikes initiated by the Communist parties in Western Europe in 1947 and 1948 as proof that the Communists had become the new fifth column within democracy.[92]

88. R. Hemmerijckx, "The Belgian Communist Party and the Socialist Trade Unions," in *Comrades and Brothers: Communism and Trade Unions in Europe*, ed. M. Waller, S. Courtois, and M. Lazar (London, 1991), 124–42; M.-P. Dhaille-Hervieu, *Communistes au Havre: Histoire sociale, culturelle et politique (1930–1983)* (Mont Saint-Aignan, France, 2009), 163–92.

89. "French Socialists Debate Communist Offer," *The Times*, 18 November 1946, 6; Conway, *Sorrows of Belgium*, 197–200.

90. See, for example, G. Saragat, *Socialismo democratico e socialismo totalitario: Per l'autonomia del Partito Socialista* (Milan, 1946), 20–25; S. M. Di Scala, *Renewing Italian Socialism: Nenni to Craxi* (New York, 1988), 47–65. See also pp. 183–84.

91. See also pp. 156–58.

92. J. Nevakivi, "From the Continuation War to the Present," in *From Grand Duchy to a Modern State: A Political History of Finland since 1809*, by O. Jussila, S. Hentilä, and

In sum, democracy was no longer what united the erstwhile war-time allies, but what divided them—politically, philosophically, and territorially—from each other. This divergence between, on the one hand, a Communist language of popular or progressive democracy based around the will of the people and, on the other, a Western European commitment to the values of democratic pluralism acquired definition through the journalistic polemics and electoral campaigns of the later 1940s. As the end of one war was replaced by the prospect of another, events dangerously close to home in central Europe—notably the Soviet blockade of the Allied military zones in Berlin and the creation of the German Democratic Republic—and by the end of the decade further afield in China and Korea gave an apparent urgency to the need for democratic forces to unite to resist the threat posed by Soviet-directed subversion.[93]

The emotional depth of anti-Communism in the western half of Europe was, however, always more than simply a response to Soviet ambitions, real and imagined. It also became part of a cultural identity. Much of the population had come to regard the purposes and methods of Communism as the antithesis of the social, political, and ideological character of Western Europe.[94] This anti-Communism was reinforced by the propaganda of the United States, and of many European political groups. But it derived its plausibility from the wider evolution that had taken place during and after the war towards a more conservative-minded mentality, in which radical social or political change of any kind was perceived as alien to the moderate values of Western Europe. In comparison to the stark and often violent confrontations of the interwar years, the politics of post-war Europe operated in a narrower spectrum, within which a commitment to democracy, and the concomitant values of individual freedom, became a key badge of identity. Consequently, the rejection of Communism—with its somewhat caricatured commitment to radical political change, spirit of political militancy, and ruthless control of all of the instruments of power—was an integral part of this shared understanding of democracy.[95]

Not all, however, benefited equally from this anti-Communist consensus. For parties of the left, and especially the majority of Socialists who rejected an alliance with the Communists, it was always difficult to differentiate their Socialist goals—those of a socialism that was respectful

Nevakivi (London, 1999), 234–35; Major, *Death of the KPD*, 259–77; J.-P. Gault *Histoire d'une fidélité: Témoignage chrétien, 1944–56* (Paris, 1964), 283–95.

93. L. Reichold, *Geschichte der ÖVP* (Graz, 1975), 188.

94. Greenberg, *Weimar Century*, 17.

95. See in this respect pp. 159–60.

of liberal values and traditions—from those of Communism, especially in the face of the polemical attacks of their electoral opponents. Conversely, the momentum of anti-Communism reinforced the political and ideological identity of movements of the political centre-right, and most notably the new parties of Christian Democracy. The strong performances by the Christian Democratic Party in Belgium (the CVP-PSC), the Mouvement républicain populaire (MRP) in France, and the Christian Democrats (DC) in Italy in elections held during the first half of 1946 demonstrated that not everybody had been radicalized towards the political left by the war. Instead, Christian Democracy provided a rapidly expanding pole of attraction, especially in Catholic areas of Western Europe, for those sections of the population, particularly middle-class and rural voters, attracted by its message of legality, order, and social capitalism, combined with a latent or explicit anti-Communism.[96]

The key event in this political transition was the general elections held in Italy in April 1948. Against the backdrop of the wider conflicts of the Cold War, including what was perceived as the Communist coup in Prague in February 1948, the Christian Democrats led by the prime minister, de Gasperi, and the Communists of Togliatti (allied for once in a rather slender Popular Front with the majority Socialist party led by Nenni) mobilized their supporters through mass rallies, poster campaigns, and, in the case of the DC, the emphatic support of the Catholic hierarchy. The result of what the Socialist Giuseppe Saragat termed "a choice of civilizations" proved to be decisive—48.5 per cent voted for the DC and 31 per cent for the Communist-led Popular Front—and the possibility of a transition to some form of people's democracy rapidly evaporated.[97] In some ways, the election campaign demonstrated the ways in which the Cold War had curtailed democratic freedoms: behind the scenes, the American government gave substantial financial assistance to de Gasperi's Christian Democrats, and the Italian Ministry of the Interior used its powers to disrupt the activities of Communist militants. But in other ways the election was an emphatic victory for democracy. The campaign was largely peaceful; more than twenty-seven million male and female Italians—a remarkable 92% of the electorate—voted in a free and orderly manner; and the principal loser, Togliatti, praised the calm and civic sense displayed by the electors. When a potential assassin wounded the Communist leader in July 1948, party

96. Conway "Age of Christian Democracy," 43–67. Re. the concept of social capitalism, see K. van Kersbergen, *Social Capitalism: A Study of Christian Democracy and the Welfare State* (London, 1995).

97. Ginsborg, *History of Contemporary Italy*, 118; Rizi, *Benedetto Croce*, 252.

FIGURE 3. V for Victory, and V for Vote: men reading the press during the Italian elections of April 1948. Hulton Deutsch/Corbis Historical via Getty Images

supporters briefly occupied factories and a number of public buildings in some northern cities; but, calmed by a call for order issued by Togliatti from his hospital bed, these extralegal activities soon came to an end.[98]

The Italian election campaign of 1948 thus demonstrated the limitations—but also the resilience—of democratic structures in Western Europe. As Togliatti's words indicated, respect for the rules of the electoral game was shared by the Communist leader and his Christian Democratic opponent.[99] Both accepted the legitimacy of the opposing camp; and democracy provided not only a means of winning power, but also of coming to terms with defeat. In Togliatti's case, his attitude no doubt owed much to his recognition that any attempt to challenge the Italian state would have been doomed to fail. But his pursuit of a legalist and non-insurrectionary course also drew on more than twenty years of Communist activism and his sincere belief that a revolutionary transition to Communism—in effect a repetition of 1917—would not provide the basis for a durable socialist regime in a Western European context. Communists could not grab power, but had to win it, through encouraging the

98. Ventresca, *From Fascism to Democracy.*

99. M. Del Pero, "Containing Containment: Rethinking Italy's Experience during the Cold War," *Journal of Modern Italian Studies* 8 (2003): 549.

development of progressive trends within democracy. As early as 1936, he had developed his idea of a "democracy of a new type" in response to the events of the Spanish Civil War, where he had been sent as a representative of the Comintern. This was, in effect, the strategy he sought to implement in Italy from 1943 onwards, placing the rapidly expanding PCI at the centre of the Resistance, the trade unions, and the new post-Fascist political system.[100] It was a policy that also had the approval of the Comintern and of Stalin, who in December 1947 bluntly replied to an Italian Communist emissary impatient for revolution that "Today, it is not possible."[101]

At heart, however, it also accorded with the ambitions of the Communist leaders of Western Europe, such as Togliatti, for whom the goal of a democratic transition to socialism was always more than a tactic. This was not a universal attitude. There were always those within Communist ranks who resented the social and political compromises imposed by seeking to build a coalition of allies, and who regarded participation in parliamentary democracy as an abandonment of Communist ideals.[102] The problem, however, that always confronted those who advocated going "beyond democracy" was the evident unreality of an insurrectionary strategy. The strike waves that occurred regularly during the post-war years demonstrated the grievances felt by many workers who believed, with real justification, that they were not receiving their share of the fruits of economic recovery;[103] but the workers tangibly lacked the resources to serve as the agents of a wider change of political regime. Compared with the spectacle of real insurrection as manifested by the anti-Stalinist demonstrators in Budapest in 1956 or by the opponents of French rule in the cities of Algeria in the later 1950s, the idea of a revolution of the left in Western Europe appeared rather suddenly to have been consigned to the past tense.

Communist attitudes to democracy during the post-war decades therefore rested on an ever more tangible disjuncture between words and actions. On the one hand, they used every opportunity to denounce, often with real virulence, the actions of American, capitalist, and neo-fascist forces who had stolen the democratic freedoms fought for in the wartime struggle against Nazism, and had transformed the countries of Western

100. Urban, *Moscow*, 122–23.

101. Ventresca, *From Fascism to Democracy*, 153–54. Re. Communist strategy more generally, see R. Mencherini, *Guerre froide, grèves rouges* (Paris, 1998), 235–52.

102. A. Marty, *L'affaire Marty* (Paris, 1955), 218–45; Conway, *Sorrows of Belgium*, 231–32.

103. See pp. 233–34.

Europe into "vassal states" of the United States.[104] On the other hand, they participated in the democratic process at the national and local levels, with all that entailed in terms of the pursuit of votes and alliances, as well as the exercise of power and respect for legal procedures. The Communists therefore continued to act as democrats, encouraging their followers to make use of their legal freedoms, even as they denounced the absence of democracy.[105] The almost schizophrenic attitude that this duality fostered was exacerbated by the suffocating influence exercised over the Western European parties during the late Stalinist years by the Comintern. The ever more virulent tone of the campaigns led by the Communist parties for democracy and peace (in opposition to the American imperialist occupation of Europe and the war in Korea) coupled with ritualistic references to the wisdom of Stalin and to the Soviet Union as "the country which acts as the guide of democracy and peace"—le pays qui est le guide du camp de la démocratie et de la Paix dans le monde—lacked political plausibility, and prevented the Western European Communist parties from articulating an alternative discourse of democracy.[106]

This oppositionist stance led the Communists, almost despite themselves, out of the democratic mainstream. Police infiltration and the regular revelations—however far they were manipulated by the Soviet leadership—of traitors within Communist ranks encouraged a return to the siege mentality of the war years, in which current political events were interpreted through the prism of references to occupation, resistance, and betrayal. They had been drawn into a world of distorting mirrors in which conspiracy theories and empty slogans took the place of engagement with the rapidly modernizing social and political landscapes of Western Europe.[107] This was reinforced by the way in which the Western European Communist parties tacked repeatedly in response to the changing winds from the Soviet Union after the death of Stalin and the Soviet-led

104. E. Lalmand, *Reconquérir l'indépendance nationale: Sauver la paix. Rapport présenté au Xe Congrès national du PCB, Bruxelles, 23-24-25-26 mars 1951* (Brussels, 1951), 7-13, 25-34; P. Robrieux, *Histoire intérieure du Parti communiste*, vol. 2 (Paris, 1981), 297-354.

105. PCB, *Démocrates, la loi est pour vous. Faites-la respecter* (Brussels, [early 1950s]).

106. E. Lalmand, *Notre lutte pour l'indépendance nationale, la démocratie et la paix* (Brussels, 1952), 1-2, 18-19, 64; H. Footitt, "American Forces in France: Communist Representations of US Deployment," *Cold War History* 11 (2011): 85-98; A. Brogi, *Confronting America: The Cold War between the United States and the Communists in France and Italy* (Chapel Hill, NC, 2011), 123-25.

107. See E. Morin, *Autocritique* (Paris, 1959), for the disabused view of a former Communist. See also the perceptive comments of M.-P. Dhaille-Hervieu in *Communistes au Havre*, 215-25.

armed intervention in Hungary in 1956. Events in Budapest in the autumn of that year were in this respect a defining moment for the relationship between Communism and democracy, most especially in France. At the liberation, a phalanx of leading intellectuals had embraced, either explicitly or more loosely, the political mentality of the French Communist Party. For Sartre and many others, the Communists became—whatever their shortcomings—the necessary vehicle for a politics that went beyond the limited democracy of the Fourth Republic. That possibility was largely destroyed by the spectacle of the violent repression conducted by Soviet troops on the streets of Budapest. Some chose to justify the Soviet intervention as necessary to pre-empt the resurgence of fascism; but such language, with its resonances of the war years and the 1930s, had an evident obsolescence, and for many more 1956 proved to be a decisive parting of the ways.[108]

Henceforth, Communism would be more important in the democratic politics of Western Europe as an ideological alternative than as a political movement. The Communist parties of France and Italy remained a powerful presence, able to rally votes and to exert their influence within particular localities and trade unions. They drew in new recruits, too, often from intellectual backgrounds, for whom their fundamental differentness and refusal to adopt the facile electoralism of the other political parties constituted a major element of their appeal.[109] But Communism no longer possessed a realistic strategy for acquiring political power. The parties found themselves, not for the first time, pursuing the chimera of a large democratic alliance with the Socialists and other progressive forces at the same time as their actions and statements were reinforcing the gulf in policy and above all in mentality between the Communists and these other political forces.[110] This was most striking in Italy, where the principal Socialist party, the PSI, finally decided in 1956 to abandon the policy of alliance with the Communist PCI that Nenni had followed with remarkable determination during the previous decade, presenting his new

108. S. Khilnani, *Arguing Revolution: The Intellectual Left in Postwar France* (New Haven, CT, 1993), 34–45, 68–69; M. S. Christofferson, "French Intellectuals and the Repression of the Hungarian Revolution of 1956: The Politics of a Protest Reconsidered," in *After the Deluge: New Perspectives on the Intellectual and Cultural History of Postwar France*, ed. J. Bourg (Lanham, MD, 2004), 253–76.

109. See, notably, P. Robrieux, *Notre génération communiste, 1953–1968: Essai d'autobiographie communiste* (Paris, 1977); M. Ozouf, *Composition française: Retour sur une enfance bretonne* (Paris, 2009), 170–80.

110. G. Ross, *Workers and Communists in France: From Popular Front to Eurocommunism* (Berkeley, CA, 1982), 91–94; Urban, *Moscow*, 218–24.

anti-Communist policy as "the definitive choice for democracy" (la scelta definitiva della democrazia) by the PSI.[111]

Communism, it seemed, had rather suddenly become old-fashioned. The emphasis placed by Communist parties on a stark dichotomy of progressive and reactionary forces, and of a decisive transition to socialism led by a vanguard party,[112] no longer fitted with the more amorphous frontiers of the protest politics of the later 1950s and the 1960s. Campaigns against nuclear weapons or in favour of the liberation of women and colonial peoples gave rise to new political alliances, within which the Communists were often tangibly ill at ease.[113] The consequence was to create a bifurcation between the political and intellectual left. While the Communist parties lost much of their purchase within European politics during the 1960s, Marxism would flourish, almost as never before, as the principal intellectual resource of those who opposed the democratic status quo. Liberated from the tutelage of the Communist parties (and indeed of the Soviet Union), Marxist ideas played a major part in challenging post-war democratic norms. They did so, however, from outside the realm of conventional political debate. As such, Marxism had become a counter-discourse about western democracy, rather than its political rival.[114]

{≈≈≈⟩⦅≈≈≈}

The post-war marginalization of Communism laid the basis for the top-down democratic reconstruction that occurred in Western Europe during the later 1940s. Between 1946 and 1949 France, Italy, and Germany received new constitutions, elections were held on inclusive franchises (including the participation for the first time of the female majority of the adult electorate in France, Belgium, and Italy), and substantial new state and parastatal structures were put in place, including much-expanded welfare institutions and forms of economic corporatism. Taken together, these changes amounted to the most substantive moment of political and constitutional change in Europe between 1918 and 1989. Political democracy received rather rapidly a new mould that, with the exception of the

111. P. Nenni, *Il socialismo nella democrazia* (Florence, 1956), 49–73, 96–97; A. De Grand, *The Italian Left in the Twentieth Century: A History of the Socialist and Communist Parties* (Bloomington, IN, 1989), 126–30.

112. See, for example, *Histoire du Parti communiste*, 607.

113. See, for example, J.-J. Becker, "L'intérêt bien compris du Parti communiste français," in *La guerre d'Algérie et les Français*, ed. J.-P. Rioux (Paris, 1990), 235–44; L. Magri, *The Tailor of Ulm: Communism in the Twentieth Century* (London, 2011), 134–37.

114. See pp. 269–71 and 283–84.

inglorious collapse of the French Fourth Republic in 1958, would endure largely unchanged until at least the 1970s, and in many of its essentials until 1989 and beyond.

There was much about this process of constitutional refoundation that was emphatically democratic, as was demonstrated by the considerable energies invested by all parties in the drafting of the new Italian constitution inaugurated in 1948, with its commitments to removing all obstacles to full social and economic equality.[115] These were not empty words. The democracy of the post-1945 era was a sincere and serious project that marked the final acceptance of universal suffrage as the basis of rule.[116] But it was also a managed one, carried through not by the people but by an elite of politicians, civil servants, and public administrators, who were initially its architects and subsequently its ruling class.[117] Inspired by the projects of state reform widely advocated in the 1930s and the war years, as well as by the models provided by the American New Deal and Allied occupation regimes, they melded together state authority and parliamentary representation in the form of a more structured democracy. The democratic mandate provided by elections and the assemblies of parliamentary government was buttressed by efficient public institutions. Above all, the new democracy was intended to be emphatically modern. The collapse of the parliamentary regimes of the interwar years in the face of internal disaffection and external invasion had convinced the democracy-builders of post-war Europe of the need for a strong centralized state. Staffed by an expanded, depoliticized, and more technically qualified bureaucracy, this state was intended to act as the social manager, asserting the primacy of the national interest over the pressures exerted by sectional interest groups, but also assuming the wide range of managerial functions essential to the functioning of a modern society and economy.[118] The most important changes in the structures of post-war democracy were therefore

115. M. Tambor, "'An Essential Way of Life': Women's Citizenship and the Renewal of Politics in Italy," in *After Fascism: European Case-Studies in Politics, Society and Identity since 1945*, ed. M. Berg and M. Mesner (Vienna, 2009), 209–14; B. Thomassen and R. Forlenza, "Catholic Modernity and the Italian Constitution," *History Workshop Journal* 81 (2016): 231–51.

116. P. Rosanvallon, *Le sacre du citoyen* (Paris, 1992), 449–55.

117. The coherence of the elite emerges clearly from Philip Nord's prosopographic study *France's New Deal*. See also G. Elgey, *La République des illusions 1945-1951, ou La vie secrète de la IVe République* (Paris, 1965), 302–3; and C. Andrieu, "Introduction: Politiques de Pierre Sudreau," in *Pierre Sudreau, 1919-2012: Engagé technocrate, homme d'influence*, ed. Andrieu and M. Margairaz (Rennes, 2017), 65–81.

118. H. Finer, *Road to Reaction* (London, 1946), 131.

not constitutional reforms but the reshaping of the internal mechanisms of the state. More effective forms of taxation were introduced, and younger and better qualified staff recruited to replace the overly politicized state officials of the interwar years. New public institutions too were created, such as the French *Commissariat général du Plan*, which assumed responsibility for the state's expanded social and economic functions.[119]

This was therefore a democracy built to last. The hierarchical models of administration introduced after the war privileged those who stood at the centre rather than the periphery. Thus, with the important (and Allied-directed) exception of West Germany, a federalization of the structures of government was avoided: policy was defined by the central state bureaucracy, and then implemented through the subordinate layers of state and provincial administration and, ultimately, local government.[120] Moreover, the state itself was increasingly centralized: rather than individual ministries, it was the office of the prime minister—most notably in the West German case the all-powerful Office of the Chancellor—that directed the machinery of government. This *Kanzlerdemokratie*, as it came to be termed during Adenauer's lengthy period of office as the inaugural chancellor of West Germany in the 1950s and early 1960s, created a new culture of professional governance.[121] Rather than the notables, lawyers, and parliamentary orators of the past, the post-war democracies drew on the skills and expertise of the increasingly large proportion of the university-educated population employed in state institutions. Nowhere was this change more evident than at the level of local government. The post-war decades were in many ways a golden age for Western Europe's thousands of communes and town and city councils, as rapidly expanding state budgets enabled local elected officials and their more professional bureaucracies to carry out ambitious projects of infrastructural development and social-welfare provision, including meeting the urgent need for housing. In turn, however, local government lost much of its autonomy: communities were no longer in any meaningful sense self-governing, and became dependent on the finance, expertise, and plans provided by the central state bureaucracy.[122]

119. P. Mioche, *Le Plan Monnet: Genèse et élaboration, 1941–1947* (Paris, 1987). See also A. J. Nicholls, *Freedom with Responsibility: The Social Market Economy in Germany 1918–1963* (Oxford, 1994), 11–14.

120. A. Pelinka and M. Welan, *Demokratie und Verfassung in Österreich* (Vienna, 1971), 49–52.

121. A. Doering-Manteuffel, *Die Bundesrepublik Deutschland in der Ära Adenauer: Aussenpolitik und innere Entwicklung, 1949–1963* (Darmstadt, 1983), 24–29.

122. For a good example of this process, see R. Wakeman, *Modernizing the Provincial City: Toulouse, 1945–1975* (Cambridge, MA, 1997).

The institutional architecture of the new democracies was remarkably uniform. Rather in the manner of the concrete apartment blocks built to house the millions of Europeans in need of new homes, the political structures of the new states had something of a simplified and ready-made character. Elections, held by universal suffrage, decided the composition of national parliaments, composed of a single, directly-elected chamber, supplemented in some cases by a second, "higher" chamber with generally very limited powers.[123] These, in turn, determined the formation of governments, almost invariably composed of a coalition of parties, which relied for their existence on being able to command a majority of the votes needed to pass their legislation in the lower house of parliament. Republicanism provided the explicit or tacit constitutional model;[124] monarchs were reduced to a ceremonial role or, as in Italy, were disposed of entirely. Similarly, presidents, elected not by the people but by parliament or an enlarged electoral college of political notables, were honorific figures, chosen on the basis of their seniority or, in some cases, their consensual anonymity. On constitutional issues, the direct will of the people was expressed through the holding of referenda, as occurred with the establishment of the French and Italian republics in 1946. But these exercises in direct democracy were used very sparingly. The appropriate channel for the expression of the will of the people was through the periodic elections by which, with due seriousness of mind, the peoples of Europe chose their representatives to do the business of government for them.[125]

The central authority of the state within post-war democracy was, however, supplemented and in some ways complicated by the roles assumed by a range of other bodies. The effective disappearance of legitimate state governance that had occurred in many areas of Europe during the latter war years reinforced the role of local notables and business figures, as well as of social institutions, especially the churches and trade unions, which had taken over responsibility for crucial wartime tasks such as the provision of food and welfare. This informal power did not disappear at the end of the war, and it carried over into the active involvement of these bodies in the business of post-war government. Indeed, through the creation

123. See, for example, the Danish constitutional reform of 1953: Lidegaard, *Short History of Denmark*, 226.

124. K. Renner, "Gesellschaft, Staat und Demokratie" (18 November 1948), in *Für Recht und Frieden: Eine Auswahl der Reden des Bundespräsidenten Dr. Karl Renner* (Vienna, 1950), 114.

125. See pp. 131–34.

of corporatist structures with responsibility for areas of socio-economic decision-making, a plethora of sectional organizations, professional lobby groups, and associations of experts acquired a recognized and tangible role in the making of public policy.

The underlying tension that this created between state-focused and more corporate forms of government was evident across a number of fields of policy-making during the post-war years: bureaucrats created uniform models, which were revised or indeed reversed by the intervention of a variety of interested parties. The impact this could have on governance was well illustrated by the case of welfare reform. Ambitious projects for the rationalization of welfare provision had been developed in many European states during and after the Second World War, with the intention of ensuring more universal welfare provision.[126] However, the implementation of these plans rarely proved to be straightforward. This was most strikingly so in the case of France. The bold vision of a single social-security system developed in London from 1942 onwards by a cohort of Free French officials—many of whom had initially devised their plans while working for the Vichy regime—was eroded after the liberation by the lobbying of employers, farmers' organizations, and myriad other interest groups who wished to retain elements of the pre-existing structures of provision and, particularly, of delivery.[127] In France, as in much of Western Europe, the "welfare democracy" that came into existence after the Second World War was therefore a complex hybrid creation, in which principles of universality and, more especially, of equality were complicated by various forms of exemption, special funding, and differential provision.

Despite the rapid post-war expansion in its financial and material resources, the state was far from being all-powerful within post-war democracy. In some spheres of policy-making, direct control by the state retreated, as corporatist institutions such as wage councils and economic planning bodies, composed of the representatives of workers, employers, and other interested parties, assumed a more direct role in the management and regulation of wages, prices, and welfare provision. In Austria, for example, the political alliance between Socialists and Christian Democrats

---

126. D. de Bellefroid, "The Commission pour l'Etude des Problèmes d'Après-Guerre (CEPAG) 1941-1944," in *Europe in Exile: European Exile Communities in Britain 1940-45*, ed. M. Conway and J. Gotovitch (Oxford, 2001), 128-29; Lidegaard, *Short History of Denmark*, 236-39.

127. P. V. Dutton, *Origins of the French Welfare State: The Struggle for Social Reform in France, 1914-1947* (Cambridge, UK, 2002), 184-225; E. Jabbari, *Pierre Laroque and the Welfare State in Postwar France* (Oxford, 2012), 132-55.

found its social equivalent in the creation of a quasi-legal Economic Commission, the *Wirtschaftskommission*, composed of the representatives of the trade unions, employers, and farmers' organizations, which from 1947 effectively excluded the central state from responsibility for many areas of socio-economic policy-making.[128] Elsewhere, the subordination of the state to such social interest groups was less emphatic; but almost everywhere the expansion of corporatist institutions blurred the distinctions between state and society. Rather than subordinating society to its rule, the post-war democratic state drew an increasingly professionalized cadre of trade-union officials, employers, and other social professionals into a collaborative ethos of governance.[129]

In addition, there were the political parties. The post-war democracies were, above all, party democracies, or indeed "a state of parties."[130] For many contemporaries, the most striking difference between the pre-war and post-war regimes was the dominant role that parties assumed within politics. This ascendancy of the parties was at the expense of parliaments. National parliaments constituted the principal symbols of the recovery of freedom, and in times of crisis they became the arena of fierce conflicts and on occasion of close-run votes. In general, however, parliamentary culture after the Second World War lacked the air of drama that had often characterized the parliaments of interwar Europe. Proceedings were more formal, and also more predictable, as much of the substantive power was transferred from the floor of parliament to the offices and committees of the parties. This was deliberate: in its institutional structures, the French Fourth Republic might have resembled its pre-war predecessor, but the intention was that the stability provided by internally disciplined parties would prevent a return to the short-lived governments of the Third Republic.[131] The leaders of the principal parties were therefore the most powerful figures within the democratic politics of post-war Europe. They were the men who brokered coalitions, made the key political decisions, both within and outside government, and who provided, as a political-science textbook of 1960 explained, the "vital link between mass populations and the vast apparatus of omnicompetent government."[132]

128. Herz, "Compendium of Austrian Politics," 571, 614–18; J. Lewis, *Workers and Politics*, 104–23.

129. See pp. 138–41.

130. Ventresca, *From Fascism to Democracy*, 41–42.

131. D. Thomson, *Democracy in France: The Third and Fourth Republics*, 2nd ed. (Oxford, 1952), 229–37; Rioux, *Fourth Republic*, 107–11.

132. H. Finer, *The Major Governments of Western Europe* (London, 1960), 9.

The ascendancy of party-political hierarchies—what Léo Hamon termed "l'âge des appareils"[133]—contributed to the somewhat muted tone of post-war democratic politics. The new cohorts of political figures who came to the fore in the post-war decades appeared to contain few outstanding individuals, less because of a fundamental lack of talent than because the political system, especially at the national level, no longer encouraged such figures to emerge. A capacity to communicate with the electors mattered less than managerial competence and negotiating skill. Both in the coalition governments of the period and in the bureaucratic structures of the political parties, reliability and an ability to master the complex, often technical, dossiers of public policy-making mattered more than personal charisma or the somewhat outmoded talents of parliamentary oratory.[134] Unsurprisingly, those political leaders who did stand out in the politics of post-war Europe were therefore men of quiet and predominantly conciliatory talents. The long-lasting prime minister of Sweden in the post-war decades Tage Erlander, the Dutch prime minister from 1948 Willem Drees, and Achille Van Acker, who was prime minister of Belgium on a number of occasions in the 1940s and 1950s, were all figures whose popularity rested on their careful manipulation of a reassuring image of pragmatic common sense and sober reliability.[135] Western Europe, in that sense, got the political leaders that it deserved, or, more exactly, those best suited to the political system.

This was reinforced by the political immobility of the post-war era. Those parties that established themselves as the principal political forces after the liberation tended—the precipitate decline of the MRP in France in the 1950s excepted—to remain in place throughout the subsequent consolidation of the new democracy. Parties had largely ceased to be mass-mobilizing movements, and had become essentially cadre institutions, dominated by closed elites, who took decisions at some remove from the relatively passive membership. The dominance of this political class was

133. L. Hamon, *De Gaulle dans la République* (Paris, 1958), 29.

134. See, for characteristic examples, F. Lafon, "Des principes du molletisme," and A. Michel, "Guy Mollet en parlement," in *Guy Mollet: Un camarade en République,* ed. B. Ménager, P. Ratte, J.-L. Thiébault, R. Vandenbussche, and C.-M. Wallon-Leducq (Lille, 1987), 59–91 and 285–97; G. Kwanten, *August-Edmond De Schryver 1898–1991: Politieke biografie van een gentleman-staatsman* (Leuven, 2001); G. Eyskens, *De memoires* (Tielt, Belgium, 1993).

135. O. Ruin, *Tage Erlander: Serving the Welfare State, 1946–1969* (Pittsburgh, PA, 1990); H. Te Velde, *Stijlen van leiderschap: Persoon en politiek van Thorbecke tot Den Uyl* (Amsterdam, 2002), 158–63, 179–86; J. Vercleyen, *Témoignage sur Achille Van Acker* (Brussels, 1967), 79–88.

assisted by the systems of proportional representation that were adopted across much of Western Europe, and which had the effect of minimizing the impact of shifts in electoral popularity. In some states, most members of parliaments were elected on party lists, whereby the electors cast their votes for a list of candidates proposed by the party, ensuring that much of the real power over who was elected to parliament lay with the party officials (who decided the rankings of candidates) rather than with the individual voters.[136] Elections consequently lost some of their centrality in political life. Defeat or victory was measured less in the drama of electoral results than in more subtle shifts of influence within party institutions, or changes of political coalition. This immobility reinforced, too, the stability of the political class. Politics became a somewhat predictable career, whereby successful politicians advanced through successive levels of the representative hierarchy—from local council to parliament or ministerial office—largely as a consequence of their status within their party rather than their wider public profile.[137]

This evolution towards a bureaucratized and predictable politics was particularly marked in the case of the Christian Democratic and Socialist parties. Both were milieu parties, which operated within wider associational structures such as trade unions and, in the case of the Christian Democrats, the highly imposing edifice of Catholic (and to a lesser extent Protestant) social, spiritual, and economic associations.[138] These affiliated institutions provided the basis for the recruitment of their cadres, and acted as the interface between the parties and the wider society. The consequence was to prioritize issues of policy and of material interest over ideology. The Socialist and Christian Democratic parties made much of their commitment to distinctive political philosophies; but, in reality, these impinged only intermittently on the more pragmatic business of government. Both were essentially coalitions—albeit ones bonded by a sense of underlying affinity—within which regional and sectional interest groups jockeyed for advantage. Policy-making in these circumstances was often an arduous and incremental process, as trade unions, producers, and a variety of other interest groups sought to influence party programmes and nominate their supporters to positions of responsibility. As an American official commented wryly of the Catholic ÖVP in Austria, this internal

136. Elder, Thomas, and Arter, *Consensual Democracies?* 143–51; Herz, "Compendium of Austrian Politics," 562.

137. R. Aerts, H. De Liagre Böhl, P. De Rooy, and H. Te Velde, *Land van kleine gebaren: Een politieke geschiedenis van Nederland 1780–1990* (Nijmegen, 1999), 267.

138. See pp. 185 and 190–91.

competition between its competing interests on occasions simply brought the party to "a dead stop."[139]

Such tensions were scarcely new in the world of mass politics. Ever since the pioneering analysis of Robert Michels in Imperial Germany prior to the First World War,[140] political scientists had been drawing attention to the way in which internal party structures were often oligarchical in ethos and practice. In an age of democracy, however, the absence of internal party democracy was particularly visible. For all their protests that they were mass-membership movements, almost all of the major parties in post-war Europe were essentially top-down institutions, in which the individual members had little real power.[141] This reflected the dominance of party bureaucracies, as well as of affiliated organizations, but also the changing nature of political debate. From time to time, issues came to the fore—such as nuclear weapons, or indeed the position of the Catholic Church in public life—that aroused passions and provoked political controversy. But, more generally, the impact of rapid socio-economic changes, and more especially the key role that the state assumed in the management of society, drew the political parties into technical issues of economic policy-making, where divisions of ideology or even of social class mattered less than the interplay of sectional interests.

The consequence was to encourage a self-consciously pragmatic ethos of government that became the defining characteristic of post-war politics. In the views of many, the more complex and technological society being created by rapid economic growth had changed the nature of governance: the challenge for governments lay in resolving problems of economic and social management, rather than the clash of opposing world views. This somewhat depoliticized vision of modern government found its intellectual expression in the slogan coined by Daniel Bell, and subsequently taken up by Raymond Aron and many other liberal commentators: "the death of ideology."[142] Especially with the marginalization of Communism, the ideologically rooted divisions of mid-century Europe appeared to have lost much of their former sting. Instead, foreshadowing Aron's comments in Berlin in 1960, Bell declared that the "ideological age had ended." The

139. Herz, "Compendium of Austrian Politics," 585.

140. R. Michels, *Political Parties: A Sociological Study of the Oligarchical Tendencies of Modern Democracy* (New York, 1962). See especially the introduction by S. M. Lipset: 15–39.

141. See the contemporary empirical study, S. H. Barnes, *Party Democracy: Politics in an Italian Socialist Federation* (New Haven, CT, 1967).

142. D. Bell, *End of Ideology*. See also C. Waxman, ed., *The End of Ideology Debate* (New York, 1968).

regimes of the western world had adopted a new model of incremental change based on "a rough consensus . . . : the acceptance of a Welfare State; the desirability of decentralized power; a system of mixed economy and of political pluralism."[143] As Carl Schorske wrote in his influential essay of 1967, with reference to the very different politics of the 1890s, Europe had arrived at a "politics in a new key."[144]

Such formulations were revealing of the comfortable world inhabited by many post-war intellectuals and academics, sheltered from the uncertainties and material hardships that continued to dominate the lives of many less privileged Western Europeans. But they were indicative also of the way in which the bandwidth of democratic politics had narrowed considerably during the first fifteen years of the post-war era. Between 1945 and the early 1960s, Communism was only one of the political losers. So too were political ideologies of the nationalist right. During the early post-war years, a range of political movements of the right had emerged, including the Gaullist Rassemblement du peuple français (RPF), the royalist supporters of King Leopold III in Belgium, and a number of protest parties that had some success in regional elections in the first years of the German Federal Republic. These, however, proved to be a transient presence. The populist rhetoric of nationalism did not emerge as a major strand of politics, as it had done in many European states during the 1920s and 1930s. In particular, the crises of the European colonial empires in Asia and Africa during the later 1940s and 1950s failed to impact significantly on European politics. The challenges to Dutch rule in the East Indies, British authority in India, and French administration of Indochina presented the European states with substantial problems, but they did not generate a surge in popular support for the nationalist right. Empire, it seemed, was too far away to disrupt democratic politics; and it was only when it came much closer with the crisis of French rule in Algeria from the mid-1950s onwards, and the consequent radicalization of the *pied noir* settlers in Algeria against the governments of metropolitan France, that the retreat from empire provoked a domestic political crisis.

There was no inevitability to this failure of the nationalist right. While the demise of the Third Reich and its satellite regimes and allies destroyed the credibility of certain forms of racial extremist politics, many of the

143. D. Bell, *End of Ideology*, 373. See also the sceptical comments of Reinhard Bendix on Bell's thesis, in an essay initially published in 1964: R. Bendix, *Embattled Reason: Essays on Social Knowledge* (New York, 1970), 18–61.

144. C. Schorske, "Politics in a New Key: An Austrian Triptych," *Journal of Modern History* 39 (1967): 343–86.

social attitudes that had provided the basis for the extreme-right politics of the interwar years, such as anti-Semitism and resentment of the privileges of a political elite, remained very much present.[145] Moreover, despite the purges after 1945, many of the intellectual and journalistic figures who had been the principal tenors of polemical right-wing ideas in the interwar years were able to regain their positions, albeit in more moderate guises, within post-war cultural life.[146] And yet the old politics of the nationalist right did not recover mass support. In West Germany, most notably, the early success of the neo-right parties faded rapidly during the 1950s.[147] The rhetoric of aggrieved nationalism that had been such a powerful force behind the right-wing parties of the Weimar Republic lacked plausibility in the more integrated context of Cold War Europe. Whoever the French and Germans sought to hold responsible for their grievances in the post-war years, their principal target was generally not on the other side of the Rhine. Moreover, in Germany and elsewhere in Western Europe, the oppositional politics of economic and social protest that had provided the lifeblood of the extreme-right movements of the interwar years no longer possessed the same force. The militants and electorates of former movements of the authoritarian right in France, such as the Parti social français, migrated instead into the democratic mainstream, featuring prominently among the supporters of the MRP and the Gaullist RPF in the immediate post-war years.[148] Whereas previously farmers, small businessmen, and students had mobilized behind parties of the nationalist right in demanding fundamental political change, they now preferred to lobby within the established political structures.[149] Thus, even when a protest movement such as Poujade's Union de défense des commerçants et artisans (UDCA) succeeded in rallying electoral support in France in the 1950s through its denunciation of the political elite, it lacked the social and political implantation that would have converted its ephemeral electorate into a more permanent presence.[150] The world of the

145. R. Vinen, "The End of an Ideology: Right-Wing Antisemitism in France, 1944–1970," *Historical Journal* 37 (1994): 365–88.

146. J. Wasserman, *Black Vienna: The Radical Right in the Red City, 1918–1938* (Ithaca, NY, 2014), 220–22.

147. R. Stöss, *Politics against Democracy: Right-Wing Extremism in West Germany* (Providence, RI, 1991), 91–92.

148. S. Kennedy, *Reconciling France against Democracy: The Croix de Feu and the Parti Social Français, 1927–1945* (Montreal, 2007), 260–65.

149. See pp. 216–18.

150. C. Crespin, "Le poujadisme en Normandie: Un mouvement éphémère," *Annales de Normandie* 67 (2017): 93–115. Re. Poujade, see also pp. 128–29.

populist right consequently remained confined to the margins of political debate, addressing its messages to restricted milieux of embittered former soldiers, contrary-minded journalists, and those nostalgic for the Third Reich, who constituted the self-limiting audience for its ideas.[151] Maurice Bardèche—one of the few right-wing intellectuals to attract a significant audience in the post-war years—recognized the political impotence of the extreme right, mocking "le pullulement anarchique de petits groupes qui ne sont découragés ni par la faiblesse de leurs effectifs ni par la pauvreté de leurs résultats."[152]

The one major opportunity for the nationalist right to break into the mainstream of European political life appeared to be the political and constitutional crisis that enveloped France in May 1958. The refusal of French settlers and officials in Algeria to accept the decisions of the government in Paris led to the collapse of the Fourth Republic and its replacement, after a nervous period of political vacuum, by the appointment of Charles de Gaulle as prime minister on 1 June. He was vested by parliament with exceptional powers for six months to address the crisis in Algeria, and create a new constitutional structure. This was much more than simply another governmental crisis. The sudden eruption of the violent street politics of Algiers into the politics of mainland France led to social mobilization and state repression on a scale unequalled in the politics of Western Europe between the later 1940s and 1968.[153] Moreover, there were many— especially in Algiers, but also among the general's entourage—who initially hoped that de Gaulle's assumption of power would open the way to some form of authoritarian or neo-Bonapartist revolution. However, the window for radical political change proved to be transitory. De Gaulle was by temperament and conviction anything but a revolutionary, and he used his position of power distinctly cautiously. The founding of the new Fifth Republic in 1958 was a rather careful exercise in political consolidation, motivated by the fear that the events in Algeria might initiate an unravelling of state authority equivalent to that which had occurred after the German invasion of France in the summer of 1940. De Gaulle's concern was not to overthrow power but to reassert it, notably by investing the

151. J. Algazy, *La tentation néo-fasciste en France 1944–1965* (Paris, 1984), 76–92.

152. "the anarchic multiplication of little groups which are discouraged neither by the small numbers of their supporters, nor by the poverty of their impact": M. Bardèche, *Qu'est-ce que le fascisme?* (Paris, 1961), 98. Re. Bardèche, see Algazy, *Tentation néo-fasciste*, 199–221.

153. O. Rudelle, *Mai 58: De Gaulle et la République* (Paris, 1988); R. Rémond, *1958: Le retour de de Gaulle* (Brussels, 2008).

executive authority of the state with greater independence from parliament. He drew many (though not all) of the leading political figures from the Fourth Republic into negotiations, which led to the creation of what remained a tangibly democratic regime. Above all, his recognition in 1961— after having initially tried to achieve the opposite—that a pacification of Algeria was impossible, led him to reach an agreement with the nationalists of the Front de libération nationale (FLN) through the Evian Accords of March 1962, which led to Algerian independence. His willingness to conclude what his erstwhile close ally Jacques Soustelle angrily denounced as a "Munich nord-africain" marked his final divorce from those radical elements in Algeria and the army, whose rebellion against the Republic in 1958 had provided the springboard for his return to power.[154]

De Gaulle had a much shrewder sense of what was politically possible in 1958 than had many of his more hot-headed supporters. His decision to embed the new Republic, and his own position as its founding president, within the established structures of the state owed more to his sense of pragmatism than to any distinctive Gaullist creed.[155] For all of the skill with which he had manipulated the crisis of May 1958 to his advantage,[156] de Gaulle did not possess a ready-made constitutional alternative. He was probably as surprised as anybody else by his return to office; and he contented himself with embracing the familiar rituals of French republicanism, promising to protect what he described in characteristically vague terms as the "libertés traditionnelles de la France."[157] He was careful too to surround himself with figures who embodied in their biographies the continuity of the French state. Thus, he entrusted Michel Debré with devising the constitution of the new Republic. Debré was a senior civil servant who had been one of the principal architects of the re-establishment of state authority during the summer of 1944. But he had long been a prominent critic of the way in which the dependence of governments of the Fourth Republic on electoral fortunes and party alliances had frustrated the initial ambition of reformers at the liberation to carry through the effective modernization of the French state.[158]

154. S. Berstein, *The Republic of de Gaulle* (Cambridge, UK, 1993), 51–57; J. Soustelle, *La page n'est pas tournée* (Paris, 1965), 8.

155. J.-M. Domenach, "Democratic Paralysis in France," *Foreign Affairs* 37 (1958): 34.

156. J. Jackson, *A Certain Idea of France: The Life of Charles de Gaulle* (London, 2018), 453–76.

157. O. Rudelle, "Gaullisme et crise d'identité républicaine," in *La guerre d'Algérie et les Français*, ed. J.-P. Rioux (Paris, 1990), 200–201. See also Rudelle, *Mai 58*, 283–93.

158. M. Debré, *La République et ses problèmes* (Paris, 1952). Re. Debré, see also J. Perrier, *Michel Debré* (Paris, 2010), 114–24, 175–95; Chapman, *France's Long Reconstruction*, 209–59.

Unsurprisingly, the new constitution, announced on 4 September 1958 and approved by just short of 80 per cent of votes in a referendum hastily organized later the same month, marked a substantial reconfiguration of presidential, executive, and parliamentary authority. The president would be elected by a college of political notables rather than by parliament, and had wide powers to hold referenda, invoke emergency powers, appoint the prime minister, and dissolve parliament. Ministers, too, would be responsible to the prime minister rather than to parliament, from which they were required to resign before taking up their ministerial office. Parliament consequently was reduced, or restored, to its core status as a legislative body, and its approval remained required for the budget and for all pieces of legislation.[159] But, for the defenders of the parliamentary model of republican governance, the separation of the executive and the legislature was unacceptable, prompting an influential group of French officials and politicians to declare that the new constitution was "at odds with all of the evolution of western democracy" (à rebours de toute l'évolution de la démocratie occidentale).[160] However, for its advocates, and above all for de Gaulle himself—who was duly elected as the first president of the new republic in December 1958—the constitution was designed to end the interminable partisan wrangling that they claimed, with some exaggeration, had characterized the Fourth Republic. Instead, the new separation of powers—reinforced by the creation of a Constitutional Council to rule on the legal aspects of legislation—would deliver effective and technocratic governance.[161]

Yet, it is also notable what did not change in 1958. Parliament remained firmly in place, and all of the principal political parties, with the exception of the Communists, gave their approval to the new constitutional structure. There was too much weight of established practice for the new constitution to mark a sudden rupture. Debré—who was chosen by de Gaulle to be the first prime minister of the Fifth Republic in January 1959—was at pains to reject any idea that the new regime marked an abandonment of democracy. Instead, he insisted with some force, if a little vaguely, that the new regime would operate within the political and legal confines of

159. For a clear account of the political and constitutional changes of 1958, see N. Atkin, *The Fifth French Republic* (Basingstoke, UK, 2005), 34–42.

160. C. Andrieu, *Pour l'amour de la République: Le Club Jean Moulin, 1958–1970* (Paris, 2002), 421. See also A. Chatriot, *Pierre Mendès-France: Pour une république moderne* (Paris, 2015), 163–68.

161. Berstein, *Republic of de Gaulle*, 8–11.

"légitimité démocratique."[162] The continuities, too, were ones of personnel and of mentalities. Many of the leading figures in the new regime had
been active in the Fourth Republic, albeit in ministries and other state
institutions rather than in parliament. They welcomed the greater freedom that the new constitutional structure accorded them to enact policies of modernization, which they had been advocating, in some cases,
since the war years. But they also had a shrewd awareness, reinforced
by the failures of the Vichy state, that durable reforms could not simply
be enacted by decree. Thus, the new regime maintained the established
democratic practices of consultation and collaboration with parliamentarians, elected local officials, and a much wider range of interest groups and
socio-economic organizations.[163]

{⚬⚬⚬⚬}

The mature model of democratic governance that emerged in Western
Europe was therefore one where power was more shared than imposed.
The classical model of democracy emanating from the single source of a
parliament composed of the elected representatives of the people appeared
outmoded in complex societies, where governance had become more diffuse and more multilayered. The consequence was a striking inversion of
the qualities with which democracy was associated. Whereas it had formerly
operated within the templates of popular rule, progressive change, and the
ideological conflicts inherited from the French Revolution of 1789 and the
nineteenth century, democracy was now presented as distinctively modern
and non-partisan. Its qualities were those of partnership between erstwhile
foes, the effective management of socio-economic challenges rather than
their exploitation, and above all the privileging of stability over change.[164]

This value shift was well expressed by the expanding discipline of
political science in Western Europe and North America during the 1960s.
For the cohort of political scientists who came to the fore after 1945, the
modern democracies of western states were not the product of past history,
but very much present-day institutions, which reflected the contemporary
reality of western societies.[165] This was evident too in their methodology:

162. M. Debré, *Refaire une démocratie, un état, un pouvoir* (Paris, 1958), 34.

163. Chapman, *France's Long Reconstruction*, 241–47.

164. Strote, *Lions and Lambs*, 12–14, 268–74.

165. Finer, *Major Governments*. Re. Finer, see also M. Conway, "Democracy in Western
Europe after 1945," in *Democracy in Modern Europe: A Conceptual History*, ed. J. Kurunmäki, J. Nevers, and H. Te Velde (New York, 2018), 231–33.

political science was a neutral empirical discipline, based on the analysis of quantitative data and the institutions that constituted the political machinery. By studying comparatively these nation-state democracies
across a world that remained, either tacitly or explicitly, primarily western
and northern in its contours, this generation of political scientists aimed to
identify the key factors that enabled these democracies to provide effective
rule and, above all, stability. As the influential Dutch-born political scientist Arend Lijphart commented in a paper written in 1967, "the question
of stability has become the dominant concern of contemporary comparative studies of democratic systems."[166] Lijphart's use of the term "system"
was characteristic of the age, but also of this way of thinking. For him and
for his colleagues of the same generation, such as the Norwegian political
scientist Stein Rokkan, democracy was not a specific political regime, but
an all-encompassing form of rule. Democracy had become the common
system of management in what, again in the language of the time, they
termed the "advanced" western societies.[167]

Thinking outside of democracy, according to this logic, had become
effectively impossible. Accidents might happen—regimes, such as the
French Fourth Republic, might collapse under particular pressures, or
be overthrown, as occurred in Greece after the coup by the colonels in
April 1967—but these were no more than minor disruptions from the
predominant trend of western societies towards a sophisticated and
essentially unassailable democracy. Even in the authoritarian time warp
of Francoist Spain, the development of a more sophisticated negotiation
between different institutions and factions had created what one observer
termed a "pseudo-democratic tendency."[168] Thus, when two academics,
Ernest Gellner and Ghita Ionescu, organized a conference in London in
1967 to discuss the "anti-politics" of populism, subsequently published as
an influential collection of essays, what was most striking was the absence
of any discussion of Western Europe. For them, as for many others, the
populism that had driven the electoral success of Hitler and many others
in the early decades of the twentieth century had become a phenomenon

166. A. Lijphart, "Typologies of Democratic Systems," in *Politics in Europe: Comparisons and Interpretations*, ed. Lijphart (Englewood Cliffs, NJ, 1969), 51.

167. E. Allardt and H. Valen, "Stein Rokkan: An Intellectual Profile," in *Mobilization,
Center-Periphery Structures and Nation-Building*, ed. P. Torsvik (Bergen, 1981), 11–38. See
also the instructive career of Maurice Duverger: V. Hoffmann-Martinot, "A Short Biography of Maurice Duverger," *French Politics* 3 (2005): 304–9.

168. J. Amodia, *Franco's Political Legacy: From Dictatorship to Façade Democracy*
(London, 1977), 39.

limited to Latin America and the Third World.[169] This was not just a certain European arrogance. It was based on the widely shared assumption that the ascendancy of democracy was inseparable from indices of socio-economic progress. What had begun as the specific regime of Western Europe and North America was destined to emerge elsewhere, as a rising tide of material and social development floated the states of the post-colonial world into the ranks of the advanced societies. Such determinism might appear simplistic, but it reflected the way that the post-war consolidation of democracy had come to appear inseparable from the rapid material development of Western Europe. Neither was cause or consequence. Together they constituted a melding of politics, governance, and socio-economic order that would prevent any return to the violent politics of the recent past.[170]

This interpenetration of society and regime was confirmed by the way that the politics of the 1960s appeared to have lost their adversarial character. Everybody, it seemed, was now a participant in the exercise of power in ways that blunted political antipathies, and excluded fundamental challenges to the status quo. This culture of shared power was well expressed by the vogue among political scientists in the 1960s and 1970s for the phenomenon of "pillarization." Again, Lijphart was the most enthusiastic exponent of the concept. Taking initially the example of his native Netherlands, which he subsequently extended to other European states, he argued that the ideological and social conflicts of the past had been overcome by a system of shared governance, whereby the "pillars" of the Socialist, Catholic, Protestant, and Liberal associational worlds enjoyed considerable autonomy, while also collaborating on issues of shared concern.[171] This was more than an empirical observation. For Lijphart and those political scientists who followed him in his increasingly ambitious studies of democratic systems across the world, "non-majoritarian" democracy, and the culture of power-sharing that it fostered, provided the means of establishing a more effective regime than the rule of an electoral or parliamentary majority, with the consequent abrupt shifts in power and lack of respect for political opponents.[172]

169. G. Ionescu and E. Gellner, eds., *Populism: Its Meanings and National Characteristics* (London, 1969). See also pp. 128–31.

170. See also pp. 294–95.

171. A. Lijphart, *The Politics of Accommodation: Pluralism and Democracy in the Netherlands* (Berkeley, CA, 1968).

172. A. Lijphart, *Patterns of Democracy: Government Forms and Performance in Thirty-Six Countries*, 2nd ed. (New Haven, CT, 2012). See also the essays in the *Festschrift* published in honour of Lijphart: M.M.L. Crepaz, T. A. Koeble, and D. Wilsford,

Pillarization was very much a concept of its age, which, as its critics were quick to point out, ignored the extent to which the collaborative democracy it celebrated relied upon the suppression of tensions within each pillar.[173] But it did have a point. The occasional and somewhat ritualized outbursts of electoral or partisan hostilities excepted, the democratic politics of the 1950s and 1960s in many areas of Western Europe did have the air of negotiation rather than of combat. In party politics, hopes of a decisive electoral victory, and still more of the categorical defeat of one's opponents, receded rapidly. Each party attempted to maximize its electoral score, in order to put itself in a position of strength vis-à-vis its interlocutors. But in the end everybody was obliged to accept the need for coalition government, and what Aron referred to with some irony as the "carrousel des ministres."[174] In this way, the so-called Westminster model, with its sharply drawn antipathy between two dominant parties, seemed increasingly at odds with the culture of power sharing that prevailed in much of Western Europe.[175] This was perhaps most explicit in Switzerland and in Austria, where the immobile politics of the Grand Coalition of the People's Party (ÖVP) and the Socialist Party (SPÖ) from 1945 to 1966 in effect divided power within the post-war Austrian republic between its two principal political and social forces. The consequent so-called *Proporz* system, with its careful sharing out of influence within state institutions between the two parties, entrenched their ascendance, but also essentially removed the people from the political process.[176]

This ethos of shared governance contributed to the stability, if not always to the effectiveness, of post-war democratic regimes. At its best, collaboration facilitated an equitable distribution of the resources of government, as well as a consensual approach to decision-making at the national and, increasingly, the European levels.[177] At its worst, however,

---

eds., *Democracy and Institutions: The Life Work of Arend Lijphart* (Ann Arbor, MI, 2000), especially the essays by D. Wilsford, "Studying Democracy and Putting it into Practice: The Contributions of Arend Lijphart to Democratic Theory and to Actual Democracy," 1–7, and A. Lijphart, "Varieties of Nonmajoritarian Democracy," 225–45.

173. M.P.C.M. van Schendelen, "The Views of Arend Lijphart and Collected Criticisms," *Acta Politica* 19 (1984): 19–55. It should be noted also that Lijphart silently abandoned his use of the term in his later work. For example, it does not feature in his *Patterns of Democracy*.

174. Raymond Aron, *Démocratie et totalitarisme* (Paris, 1965), 10.

175. S. Hellemans, *Strijd om de moderniteit* (Leuven, 1990).

176. G. Lehmbruch, *Proporzdemokratie* (Tübingen, Germany, 1967); Pelinka and Welan, *Demokratie und Verfassung*, 45–48, 325–27; O. Rathkolb, *The Paradoxical Republic: Austria, 1945–2005* (New York, 2010), 30–53.

177. Re. European integration, see pp. 143–45 and 212–15.

this culture of partnership encouraged a lowest-denominator pragmatism, whereby power, and the fruits of political influence, were shared around between parties and the interests they represented.[178] Power-sharing blunted conflicts, both old and new; but issues of principle, it seemed, mattered less than discovering an expedient means of getting things done. This was evident at many levels in post-war government, and contributed to the relative weakness of debate and a language of moral authority in the democratic politics of the post-war era. Politics based on choice and moral leadership appeared to have been effaced by a bureaucratic culture of governance, which in fields such as social legislation was often unconsciously discriminatory in its treatment of women or of those such as recent immigrants who did not fit easily within conventional societal norms.[179] Western European politics was thus more obviously inclusive than it was either participatory or egalitarian.

{∗∗∗∗∗∗∗∗}

The most striking example of the weakness of this moral dimension in post-war politics concerns the legacies of the Second World War. The many unresolved problems left over from the war years were closed down in favour of pressing forward, often somewhat obsessively, with the challenges of the future. The ambition that a new era of justice would emerge from the sufferings of the war had been central to the aspirations of the liberation.[180] But any hope of a general settling of accounts rapidly dissipated during the post-war years, as the initial energy of prosecution and purging was frustrated by the enormous scale of the task, the pragmatic dictates of economic reconstruction, and the slowness of legal processes. Thus, in both Austria and West Germany, the initial scope of denazification was radically reduced to the prosecution of an ever smaller cluster of guilty men designated as having been the true agents of the Nazi system. At the same time, amnesties allowed the reintegration of the large majority of those who had been party members

178. See the disabused, if retrospective, presentation of the conduct of politics in the French Fourth Republic in G. Elgey, *La République des contradictions 1951–1954* (Paris, 1968), 9–14.

179. See, for example, R. Chin and H. Fehrenbach, "German Democracy and the Question of Difference," in *After the Nazi Racial State: Difference and Democracy in Germany and Europe*, by Chin, A. Grossmann, and G. Eley (Ann Arbor, MI, 2009), 102–36.

180. See pp. 30–31. See also Deak, Gross, and Judt, *Politics of Retribution*, and Koreman, *Expectation of Justice.*

and bureaucratic officials, or whose actions could be attributed to the disciplines and circumstances of war.[181]

This too was, in part, democratic. The scaling down and subsequent effective abandonment of the prosecution of those responsible for the crimes committed during the war years owed much to the pragmatic attitudes of those in power. Local officials and Allied authorities tended to regard the investigation of past crimes as at best an irrelevance and at worst a threat to the consolidation of the post-war regimes.[182] But, at heart, the reluctance to dig too deeply into issues of responsibility for past actions was a policy with which the large majority of Western Europeans came to concur. Demands for the prosecution of wartime collaboration largely disappeared from public debate by the end of the 1940s, as initial hopes of some form of rapid and transparent justice were replaced by widespread cynicism at the motives that lay behind particular prosecutions. A prevalent belief developed that the purges were directed disproportionately against the so-called "small fry" rather than those who had the money or influence to protect themselves from prosecution. This was especially so in West Germany and Austria, where the attempts of the Allied authorities to direct measures of denazification rapidly came to be resented as an illegitimate intervention in the affairs of local communities. Instead, the political parties—the Communists excepted—vied for electoral advantage by defending those threatened by a more thoroughgoing purge of the mass of state officials and party members.[183]

Democracy worked predominantly against any coming to terms with the legacies of the Nazi and wartime past. In the new circumstances of a recovered but still fragile normality, it was much more attractive to efface past divisions through the construction of inclusive national discourses of collective suffering, patriotism, and the recovery of freedom. The war therefore came to appear to be further away in post-war Europe than it really was. At a time when many lives remained indelibly marked, and deeply (but also often quietly) traumatized, by the events of the war and its aftermath, there was little public appetite for a comprehensive

181. N. Frei, *Adenauer's Germany and the Nazi Past: The Politics of Amnesty and Integration* (New York, 2002), xi–xiii, 311–12; S. Niederacher, "Die Entwicklung der Entnazifizierungsgesetzgebung," in *Entnazifizierung zwischen politischem Anspruch, Parteienkonkurrenz und Kaltem Krieg*, ed. M. Mesner (Vienna, 2005), 13–36.

182. Conway, *Sorrows of Belgium*, 131–32, 341–42; Frei, *Adenauer's Germany*, 308–9.

183. R. Knight, "Denazification and Integration in the Austrian Province of Carinthia," *Journal of Modern History* 79 (2007): 580–612; S. Niederacher, "Die öffentliche Rede über Entnazifizierung, 1945–1949," in *Entnazifizierung zwischen politischem Anspruch, Parteienkonkurrenz und Kaltem Krieg*, ed. M. Mesner (Vienna, 2005), 37–58.

reckoning with the difficult issues it raised.[184] Coming to terms with the past—a phrase that lacked any defined meaning—was a challenge that post-war European societies were poorly equipped to address. Rulers and ruled alike preferred instead to knit together elements of the war years to construct a usable past.[185] The rituals of commemoration enacted by the state authorities, in collaboration with the institutions of civil society, packaged the memory of the war into simple dichotomies—of perpetrators and victims, of male soldiers and female civilians, and of compatriots and foreigners—that avoided addressing the complexity of the actions of individuals and institutions during the preceding years.[186] None of this was straightforward to achieve, but over time it did largely succeed in creating a culture of commemoration of the wartime past. This served as a foundational narrative for the post-1945 present as well as embedding remembrance of the war within the civic and associational structures of post-war societies: the war would not be forgotten, but its memory would serve to unite rather than divide.[187]

It is tempting to see in the stories that Europeans told one another about the war years the manifestation at the societal level of the difficulties experienced by individuals in digesting the experiences of the war. As Norbert Frei has persuasively argued, the creation of national narratives of remembrance responded to the "collective psychic needs" of European populations who were seeking, however unconsciously, to evade the unmanageable nature of their recent past.[188] By occluding the extent of wartime collaboration, as well as the complicity of state authorities and of occupied populations in the implementation of the Holocaust, European populations and their leaders were engaged in a collective policy of denial. Its long-term consequence would be the bundle of unresolved issues and sense of collective guilt that would return to bedevil Western European

184. O. Wieviorka, *Divided Memory: French Recollections of World War II from the Liberation to the Present* (Stanford, CA, 2012), 35.

185. See the intelligent reflections of Frank Biess in *Homecomings: Returning POWs and the Legacies of Defeat in Postwar Germany* (Princeton, NJ, 2006), 228–29.

186. The now classic account of the construction of post-war official memory is Rousso, *Vichy Syndrome.*

187. Lagrou, *Legacy of Nazi Occupation*; Moeller, *War Stories*, 6–8, 12–14; R. G. Moeller, "Sinking Ships, the Lost *Heimat* and Broken Taboos: Günter Grass and the Politics of Memory in Contemporary Germany," *Contemporary European History* 12 (2003): 147–81; E. Heineman, "Gender, Sexuality and Coming to Terms with the Nazi Past," *Central European History* 38 (2005): 41–74.

188. Frei, *Adenauer's Germany*, 307. See also Knight, "Denazification and Integration," 575–76.

societies from the later 1960s onwards.[189] Collective memory, however, obeys logics different from those of individual psychology; and, though such psychological explanations have an obvious plausibility for certain actors and groups, the ways in which post-war societies addressed and evaded their wartime past was the product of a complex interrelationship between state policies, popular attitudes, and the activism of particular interest groups.

The memory of the war was a contested phenomenon that reflected the character of post-war democracy, both in its possibilities and in its limitations. Europeans did not in their large majority choose the way in which the war was remembered after 1945. As schoolchildren, but also as adult citizens, they were enrolled in rituals of commemoration that, through their patriotic discourses and their celebration of the values of discipline, heroism, and sacrifice, were designed to serve the interests of the state and of social order. But memory was never simply a matter of state manipulation and control. The personal memories of individuals, but also those of families and of particular communities, found their own spaces within post-war commemoration. Sometimes these took the form of the construction of counter-memories that defied the narratives of the state authorities.[190] But, more often, these particular forms of memory remained within the boundaries of the patriotic rhetoric of the post-war era. By inflecting these rituals with their own emphases, groups such as former soldiers, resisters, prisoners of war, or deportees customized the official script to serve their own purposes. In a similar way, local communities used the construction of war memorials and the choreography of rituals of commemoration, such as the renaming of streets and squares, to locate the national within the textures of the local.[191]

Memory therefore was also a democratic space, characterized by a jostling for influence—sometimes at a national level, but generally in more local and specific spheres—among a plethora of overlapping forms of remembrance, each of which displayed its own forms of selectivity. As memory of the war could never be either neutral or all-encompassing, the hierarchies accorded to both heroes and victims were themselves the

189. S. R. Suleiman, *Crises of Memory and the Second World War* (Cambridge, MA, 2006), esp. 4–8; T. Judt, "The Past is Another Country: Myth and Memory in Postwar Europe," in Deak, Gross, and Judt, *Politics of Retribution*, 305–13.

190. K. Aerts and B. De Wever, "Het verzet in de publieke herinnering in Vlaanderen," *Journal of Belgian History* 42 (2012): 78–107.

191. J. Foot, *Italy's Divided Memory*, 8–17. See also the collection of studies of the local textures of memory in Belgium in E. Peeters and B. Benvindo, eds., *Les décombres de la guerre: Mémoires belges en conflit, 1945–2010* (Waterloo, Belgium, 2012).

consequence of a surrogate form of election, in which the present generally had greater influence than did the past. Unsurprisingly, the principal
losers in this contest were those groups whose memories of the war did not
sit easily with the character of post-war societies. The selective pantheon
of dutiful soldiers, patriotic Resistance fighters, and anonymized innocent civilian victims—notably women and children—offered little space
for the commemoration of those, such as Communist militants, immigrant Resistance fighters, or female victims of rape, who did not fit easily
into these categories.[192] Most prominent, at least in retrospect, among
these absentees were the Jewish victims of Nazi extermination policies.[193]
The prominence that memory of the Holocaust subsequently attained in
memory of the Second World War has made its relative absence during
the decades immediately following the war appear all the more remarkable, and the foremost demonstration of the failure of post-war societies to
come to terms with wartime atrocities, and their own complicity in them.
There is much that is justified in such accusations. Few Europeans—
including some of those who had directly experienced Nazi policies of
extermination—were particularly eager to dwell on the issues of individual
and collective responsibility that Nazi policies raised, especially if they had
the potential to undermine narratives of national solidarity or impinge
on material rights.[194] This was, however, especially so when these issues
concerned a Jewish minority, whom many post-war Europeans continued
to regard, as a consequence of their ethnicity, politics, or immigrant background, as being somewhat less than fully national citizens.

The lack of receptivity to the recognition of Jewish victimhood owed
much to these long-standing forms of societal prejudice—but it was reinforced by the patterns of democratic politics.[195] Democratic universalism privileged the rights of majorities over those of minorities, and the
bureaucratic culture of post-war governance preferred the clarity of

192. J. C. Simmonds, "Immigrant Fighters for the Liberation of France: A Local Profile
of Carmagnole-Liberté in Lyon," in *The Liberation of France: Image and Event*, ed. H. R.
Kedward and N. Wood (Oxford, 1995), 29–41; R. Gildea, *Fighters in the Shadows. A New
History of the French Resistance* (London, 2015), 1–19, 205–39; J. Mark, "Remembering
Rape: Divided Social Memory and the Red Army in Hungary, 1944–1945," *Past and Present*
188 (2005): 133–61.

193. Wieviorka, *Divided Memory*, 72–75.

194. P. Lagrou, "Victims of Genocide and National Memory: Belgium, France and the
Netherlands, 1945–1965," *Past and Present* 154 (1997): 181–222. For an example of a survi-
vor's reluctance to dwell on the wartime past, see P. Steinberg, *Speak You Also: A Survivor's
Reckoning* (London, 2001).

195. M. M. Feinstein, *Holocaust Survivors in Postwar Germany, 1945–1957* (Cambridge,
UK, 2010), esp. 33–43.

uniform citizenship to the acknowledgement of ethnic and cultural difference. Consequently, the populations of Western European states had
difficulty in recognizing, or respecting, the forms of difference within their
own ranks. The patriotic rhetoric of the post-war years, as well as the population transfers and exterminations that had taken place during the war
years, had the consequence of creating societies that were more homogeneous in their composition, but more especially in their self-image.
Consequently, the universalist democratic cultures that developed after
1945 circumscribed the granting of specific rights to groups. The issue of
minority rights had become closely associated since the 1920s with Germany, and its protection and sponsorship of a wide range of supposedly
Germanic ethnic groups well beyond the frontiers of the Reich.[196] Many
of these populations had been swept away by the events of the latter war
years, while others had been discredited by their wartime espousal of collaboration. In the new democratic cultures of the nation-states of Western
Europe, there was therefore an assumption of sameness. All citizens were
henceforth equal, and forms of difference had to be subordinated to the
democratic will of the majority.

The emphasis on civic equality was a consequence of these attitudes,
but so too were the forms of social intolerance that also emerged in European culture after the war. Fitting in, both self-willed and imposed, characterized the rather conformist spirit often associated with the immediate
post-war decades. This created particular difficulties for those groups—
be they sexual minorities or members of particular linguistic or ethnic
communities—who stood out from the crowd. These problems were, however, particularly acute for those large numbers of immigrants from the
margins of Europe or beyond who arrived in Western Europe during the
1950s and 1960s. The presence of significant new population groups, iden-
tifiable not only by their skin colour but also by their different languages,
family structures, religious cultures, and forms of clothing and diet, was
disruptive not only of social norms but also of the self-image of Western
European states. One of the most pervasive consequences of the war years
and of the post-war partition of the European continent had been to reinforce the image of Western Europe as a homogeneously European and

196. U. von Hirschhausen, "From Minority Protection to Border Revisionism: The
European Nationality Congress, 1925–38," in *Europeanization in the Twentieth Century.
Historical Approaches*, ed. M. Conway and K. K. Patel (Basingstoke, UK, 2010), 87–109; S.
Carney, *Breiz Atao! Mordrel, Delaporte, Lainé, Fouéré: Une mystique nationale (1901–1948)*
(Rennes, 2015), 274–96, 383–501.

white society.[197] Whatever other forms of diversity—cultural, historical, and linguistic—it encompassed, the smaller and more inward-looking Europe that emerged from the war defined itself against those whom it regarded as non-European. This was evident in the hostility towards those colonial and black American soldiers who contributed to the liberation of Europe, as well as towards those—Roma, non-assimilated Jewish populations, and economic migrants from the borderlands of southern Europe—who constituted isolated symbols of diversity in post-war societies.

The prejudices and racist attitudes that these groups often encountered were far from novel, but the form that they took reflected the particular nature of the post-war societies. The arrival of economic migrants, from former colonial territories as well as from North Africa and Turkey, that gathered pace during the 1950s and 1960s was often encouraged by the state and by companies, eager to address post-war labour shortages. But they had not been invited by European populations, who often regarded them as threatening to social cohesion and economic prosperity. Such hostility could, at times, take violent forms—especially when, as in the case of Algerians in France, it was associated with an insurrection against the French state.[198] But more often it operated within the democratic norms of the post-war order. At a national level, the laws of citizenship and of residence were redefined to circumscribe the numbers of immigrants who could enjoy full rights of nationality and of citizenship. At the local and municipal level, housing and education provision were designed in ways that served to emphasize the differentness, and even segregation, of minorities defined as non-European. These policies, and the popular attitudes that they simultaneously expressed and reinforced, demonstrated the frontiers of citizenship in post-war Europe. The protection of the interests of the enfranchised majority took precedence over the individual and collective rights of those regarded as outsider minorities.

{≈≈≈}

How the war was remembered, and more generally the forms of selectivity that such memory embodied, cannot therefore be understood in isolation from wider social and cultural attitudes, and from the culture of post-war democracy. The shadows that continued to be cast over a Europe

197. R. Chin, *The Crisis of Multiculturalism in Europe: A History* (Princeton, NJ, 2017), 24–25.

198. J. House and N. Macmaster, *Paris 1961: Algerians, State Terror and Memory* (Oxford, 2006), 184–215.

experiencing what amounted to life after mass death contributed to the reluctance to reopen past wounds.[199] Awkward questions were not welcomed; but nor were they frequently posed. The discipline imposed by state authorities was reinforced by the self-discipline of citizens. Rulers and ruled collaborated in an attitude of restraint that Frank Biess has described as the "emotional regime" of West German democracy.[200] This is a term that had a particular resonance for the newly established Federal Republic, which found its national self-identification in the image of a society rebuilding itself through the discipline of labour out of the rubble of bombing, invasion, and national defeat.[201] The distrust that surrounded excessive displays of emotion and the value placed on correct forms of behaviour were expressive of the often difficult process whereby former combatants and victims were reintegrated into the regulated norms of German peacetime society.[202] But these phenomena were far from exclusively German. Everywhere in post-war Europe, there was a concern to reassert the values and symbols of civilized society, as reflected in the widespread adoption of norms of middle-class behaviour, and the disproportionate ire focused against those, be they unmarried mothers or disorderly teenagers, who appeared not to respect those norms.

The post-war reluctance to challenge boundaries also had more directly political consequences. This "controlled democracy"—to borrow the term that Oliver Rathkolb has used to describe post-war Austria[203]—was one in which heretics, of various kinds, often found it difficult to make their voices heard. The polarization that had undermined the Weimar Republic and had led the Austrian and Spanish republics into civil war in the 1930s was replaced by a political system that valued compromise

199. The idea of life after death provides the defining framework of Bessel and Schumann, *Life after Death.*

200. F. Biess, "Feelings in the Aftermath: Toward a History of Postwar Emotions," in *Histories of the Aftermath: The Legacies of the Second World War in Europe,* ed. Biess and R. G. Moeller (New York, 2010), 43.

201. D. Wierling, "Generations as Narrative Communities: Some Private Sources of Public Memory in Postwar Germany," in *Histories of the Aftermath: The Legacies of the Second World War in Europe,* ed. F. Biess and R. G. Moeller (New York, 2010), 104; R. G. Moeller, "Winning the Peace at the Movies: Suffering Loss and Redemption in Postwar German Cinema," in *Histories of the Aftermath: The Legacies of the Second World War in Europe,* ed. F. Biess and Moeller (New York, 2010), 139–55.

202. P. Betts, "Manners, Morality and Civilization: Reflections on Postwar German Etiquette Books," in *Histories of the Aftermath: The Legacies of the Second World War in Europe,* ed. F. Biess and R. G. Moeller (New York, 2010), 196–214; Van Rahden, "Clumsy Democrats," 485–504; Biess, *Homecomings,* 97–125.

203. Rathkolb, *Paradoxical Republic,* 30.

and partnership more highly than the frank expression of differences. Suddenly everybody appeared to agree more than they disagreed, and to find virtue in doing so.[204] As a consequence, parliamentary politics, as satirized by the West German writer Wolfgang Koeppen in his 1953 novel *Das Treibhaus* (*The Hothouse*), became a contrived game in which the personal reputations of politicians—but no real issues of substance—were at stake.[205] This was of course only a partial truth. It neglected new and often intense sources of political division, over European defence policy or over the politics of colonial retreat, which emerged during the 1950s.[206] But the years between the Second World War and the mid-1960s did have something of the character of a lull: past storms had blown themselves out, while the socio-political conflicts that would manifest themselves at the end of the 1960s had yet to acquire real definition. Restraint also generated a new respect for those in power. In contrast to the virulent verbal (and occasionally physical) attacks on political figures that had been commonplace in interwar Europe, there was a new-found respectability to politics in the post-war years.[207] The political process had acquired a new politeness, as expressed in the formality of speeches in the parliamentary chamber, the serious tone of the quality newspapers, and the rituals of public meetings and orderly demonstrations. The self-conscious maturity of this democratic politics distinguished Europe from the destructive conflicts of the recent past, and also delegitimized those violent actions that transgressed the narrowed confines of acceptable political debate.[208]

These constraints led the young Jürgen Habermas to denounce in 1961 what he termed the "Wahlmonarchie" (electoral monarchy) that had established itself in Western Europe. Europeans had become the subjects of an omnipotent executive power, rather than democratic citizens.[209] He was not alone in expressing these views. A range of critiques of the

204. See, for example, the comments of Gottfried Heindl in 1958 cited in R. Kreichbaumer, *Parteiprogramme im Widerstreit der Interessen: Die Programmdiskussion und die Programme von ÖVP und SPÖ 1945–1986* (Vienna, 1990), 374. See also Lidegaard, *Short History of Denmark*, 219–21.

205. W. Koeppen, *Das Treibhaus* (Stuttgart, 1953).

206. Most notably of course the Algerian War. See pp. 273–76.

207. It is difficult to think of an equivalent to the violent assault on the French Socialist leader (and future prime minister) Léon Blum by Action française activists in the streets of Paris in February 1936: C. Millington, *Fighting for France: Violence in Interwar French Politics* (Oxford, 2018), 94.

208. See pp. 219–21.

209. Van Rahden, "Clumsy Democrats," 498; M. G. Specter, *Habermas: An Intellectual Biography* (Cambridge, 2010), 62–63.

shortcomings of post-war democracy were voiced in the first half of the 1960s.[210] Nor were such criticisms new. The Western European Communist parties had long denounced the capitalist inequality and, more especially, state repression that lurked beneath the veneer of democratic pluralism.[211] This overweening power of the state, and the way in which it impinged upon individual freedoms, was a tangible element of the post-war European order, in the west as well as the east. State bureaucracies contained too many ambitious police and security officials who had become accustomed during the war years to acting without effective democratic control.[212] Ministries of the interior were too powerful, and the supposed need for public order was used too readily to ignore the rights of citizens, and to justify the "exceptional" powers deployed to arrest awkward individuals, repress subversive organizations, and expand a semi-visible culture of surveillance.[213] This might not—the case of the civil-war Greek state excepted[214]—have been the heavy-handed state repression experienced by many Europeans during the previous decades. But it hurt all the same, and was all the more effective for being implemented within the legalism of a democratic order.

Above all, there was the Cold War. Fears of Soviet-sponsored Communist subversion escalated rapidly among those in authority during the strike waves that broke out in Western Europe in the autumn of 1947, the largely unanticipated Communist seizure of power in Czechoslovakia in February 1948, and the blockade of Berlin by the Soviet authorities later in the same year. As a consequence, Western Europe was jolted in little more than a year from post-war liberation into an atmosphere of pre-war mobilization. The intimidating might of a bloc of Soviet-controlled states of four hundred million people, as de Gaulle warned the French people, lay only five hundred kilometres from the eastern frontiers of France—or, as he tried to express it in more accessible terms, less than the distance of two stages of the Tour de France.[215] The external threat supposedly posed by the Red Army and its allies also provided the justification for policies of

210. See pp. 262–63.

211. See pp. 60–61.

212. Laborie, "Libération de Toulouse," 149–73; Conway, *Sorrows of Belgium*, 161.

213. Major, *Death of the KPD*, 298–301; H. Reiter, "Police and Public Order in Italy: The Case of Florence," in *Policing Protest: The Control of Mass Demonstrations in Western Democracies*, ed. D. Della Porta and Reiter (Minneapolis, 1998), 150–59; see also pp. 207–8.

214. D. H. Close, "The Reconstruction of a Right-Wing State," in *The Greek Civil War, 1943–1950: Studies of Polarization*, ed. Close (London, 1993), 156–89.

215. C. Purtschet, *Le rassemblement du peuple français 1947–1953* (Paris, 1965), 181–82.

state repression towards the Communist enemy within. As a consequence, anti-Communism evolved from a political opinion to an institutionalized state practice. The use of the police and the burgeoning officialdom of the intelligence agencies to block Communist activities, undermine their political campaigns, and infiltrate the parties and (in the language of the time) their "front" organizations, intensified rapidly during the late 1940s, driven by the fear that a Communist-led destabilization of Western Europe had already begun.[216]

Democracy, so the logic of the time dictated, needed to defend itself and, if necessary, to do so by force.[217] Raymond Aron was one of the many who succumbed to the fears of the moment. In a book entitled *Le grand schisme*, which he wrote hurriedly during the bleak winter of 1947–48, Aron traced the divorce that had developed since the war between Communism and democracy. The two were opposites, but also enemies, neither of which could tolerate the existence of the other in the long term. Central to this mentality of democratic defence was the concept and language of totalitarianism, which equated the present Communist danger with the Nazism of the recent past. Thus, Aron declared that Stalinist Communism was as radically opposed to what he termed the Christian and liberal traditions of the West as Nazism had been. On this basis, the French Communists were in effect the new collaborators, who as a consequence of their dependence on the will of Moscow acted as spies, saboteurs, or traitors within France. The time had therefore come, Aron declared, to question whether they should be allowed to participate in the freedoms of a democratic society: "Par la faute de l'Union Soviétique, l'Europe entière est engagée dans une lutte à mort dont l'enjeu est le salut de l'Occident. A l'est de l'Europe, il n'y a plus de parti 'américain'. On n'accordera pas indéfiniment au parti 'russe', à l'ouest, une tolérance illimitée."[218]

216. M. Herz, "Conversation with Dr. Max Pammer, Chief of the Political Section (Staatspolizeiliche Abteiling) of the Austrian Ministry of the Interior" (6 April 1948), cited in R. Wagnleitner, ed., *Understanding Austria: The Political Reports and Analyses of Martin F. Herz, Political Officer in the US Legation in Vienna, 1945-1948* (Salzburg, 1984), 370–74; R. Van Doorslaer and E. Verhoeyen, *L'assassinat de Joseph Lahaut: Une histoire de l'anticommunisme en Belgique* (Antwerp, 1987).

217. M. Debré, "Combattre le communisme" (18 March 1950), republished in Debré, *République et ses problèmes*, 71–73.

218. "Because of the actions of the Soviet Union, the whole of Europe is engaged in a struggle to the death, on which will depend the survival of the West. In the east of Europe, there is no longer an 'American' party. We will not accord indefinitely to the 'Russian' party in the west an unlimited tolerance": Raymond Aron, *Le grand schisme* (Paris, 1948), 8–9, 235–36 (quotation); Rizi, *Benedetto Croce*, 109, 169.

As Aron's alarmist rhetoric indicated, the Cold War elevated democracy as the defining characteristic of Western Europe, while also restricting its exercise to those who were willing to subscribe to a particular definition of its values. More immediately, it also subordinated the sovereignty of the Western European states to a new alliance with the United States. The creation of NATO and the expansion of CIA-sponsored intelligence and security operations in Western Europe during the late 1940s brought the full weight of American diplomatic, economic, and military might into the politics of Western Europe.[219] The durable inequality of that relationship imposed a limited state sovereignty on the European democracies, as well as reinforcing the influence of American companies in the economies of Western Europe, and integrating the armed forces of the European states into a military alliance that operated outside of democratic control.[220] During the most intense period of the Cold War from the warlike manoeuvrings of 1947–48 to the building of the Berlin Wall in 1961, Western European democracy became the territorial and ideological front line of the American campaign against Soviet expansionist ambitions. The urgent need to defend freedom and democracy in Western Europe justified interventions, both public and more clandestine, in the operation of that democracy. Building on what they believed to have been their success in averting a Communist victory in the Italian election of April 1948, a range of American governmental agencies launched what W. Scott Lucas has termed a "total strategy" intended to marginalize all elements of Communist influence within what they now regarded as the western bloc.[221] Democracy, and indeed "civilization" itself, changed its shape: it was no longer European, but "western," thereby providing the basis for both the admission of the German Federal Republic to the NATO alliance and the durable commitment of the US armed forces to the defence of Western Europe.[222] This "atlanticization" of democracy extended too

219. T. Barnes, "The Secret Cold War: The CIA and American Foreign Policy in Europe 1946–1956," *Historical Journal* 24 (1981): 399–415, and 25 (1982): 649–70.

220. D. Ellwood, "Italy, Europe and the Cold War: The Politics and Economics of Limited Sovereignty," in *Italy in the Cold War: Politics, Culture and Society 1948-58*, ed. C. Duggan and C. Wagstaff (Oxford, 1995), 25–46.

221. K. Mistry, "Re-thinking American Intervention in the 1948 Italian Election: Beyond a Success-Failure Dichotomy," *Modern Italy* 16 (2011): 179–94; W. S. Lucas, "Beyond Freedom, beyond Control: Approaches to Culture and the State-Private Network in the Cold War," in *The Cultural Cold War in Western Europe 1945–1960*, ed. G. Scott-Smith and H. Krabbendam (London, 2003), 57.

222. P. T. Jackson, *Civilizing the Enemy: German Reconstruction and the West* (Ann Arbor, MI, 2006).

to the spheres of culture and propaganda. Abstract art, modernist music, and the liberal intellectuals of institutions such as the Congress for Cultural Freedom (CCF) all became enrolled in an American-directed and often American-funded cultural offensive intended to demonstrate the superiority of the values of a free society.[223] Conversely, for their Marxist intellectual opponents in this Cold War *Kulturkampf*, the United States became the new imperialist power, which, like a giant spider, used its political and military agents and local collaborators to bring about the "Marshallization" of Western Europe and suppress strivings for independent sovereignty.[224]

The concept of a soft imperialism is one that is easy to apply to Western Europe during the early years of the Cold War, when the imbalance between the limited military forces of the Western European states and the protective, and constraining, might of the United States was a flagrant reality. However, this does not reflect the full complexity of the relationship between the USA and Western Europe. Power did not always flow in one direction, and Western European states rarely acted simply as clients of the United States.[225] In the sphere of popular culture, America might indeed have acquired something of the character of the "irresistible empire" invoked by Victoria de Grazia: a dazzling new civilization where everything was larger, more modern, and more prosperous than in an exhausted Europe.[226] But this was an image of America that excluded politics. European images of America were of a land without politics, a land to which emigrants travelled to be liberated from the constraints of the political community and to pursue their personal dreams.[227] In the political sphere, there remained a sense of distance between Western Europe and the United States. In 1952, the American-based French Catholic intellectual Jacques Maritain referred to the Atlantic as the successor to the Mediterranean of the Classical age: a sea with two shores,

223. Brogi, *Confronting America*, 81. See also pp. 3–4.

224. L. Goretti, "Truman's Bombs and De Gasperi's Hooked Nose: Images of the Enemy in the Communist Press for Young People after 18 April 1948," *Modern Italy* 16 (2011): 159–77; G. Ross, *Workers and Communists*, 50–69.

225. J. M. Hanhimäki, "Europe's Cold War," in *The Oxford Handbook of Postwar European History*, ed. D. Stone (Oxford, 2012), 285–88.

226. V. De Grazia, *Irresistible Empire: America's Advance through Twentieth-Century Europe* (Cambridge, MA, 2005); D. Ellwood, *The Shock of America: Europe and the Challenge of the Century* (Oxford, 2012); A. Pasquier, *Amérique 44* (Brussels, [1944 or 1945]). See also p. 250.

227. M. Dekeyser, *De amerikaanse droom* (Leuven, 1978).

but around which ideas flowed freely.[228] The image was an arresting one, but it did not gain a wider currency. Democracy did not travel easily in either direction across the Atlantic in the post-war years, and the democratic institutions of the United States and of Western Europe remained throughout the post-war decades obstinately distinct in their structure and temperament.

Notions of a common western or Atlantic democracy remained for the most part a dream of Europhile American policy-makers. European political figures, it seemed, felt no need of lessons from Americans in democracy, and—at least until the 1960s—tended to regard with some disdain the workings of American politics.[229] For most non-Communist political leaders, the United States remained during the Cold War an offshore resource: primarily of military protection, but also of finance (most notably through the enormous volume of assistance channelled into the states of non-Communist Europe through the European Recovery Program, the ERP) and economic innovation. This led a range of Western European elites to travel to the United States, funded by the US State Department and other bodies, with the purpose of learning about American methods of production, management, and administration.[230] But the learning process was almost always more selective than general; and, when it came to doing politics, neither Western European leaders nor, it seemed, their populations were eager to imitate American ways of conducting democracy.[231]

This was especially so when American policy-makers appeared to be too visibly concerned to mould Western Europe according to an American design. Patriotic sensibilities and calculations of economic and partisan interest often militated against impeccably anti-Communist politicians such as De Gasperi acceding to American pressure, especially when it was presented in the high-handed manner of the American ambassador to Rome during the early years of the Eisenhower presidency, Clare Boothe Luce.[232] Similarly, American attempts to use the structures of the ERP to

228. F. Michel, *La pensée catholique en Amérique du Nord: Réseaux intellectuels et échanges culturels entre l'Europe, le Canada et les Etats-Unis (années 1920–1960)* (Paris, 2010), 549–60.

229. Scott-Smith, "Intellectual Atlantic Community," 132–45; Brogi, *Confronting America*.

230. G. Scott-Smith, *Networks of Empire: The US State Department's Foreign Leader Program in the Netherlands, France and Britain, 1950–1970* (Brussels, 2008).

231. See pp. 146–47.

232. M. Del Pero, "American Pressures and Their Containment in Italy during the Ambassadorship of Clare Boothe Luce, 1953–1956," *Diplomatic History* 28 (2004): 407–39, and "Containing Containment," 533–41. See also Brogi, *Confronting America*, esp. 146–56.

bring about changes in European economic structures were largely a failure. European state officials, businessmen, and trade unionists would seize
upon particular American methods where they had a particular interest in
doing so, but there was little wish to adopt more generally what was perceived to be the alien American model of high productivity and corporate
labour relations.[233] As the secretary of state John Foster Dulles remarked
with somewhat weary understatement in 1954, "the pre-supposition of
dependence of our allies on the United States . . . has turned out not to be
so great as had been thought at the end of the war."[234] What Geir Lundestad defined as the "empire by invitation" that emerged in Western Europe
during the Cold War therefore always had clear limits, and served purposes that were often more European than American.[235] Indeed, democracy became one of the means by which from the end of the 1950s onwards
the Western European states demonstrated their autonomy from the
United States. The construction of European political institutions, such
as the European Economic Community (EEC), which operated independently of the United States, encouraged a flowering of rhetoric celebrating
the democratic heritage of Europe. Democracy, according to this language,
had been "made in Europe," even if it had subsequently been exported
across the Atlantic, as well as to various European settler societies.[236]

The confidence with which Western European political leaders developed these arguments reflected their sense that they stood on solid
ground. By the mid-1950s, the process of post-war reconstruction was
essentially complete. The infrastructure and buildings had been largely
rebuilt, economic growth was accelerating, and the authority of the state
had been re-established. In addition, they appeared to have created a stable form of democracy. Electoral rules were on occasions bent, judicial
rights neglected, and the ubiquitous Cold War rhetoric of freedom used
to justify exceptional police actions within and, more especially, outside
of Europe in the remaining territories of empire.[237] However, the stability

233. B. A. Mackenzie, *Remaking France: Americanization, Public Diplomacy and the
Marshall Plan* (New York, 2005), 232–39; D. Ellwood, "The Message of the Marshall Plan,"
in *Selling Democracy, Friendly Persuasion*, ed. R. Rother (Berlin, 2006), 7–15.

234. Quoted in W. Hitchcock, *France Restored: Cold War Diplomacy and the Quest for
Leadership in Europe, 1944–1954* (Chapel Hill, NC, 1998), 7–9 and 207 (quotation).

235. G. Lundestad, "Empire by Invitation?: The United States and Western Europe,
1945–1952," *Journal of Peace Research* 23 (1986): 263–77.

236. See pp. 147–49.

237. B. Grob-Fitzgibbon, *Imperial Endgame: Britain's Dirty Wars and the End of
Empire* (Basingstoke, UK, 2011); C. Elkins, *Britain's Gulag: The Brutal End of Empire in
Kenya* (London, 2005). See also p. 274.

was undeniable. In comparison with the numerous instances during the interwar years when parliamentary regimes had been overthrown by military uprisings, presidential coups, and a range of nationalist and anti-parliamentary movements, the immobility of post-war democracy was its most striking feature. That was above all the case in Germany. The transition from the violent politics of the recent past to the predominantly moderate temper of the politics of the Federal Republic in the 1950s and early 1960s appeared to contemporaries—Aron included—to be the most remarkable manifestation of the changed political spirit of the age.[238] Only in France amidst the crisis provoked by events in Algeria in 1958 did a political regime simply collapse, though here again, as we have seen, what was most striking was the care with which the transition from the Fourth to the Fifth Republic was conducted within a framework of republican legalism. Democracy was never more carefully respected than when it was least evident.[239]

There were many reasons for this regime stability, most notably the relative prosperity generated by high levels of economic growth from the end of the 1940s onwards. But central to it too was the investment of the rulers themselves in the project of democratic reconstruction. The new "classe politique" highlighted by Raymond Aron preferred to wear their ideology lightly.[240] Their skills were primarily technical and managerial ones. In contrast to their predecessors, they eschewed grandiose rhetoric and were inclined to measure their achievements in terms of percentages of economic growth, numbers of houses built, or kilometres of motorways constructed. As the next chapter will argue, their understanding of democracy was often cautious and unimaginative, rooted in a nervous preoccupation with learning the lessons of past excesses. Confronted by the complex challenges of post-war reconstruction, they evaded democratic accountability through opaque processes of decision-making that privileged the authority of government institutions over the will of the people. Moreover, they neglected the challenge of creating a more egalitarian and social democracy in favour of policies that largely reinforced the pre-existing hierarchies of European societies.

Especially when viewed in retrospect, the missed opportunities of 1945 appear the most evident. Western Europe's mid-century turning point failed to be a radical new departure; and, far from achieving what was

238. M. Oppermann, *Raymond Aron und Deutschland: Die Verteidigung der Freiheit und das Problem des Totalitarismus* (Ostfildern, Germany, 2008), 387–402.

239. See pp. 75–77.

240. Raymond Aron, "Institutions politiques de l'occident," 26–27.

sometimes referred to in West Germany as a *Demokratiewunder*, the rulers of post-war Western Europe restored too much and challenged too little.[241] Disillusionment is of course inseparable from moments of substantial political change, and there were at the time many at all levels of society who regretted the absence of a more emphatic rupture.[242] But, as this chapter has sought to demonstrate, the weakness of such perspectives lies not so much in their accounts of the shortcomings of the post-war democratic order as in their exaggerated sense of the potential of liberation. Western Europe's transition to democracy in the 1940s was not a failed revolution. It was from the outset a managed process, implemented largely from within the established structures of power, which was concerned not so much to enact rule by the people as to construct a democracy that worked, and endured. And, measured by those criteria, it was indeed successful.

241. Re. *Demokratiewunder*, see W. Rüegg in W. Krönig and K.-D. Müller, eds., *Nachkriegs-Semester: Studium in Kriegs- und Nachkriegszeit* (Stuttgart, 1990), 5. See also Forner, *German Intellectuals*, 279–80.

242. For examples of contemporary critiques of the "failure" of post-war democratic reconstruction, see Mazower, *Dark Continent*, 316; R. Krieg, *Catholic Theologians in Nazi Germany* (New York, 2004), 130.

CHAPTER TWO

Thinking Democracy

THE NEW MODEL OF A STABLE DEMOCRACY

SOMETIMES SILENCES CAN BE SIGNIFICANT. The most remarkable feature of the term "democracy" was its relative absence from the rhetoric of liberation. Whatever causes the Second World War had been fought for, democracy, it seemed, was not foremost among them. In the lexicon of European liberation four overlapping terms predominated: freedom, liberty, people, and nation—or its subtle but significant variants of homeland and motherland. Take, for example, the tract issued during the liberation of Paris in August 1944 by those who would subsequently launch the major Catholic political party in post-war France, the MRP. It is a very typical example of the political rhetoric of the time, spinning together a distinctly French political language of the Republic, of liberty and freedom, and of the *peuple*, defined against privileged elites. Of democracy, however, there is not a word.[1] This example is trivial, but it could be repeated many times over with reference to the ephemeral and more formal literature of the liberation era. Democracy was rarely mentioned by name, and even less frequently as a concept. Moreover, when it did appear, it was often in an almost perfunctory way, with democracy becoming a form of political shorthand, a means of articulating opposition to an authoritarian or fascist order, or indicating support for a regime of independence and self-government. In a major speech given on 8 May 1946 to mark the first anniversary of the end of the war, the Austrian chancellor, Leopold Figl,

---

1. "Paris est libre!" [August 1944], republished in P. Letamendia, *Le Mouvement républicain populaire: Histoire d'un grand parti français* (Paris, 1995), 50. See also Andrieu, *Programme commun de la Résistance*, 109–10.

launched into a long list of the benefits of freedom and national independence that had flowed from the defeat of Nazism, before concluding with a passing reference to the fact that 8 May 1945 had also been the "victory of Democracy over Dictatorship" (Sieg der Demokratie über Diktatur).[2]

Of course, this absence can be exaggerated. As discussed in chapter one, Communists across Europe were vocal during the post-liberation years in their support for a people's democracy.[3] And, even when the term was not used, calculations about the nature of the future political regime were often tangibly present. The rhetoric of liberation was effusive and improvised. But it contained within it many nuances and downright conflicts of meaning, which reflected the struggles for power and for ownership of the process of liberation that underlay the celebration of national union. Liberation had been so long delayed in many areas of Western Europe that, by the time it occurred, minds had long moved on to what would happen next. In this highly uncertain environment, political actors did not necessarily say everything that was on their minds. Even though the lexicon of liberation was often narrow and repetitive, there were subtly different ways of deploying the same terms. Through the weightings—or simply the order of preference—that political figures accorded to the victory of freedom or the defence of liberty, to the achievement of social justice or the restoration of a legal order, they were sending messages as to the nature of the political regime they believed should emerge after the war.

Nevertheless, the relative silence that surrounded the term democracy in 1945 was interesting and significant. The purpose of this chapter is to explore the reasons for that silence, and to analyse how a discussion about democracy did gradually develop, often in rather guarded ways, during the post-war years. That debate revealed many nuances of emphasis, which reflected the diversity of national and ideological traditions within Europe. But it was also remarkably unitary. This might appear surprising: Socialists and Christian Democrats, for example, had set off from very different starting points, and over the previous half-century had articulated opposing visions of democracy, when not rejecting it entirely. Yet, after 1945, there was a marked convergence in their conception of democracy, of how it should operate, and more especially of the dangers that needed to be averted. As a consequence, Western Europe arrived during the post-war years at something close to an agreed model of democracy.

2. L. Figl, "Wer hat wen befreit?" (8 May 1946), in *Leopold Figl: Ansichten eines grossen Österreichers*, ed. R. Prantner (Vienna, 1992), 54–55.

3. See pp. 52–53.

In the beginning, however, was silence; or rather the noise of the slogans of liberation. The chaos of the months preceding and following liberation was hardly conducive to reflection on the nature of the political system that would follow the defeat of the Third Reich and its collaborationist allies. In the innumerable clandestine tracts and newspapers, songs, and scrawled slogans that served as an alternative public space in German-occupied Europe during the final years of the war, direct opposition to the occupier predominated. Resisters acted more on instinct than ideology, finding in the direct rhetoric of patriotism, hatred of the occupiers (and, in particular, their local agents), and, in the case of France, republicanism, the immediate resources that gave a meaning to their actions and, for those who fell or were executed, the sacrifice of their lives.[4] The terms that they deployed—notably "liberation" and "revolution"—were little more than rallying cries. The exigencies of the time, but also the enormous uncertainty that surrounded the post-war future, discouraged any sustained reflection as to what content these terms might acquire, beyond the absence of alien occupation.[5] The nature of the political system that would follow the war was something that could be left until the more urgent goals of victory, justice, and material security had been attained.

There were, however, other and less circumstantial reasons for this silence. Any discussion as to what kind of democracy Europeans were seeking to achieve risked raising awkward memories of past democratic experiences. Between 1920 and 1940—however one establishes the definitions—the majority of European states had in one way or another moved from a parliamentarian to an authoritarian model of government.[6] Though often carried out by executive coup, military intervention, or, in the case of Spain, a bloody civil war, these political transitions had rarely lacked some basis in popular support. This was especially so of the political changes that had occurred in 1940 in the heart of the area that after the war would become Western Europe. The military victory of the armies of the Third Reich in the Netherlands, Belgium, and France in May and June 1940 had appeared to many of the citizens of those states to have proven the inferiority of multiparty parliamentary government in the face of new models of authoritarian politics. Thus, in all three of these defeated states, projects of New Order reform were initiated, which in France led to the collective decision

4. F. Marcot, "Voix d'outre-tombe," in *Lettres de fusillés*, ed. G. Krivopissko (Paris, 2003), 17–19; *Visioen en werkelijkheid*; Morgan, *Fall of Mussolini*, 180–88.

5. M. Sueur, "Approche lexicographique du mot libération dans *La voix du nord* clandestine (avril 1941–août 1944)," *Revue du Nord* 57 (1975): 347–64.

6. Luebbert, *Liberalism*; Capoccia, *Defending Democracy*.

of the Chamber of Deputies and the Senate, taken at Vichy in July 1940, to entrust the direction of the French state to Marshal Pétain.[7] These changes were undertaken without any popular mandate, but they reflected the widespread belief in the summer of 1940 that parliamentary democracy— as it had developed since the First World War—had ended in inglorious collapse.[8] The future, it was assumed, lay with new structures of organization and representation; while those politicians and other elite figures who had fled from the German advance to establish exile regimes in the somewhat tenuous safety afforded by London in 1940 appeared initially to be little more than the remnants of an outmoded *ancien régime*.[9]

This political current went rapidly into reverse over the course of the subsequent years. Almost everything that happened in Europe after 1940 served to demonstrate to Europeans that authoritarian rule could be distinctly worse than its alternatives. Nazi policies of exploitation and oppression, as well as the tangible failure of New Order political projects such as the Vichy Regime in France to effect meaningful change or respond to the expectations of their populations, led to a durable change in attitudes in Western Europe around 1942. A tide turned during that crucial year of the war, not only on the battlefields of Russia and North Africa, but in the terms of European political debate. This led within the space of a few months to the demise of the enthusiasm for authoritarian state reforms and a corporatist reordering of society that had dominated political and intellectual discussion over the previous decade.[10] In its place, there emerged a new political rhetoric of legality, accountability, and guarantees of individual freedom, within which an aspiration to democracy—in spirit if not yet in name—gradually took shape.[11]

This change was reflected in the language of resistance, and also in the wider sense of communities rejecting the rulers imposed on them and recovering their sovereignty. Europeans, it seemed, were rebuilding their

7. See, notably, J. Jackson, *France: The Dark Years 1940–1944* (Oxford, 2001), 132–36; F. Kupferman, *Laval 1883–1945* (Paris, 1987), 232–36.

8. F. Ibrugger, *Au fond, qu'est-ce que la démocratie?* (Paris, 1941). See also the analysis of political attitudes in J. Gérard-Libois and J. Gotovitch, *L'an 40* (Brussels, 1971), 167–325.

9. Conway, "Legacies of Exile," 255–56, 259–61; Conway and Romijn, *War for Legitimacy*, 67–107.

10. See, for example, Z. Sternhell, *Neither Right nor Left: Fascist Ideology in France* (Berkeley, CA, 1986).

11. F. Bédarida, "Vichy et la crise de la conscience française," in *Le régime de Vichy et les Français*, ed. J.-P. Azéma and F. Bédarida (Paris, 1992), 77–96; P. Laborie, *L'opinion française sous Vichy* (Paris, 1990), 262–81; P. Struye, *L'évolution du sentiment public en Belgique sous l'occupation allemande*, ed. J. Gotovitch (Brussels, 2002), 185–86, 228–30.

democracy from the roots up, choosing the structures and leaders that matched their rather truculent mood of distrust.[12] At the same time, this shift in political fashion was also evident in the attitudes of those elites, notably within the judiciary, the civil service, and industry, who had been among the most enthusiastic supporters of the authoritarian regimes established in the aftermath of the defeats of 1940. They now passed, often almost without a break, into participating in the committees and planning bodies that proliferated around internal Resistance groups and the exile regimes.[13] This change of camp, however opportunist it might have been on the part of some, proved to be of durable significance. In particular, it brought much of the high personnel—the *grands corps*—of the state over into the camp of democracy and laid the basis for what Zygmunt Bauman retrospectively termed the "social engineering state." For the next thirty years a wide range of civil servants, economic experts, and technocratic planners who had formerly looked to authoritarian models sought instead to achieve their projects of social, economic, and bureaucratic modernization within the framework of parliamentary democracy.[14]

None of this, however, implied a simple rehabilitation of the democratic past. Democracy—not as an ideal but as a lived experience—remained associated in the minds of the populations of Western Europe, and more especially of their more conservative-minded leaders, with predominantly negative memories of governmental instability, violent social conflict, and, in the case of Germany in 1918 and France in 1940, national defeat: one a democracy born of defeat and the other a democracy that led to defeat.[15] Unsurprisingly, there was little political nostalgia in 1945. Everybody, it seemed, looked forward. Discussions in the clandestine press of the new political regime that should emerge in the aftermath of the war were always at pains to emphasize the differentness of the democratic order of the future from that of the past.[16] "A parting of the ways," the Czechoslovak

12. Forner, *German Intellectuals*, 74–75; Pius XII, "Democracy and Peace," 302.

13. Mioche, *Plan Monnet*, 71–72; Jabbari, *Pierre Laroque*, 4, 156–63; P. Péan, *Une jeunesse française* (Paris, 1994). See also T. Grosbois, "Le renseignement économique et financier en Belgique occupée: L'exemple du Groupement d'études économiques," in *La Résistance et les Européens du Nord* (Brussels, 1994), 183–207.

14. Z. Bauman, *Memories of Class: The Pre-history and After-Life of Class* (London, 1982), 165–67; J. Clarke, *France in the Age of Organization: Factory, Home and Nation from the 1920s to Vichy* (New York, 2011), 164–69; G. Brun, *Technocrates et technocratie en France (1914–1945)* (Paris, 1985), 281–88.

15. Groth, *Democracies against Hitler*, 1–14.

16. A. F. Luyendijk, "Ontnuchterd radicalisme," in *Visioen en werkelijkheid*, 38–46; M. Corthals, "Welke toekomst voor een bevrijd België?" *Belgisch Tijdschrift voor Eigentijdse Geschiedenis* 48 (2018): 49–53.

president Edvard Beneš declared resonantly at the reopening of parliament in Prague on 28 October 1945, had occurred "in modern society," which would give birth to "a society of universal outlook, consistently democratic and [more just] in the social and economic sphere than the old."[17] The new democracy, so everybody seemed to agree, would be "new," "broader," and "more social," and not a restoration of what the British Labour Party politician Richard Crossman referred to as the "callow . . . materialist" democracy of "that dreary armistice between the wars."[18] The war, in a frequently used formula of the time, must not prove to have been a parenthesis, but the starting point of a much broader process of renewal—what de Gaulle termed, with his rather empty grandiloquence, "la rénovation nationale par la démocratie et dans la liberté."[19]

From the outset, the project of post-war democracy was therefore conceived in opposition not so much to the discredited fascist and authoritarian models of the war years but to the ghosts of past democratic failures. The "adventure" of democracy, one Belgian Catholic writer commented in 1946, had failed after 1918; the question now was whether it would be more successful on this occasion.[20] The answer took different forms within Europe's national political cultures. In some cases, this relaunching of democracy was presented as a return to long-standing traditions of independence and freedom. This was notably the case in Belgium and the Netherlands. As an influential Dutch pamphlet of 1945 declared, the urgent task was for a fundamental *vernieuwing*—renewal—that would restore the popular character of the Dutch people through the recreation of what it termed "our Dutch historic institutions"—onze Nederlandsche historische instellingen.[21] Much the same patriotic rhetoric of purging the recent past through returning to more historic freedoms was evident in Belgium, where the founding constitution of the state in 1831 was rediscovered as a

17. Speech of Edvard Beneš, in *The Opening of the Prague Parliament: Message of President Dr. Edvard Beneš to the National Assembly of the Czechoslovak Republic* (Prague, 1946), 25. This was the continuation of themes that Beneš had articulated in exile: Orzoff, *Battle for the Castle*, 204.

18. R.H.S. Crossman, introduction to *The God that Failed: Six Studies in Communism*, by A. Koestler. I. Silone, A. Gide, R. Wright, L. Fischer, and S. Spender (London, 1950), 10–11.

19. "national renovation through democracy and with liberty": C. de Gaulle, *Discours et messages* (Paris, 1970), 1: 304 (quotation), 279–81.

20. G. Hoyois, "La réponse des peuples à la démocratie," in *Les lignes de faite de la démocratie: XXVIIIe semaine sociale wallonne, 1946* (Courtrai, Belgium, n.d.), 234.

21. Pompe, *Bevrijding*, 9 (quotation), 85–130.

charter of Belgian traditions of self-government, in opposition—implied or explicit—to the party politics of the interwar years.[22]

In northern Europe, too, concepts of national identity provided a bridge between the old and the new. The idea of "Nordic democracy," as an expression of the particular democratic spirit and social structure of the people of Scandinavia, had initially developed in the 1930s in response to the threat from Nazi Germany. But in the post-war years this theme acquired a much wider currency. According to this version of history, Nordic democracy was the expression of the collective folkish mentality forged by the struggles of the Scandinavian nations—now expanded to include the rather different case of Finland—for independence from alien rule and monarchical despotism. A democratic attitude was, thus, "natural" to the Nordic people, and reflected the long-term development of egalitarian social structures in Scandinavian society, stretching back, in some of its more fanciful formulations, to the Viking era.[23]

Not all pasts were, however, so readily capable of being turned to such purposes. In Czechoslovakia, the recovery of national freedom in 1945 was presented as the renewal of a historic Czech tradition of self-rule that had originated with the Hussite revolt but had reached its full expression during the presidency of Tomáš Masaryk after the First World War.[24] However, given the inglorious final phase of the Czechoslovak republic after the state's dismemberment as a consequence of the Munich agreement of 1938, this was accompanied by strong criticism of the oligarchical character of the pre-war republic. Thus, the rebirth of an independent Czechoslovakia could not be a simple restoration, but needed to be accompanied by a wide-ranging democratic transformation of society.[25] During his wartime exile in London, President Beneš had already given voice to this aspiration, promising that the new regime would be "a new fresh democracy." This was reinforced by the Košice Programme, issued by the National Front of all of the principal political parties on 4 April 1945, shortly before the end of the German occupation. Intended as the founding

22. Conway, *Sorrows of Belgium*, 249–52.

23. See notably J. A. Lauwerys, *Scandinavian Democracy: The Development of Democratic Thought and Institutions in Denmark, Norway and Sweden* (Copenhagen, 1958); Jakobsen, "Inventions and Developments," 322–24; J. Kurunmäki and J. Strang, "Introduction: 'Nordic Democracy' in a World of Tensions," in *Rhetorics of Nordic Democracy*, ed. Kurunmäki and Strang (Helsinki, 2010), 9–36.

24. J. De Graaf, "European Socialism between Militant and Parliamentary Democracy: A Pan-European Debate, 1945–8," *European Review of History: Revue européenne d'histoire* 26 (2019): 342.

25. Orzoff, *Battle for the Castle*, 20–22, 209.

charter of the post-war regime, it laid down an ambitious programme of political and social changes that would define the "popular character" of the new democracy.[26]

In France and Italy, too, the emphasis was emphatically on the new. Memories of the French Third Republic and of the pre-1922 parliamentary regime in Italy were associated with corruption, personal opportunism, and a disruptive factionalism that had failed to address the needs of the country and the concerns of the population. Both had been, in the phrase of the Italian anti-Fascist exile Gaetano Salvemini, "imperfect democracies," in which the illusory notion of the sovereignty of the people had provided a façade for the actions of political manipulators, such as the long-time pre-Fascist prime minister of Italy, Giovanni Giolitti.[27] The consequence, as the Italian historian Federico Chabod argued in a highly influential series of lectures on Italy's recent history, initially given in Paris in 1950, was not so much that Fascism had won, but that the parliamentary regime had simply failed to comprehend the nature of the challenge it faced.[28] Similar ideas were voiced in France, where the new energy that republicanism had acquired as a result of the war years went hand in hand with a determination to ensure that the new republic would be very different from the pre-war Third Republic. This ambition was well articulated by the political scientist François Goguel in his study of the politics of the Third Republic written during his wartime detention in a German prisoner-of-war camp, and published in 1946 after his return to liberated France. Goguel analysed what he deplored as the decadence and "the fierce character"—le caractère forcené—of the political disputes that had characterized the final years of the Third Republic. France, he argued, had become stuck in the bipolar conflicts of right and left, and he concluded his study with a plea for the new republic to foster a civic spirit and a more effective state culture that would prevail over sectional interests.[29]

Such historical analyses had a particular resonance in Germany. The Weimar Republic could hardly be held responsible for the fate that befell

26. *Košický vládní program: program nové československé vlády Národní fronty Čechů a Slováků* (Prague, 1974); Speech of Josef David, president of the Provisional National Assembly, in *Opening of the Prague Parliament*, 54; Suda, *Zealots and Rebels*, 181–85; Orzoff, *Battle for the Castle*, 204.

27. G. Tintori, "An Outsider's Vision: Gaetano Salvemini and the 1948 Elections in Italy," *Modern Italy* 16 (2011): 139–57.

28. F. Chabod, *L'Italie contemporaine: Conférences données à l'Institut d'études politiques de l'Université de Paris* (Paris, 1950), 52–58.

29. F. Goguel, *La politique des partis sous la IIIe République* (Paris, 1946), 2: 330–44.

Germany after the directly elected president invited the leader of the largest single party in the Reichstag to form a coalition government with a parliamentary majority in January 1933. And yet that is overwhelmingly what took place after 1945: Weimar—and not the Third Reich—was seen as a warning from history, and a demonstration of what went wrong when democratic structures were destabilized by the actions of demagogic forces (of right and left) who played upon the emotions of the people. Thus, the Federal Republic was designed from the outset almost as an "anti-Weimar," as reflected in its carefully calibrated constitution, its avoidance of a powerful presidential office, and in the powers devolved to its federal states. Throughout the 1950s, Weimar remained a consistent and negative point of reference for politicians and intellectual elites alike, the memory of which constrained them to adopt a consciously moderate politics of centrist governance. Having learned from this past history, the Federal Republic's political leaders sought to use their maturity and self-restraint to avoid the polarization that had undermined Germany's previous experience of democracy.[30]

Nor did the distant past appear to offer more attractive political models. One of the more obvious anniversaries of the immediate post-war years was the centenary of the revolutions of 1848. The inspiration that the constitutions, universal (male) suffrage, and civic and social emancipation of the revolutions might have provided for the democracies of 1948 was, however, for the most part referred to only rarely in public discourse.[31] In Italy, the Popular Front of Communists and left Socialists used Garibaldi in the elections of April 1948 as a symbol of popular Italian nationalism, striving to drive the Americans out of the Italian peninsula, as Garibaldi had fought to expel the Habsburgs a hundred years earlier. Its impact, however, was only limited, and was at odds with the much more critical approach to the entire project of the *Risorgimento* provoked by the posthumous publication of Antonio Gramsci's prison notebooks in 1949.[32] In Germany, or more exactly in the western zones

---

30. F. R. Allemann, *Bonn ist nicht Weimar* (Cologne, 1956), esp. 7, 411–40; S. Ullrich, *Der Weimar-Komplex: Das Scheitern der ersten deutschen Demokratie und die politische Kultur der frühen Bundesrepublik 1945–1959* (Göttingen, 2009); Depkat, *Lebenswenden und Zeitenwenden*, 370–94; Suri, *Henry Kissinger*, 7–10. The enduring legacies of Weimar are the central focus of two monographs: Greenberg, *Weimar Century*, and Strote, *Lions and Lambs*.

31. K. Renner "30 Jahre Republik Österreich" (12 November 1948), in *Für Recht und Frieden*, 75.

32. Ventresca, *From Fascism to Democracy*, 199–200; L. Riall, *Garibaldi: Invention of a Hero* (New Haven, CT, 2007), 9–10.

that would become the Federal Republic a year later, there was remarkably little public acknowledgement of an anniversary that recalled all too directly the cycle of revolutionary upheavals from which Germany was seeking to escape. In historical works too, the tone was very similar: the German revolution of 1848 had been a failure, initiated by an inexperienced political elite who had little comprehension of the aspirations of the population, and who had rapidly fallen victim to the reactionary forces of the Prussian state but also to the conservative attitudes of the middle classes.[33] German democratic republicanism was perceived as predominantly a history of political failures. It was only by going back to the Reformation of the sixteenth century, or by abandoning the national for the more local frames of reference provided by the inclusive language of *Heimat*, that it was possible to recover more positive definitions of inclusive self-government.[34]

In France, which continued to regard itself as the birthplace of the revolutions of 1848, the centenary (which coincided with that of the publication of Marx's *Communist Manifesto*) was marked more positively. It prompted the publication of a number of Communist historical works, which combined praise of the ideals of the revolution with criticism of its confused class character.[35] More interesting, however, was the publication by the former Resistance publisher Editions de Minuit of an ambitious two-volume global history of the revolutions. Seeking to escape from the narrow nationalism of the recent past, the essays written by an international team of scholars presented a largely favourable image of the ambitions of the revolutionaries of 1848: "jeunesse magnifique, qui croyait à la liberté, à l'égalité, à la fraternité, qui croyait qu'on aboutirait à l'union des peuples par la libération de chaque nation particulière."[36] Even here, however, the revolutions were not presented as a model for the present day, but as the symbol of a past era of idealism that had been defeated by the self-interested actions of the bourgeoisie and more

33. J. Droz, "Travaux récents sur la révolution de 1848 en Allemagne," *Revue d'histoire moderne et contemporaine* 1 (1954): 145–55.

34. A. Weber, "Freier Sozialismus: Ein Aktionsprogramm," in *Freier Sozialismus*, by A. Mitscherlich and Weber (Heidelberg, 1946), 40–43; C. Applegate, *A Nation of Provincials: The German Idea of Heimat* (Berkeley, CA, 1990), 242–43.

35. E. Tersen, "Les révolutions de 1848," *Revue historique* 201 (1949): 272–89; *La pensée* 18 (May–June 1948).

36. "a magnificent youth, who believed in liberty, equality, and fraternity, and who believed that the union of peoples would be achieved by the liberation of each individual nation": F. Fejtö, ed., *1848 dans le monde: Le printemps des peuples* (Paris, 1948), 1: 49.

especially by the reactionary role played by the two great powers of the era, England and Russia.[37]

⟨⸺⟩

The spirit of 1945 could therefore hardly have been more different from that of 1848. Democracy after the Second World War was a work of disabused maturity rather than of youthful enthusiasm, implemented for the most part by politicians and state officials whose cautious support for democracy was the product of hard-won and often painful experience. The public figure who declared as early as the spring of 1947 that "There may be no good political regime, but democracy is surely the least bad of the alternatives" was not, as is often claimed, Winston Churchill but Albert Camus, writing in the French intellectual review *Combat*.[38] The view to which he gave expression—that democracy was not so much a good in itself as a bulwark against the dangerous adventurism of other political models—was widely shared among non-Communist political and intellectual figures in the post-war years. Democracy had failed in the past, and it might fail again. But, as the German exile from Nazism Karl Loewenstein commented in somewhat resigned tones in 1946: "There is no other solution than to try again. There is no other key than faith in democratic legitimacy."[39]

The prevalence of these attitudes helps to explain the lack of celebration that accompanied the reintroduction of democracy into European political life. The rulers of democratic Europe were not, and could not have been, new men: regardless of whether they had held significant political office prior to 1945, their attitudes had been moulded by a host of personal experiences as well as by the wider events through which they had lived—and which they had survived. For this generation of predominantly middle-aged, middle-class, and male political figures who assumed the responsibility of creating a durable democratic structure in post-war Europe, the objective was not to inaugurate a new era of freedom, but more prosaically to avoid past mistakes, to learn from recent

37. Fejtö, *1848 dans le monde*, esp. 2: 456–59.

38. A. Camus, "Democracy and Modesty" (30 April 1947), in J. Lévi-Valensi, ed., *Camus at Combat: Writing 1944–1947* (Princeton, NJ, 2006), 287. Churchill used the same phrase, indicating that he was citing somebody else but without attributing it explicitly to Camus, in a debate in the House of Commons later that year: 444 Parl. Deb. H. C. (5th ser.) (1947) col. 207.

39. K. Loewenstein, *Political Reconstruction* (New York, 1946), 136.

experiences—notably the Anglo-American models of government that had played such a role in defeating the Third Reich—and to pre-empt, as best they could, the dangers of a distinctly uncertain future.

This cautious mentality drew the political elite of post-war Europe towards the safety-first definition of the practice of democracy described in the previous chapter. They inhabited, and more importantly believed themselves to inhabit, a Europe in ruins—in the evocative phrase of Jean-Pierre Rioux, "une Europe exsangue" (a Europe drained of its lifeblood).[40] Evocations and metaphors of ruins were everywhere in Europe in 1945. In material terms, but also politically and intellectually, Europe needed to be rebuilt from the fratricidal conflicts that had brought the continent to the verge of its modern extinction.[41] Visual images were a key component of this vision of Europe. The still photography and movie newsreels of the era were saturated with images of ruins, and of the people who inhabited them, framing the way in which Europeans perceived the world around them. The physical destruction caused by Allied bombing and urban fighting merged with images of emaciated camp survivors and the millions of displaced persons (DPs) in central Europe to forge a stark sense of an atomized society. This was encapsulated most strikingly in the archetypal and enduring image of the *Trümmerfrauen*, the so-called "rubble women," labouring to rebuild their homes and lives amidst the desolate landscape of Germany's ruined cities.[42]

In retrospect, what Paul Steege has termed the "before-and-after postcard" of Europe's subsequent recovery has come to define memories of 1945.[43] The sheer scale of post-war reconstruction, which, in the case of West Germany, built a new economy and society almost literally over the top of the ruins left by the war, has served to fix the ruined urban landscapes of 1945 as the point of departure in numerous memoirs and fictionalized accounts of Europe's post-war development.[44] More immediately, however, this image—which was only partially accurate—of a continent in ruins conveyed much more than a literal meaning: it served, too, to

40. J.-P. Rioux, "L'héritage difficile ou les contraintes de la libération," in Bloch-Lainé and Bouvier, *France restaurée*, 15.

41. S. de Madariaga, *Victors, Beware* (London, 1946), 10; J. Solchany, *Comprendre le nazisme dans l'Allemagne des années zéro (1945-1949)* (Paris, 1997), 257-303.

42. A. Grossmann, "Trauma, Memory and Motherhood: Germans and Jewish Displaced Persons in Post-Nazi Germany, 1945-1949," in Bessel and Schumann, *Life after Death*, 93-127; J. Evans, *Life among the Ruins*, 16-45.

43. Steege, *Black Market, Cold War*, 13.

44. See the intelligent analysis in A. Fuchs, *Phantoms of War in Contemporary German Literature, Films and Discourse* (Basingstoke, UK, 2010), esp. 1-16.

justify predominantly conservative logics of rescue, reconstruction, and the restoration of moral norms. The immediate priorities of hunger and homelessness had to be addressed, but there was also a perceived need to impose law, social order, and authority on populations who had lost their moral coordinates amidst the chaos of war.[45] The language of a crisis of morality was pervasive after the war. The spectacle of millions of Europeans living without the frameworks of family, housing, or reliable means of subsistence generated powerful anxieties about crime, sexual promiscuity, and a wild youth—a *jeunesse sauvage*—who had grown up without the disciplines provided by family and schooling. The priority given to austerity was therefore as much moral as economic. Only by depriving the populations of Europe of the facile pleasures of immediate consumption would they be re-educated in the necessary virtues of self-restraint, hard work, and service to the nation.[46]

This language of moral crisis served various purposes. Most immediately, it justified the reimposition of structures of law and state authority; as well as contributing to the new esteem that Christianity—and more especially Catholicism—enjoyed in the post-war era. Amidst a ruined landscape, Europe's historic church buildings acquired a visibility that seemed expressive of the way in which the moral truths of Christianity had a value that surpassed the frontiers of religious practice.[47] Democracy, too, was inflected by this language of moral crisis. It was regarded less as a political principle than an instrumental device—the means by which the surviving populations could be remade into citizens. By bringing them back into the fold, the energies of the people could be directed towards the collective challenge of national reconstruction, as well as preventing the enemies of democracy—both communism and the widely felt threat of a renascent fascism[48]—from playing on their emotions and material sufferings.

The underlying problem, however, was that democracy was a difficult tool to manage. The experiences of the recent past demonstrated that democracies needed vigilant leadership and direction to keep them from succumbing not only to subversion by ill-intentioned forces but also to the excesses and strains inherent to a volatile mass politics.[49] This was a point made forcefully by Raymond Aron. The time that he had spent in

45. J. Evans, *Life among the Ruins*, 12–15.
46. Re. the moral panic about children and youth, see Zahra, *Lost Children*, 17–23.
47. Strote, *Lions and Lambs*, 13–14.
48. *Combat*, December 1947, as quoted in Algazy, *Tentation néo-fasciste*, 92–94.
49. De Madariaga, *Victors, Beware*, 38–41.

Germany during the final years of the Weimar Republic had left him with a deep distrust of mass politics. For him, right and left had been equally guilty of exploiting the institutions of Weimar for their own ends, rather than valuing democracy in itself. Thus, the democratic regimes of the post-war era must not be left to find their own balance, but must consciously be fashioned in ways that imposed compromise and moderation.[50]

There was therefore little enthusiasm after 1945 to return to the democratic radicalism of the past. The French Revolution of 1789—and more especially the example it provided of the people seizing power forcibly from the monarch, Church, and aristocracy—was very far from the mentality of the democracy-makers of the post-war era. They were more concerned to constrain popular participation than to celebrate it. Much the same was also true of the language of popular nationalism. The history of the development of democracy in Europe since 1789 had been inseparable from the ideal of the collective sovereignty of peoples, breaking free from despotism or alien rule, and establishing institutions of national government, which in turn guaranteed and fulfilled the freedom of their citizens. Nationalism, however, was a newly awkward concept in Western Europe after 1945. The nation was what the war had been fought for (on both sides), as was evident in the patriotic euphoria of liberation and the more solemn ceremonial of the reinauguration of national parliaments and institutions. The nation, moreover, provided the emotional community that bound together those who had died in the war and the new generations of the post-war future.[51] However, the rhetorical language of nationalism—of the territory of the *patrie*, of the people in arms, or of the ethnic or racial community of the *Volk*—had awkward political resonances after 1945. In some areas of Europe the nation was associated with the actions and crimes of the authoritarian and fascist regimes of the recent past, while elsewhere nationalism was tied to the volatile memory of insurrectionary resistance against Nazi rule.

Unsurprisingly, there was a consciously new sobriety to the nationalism of the post-war period, as expressed in the state-policed rituals of commemoration of the fallen soldiers of the two world wars.[52] Rulers were conscious of the need to take control of nationalist sentiments, and

50. Oppermann, *Raymond Aron und Deutschland*, 343–63. I have written about the fear of the fragility of democracy in M. Conway, "On Fragile Democracy: Contemporary and Historical Perspectives," *Journal of Modern European History* 17 (2019): 422–31.

51. Pompe, *Bevrijding*, 85–130; *Košický vládní program*, 13. I am indebted to Jan Indracek for his translation of this latter text.

52. Rousso, *Vichy Syndrome*, 221–26.

to channel them away from visions of the sovereign people and towards the patriotic duties that citizens owed to their state. The nationalism of the post-war era was therefore more about the state than the nation, as reflected in the widespread adoption of the neologism of the "nation-state." With the rapid increase in the role that the state played in the lives of individuals during the post-war decades, membership of the nation came to be defined primarily by the state, through its power to decide who was allowed to acquire nationality and through its control of the benefits that derived from citizenship. This did not mean that the nation had ceased to matter. Nations, along with states, needed to be reconstructed after 1945, and nowhere more so than in the case of those nations that had experienced the collective humiliation of military defeat. The reintegration of former soldiers and prisoners of war into European societies after the Second World War was a substantial challenge, and one that had long-lasting legacies through the pensions, systems of healthcare, and other material benefits that these veterans were accorded. This was, of course, especially true in the German Federal Republic, where the sufferings of the war years, and of national defeat in 1945, were followed by the forcible division of the country, mass migration from the eastern territories, and its reorientation towards a Western European identity.[53] There was therefore a need, in Germany as well as elsewhere, for the construction of new national narratives that, through the careful reconfiguration of the recent past under the symbolic carapace of flag, anthem, and history, would express the post-war reconstruction of the nation without giving renewed oxygen to the demons of the preceding decades.[54]

As a consequence, the nationalism of the post-1945 era assumed new democratic clothes. Everywhere, it seemed, histories were recast to provide narratives that presented where nations had ended up as where they had always been intending to go. Some of these narratives were more successful than others;[55] but common to all was the desire to incorporate and domesticate nationalism within a democratic language of self-government and universal citizenship. This did not prevent the continuity

53. J. Diehl, *The Thanks of the Fatherland: German Veterans after the Second World War* (Chapel Hill, NC, 1993). The historical literature on the construction of a usable past within the Federal Republic is substantial. See notably Moeller, *War Stories*, esp. 2–14.

54. M. M. Feinstein, *State Symbols: The Quest for Legitimacy in the Federal Republic of Germany and the German Democratic Republic, 1949–1959* (Boston, MA, 2001), 1–15, 33–34, 85–122. See also H. Klitzing, *The Nemesis of Stability: Henry A. Kissinger's Ambivalent Relationship with Germany* (Trier, 2007).

55. The case of Austria stands out as a particularly awkward one: see, for example, L. Figl, "Wer hat wen befreit?"

of more-popular forms of nationalism, such as the surge in passions generated by international sporting events, which seemed to serve almost as a compensation for the displacement of such mobilizations from the political realm.[56] Nor did it exclude more atavistic elements of national chauvinism, evident in attitudes towards the children born of liaisons with foreign soldiers, or the racist assumptions that surrounded attitudes towards immigrant "non-European" populations during the 1950s and 1960s.[57] But, with some exceptions,[58] these social prejudices operated largely outside of the mainstream of political debate, and did not destabilize the newly democratic languages of nationalism, in which loyalty to the nation-state went hand in hand with projects of reconciliation and international understanding. This matched, moreover, the reality of a rapidly modernizing Western Europe where people—especially the young middle class—mixed with one another and moved relatively easily across national frontiers.[59] As a consequence, the harder edges of national difference were eroded, and the nation itself was no longer such an exclusive or all-demanding element of personal and collective identity. This in turn changed the way in which ethnic and linguistic groups in Western Europe after 1945 justified their demands for greater independence. No longer was it sufficient to invoke the collective will of a people for freedom. Instead, as in the case of the Flemish Nationalists in Belgium, they were obliged to adopt a new political rhetoric that articulated demands for linguistic rights and self-government through the democratic language of human rights and individual freedom.[60]

Democracy, as conceived by those in authority, was therefore less a form of popular rule than the means—the method, the mentality, and the

56. Such as the so-called "Miracle of Bern" when the newly founded West German football team won the World Cup in 1954: Heineman, "Gender," 43–53.

57. K. Ericsson and E. Simonsen, eds., *Children of World War II: The Hidden Enemy Legacy* (Oxford, 2005); H. Fehrenbach, "Black Occupation Children and the Devolution of the Nazi Racial State," in *After the Nazi Racial State: Difference and Democracy in Germany and Europe*, by R. Chin, A. Grossmann, and G. Eley (Ann Arbor, MI, 2009), 30–54.

58. C. Schofield, *Enoch Powell and the Making of Postcolonial Britain* (Cambridge, UK, 2013).

59. R. I. Jobs, *Backpack Ambassadors: How Youth Travel Integrated Europe* (Chicago, 2017); A. Vion, "Town-Twinning in France during the Cold War," *Contemporary European History* 11 (2002): 623–40; F. Mehring, "Friendly Persuasion, Self-Americanization and the Utopia of a New Europe," in *Selling Democracy, Friendly Persuasion*, ed. R. Rother (Berlin, 2006), 43.

60. V. Walgrave, *Onze Vlaamse Volksbeweging* (Tielt, Belgium, 1949); B. De Wever, "Het Vlaams-Nationalisme na de tweede wereldoorlog," *Bijdragen tot de eigentijdse geschiedenis* 3 (1997): 277–90.

language—through which the state transacted its business with society more widely. As the German student radical Rudi Dutschke subsequently observed with some virulence, democracy did not exist after 1945 to be celebrated but to serve the purposes of the administrative state.[61] This was a perspective with which a good number of state officials might, in their more unguarded moments, have been inclined to agree. As the Gaullist bureaucrat Michel Debré was reported to have commented pessimistically towards the end of his life: "La démocratie s'est installée en France contre le pouvoir. Peut-être ne nous sommes-nous jamais guéris de ce fait capital. . . . C'est là que gît la contradiction de la République."[62] The means of resolving that contradiction was to establish clear hierarchies of authority, and more especially to define a visible but delineated role for the people. Thus, the solemnity of post-war parliamentarism was intended to convey its dual role as the assembly of the people's elected representatives and as a forum of authority where its members conducted their debates insulated, both literally and metaphorically, from the sounds of the street.[63]

Similar concerns were apparent too in the rather formalized character of post-war elections. As Robert Ventresca has perceptively argued with reference to the case of Italy, elections were as much cultural as political events in the post-war democracies.[64] Partly because of the complexity of the proportional electoral systems that became the norm in much of Europe, elections lost much of the element of surprise: success or failure was measured not in the drama of the results from constituencies but in incremental shifts in the balance of power between political forces. Elections became ritualized events, in which the individual gesture of casting one's vote was more important than its consequences. The turnout in elections was, therefore, celebrated more than the outcome.[65] The image of sober queues of citizens—many of them female—outside polling stations was the riposte to the manipulated plebiscites of the Communist east, as well as a demonstration of the seriousness of purpose of the citizens of the Western European states. By waiting patiently to cast their ballots

61. R. Dutschke, *Ecrits politiques* ([Paris], 1968), 57.

62. "Democracy established itself in France against the executive power. Perhaps we never got over this fundamental fact. That is where the contradiction of the Republic lies.": Perrier, *Michel Debré*, 199.

63. See below, p. 134.

64. Ventresca, *From Fascism to Democracy*, 10–13.

65. The turnout was indeed impressive in the immediate post-war elections: 94% of the Austrian electorate voted in the first post-war elections in November 1945, and 92% in the elections of April 1948 in Italy: J. Lewis, *Workers and Politics*, 75–79; Ventresca, *From Fascism to Democracy*, 215.

FIGURE 4. Female suffrage: a woman votes in Paris in the elections for the National Assembly on 10 November 1946. AFP/AFP via Getty Images

against the backdrop of reassuringly unchanging rural landscapes or of cities under reconstruction, the people were endorsing the parliamentary regimes, before withdrawing to allow their elected representatives to conduct the serious and complex business of government.[66] The space that this created between the electorate and the exercise of power was reinforced too by the changing character of election campaigns. The mass meeting and direct contact between candidates and electors were gradually superseded during the post-war decades by the new media of advertising, radio, and eventually television. These distanced the people from direct participation in politics. Instead, they were the audience, or the spectators, of a process that happened elsewhere.[67]

Consequently, the democracies of the post-war decades retained, at least until the upheavals of the 1960s, something of an anti-popular ethos. Put rather starkly, the people had to be made to fit the democracy, rather than vice versa. The experience of Nazism was necessarily central to this

66. Conway, *Sorrows of Belgium*, 276–82.
67. J. Lawrence, *Electing our Masters: The Hustings in British Politics from Hogarth to Blair* (Oxford, 2009), 162–69.

attitude. The undeniable fact that millions of Germans had freely cast their votes for Hitler and the National Socialist German Workers' Party (NSDAP) could not but influence the wariness with which the popular exercise of democracy was regarded. In post-war Germany and elsewhere, the Nazis were reviled not for their destruction of a vibrant and sophisticated democracy but for the way in which they had demonstrated the weakness of any regime that relied on the democratic will of the people. Those, such as the young Henry Kissinger, who had lived through those years in Germany and deemed themselves fortunate to have survived, saw in mass support for the NSDAP the inherent vulnerability of all democracies.[68]

Analysis of Nazism after 1945 therefore focused primarily upon its manipulative techniques and psychological appeal. Rather than presenting the NSDAP as the heir to a tradition of anti-democratic nationalist politics in Germany stretching back to the pre-1914 *Kaiserreich*, the party was perceived as the manifestation of a distinctively modern style of mass politics. Lacking in intellectual or political coherence, the Nazis had worked on the passions and prejudices of the people to lend them initially their electoral support and subsequently their consent.[69] The lesson of the Third Reich was clear: all modern populations were potentially susceptible to manipulation by demagogic opportunists who exploited what the psychologist Erich Fromm described in his influential text *The Fear of Freedom* (1942) as the isolation and powerlessness of the individual in modern society. Confronted by forces beyond their control, and unable to develop a positive sense of their own identity, modern citizens were inclined to engage in what Fromm termed a "totalitarian flight from freedom," by rallying to modern charlatans who provided an illusory sense of security.[70] This conviction that, in the words of Kissinger, "modern mass society starves the individual emotionally" became a widely shared assumption of the age. Democracy was consequently seen as doubly vulnerable: to the

68. Suri, *Henry Kissinger*, 16–51. For similar attitudes, see also de Madariaga, *Victors, Beware*, 36–38; H. Trevor-Roper, preface to Z. Stypulkowski, *Invitation to Moscow* (London, 1951), xiii; De Graaf, "European Socialism," 335; Lijphart, "Typologies of Democratic Systems," 51.

69. P. Nathan, *The Psychology of Fascism* (London, 1943); W. A. Brend, *Foundations of Human Conflicts: A Study in Group Psychology* (London, 1944); K. Sears, *Opposing Hitler: Adam von Trott zu Solz, 1909–1944* (Brighton, UK, 2009), xiii; J.-W. Müller, "European Intellectual History as Contemporary History," *Journal of Contemporary History* 46 (2011): 577–78.

70. E. Fromm, *The Fear of Freedom* (London, 2001), ix. See also G. Mosse, *The Culture of Western Europe* (London, 1963), 6–7.

actions of political adventurers, and to the weaknesses within the people. The response, too, must be twofold. Institutions must protect democracy against its enemies, while the people needed to be vigilant in their defence of "reason, moderation and political democracy"—primarily, it seemed, as protection from themselves.[71]

Nazism was not, however, the only such warning of the power of the masses.[72] In much of western and central Europe, the events of the liberation had left a distinctly ambivalent legacy: the euphoria of emancipation from Nazi rule was intertwined with strong and often personal memories of what were referred to somewhat euphemistically as the "excesses" of the era. The daily currency of crime, physical violence, and rape that had developed in some areas of Europe in the liberation period as a consequence of the collapse of effective police structures had been an education for many Europeans in the way in which lives could be disrupted (or ended) by acts of violence.[73] It also generated a durable anxiety about the arbitrary exercise of popular power. As the Danish sociologist Svend Ranulf commented in 1948, the excesses committed by some Resistance groups at the end of the war had resembled Nazism through what he termed their "proto-fascist" actions, demonstrating how easily mass politics could veer into mob violence rooted in community tensions and the dictatorship of emotions.[74]

Seen in this way, the events of the liberation became another warning of the dangers of arbitrary power, and of the need to construct barriers within democracy against surges in popular passions. The unpopularity of the acts of popular justice carried out after the liberation by predominantly young Resistance fighters, as well as the powers assumed by local committees, such as the so-called National Committees in Czechoslovakia, were used by governments to justify the restoration of the predictable hierarchies of state power and of a legal order.[75] Again, however, the impact of this dark perception of the liberation went deeper than its unsubtle

71. Klitzing, *Nemesis of Stability*, 84; Mosse, *Culture of Western Europe*, 422; K. Renner, "Die Demokratie ist der Friede!" (Christmas 1949), in *Für Recht und Frieden*, 281.

72. J.-W. Müller, *Contesting Democracy: Political Ideas in Twentieth-Century Europe* (New Haven, CT, 2011), 126–27.

73. Much of the memoir and fictionalized literature of the war emphasizes the traumatic impact of almost random acts of violence. See, notably, A. Polcz, *One Woman in the War: Hungary 1944–1945* (Budapest, 2002), and E. Morante, *La storia: Romanzo* (Turin, 1974).

74. S. Ranulf, *On the Survival Chances of Democracy* (Copenhagen, 1948).

75. Conway, *Sorrows of Belgium*, 90–92; speeches of Edvard Beneš and Zdenek Fierlinger, in *Opening of the Prague Parliament*, 27–28 and 76–77.

instrumentalization by those in authority. The memory of the era soon acquired a darker hue, associated with the unpredictability of crowds, and the excesses fuelled by alcohol, guns, and an unrestrained sexuality. Direct experience was less important in this respect than rumours and imaginings. Visual images played a major part in this process. The end of the Second World War was the first moment of popular politics in European history to be captured, and thereby framed, by mass photography. As such, it generated a repertoire of images of public disorder that rapidly came to define what Europeans believed had happened at the liberation. Turbulent crowds gathering in streets and squares, young men armed with guns, the unpredictability of criminality and improvised authority, and above all the spectacle of women having their heads shaved by an avenging mob became the images by which the liberation was remembered and, more importantly, reproduced.[76]

These perceptions could take on a distinctly reactionary and anti-popular tone reminiscent of late nineteenth-century fears of the irrationality of the crowd, as expressed in Robert Aron's distinctly lurid account of "the outpouring of popular passions"—le déchaînement des passions populaires—during the liberation of France.[77] This too was the message of William Golding's dystopian novel, *Lord of the Flies* (1954), which through the allegorical device of a group of children left to fend for themselves after an air crash on a deserted island appeared to demonstrate that unregulated popular power led only to the collapse of community and the triumph of brute force.[78] But, expressed in rather more intellectual terms, the latent potential for violence also provided the basis for a new conservative definition of democracy. Hannah Arendt's gloomy sense of living in an age of "monstrosities" was rooted in her distrust of the passions unleashed by mass politics that had culminated in the horrors of the Third Reich.[79] Ideologies were, for her and others, the root of the problem. They were reservoirs of passions that, like the religions of bygone times, could lead people and societies to take leave of their senses.[80] There was therefore

76. See the images, taken by Allied war photographers, in C. Laurens, "'La femme au turban': Les femmes tondues," in *The Liberation of France: Image and Event*, ed. H. R. Kedward and N. Wood (Oxford, 1995), 155–79; and R. Whelan and C. Capa, eds., *Robert Capa Photographs* (London, 1985), 162–79.

77. Robert Aron, *Histoire de l'épuration*, vol. 1, *De l'indulgence aux massacres* (Paris, 1967), 7, 433–35.

78. W. Golding, *Lord of the Flies* (London, 1954).

79. H. Arendt, *Men in Dark Times* (London, 1970), vii–x; D. Villa, ed., *The Cambridge Companion to Hannah Arendt* (Cambridge, 2000).

80. D. Bell, *End of Ideology*, 371.

a need to drain the passion out of political life, in order to protect what Isaiah Berlin defined as "a limited but nevertheless real area of human freedom." This would be possible only once Europeans came to accept that the pluralism of a "negative" liberty—the liberty to be free—was preferable, and more human, than the ambitions of those who would force people to be free through enforcing the "positive" freedom of a homogeneous and therefore oppressive community.[81]

Berlin's belief that the origins of many of the dangers of the modern world lay in the intellectual principles of the radical thinkers of the Enlightenment, and more especially those of Rousseau (and his spiritual heir, Karl Marx), received powerful polemical support in Jacob Talmon's *The Origins of Totalitarian Democracy* (1952). Talmon argued that the "totalitarian messianic democracy" of the Communist world was the consequence of the dangerously utopian vision of the reconciliation of freedom and constraint forged by Rousseau and his Jacobin acolytes during the French Revolution.[82] Rousseau, indeed, was distinctly out of fashion in post-war Western Europe. For a Catholic intellectual such as Jacques Maritain, Rousseau's "very special and morbid form" of popular sovereignty as implemented during the French Revolution lay at the origins of the ills of the modern world.[83] By asserting the sovereign will of the people, Rousseau (aided by Hegel) had given birth to the modern heresy of the "cultural, ideological, caesaro-papist totalitarian State." Only by overthrowing the myth of popular sovereignty, Maritain argued, would it be possible to create an "organic democracy" that would reassert the primacy of society over the state.[84]

Maritain's approach reflected his particular Catholic conception of democracy. But the link he traced between a rather simplistic understanding of Enlightenment doctrines and the modern totalitarian state became something of a commonplace among anti-Marxist intellectuals

81. I. Berlin, *Four Essays on Liberty* (London, 1969), esp. 116–17, 171–72; J. Gray, *Isaiah Berlin* (London, 1995), 5–37.

82. J. Talmon, *The Origins of Totalitarian Democracy* (London, 1952). See also Y. Arieli, "Jacob Talmon: An Intellectual Portrait," in *Totalitarian Democracy and After*, ed. Arieli and N. Rotenstreich (London, 1984), 14–20. Berlin and Talmon discussed their shared dislike of Rousseau while Talmon was writing his book: C. Brooke, "Isaiah Berlin and the Origins of the 'Totalitarian' Rousseau," in *Isaiah Berlin and the Enlightenment*, ed. L. Brockliss and R. Robertson (Oxford, 2016), 96–98.

83. J. Maritain, *Scholasticism and Authority* (Glasgow, 1940), 90.

84. J. Maritain, *Man and the State* (Chicago, 1951), 1–27; *Scholasticism and Authority*, 89–117. See also B. Doering, *Jacques Maritain and the French Catholic Intellectuals* (Notre Dame, IN, 1983), 178–90.

in the 1950s.[85] To counter Rousseau's merging of the personal and the collective in the notion of the General Will, modern societies needed to heed the call of Alexis de Tocqueville—the centenary of whose death in 1959 prompted renewed attention to his writings—for the power of the state to be limited by the rights of the individual and the actions of local communities.[86] In this way, "totalitarianism"—a term that had initially acquired intellectual definition among Catholic intellectuals in the 1930s, in response to the twin challenges of Nazism and Bolshevism—became a concept that expressed the dangers that lurked within modern democracy. The threat was not that unscrupulous rulers would seek to establish oppressive rule—that, after all, had always been so. What was distinctive about the modern era was the way in which the notion of the sovereignty of the people contained the means for the people to succumb to their own enslavement.[87] Thus, in their highly influential essay on the modern concept of totalitarianism, *Totalitarian Dictatorship and Autocracy* (1956), Carl Friedrich and Zbigniew Brzezinski presented the totalitarian regimes of the Communist east as "the perversion of democracy": by combining the legitimacy of the democratic rule of the people with the technology of all-powerful state propaganda, the leaders of the Soviet Union had used the raw material of democratic politics to forge an unprecedented form of modern dictatorship.[88]

Converted into political practice, these arguments provided convenient justifications for those in positions of authority to build defences against the will of the people. The enthusiasm evident among certain German intellectuals in the immediate aftermath of the demise of the Third Reich to create a new democratic regime of mass participation faded rapidly

---

85. See the essays contained in L. Brockliss and R. Robertson, eds., *Isaiah Berlin and the Enlightenment* (Oxford, 2016).

86. B. Fabian, *Alexis de Tocquevilles Amerikabild* (Heidelberg, 1957), 28–57; R. Rémond, "Tocqueville et la démocratie en Amérique," in *Alexis de Tocqueville: Livre du centenaire, 1859–1959* (Paris, 1960), 180–90.

87. J. Chappel, "The Catholic Origins of Totalitarianism Theory in Interwar Europe," *Modern Intellectual History* 8 (2011): 561–90. See also Solchany, *Comprendre le nazisme*, 278–98; J.-M. Domenach, *La propagande politique* (Paris, 1950), 119.

88. C. Friedrich and Z. Brzezinski, *Totalitarian Dictatorship and Autocracy* (Cambridge, MA, 1956), 6–13. On the intellectual history of totalitarianism, see also M. Geyer with S. Fitzpatrick, introduction to *Beyond Totalitarianism: Stalinism and Nazism Compared*, ed. Geyer and Fitzpatrick (Cambridge, UK, 2009), 3–8.

over the subsequent years.[89] Instead, the ambition became to create what Jan-Werner Müller—citing the writings of the German exile from Nazism Karl Loewenstein—has termed a "disciplined democracy." This aimed to forestall the danger of majority dictatorship inherent in a regime of parliamentary democracy by establishing a panoply of constitutional and legal roadblocks. These would serve to guarantee respect for sectional rights and civil freedoms.[90] For Loewenstein, the "lenient and generous liberal democracy" of the Weimar Republic had inadvertently allowed the German people to be won over by "totalitarian pied pipers," who went on to "raze democracy to the ground." Given the enormous power of modern mass propaganda to manipulate political opinions, he argued that it was essential to restrict freedom of expression in order to protect freedom itself.[91] The influence of the ideas of Loewenstein, who went on to work for the Legal Division of the American Military Administration in occupied Germany, was visible in the structures of the subsequent Federal Republic. The Basic Law of 1949 created the legal framework within which the new German republic would operate, as well as establishing a constitutional court to enforce it. Located above the democratic process, this court used its considerable powers to forbid the expression of views—such as anti-Semitism—that it deemed to be in violation of the Basic Law. Nor did it act only against ideas. After a lengthy legal dispute, the court acted in 1956 to ban the German Communist Party, on the basis that its principles were contrary to those of democracy.[92]

The idea that law, as interpreted by judges, could be superior to the sovereignty of the people well conveyed the cautious spirit of post-war democracy. Though the benefits of a free society were real, the danger was always present that the pursuit of a good democracy could lead to

89. Forner, *German Intellectuals*, 4.

90. J.-W. Müller, *Contesting Democracy*, 146–50. The same phrase is used by others: e.g., Te Velde, *Stijlen van leiderschap*, 156.

91. Loewenstein, *Political Reconstruction*, 126–29; M. Lang, *Karl Löwenstein: Transatlantischer Denker der Politik* (Stuttgart, 2007), 238–45; Greenberg, *Weimar Century*, 169–210. Loewenstein developed these ideas first in the 1930s, during his exile in the United States from Nazism. See K. Loewenstein, "Militant Democracy and Fundamental Rights," *American Political Science Review* 31 (1937): esp. 426–28, 430–32, 644–58.

92. J. Collings, *Democracy's Guardians: A History of the German Federal Constitutional Court 1951–2001* (Oxford, 2015), esp. xxv–xxvii, 1–62; A. J. Nicholls, *The Bonn Republic: West German Democracy, 1945–1990* (London, 1997), 83–85; C. Jahr, "Fighting Anti-Semitism—Democratizing Society?: Reflections on Germany's Rocky Path towards a Civil Society after the Second World War," in *After Fascism: European Case-Studies in Politics, Society and Identity since 1945*, ed. M. Berg and M. Mesner (Vienna, 2009), 89–107; Major, *Death of the KPD*, 283–93.

its converse, through what the Italian liberal politician Giovanni Malagodi denounced as *democraticismo*, the mass politics of democratic will.[93]
Rather than a vehicle driven—who knew where—by the unconsidered
gestures of universal suffrage, democracy needed to be constrained by
free institutions and the rule of law. Nor was such thinking limited to the
domain of the nation-state. The Universal Declaration of Human Rights,
issued by the United Nations in 1948, and, at a regional level, the European Convention on Human Rights of 1950 were in their origin primarily
rhetorical gestures.[94] However, they formed part of a nascent international culture that constrained the sovereignty of the modern state within
higher principles. The crimes of rulers—above all the desire to avoid any
repetition of the acts of genocide committed by the Nazi regime and its
allies during the Second World War—provided the immediate impulse for
these initiatives. But they acquired a wider legitimacy because of the more
general nervousness within post-war intellectual and political culture as
to where the will of the people could lead.[95]

Over time, these ideas would create a discourse and practice of human-
rights law that would expand the nature of democracy while also limiting
the legislative freedom of national parliaments and governments. Most
immediately, however, the elevation of law served more obviously conservative purposes. Campaigning in the elections of the immediate post-war
years, the leaders of the new Catholic Party in France, the MRP, adopted
the slogan of *la Révolution dans la loi*—the Revolution by the law—
thereby neatly encapsulating their advocacy of an ambitious programme
of political and social change while distancing themselves from the arbitrary expressions of popular power supposedly espoused by the Communists and their allies.[96] Indeed, in its more conservative formulations, this
preoccupation with law came close to endorsing an authoritarian reconfiguration of democracy. For example, the political ideologist of the Austrian
People's Party, the ÖVP, Alfred Kasamas, declared that the votes of the
people were only the beginning of the democratic process. What mattered

93. G. Malagodi, *Massa non-massa: Riflessioni sul liberalismo e la democrazia* (Rome,
1962), 35–55.

94. S.-L. Hoffmann, "Introduction: Genealogies of Human Rights," in *Human Rights
in the Twentieth Century*, ed. Hoffmann (Cambridge, UK, 2011), 13–15.

95. S. Moyn, "Personalism, Community and the Origins of Human Rights," and G. Sluga,
"René Cassin: *Les Droits de l'Homme* and the Universality of Human Rights, 1945–1966,"
in *Human Rights in the Twentieth Century*, ed. S.-L. Hoffmann (Cambridge, UK, 2011),
85–106 and 107–24.

96. Letamendia, *Mouvement républicain populaire*, 51. See also Vinen, *Bourgeois Politics in France*, 137–72.

more was the creation of what he termed a *Rechtsordnung*: a regime of legal and judicial norms that, when combined with a separation of institutional powers, would provide a series of dykes within which the will of the people would be contained, and channelled.[97]

Democracy, for many post-war figures, was therefore inseparable from rules. While freedom without order was licence, order without freedom was tyranny, be it fascist dictatorship, Communist totalitarianism, or the amalgam provided in George Orwell's *1984*, published in 1949.[98] The nature of a free society—itself a concept born of the politics of Cold War Europe[99]—lay in the judicious combination of the two in order to foster an ethos of "responsible participation" in democracy, without allowing it to degenerate into the violent brawls of mass politics.[100] This contributed to a remarkably limited conception of the role of elections. Rather than a celebration of the will of the people, they were periodic exercises of control over the actions of rulers. In the disabused words of Karl Popper in his influential text *The Open Society*, they "are to be considered as no more than well-tried and . . . reasonably effective institutional safe-guards against tyranny."[101]

Such caution was reflected also in the changing definitions of freedom. In 1945, few had any doubts that, in the words of a Dutch tract of 1945, "vrijheid is positief": it signified freedom from want and the threat of arbitrary arrest, but also the freedom to create and participate in a new political community.[102] Within a few years, however, this positive content of freedom had been replaced by a more limited emphasis on the freedoms of the individual—what the former Communist and now strong anti-Communist John Middleton Murry summarized in 1948 as "freedom of conscience, of speech, of expression and association."[103] These freedoms provided the definition of a free society as well as the yardstick by which other societies, such as those of the Communist east and the post-colonial Third World,

97. A. Kasamas, *Programm Österreich: Die Grundsätze und Ziele der Österreichischen Volkspartei* (Vienna, 1949), 92–100.

98. G. Orwell, *Nineteen Eighty-Four: A Novel* (London, 1949); B. Crick, "*Nineteen Eighty-Four*: Context and Controversy," in *The Cambridge Companion to George Orwell*, ed. J. Rodden (Cambridge, UK, 2007), 146–59.

99. J. Middleton Murry, *The Free Society* (London, 1948).

100. Socialist Union, *Socialism. A New Statement of Principles* (London, 1952), 59–60; Te Velde, *Stijlen van leiderschap*, 165–66.

101. M. H. Hacohen, *Karl Popper—the Formative Years 1902–1945: Politics and Philosophy in Interwar Vienna* (Cambridge, 2000), 506–10.

102. Pompe, *Bevrijding*, 7–9.

103. Middleton Murry, *Free Society*, 138–48.

could be judged. The western discovery of dissident Soviet intellectuals, through the controversies surrounding the award of the Nobel Prize to Boris Pasternak in 1958 and the publication of Alexander Solzhenitsyn's *One Day in the Life of Ivan Denisovich* in English translation in 1963, as well as heavy-handed Soviet police actions during the 1960s against a range of writers, musicians, and cultural figures, reinforced this trend. The Communist societies of the east were perceived to be captive societies, as a consequence not so much of the absence of political pluralism, but of their intolerance of those who dared to write, paint, or compose music in ways that offended against socialist, or more exactly Soviet, cultural norms.[104] Freedom, such arguments implied, was always essentially personal. This was reinforced by the foundation of Amnesty International in 1961, which by its defence of the "prisoner of conscience"—persecuted by an authoritarian dictatorship of whatever political colour—provided the mirror by which the west knew itself to be free.[105]

Over the course of the post-war years, freedom came to be defined in terms that were more individual than collective. The mass protests, such as demonstrations, public meetings, and strikes, that occurred in many areas of Western Europe during the tense years of the later 1940s and early 1950s might have been seen as healthy indications of Europe's return to democracy. For many contemporaries, however, these crowd actions recalled too obviously the volatile mass politics of the interwar years, as well as the conscripted mass demonstrations of the people's democracies of the Communist east. The crowd, in its various forms, was a subject of nervousness, as reflected in the emphasis placed in much social-psychological thought of the time on the irrationality of collective actions. Crowds were different from people; they obeyed logics of "unconsciously motivated impulses," releasing forms of anger and aggression that otherwise were kept under control.[106] The freedom to protest in post-war Europe was therefore kept, often very literally, under surveillance. Strikes, mass rallies, and above all marches through the streets were constrained by a panoply of legal and bureaucratic controls, enforced by the uniformed personnel of the state. This was especially so during the Communist protest campaigns of the early 1950s. The prominent role played by the Communists in the

104. J. Rubenstein, *Soviet Dissidents: Their Struggle for Human Rights* (Boston, MA, 1980), 1–30.

105. T. Buchanan, "'The Truth Will Set You Free': The Making of Amnesty International," *Journal of Contemporary History* 37 (2002): 575–97.

106. K. Young, *A Handbook of Social Psychology* (London, 1946), 387–410. See also S. Tchakhotine, *Le viol psychique des masses: Obstacles à une vraie démocratie* (Paris, 1946).

strike waves of those years, as well as their leadership of protests against the Korean War and for international peace, frequently attracted accusations that, in the words of Karl Renner, the veteran Socialist president of Austria during a wave of industrial strikes in 1950, they were plotting an "onslaught of brutal violence and tyranny"—Ansturm von brutaler Gewalt und Tyrannei—on the authority of the democratic state.[107]

The consequence was a democracy that at times seemed uneasy with the visual presence, and sound, of the people. Rather than the slogans, emotions, and broken heads of mass demonstrations, the grievances of the people needed to be pre-empted through institutions of socio-economic negotiation that removed the need for protest, or that indeed removed the people themselves by dispersing populations from the inadequate housing and street cultures of urban centres to the apartment blocks of the more ordered suburbs.[108] This distanced perception of the people, not as the collective sovereigns of a democracy but as the objects of solicitude on the part of a well-intentioned state, was integral to the practices of the proliferating governmental agencies of the post-war years. It also found expression in the preoccupation with the pseudoscientific methods of opinion polls. The use of opinion polling by public bodies, private companies, and the major political parties expanded rapidly during the post-war years. By asking people their preferences, rulers indicated their wish to understand the views of the population, while also remaining at a certain objective distance from them.[109]

This underlying nervousness regarding the role of the people in a modern democracy was reflected in the post-war concern with the training of citizens in the practice of democracy. The functioning of a true democracy, Pius XII warned with rather magnificent condescension in 1944, "makes very great demands on the moral maturity of individual citizens."[110] This was, moreover, an aspect of democracy where the people had in the past been found wanting. They had been corrupted, or poisoned, by demagogic politics that had encouraged them to place their own interests above those of the nation, and to blame their misfortunes on the malevolent actions of their rulers.[111] Before post-war elections could be held, therefore, the Italian prime minister Alcide De Gasperi explained to US officials, it was

---

107. Rauscher, *Karl Renner*, 389; G. Ross, *Workers and Communists*, 59–75.

108. M. Young and P. Wilmott, *Family and Kinship in East London* (Harmondsworth, UK, 1962). See also p. 210.

109. A. Kruke, *Demoskopie in der Bundesrepublik Deutschland* (Dusseldorf, 2007).

110. Pius XII, "Democracy and Peace," 311 (quotation), 305–7.

111. Goguel, *Politique des partis* 2: 341.

necessary to "prepare" the Italian people for the exercise of democracy.[112] That was a task which might well take some time. The Italian anti-Fascist exile Gaetano Salvemini was convinced that a determined ten-year tutelage would be necessary to place Italian politics on the right track.[113] Training the people in the subtle virtues of what Talmon termed "empirical and liberal democracy" required the detoxification and reconstruction of the structures of civil life in Europe, as well as the inculcation of new norms of democratic behaviour in the young.[114] Reform of legal systems and of the practices of the state, as well as an intelligent propaganda campaign designed to teach people how to think critically as active citizens, all formed part of this post-war project of an "apprenticeship in democracy" (l'apprentissage de la démocratie) intended to lay the basis of a new democratic culture.[115]

Democracy was not therefore about taking people as they were, but about encouraging their development in new directions. In those societies that had been occupied by German forces, the punishment of those who had collaborated with the enemy was accompanied by a programme of retraining in their social and political responsibilities prior to their reintegration into society.[116] In central Europe, that challenge was much larger; it was not a matter of re-educating deviant minorities but of changing the national mentalities that had given rise to Nazism, and inculcating the values of free debate and democracy.[117] Whatever the initial optimism of some anti-Nazi Germans returning from exile and of Allied officials, this proved to be no easy task. Many of the somewhat heavy-handed attempts at educating post-war Germans and Austrians about the errors of their past merely served to reinforce a sense of resentful victimhood among a population who held others rather than themselves responsible for their sufferings.[118] Indeed, as opinion polls indi-

112. Brogi, *Confronting America*, 61. See also De Graaf, "European Socialism," 335; Rizi, *Benedetto Croce*, 15–16.

113. Tintori, "Outsider's Vision," 148–49.

114. Renner, "30 Jahre Republik Österreich," 86; Arieli, "Jacob Talmon," 18 (quotation).

115. H. Finer, *The Future of Government* (London, 1946), 144–56; Domenach, *Propagande politique*, 119–27; Hoyois, "Réponse des peuples," 237 (quotation).

116. D. Luyten and X. Rousseaux, "Introduction générale," in "Les professionnels du droit," ed. Luyten and Rousseaux, special issue, *Cahiers d'histoire du temps présent* 24 (2011): 30–31.

117. Weber, "Freier Sozialismus," 62–63, 87–94.

118. Moeller, *War Stories*, 6; Forner, *German Intellectuals*, 135–36; R. Knight, "National Construction Work and Hierarchies of Empathy in Postwar Austria," *Journal of Contemporary History* 49 (2014): 491–513.

cated, a substantial minority of people in Germany and Austria retained at least until the 1950s a quietly positive memory of the Third Reich, and of its leader.[119]

This did not mean that they were unrepentant fascists, or indeed necessarily opposed to democracy; but it did indicate the way that changes in legislation and judicial processes depended upon the more gradual reordering of norms of civil behaviour and citizenship. This above all required the forging of new elites, who would combine a strong sense of their social role and their wider responsibilities to society. Universities had a key role in this process;[120] but so too did the institutions of the state. An old "Prussian" civic mentality of unquestioning obedience to authority had to be replaced, in the civil service and in the newly refounded armed forces of the Federal Republic (the *Bundeswehr*), by the notion of the official as the servant of the people.[121] In the army, as in structures of education, there was a conscious attempt in the 1950s to disseminate liberal values, and encourage a democratic culture of debate and of mutual respect. What one schoolteacher termed in 1954 the "Untertanengeist"—the servile spirit—of the Wilhelmine and Nazi past had to be replaced by a spirit of participation and debate, through school councils and student newspapers, which in turn would provide a training for pupils in the virtues of active citizenship.[122]

Inevitably, these reforms were not a complete success; but they did encourage a real shift in attitudes. This owed much to broader social changes: the optimism generated by economic growth from the end of the 1940s onwards and effective programmes of welfare and housing provision, as well as the increased social and geographical mobility of the post-war years, all encouraged Germans to embrace the norms of the new political and social order. But this change was also one of values, which was particularly marked among the elites. The reproduction of hierarchical and anti-democratic attitudes that had characterized many sectors of German upper-middle-class society since the late nineteenth century came decisively to an end after 1945. In their place, there developed a new and more open value structure of citizenship—*Bürgerlichkeit*—reflected in the post-war intellectual engagement with liberalism and the emulation

119. Stöss, *Politics against Democracy*, 41–43; Rathkolb, *Paradoxical Republic*, 30–33.

120. Greenberg, *Weimar Century*, 73–75; Forner, *German Intellectuals*, 103–11.

121. Weber, "Freier Sozialismus," 69–71; U. Frevert, *A Nation in Barracks: Modern Germany, Military Conscription and Civil Society* (Oxford, 2004), 263–65.

122. S. Levsen, "Authority and Democracy in Postwar France and West Germany, 1945–1968," *Journal of Modern History* 89 (2017): 812–50, quotation at 830.

of the supposedly more democratic forms of behaviour current in other societies, and most especially the United States.[123]

⟨⟩

It was not, however, only the people who had to practise the new habits of democracy. So too did their leaders. The origins of many of the problems of the interwar democratic regimes, it was believed, lay in the actions of irresponsible political figures, who had sought to outbid each other, thereby fostering unrealistic expectations among the electors. In response, a self-conscious sobriety was evident in the politics of the post-war era. Leaders eschewed the tools of emotional rhetoric and extravagant promises in favour of modest commitments to incremental reform and to working collaboratively with one another for the general good. This was a change of political rhetoric, but also of style and of appearance. The cult of the great man was very much out of fashion.[124] Instead, politicians cultivated a certain ordinariness that, through their family life and simple pleasures—sport, traditional food, their allotment—betokened their sympathy with the mentalities of the people.[125] In contrast, those who broke with such restraint, such as the Communists, or those movements of the populist right that intermittently appeared in the immediate post-war years, were condemned as demagogues.[126]

In this new world, political leaders were not supposed to get too close to the people. Thus, for example, the Uomo Qualunque movement that developed in Italy in the later 1940s was distrusted not solely because of the post-Fascist echoes of its sloganeering, but for its adoption of the direct language of the "ordinary man" who disliked politics and wanted to be left to get on with his own life.[127] Much the same was true, too, of the Poujadist movement that emerged around the figure of Pierre Poujade and his UDCA in France in 1953. Poujade succeeded in seizing the mood of the moment with his uncomplicated demands for voters to reject

---

123. Van Rahden, "Clumsy Democrats," 485–504.

124. Riall, *Garibaldi*, 8.

125. Te Velde, *Stijlen van leiderschap*, 169–80.

126. Conway, *Sorrows of Belgium*, 197–200. Re populism, see also pp. 78–79.

127. S. Setta, *L'uomo qualunque 1944/1948* (Rome, 1975); R. Chiarini, "L'antipolitica in Italia: Un tentativo di concettualizzazione," *Storia Contemporanea* 19 (2015): 13–16; P. Corduwener, "Challenging Parties and Anti-Fascism in the Name of Democracy: The Fronte dell'Uomo Qualunque and Its Impact on Italy's Republic," *Contemporary European History* 26 (2017): 69–84.

the existing deputies: "sortir les sortants!"[128] The score of 11.6 per cent of the vote achieved by Poujade and his allies, who together constituted a list entitled Union et fraternité française (UFF) in the parliamentary elections of January 1956, was a remarkable but ephemeral achievement, which expressed the discontent of those—notably in provincial and rural southern France—who felt neglected by a Parisian political elite.[129] Poujade himself denied his movement had a political ideology, entitling a column he wrote in *Le Monde* "Notre apolitisme"; and in truth his movement offered little that went beyond the conventional rhetoric of French republican democracy. More subversive, however, was the deliberate way in which he emphasized the sovereignty of the people. He addressed the electors by the more intimate formula of *tu* in place of the more formal *vous*, and denounced the "new feudalism"—nouvelle féodalité—of politicians who had stolen the liberation from the people.[130]

The most important of such heretical voices was, however, undoubtedly Charles de Gaulle. When he first established France Libre in London in 1940, de Gaulle was careful to avoid being too specific regarding his political views. But, once he had established his provisional regime in Algiers in 1943, he began to elaborate on his vision of the new form of democracy, "renewed in its institutions and especially in its practices," that should replace the Vichy regime.[131] The themes he developed in his speeches at that time were in essence the same amalgam of ideas of executive authority and of direct democracy that he would advocate during the subsequent twenty-five years. National sovereignty, he argued, must be ensured through the establishment of an executive authority that had the means and the freedom to "carry out its duties in a manner worthy of France," while responding directly to the aspirations of the people.[132] After the liberation, de Gaulle initially sought to build support within the political elite for his ideas. But, when it became clear to him that the constitution being devised by the Constituent Assembly would privilege parliamentary rule over presidential authority, he abruptly resigned from the office of president in January 1946. Thereafter, de Gaulle's rhetorical

---

128. R. Souillac, *Le mouvement poujade: De la défense professionnelle au populisme nationaliste, 1953–1962* (Paris, 2007); D. Borne, *Petits-bourgeois en révolte?: Le mouvement poujade* (Paris, 1977).

129. Borne, *Petits-bourgeois en révolte?* 132–50; C. Leleu, *Géographie des élections françaises depuis 1936* (Paris, 1971), 85–86, 269.

130. P. Poujade, *J'ai choisi le combat* (Saint-Céré, France, 1955), 123–26, 205–8 (quotation at 125); Borne, *Petits-bourgeois en révolte?* 137–40, 181–98.

131. De Gaulle, *Discours et messages* 1: 389; Rudelle, "Général de Gaulle," 26–28.

132. De Gaulle, *Discours et messages* 1: 280 (quotation), 341.

sallies against the political parties, and through them against the entire edifice of representative democracy, acquired a harder edge. In a speech at Bayeux in June 1946 that became the manifesto for his alternative vision of France's constitutional structure, he presented a measured but wide-ranging critique of the proposed constitution of the Fourth Republic, which, by locating government in the institution and personnel of the new National Assembly, confused the necessary separation of executive and legislative power. While de Gaulle soon after withdrew from active politics, the party he created to act as a vehicle for his ideas, the Rassemblement du peuple français (RPF), became increasingly outspoken in its denunciation of the regime and its major political parties. In tones that recalled the rhetoric of right-wing critics of the Third Republic in the 1930s, de Gaulle and his supporters denounced a political elite whose rivalries were depriving France of the effective leadership it required.[133]

In stark contrast to the complexities of parliamentary government, de Gaulle's vision rested on a direct bond between ruler and ruled. In a speech given in Algiers on Bastille Day in 1943, he referred to this link as "la pure démocratie."[134] Only a strong president, able to act independently of party-political pressures, could, he repeatedly argued, serve as the embodiment of the will of "la Nation dans ses profondeurs" (the nation in its depths).[135] As this resonant language indicated, de Gaulle's conception of democracy resisted institutional definition. His almost mythic sense of his own destiny as the providential figure who through his vision and his physical presence embodied the collective will of the people represented the antithesis of the careful constitutional frameworks that dominated post-war Western Europe. In that sense, de Gaulle was very much a figure out of his time—the heir to the traditions of personalized power rooted in the nineteenth century, but which he also succeeded in transcending. Part monarch, part military saviour, and part father of the nation, de Gaulle's personal image, and his artful manipulation of it, played on a series of political discourses without allowing himself to be constrained by any.[136]

133. De Gaulle, *Discours et messages* 2: 417–18, 422–23, 503–4; Purtschet, *Rassemblement du peuple français*, 34–41. This was a theme that was of course voiced even more emphatically by many of de Gaulle's supporters. See, for example, M. Debré, "La véritable faiblesse de la démocratie" (1–2 September 1948), republished in *République et ses problèmes*, 31–35. The most obvious continuity was with the language of the interwar ex-combatant organization the Croix de Feu: see W. D. Irvine, "Fascism in France and the Strange Case of the Croix de Feu," *Journal of Modern History* 63 (1991): 271–95.

134. De Gaulle, *Discours et messages* 1: 312. See also pp. 265–66.

135. Quoted in J. Touchard, *Le gaullisme 1940–1969* (Paris, 1978), 310.

136. S. Hazareesingh, *Le mythe gaullien* (Paris, 2010), 207–22.

Whether, as Jean Touchard has suggested, this should lead us to question the general's commitment to democracy is less certain.[137] De Gaulle's vision of a presidential republic placed him at odds with much of the French political class following the liberation, but it may well have enjoyed greater support with the French people than the creation of the Fourth Republic might suggest.[138] However, de Gaulle's self-image and his determination to avoid being confined by political labels can easily lead to an exaggeration of his political radicalism. For his long-time opponents, such as François Mitterrand, de Gaulle was essentially a Bonapartist adventurer who used his position as president after 1958 to sideline representative government and transform it into what Mitterrand denounced as effectively a monarchy: a "démocratie tombée en monarchie."[139] Such formulations exaggerate the degree to which the Fifth Republic in fact marked a break from its predecessor.[140] But the accusations of dictatorial ambitions that always surrounded de Gaulle—as well as the extravagant hopes placed in him by some of his more radical supporters—indicate how democracy had assumed a defined shape during the post-war years. Democracy had edges, beyond which political leaders were not supposed to step.

Monarchs were also subject to this rule. This was well demonstrated by the failure of Leopold III to recover his constitutional role as the king of the Belgians. The bitter political dispute between Leopold and his opponents dominated Belgian politics between 1944 and 1950, starkly juxtaposing two divergent definitions of political legitimacy. Leopold had chosen to remain in German-occupied Belgium during the war, while the principal members of the government had fled initially to France and subsequently to London, where they established a government-in-exile.[141] This opened up a durable fissure in national life between the supporters and the opponents of the king. On one side was the post-war government, and most notably the powerful Socialist Party, who accused Leopold of having tried to create a New Order government during the German occupation. They used their majority in parliament to bar Leopold from returning to Belgium as monarch, when he was released from Nazi detention in Germany in May 1945, until he gave assurances of his loyalty to the constitution. On

137. Touchard, *Gaullisme*, 309–10.

138. J. Cowans, "French Public Opinion and the Founding of the Fourth Republic," *French Historical Studies* 17 (1991): 90.

139. F. Mitterrand, *La rose au poing* (Paris, 1973), 135.

140. See pp. 76–77 and 265.

141. J. Stengers, *Léopold III et le gouvernement: Les deux politiques belges de 1940* (Paris, 1980).

the other side stood Leopold, who, since succeeding his father as king in 1934, had made no secret of his dislike for the party-political system. Leopold refused to accept the conditions imposed by the government on his return, seeking instead to appeal directly to the people. Mobilizing the resources of popular monarchist sentiment, Leopold presented himself as the father of his people, who had chosen to share their sufferings through the harsh years of the German occupation and who was now the victim of unjust accusations by the politicians. This conflict—part personal and part ideological—reached its increasingly bitter dénouement when a government led by the pro-Leopold Catholic Party, the CVP-PSC, organized a consultative referendum in March 1950 on the future of the king. Leopold won by 57.7 to 42.3 per cent and, after the CVP-PSC also won a narrow overall majority in the general elections of June 1950, he duly returned to the royal palace in Brussels. However, in the face of street demonstrations and strikes provoked by his return, notably in the francophone industrial areas of southern Belgium, the commitment of the Catholic political leaders to Leopold's restoration began to evaporate. After a series of tense meetings with delegations of ministers and parliamentarians, Leopold was effectively obliged in July to agree to abdicate in favour of his eldest son, Baudhuin.[142]

The resolution of a conflict that at times had seemed to threaten Belgium's post-war recovery as a nation-state came to be widely seen—though certainly not by Leopold and his monarchist supporters—as a demonstration of the resilience of the country's constitutional structures. It also, however, marked the triumph of a parliamentary definition of democracy: the political elite, rather than the people or the monarchical laws of heredity, would decide who would be king. The highly personalized and at times sentimental campaign that built up around Leopold operated in a very different register from the constitutional legalism of his opponents. Leopold insisted that he too was acting to defend the principles of the constitution, but he presented himself as a monarch who "understood" those he referred to almost unconsciously as "his" people.[143] This paternalistic discourse—which de Gaulle unconsciously echoed in his famous but highly evasive statement of "Je vous ai compris" (I have understood you) to the crowds in Algiers in 1958—retained a considerable appeal among some sections of the population. But it was at odds with the dominant

142. J. Gérard-Libois and J. Gotovitch, *Léopold III: De l'an 40 à l'effacement* (Brussels, 1991); P. Theunissen, *1950, le dénouement de la question royale* (Brussels, 1986).

143. See, for example, Conway, *Sorrows of Belgium*, 268–75.

quasi-republicanism of post-war Europe. Monarchs, in Belgium as else-where in Western Europe, had ceased to be the embodiment of an alternative political legitimacy, and became mute symbols of the values of the nation, or participants in the highly visual culture of popular celebrity.[144]

The decision by the Belgian political elite to overrule the results of the referendum on Leopold's future was indicative too of the wider caution with which all such exercises in direct democracy were regarded after the war. In Switzerland, referenda were of course a long-established element of the political process; but elsewhere they were regarded as a tool of manipulation, and, in the words of one German politician, "a blessing to every demagogue."[145] De Gaulle was an enthusiastic advocate of their use, holding five referenda to validate the establishment of the Fifth Republic in September 1958, the granting of self-determination and subsequently independence to Algeria in 1961 and 1962, and, more controversially, the remoulding of the constitution through the direct election of the president in October 1962, before finally being defeated in a referendum on regional constitutional reforms in April 1969, which brought about the end of his political career.[146] But, the French Fifth Republic aside, there was little provision for referenda in the architecture of post-war democracy. The Belgian constitution did not allow for referenda and the experiment of 1950 was never repeated. In the Federal Republic of Germany the role that referenda and the direct election of the president had supposedly played in inciting the volatile nationalist politics of the Weimar Republic created a strong taboo against such exercises in direct democracy.[147] Even when the people were consulted, there was a reluctance to accept their view as sovereign. Provision for referenda was introduced by the reform of the Danish constitution in 1953, but politicians hesitated to use it, fearing the polarization of popular opinion that would be generated by single-issue campaigns.[148] In Sweden, the Social Democratic government did organize two referenda, albeit only advisory ones, in the 1950s. In the first, held in 1955, an overwhelming 83 per cent of those who voted rejected a proposal that driving should move from the left to the right side of the road, to bring it

144. A. Schwarzenbach, *Königliche Traume: Eine Kulturgeschichte der Monarchie von 1789 bis 1997* (Munich, 2012). Re. de Gaulle's speech in Algiers, see J. Jackson, *Certain Idea of France*, 484–87.

145. Collings, *Democracy's Guardians*, xxiii.

146. Berstein, *Republic of de Gaulle*, 11–18, 54–55, 71–78, 237–41. See also pp. 263–65.

147. Weber, "Freier Sozialismus," 72; R. Schiffers, *Elemente direkter Demokratie im Weimarer Regierungssystem* (Dusseldorf, 1971), 289–91.

148. Lidegaard, *Short History of Denmark*, 226.

into line with the practice in the large majority of European states; in 1957 a referendum on three complex proposals for a supplementary pension scheme resulted in no clear majority opinion. In both cases, however, the parliament and government felt that they knew better than the people. A few years later, parliament overruled the outcome of the first referendum, and implemented driving on the right. As the prime minister, Tage Erlander, commented: "It is obvious that referenda are a strongly conservative force. It becomes much harder to pursue an effective reform policy if reactionaries are offered the opportunity to appeal to people's natural conservatism and natural resistance to change."[149]

{⸻⸻}

The democracy of post-war Western Europe was therefore intended to be one not of direct popular sovereignty, but of representation and of intermediaries. These twin principles presented rather different aspects of democracy. On the one hand, the familiar rituals of elections and of parliaments constituted the public face of democracy; on the other, the multilayered institutions of corporatist negotiation, involving the state and a range of social organizations, served as the mechanisms whereby socio-economic decisions were arrived at in an inclusive manner. Both were regarded as essential. In particular, parliaments served as the centrepieces of the new regimes. This was perhaps most obviously so in Austria, where the reinstallation of parliament in its imposing late Habsburg building in Vienna expressed the recovery of Austrian sovereignty after the country's integration into the Third Reich as well as its freedom in the face of its Communist-ruled neighbours to the east.[150] Parliaments were in this way both national and universal; by conducting the affairs of the nation through the rituals of parliamentary motions and procedures, the post-war states demonstrated their differentness from the personal power of monarchy or dictatorship, as well as their commitment to democracy.[151]

---

149. L. Lewin, *Ideology and Strategy: A Century of Swedish Politics* (Cambridge, UK, 1988), 218–37.

150. J. Raab, "Parteiverantwortung für das Staatsganze in der Republik" (1951), in *Julius Raab: Ansichten des Staatsvertragskanzlers*, ed. R. Prantner (Vienna, 1991), 13–14.

151. Weber, "Freier Sozialismus," 66–69; De Graaf, "European Socialism," 343; D. Luyten and P. Magnette, "L'idée du parlementarisme en Belgique," in *Histoire de la Chambre des représentants de Belgique 1830–2002*, ed. E. Gubin, J.-P. Nandrin, E. Gerard, and E. Witte (Brussels, 2003), 38–41; Chatriot, *Pierre Mendès-France*, 176.

FIGURE 5. Men (and one woman) in suits: Konrad Adenauer (bottom right) meets with the West German government in Bonn. Bettmann/Bettmann via Getty Images

If, however, as everybody seemed to agree, parliaments were the essential institutions of democracy, they also had to be made to operate effectively. Thus, while insisting that parliament was essential to democracy— "on ne conçoit pas de démocratie en France sans parlement"—Michel Debré deplored the failings of the Fourth Republic. He called for a reformed electoral and constitutional system that would avoid the dangers of what he termed the "tyranny of factions," and would create an effective executive authority.[152] In the immediate post-war years, this caused some to look to Britain, where the Westminster model of a disciplined bipolar system appeared to offer an alternative to the short-lived coalitions of the parliamentary regimes of the recent past. But, as those European political figures who made the journey to London soon recognized, much of the reality of power lay not in the House of Commons but within the political parties.[153]

Thus, parties, more than parliaments, rapidly came to be seen as the essential building blocks of democracy. As the new Italian constitution of January 1948 declared emphatically: "All citizens have the right to free

152. Debré, *Refaire une démocratie*, 21–30. See the similar (if retrospective) comments of Pierre Mendès France in *Rencontres: Nenni, Bevan, Mendès France (février 1959)* (Paris, 1959), 27–36; Chatriot, *Pierre Mendès-France*, 167–68.

153. Bobbio, *Political Life*, 72–74.

association in political parties so as to participate in the democratic process, to help determine the politics of the nation."[154] These had, however, to be parties of the right kind. Responding to de Gaulle's attacks on the constitution of the new Fourth Republic, the Socialist minister of the interior, Edouard Depreux, insisted in 1946 that, in contrast to the interwar years when the intrigues of small parliamentary cliques had been responsible for many of the weaknesses of the Third Republic, the new democratic regime would be based on internally disciplined political parties.[155] This aspiration for what Chabod described as well-organized major parties was a theme adopted by a wide range of post-war figures.[156] For example, the new president of the Fourth Republic Vincent Auriol, in a speech on coming into office in January 1947, expressed the hope that the parties would come together to create "au début de chaque legislature et *pour sa durée* une majorité disciplinée autour d'un programme concret et dans une orientation politique précise."[157] This proved to be a vain hope; but the need for modern voter-oriented parties became a commonplace mouthed by all new political parties, such as the Gaullist Union pour la Nouvelle République (UNR) of the 1960s, who presented themselves as responding to the demands of their constituents, in contrast to the self-interested actions of their opponents.[158] But, for all their flaws, political parties were accepted as an unavoidable component of modern democracy. This was the theme of an influential study first published in 1951 by the French political scientist Maurice Duverger—who had himself repented of his youthful dalliance with Doriot's quasi-fascist Parti populaire français—which became through its multiple editions in effect a textbook of the party politics of post-war Europe.[159]

The central role of political parties also defined the electoral process. Majority rule was not regarded as an essential, or even a desirable, feature

154. Ventresca, *From Fascism to Democracy*, 273.

155. Chabod, *Italie contemporaine*, 169. See also Hamon, *De Gaulle*, 39–40.

156. Purtschet, *Rassemblement du peuple français*, 41–42; De Graaf, "European Socialism," 338. See also Finer, *Future of Government*, 166.

157. "at the beginning of each legislature, and *for its duration*, a disciplined majority based on a concrete programme, and a clearly defined political orientation": V. Auriol, *Journal du septennat, 1947–1954* (Paris, 1970), vol. 1 (1947), 17 January 1947, 26 (emphasis in original).

158. J. Watson, "The Internal Dynamics of Gaullism, 1958–1969" (University of Oxford DPhil. thesis, 2001), 306–73.

159. M. Duverger, *Les partis politiques* (Paris, 1951), published in English translation as *Political Parties: Their Organization and Activity in the Modern State* (London, 1954), and many subsequent editions. Re. Duverger's career and influence, see Hoffmann-Martinot, "Biography of Maurice Duverger," 304–9. See also pp. 68–71.

of a mature democracy; what mattered more was the construction of a parliamentary culture in which all of the principal political and social forces of the nation had a voice. Representation therefore took priority over transient swings of electoral fortunes, as reflected in the systems of proportional representation adopted in most European states. For some critics, such as Debré, proportional representation merely encouraged a lowest-common-denominator approach to politics, in which parliamentary dealmaking took precedence over effective governance.[160] But, for many others, the opacity of the more complex systems of proportional representation—whereby, for example, in Italy surplus votes were redistributed from constituencies to a national electoral college—was a substantial benefit. By removing the unpredictability (and excitement) of individual electoral contests, proportional representation ensured that votes were cast for parties rather than individual candidates, and that the parties were obliged to collaborate and negotiate to achieve a collective goal.[161]

These arguments in favour of electoral complexity reflected, once again, the demagogic experiences of the recent past. By denying extremist parties the momentum of a rapid electoral advance based on incoherent protest votes, proportional representation reinforced the outer barrier walls of a political culture of centrist compromise. However, this also required democracy to be embedded within society. Parliamentary regimes of the past had been, it was widely believed, simply too political, and consequently too divorced from the associational structures of society. Therefore, if the new regimes were to prove more durable, it was necessary to extend democracy into other areas of society, and to associate the principal social institutions with the democratic process. These twin goals of socio-economic democratization and of the involvement of social organizations such as trade unions and professional interest groups in the business of government became a major aspect of democracy in the post-war era. Rather than isolated legislatures seeking to assert their supremacy over society, parliaments would form part of a wider culture of representation and negotiation—what the Danish writer Hal Koch presented in his 1945 booklet "What Is Democracy?" as a democracy of dialogue.[162]

The ambition to create a "more" democratic society was a prominent feature of the liberation period. For example, "the widest democracy"

---

160. Debré, *République et ses problèmes*, 57–59.

161. Ventresca, *From fascism to democracy*, 274–83. See also pp. 79–81.

162. H. Koch, *Hvad er demokrati?* (Copenhagen, 1945). Re. Koch's ideas, see also Jakobsen, "Inventions and Developments," 320–22.

advocated in the Resistance Charter in France did not concern political change but the wish to create "a true economic and social democracy" that would encompass all areas of daily life.[163] Democracy, in such rhetoric, should no longer describe a political regime but a much wider ethos, which permeated economic, social, and human relations.[164] This goal had a particular resonance in those states where the post-war prosecution of economic collaboration became associated with the broader goal of the redistribution of economic power. Thus, in justifying the Czechoslovak National Front government's expropriation of those businesses, often owned by German-speaking Czechs, that had collaborated with the Nazi war effort, the Socialist prime minister, Zdeněk Fierlinger, announced that he wished to issue "a sort of 'magna carta'" of the new popular democracy being created in Czechoslovakia. In this new regime, democracy would not be limited to public administration and the parliamentary sphere. Instead, he declared (in a French-language publication), "la démocratie pénétrera dans toutes les branches de la production et de la distribution et où il sera par conséquent possible de parler de nouvelles formes du socialisme démocratique."[165]

The ambition of an economic democracy was, however, about more than simply the transfer of economic power. It reflected the widely held belief that the war, coming so soon after the global economic crisis of the 1930s, had marked the demise of individualist and competitive capitalism. Instead, new forms of ownership and control had to be created, both from below through the participation of the workers in the management of the enterprise and from above though creating institutions, within particular industrial sectors, as well as across the economy as a whole, that would bring together employers, representatives of the trade unions, and state officials to set the priorities for the economy. The inspirations behind these corporatist institutions that emerged in almost all European states after 1945 were varied. In part, they were a repackaging of similar bodies that had been established during the 1930s in Fascist Italy, Salazar's Portugal, and, after 1940, in Vichy France. Corporatism, however, also formed part of the post-war ambition to replace the anarchic conflicts

163. "The Resistance Charter," in Thomson, *Democracy in France*, 277; G. Ross, *Workers and Communists*, 21–23.

164. Auriol, *Journal du septennat* vol. 1 (1947), 17 January 1947, 26.

165. "democracy will penetrate in all branches of production and distribution, thereby making it possible to speak of new forms of democratic socialism": Z. Fierlinger, "Programme gouvernemental de reconstruction de l'état," in *La Tchécoslovaquie sur une route nouvelle* (Prague, 1947), 7. Fierlinger's statement reflected his policy of close alliance with the Communist Party: see Myant, *Socialism and Democracy*, 120–23.

of the nineteenth-century capitalist economy with rational structures of economic planning and social negotiation. By bringing together the triple forces of the state, of workers' organizations, and of employers, it would be possible to implement a comprehensive modernization of Europe's economic life.[166]

The extent to which these new institutions marked a break with capitalism itself was, however, less clear. For the more radical trade-union leaders who had come to the fore in many areas of Europe since the strikes of the 1930s, corporatism formed part of a process that would lead, sooner rather than later, to worker self-management of the means of production.[167] For others, however, and most obviously for the social coalition of state bureaucrats, reform-minded industrialists, and economic technocrats, who emerged as the driving force of Western Europe's post-war economic modernization and recovery, corporatist bodies were primarily a means of mobilizing economic resources and of hastening the pace of technical innovation. Thus, for these figures, the corporatist structures of negotiation at the industrial, national, and subsequently European levels were intended to stabilize capitalism by pre-empting cycles of boom and slump. The state planning agencies would set the goals for the economy, while the different institutions of corporatist negotiation would determine the most effective means of delivering those targets. In this way, corporatism would also provide a means of mediating conflicts between labour and capital, as well as between industrial sectors and nation-states, which, from a post-1945 perspective, had been the principal source of economic, and consequently social, instability since the late nineteenth century.[168]

Common to all of these variously titled economic councils, chambers, and workplace committees was also the belief that they were democratic. The replacement of Darwinian struggles between conflicting interests by institutions of social negotiation would create an economic parliament to sit alongside the political democracy of parliament. Moreover, by associating powerful social organizations such as trade unions, consumer groups, and farmers' leagues with the processes of state decision-making, corporatism was intended to prevent a return to the oppositional and even insurrectionary social politics that had developed in many regions during the interwar years. Those who had formerly been on the outside now

166. See, for example, J. Monnet, *Mémoires* (Paris, 1976), 280–82.

167. Hemmerijckx, *Van Verzet*, 83–123; R. Hemmerijckx, "Le Mouvement syndical unifié et la naissance du renardisme," *Courrier hebdomadaire du CRISP* 1119–20 (1986).

168. R. Kuisel, *Capitalism and the State in Modern France* (Cambridge, UK, 1981), 187–247; Nicholls, *Freedom with Responsibility*, 136–205.

found themselves within the institutions of decision-making, able to voice their concerns, and influence the making of socio-economic policies.[169] This "semi-sovereign state," to use the formula coined by Peter Katzenstein with regard to West Germany, might have lost some of its executive autonomy, but it had gained a plethora of willing collaborators.[170]

Democratic corporatism contributed more to social stability than to the empowerment of workers. The hopes of trade-unionists—and indeed of some state officials—that corporatism would change the relations of power within the workplace, by abolishing the sovereignty of employers and obliging them to respect the opinions and interests of their workers, faded over the post-war years.[171] The rapid rate of economic growth achieved in many European states during the 1950s did not remove worker discontent—as was evident in the strikes and other forms of industrial conflict during the post-war years[172]—but it gave a new self-confidence to employers and managers. Corporatism therefore proved to be more about representation than power. Rather than constraining the autonomy of companies, it created a new culture of decision-making. Employers and trade-union officials, as well as in some cases the representatives of producers and of consumers, became accustomed to meeting regularly to reach agreements over the allocation of raw materials, the setting of salary levels, and in some cases of prices, and a wide range of issues relating to the material conditions of workers within and outside the workplace. The consequence was a continuous but incremental reformism. Employees benefited from increased wage levels and social benefits, whilst the larger issues of industrial and economic decision-making remained in the hands of employers and state officials.[173]

Perhaps more significant than their relatively modest results was, however, the way in which these corporatist institutions contributed to the non-confrontational ethos of a "democracy of negotiation."[174] By bringing

169. D. Luyten, *Sociaal-economisch overleg in België sedert 1918* (Brussels, 1995).

170. P. Katzenstein, *Policy and Politics in West Germany: The Growth of a Semisovereign State* (Philadelphia, 1987).

171. A. Steinhouse, *Workers' Participation in Post-Liberation France* (Lanham, MD, 2001).

172. See pp. 233–34.

173. I. Theien, "Shopping for the 'People's Home': Consumer Planning in Norway and Sweden after the Second World War," in *The Expert Consumer. Associations and Professionals in Consumer Society*, ed. A. Chatriot, M.-E. Chessel, and M. Hilton (Aldershot, UK, 2006), 137–49; A. Renard, *Vers le socialisme par l'action* (Liège, 1958).

174. D. Skenderovic and C. Späti, *Les années 68: Une rupture politique et culturelle* (Lausanne, 2012), 29.

the representatives of different economic interests within a framework of structured discussion, the corporatist bodies of the post-war era reduced, if they could not entirely remove, the prevalence of strikes, lock-outs, and direct action by producers, which had been such a disruptive feature of economic life during the early decades of the twentieth century.[175] This was a role that these representatives were on the whole eager to assume. The emergence in many areas of Western Europe over the previous decades of an increasingly well-organized range of professional associations had created a new cadre of social bureaucrats who were well qualified to take on managerial responsibility for issues of economic and social policy-making. Among the trade-union officials who came to the fore after 1945, and also a younger and more professionally trained generation of reform-minded employers, the dominant mentality was no longer the defence of sectional interests at all costs. They shared in a new mentality of co-management, which, though it did not exclude the need for tough negotiation, reflected the widespread belief that the simple victory of one interest over all others was no longer desirable or possible in economic and industrial relations. Instead, in this new culture of what the Norwegian political scientist Stein Rokkan termed "corporate pluralism," decisions were arrived at through a quasi-continuous process of negotiation and compromise.[176]

The tensions between this economic corporatism and political democracy became more visible with the passage of time. On the one hand, the presence of economic interest groups within the process of government appeared to offer a more effective form of representation than the individual suffrage of the past. Indeed, many modernizing reformers advocated replacing outmoded parliamentary structures—such as the upper houses of parliament—with corporatist chambers that would represent the principal interest groups of the economy.[177] On the other hand, these corporatist institutions replaced the direct transmission belt of democratic power from electors to their parliamentary representatives with a more diffused structure of decision-making in which trade-union leaders, employers' representatives, and other social bureaucrats assumed responsibility for an increasing range of issues, including setting wages and prices, working conditions, and social-security provision.

175. See also pp. 67–68.
176. S. Rokkan, "Norway: Numerical Democracy and Corporate Pluralism," in *Political Oppositions in Western Democracies*, ed. R. A. Dahl (New Haven, CT, 1966), 105–14; F. G. Castles, *The Social Democratic Image of Society: A Study of the Achievement and Origins of Scandinavian Social Democracy in Comparative Perspective* (London, 1978), 30–31.
177. See p. 267.

Thus, rather than broadening democracy, corporatism generated over the course of the long era of post-war economic growth what by the 1970s was increasingly criticized as a process of "de-democratization." The participation of representatives of economic interest groups in the repeated compromises of corporatist decision-making effectively excluded the expression of the grievances of those whom they claimed to represent.[178] This was especially so in the trade unions. The post-war expansion of corporatist institutions at the national and, subsequently, international levels through organizations such as the International Labour Organization (ILO) and the Economic and Social Council (ESC) of the EEC reinforced the power of a new class of professional trade-union officials who by dint of these responsibilities no longer had meaningful contact with their members.[179] The resentments that this generated would become apparent in the resurgence in more local forms of workplace militancy in the 1960s and 1970s, as well as in the emergence of new populist movements that claimed to speak in the name of "ordinary" people.[180] In the immediate post-war decades, however, corporatism was regarded as an important element of the way by which the values of democracy would be diffused through society. By associating the associational culture of modern life with the decision-making processes of government, the ambition was to embed democracy within European society, and at the same time to bring society into democracy.[181]

{≈≈≈⟫Ⓦ⟨≈≈≈}

The project of democracy was never, however, exclusively national and social; it was also intended to be international. There was a widely felt need to create an international democratic order in the immediate post-war years. By creating a true community of nation-states, operating according to agreed rules of behaviour, it would be possible to reconcile former foes, and prevent a return to the aggressive nationalism of the interwar

178. W. Falla, *Zwischen Integration und Klassenkampf: Sozialgeschichte der betrieblichen Mitbestimmung in Österreich* (Vienna, 1981), 182–202. See also p. 263.

179. See, for example, J. Lewis, *Workers and Politics*, 104–81; M. Roseman, *Recasting the Ruhr, 1945–1958: Manpower, Economic Recovery and Labour Relations* (Providence, RI, 1992), 294–98, 301–6.

180. See pp. 289–90 and 302–3; H.-G. Betz, *Radical Right-Wing Populism in Western Europe* (Basingstoke, UK, 1994), 1–9.

181. See the comments in R. Alapuro, "Conclusion: How History Matters in Putting Nordic Associations into a European Perspective," in *Nordic Associations in a European Perspective*, ed. Alapuro and H. Stenius (Baden-Baden, 2010), 215–40.

years that had proved to be so destructive of democracy.[182] The United Nations (UN), and its affiliated organizations—notably, in the later 1940s, UNESCO[183]—were unsurprisingly the focus of much of this democratic internationalism. The UN, it was intended, should act as the policeman of the new democratic order by enforcing rules of peaceable diplomacy. At the same time, its General Assembly was intended to serve as a global parliament. The idea of an international parliament, based on the principle of one state, one vote, had a long prehistory in international relations. However, the way in which the Assembly operated reflected strongly the western culture of democracy as it emerged after 1945.[184] By submitting its decisions to public votes, guided by a bureaucracy of expert advisors, the UN resembled in its principles and inspiration the democracy constructed at a national level in Western Europe. This also helps to explain the problems it encountered. Its operation as an international democracy of sovereign states was undermined by the Cold War rivalries of the United States and the USSR. But the western character of the UN was also contested from its inception by voices from Africa and Asia concerned to advance a different agenda of democratic issues, such as global social development, and the collective rights of colonized peoples to self-determination.[185]

In response, European ambitions for a new democratic order retreated from the global to the European level. The establishment of the successive institutions of transnational European cooperation—the Council of Europe, the European Coal and Steel Community (ECSC), and finally the EEC by the Treaty of Rome of 1957—provided a less threatening and more manageable context within which a transnational framework for democracy could be nurtured. This interconnection of the languages of Europe and of democracy was one of the more surprising features of the post-war era. In so far as ideas of European integration had developed during the interwar years, they had tended to be espoused by those, notably on the right, who opposed parliamentary democracy.[186] Moreover, during the war years, the rhetoric of Europeanism was deployed much more wholeheartedly in the propaganda of the Third Reich and its

182. Camus, "Democracy and Modesty," 287–88; Pius XII, "Democracy and Peace," 251.

183. P. Betts, "Humanity's New Heritage: Unesco and the Rewriting of World History," *Past and Present* 228 (2015): 249–85.

184. Renner, "Gesellschaft, Staat und Demokratie," 139–40; "Was ist Demokratie?" (22 October 1949), in *Für Recht und Frieden*, 194–95.

185. M. Mazower, *No Enchanted Palace: The End of Empire and the Ideological Origins of the United Nations* (Princeton, NJ, 2009), 191–203; S. Amrith and G. Sluga, "New Histories of the United Nations," *Journal of World History* 19 (2008): 251–74.

186. See, for example, R. Dupuis and A. Marc, *Jeune Europe* (Paris, 1933), esp. xi–xiv.

collaborationist allies than was the case within the overwhelmingly patriotic and nationalist languages of Resistance groups.[187] This, however, changed rather abruptly after 1945. The adoption of the project of a united Europe by a broad range of European political figures of the centre-right and centre-left had various pragmatic logics. But it also reflected the convergence that occurred between the nascent identity of Western Europe and the culture of democracy. For anti-Communist Socialists, and above all Christian Democratic politicians, Europe provided an identity within which they could frame their higher loyalty to the values of democratic freedom. This was especially so for the Christian Democrats who by the end of the 1950s had become the dominant force within the politics of many Western European states. For them, Europe was a flexible transnational loyalty that expressed their long-standing antipathy to secular nationalism, as well as providing a model of the collaborative decision-making that they believed should underpin the democratic process.[188]

Even so, there remained no ambition to create a Europe that in itself was democratic. The EEC did not have a democratic mandate, beyond the fact that it was composed of democratically elected national governments. The Treaty of Rome avoided any direct reference to democracy, merely describing the signatories as a community of nation-states committed to what the treaty defined somewhat perfunctorily as "peace and liberty."[189] Democracy was therefore little more than a rather vague qualifying test for membership, to be invoked as a convenient justification for deferring the application for membership by Franco's Spain in 1962, and as a resonant-sounding motive for the decision to admit Greece as a member in 1979.[190] Moreover, the European institutions were very deliberately designed to operate above democracy rather than within it. The parliamentary institutions created by the Treaty of Rome—the European

187. M. Mazower, *Hitler's Empire: Nazi Rule in Occupied Europe* (London, 2008), 556–61; D. Gosewinkel, ed., *Anti-liberal Europe: A Neglected Story of Europeanization* (New York, 2014).

188. B. Shaev, "Liberalising Regional Trade: Socialists and European Economic Integration," *Contemporary European History* 27 (2018): 258–79; W. Kaiser, *Christian Democracy and the Origins of European Union* (Cambridge, UK, 2007); R. Forlenza, "The Politics of the *Abendland*: Christian Democracy and the Idea of Europe after the Second World War," *Contemporary European History* 26 (2017): 261–86. See also p. 191.

189. European Union, Treaty Establishing the European Community, Rome Treaty, 25 March 1957. http://eur-lex.europa.eu/treaties/index.htm.

190. V. Fernández Soriano, "Las Comunidades Europeas frente al franquismo: Problemas políticos suscitados por la solicitud española de negociaciones de 1962," *Cuadernos de historia contemporánea* 32 (2010): 153–74; E. Karamouzi, *Greece, the EEC and the Cold War, 1974–1979: The Second Enlargement* (Basingstoke, UK, 2014).

Parliament and the ESC—were not directly elected but composed of delegates sent from national institutions. Their powers were strictly limited;
and the key locus of power lay in the bureaucracy of the European Commission, which was responsible not to the European people but to the
national governments.[191]

This democratic deficit in the institutions of European integration
was, however, more evident in retrospect than it was at the time.[192] More
immediately, the intermingling of European and democratic identities
that gathered pace from the 1950s onwards was one of the ways by which
post-war Western Europeans came to regard democracy as part of their
collective identity. With the defeat of Nazism, Europeans had, almost to
their surprise, found their way back to a mainstream rhetoric of emancipatory modernization. This was expressed in eloquent terms by the Czechoslovak president Edvard Beneš in his message delivered at the reopening
of the country's parliament in October 1945, in which he celebrated his
country's return, after the sufferings of Nazi occupation, to "the path of
world evolution, of world progress, of truth, of right, of genuine humanity, of world morality and world democracy."[193] Europe had rejoined the
narrative of 1789, albeit now couched in sufficiently ecumenical terms to
incorporate those political traditions, such as Catholicism, that had formerly defined themselves against Europe's revolutionary past. The Europeanism of the post-war era—soon confined as a consequence of the Cold
War to the western half of the continent—provided a space where rhetorics
of democracy, liberty, and peace overlapped and reinforced one another.

The "Europeanizing" of democracy that occurred in the two decades
following 1945 served also to compensate Europeans for their somewhat
reduced status.[194] Europe no longer ruled the world, as demonstrated
by the translation of global governance from the Geneva of the League
of Nations to the New York of the United Nations. However, Europe
retained less-tangible forms of power. Its post-war claim to ownership of
democracy—what Herman Van Rompuy would much later term Europe's
collective status as "the Fatherland of Democracy"[195]—formed part of
a wider cultural reassertion of Western European identity. This found
expression through the post-war celebration of the heritage of Europe's

191. See pp. 212–15.
192. Re the "democratic deficit" in the EU, see p. 302.
193. *Opening of the Prague Parliament*, 25.
194. Conway and Depkat, "Towards a European History," 132–56.
195. H. Van Rompuy, "Europe, Political Democracy and the Flux of Time," in *The Road
to Political Democracy*, ed. R. Senelle, E. Clément, and E. Van de Velde (Brussels, 2012), 1007.

historical past, the civic culture of its buildings and cities, and its intellectual heroes such as Kant, Goethe, and Beethoven. Stripped of their *völkisch* representation by the Third Reich, these German-speaking intellectuals re-emerged as cosmopolitan and European figures, symbols of the quest for freedom that had characterized European history.[196] This reworking of Europe's heritage to serve purposes both European and democratic was more unconscious than deliberate. However, it provided a durable emotional basis for what Raymond Aron described in the peroration to his speech to the Berlin conference of the Congress for Cultural Freedom in 1960 as a "patriotisme de continent"—a continental patriotism.[197] Democracy formed part of what Europe was, and in some rather undefined sense what it had always been.

This helps to explain the reserve with which Europeans of all political traditions continued to regard American democracy after 1945. The United States might have been an evil imperial power for some, or the partner in an Atlantic alliance for others, but the almost universal postwar assumption appeared to be that its politics—and more especially its politicians—had little to teach Europeans. The USA was not a frequent point of reference in European discourses of democracy after 1945, reflecting the widespread sense, shared across national and ideological frontiers, that the United States remained a profoundly different and somewhat exotic society. The USA was what Western Europe liked to think *it* was not: a harsh hegemony of economic forces, a glittering but superficial social modernity, and an immature political system. American democracy was similarly opposed to that of Europe. When Europeans did refer to American democracy, it was generally through disparaging comments about the McCarthy hearings and racial inequalities. This was, of course, especially so on the part of Communists, as in Togliatti's comment in 1947 that "the Italian people would take no lessons on how to behave democratically from a country where the trade unions faced repression and where a man could be hanged for the colour of his skin."[198] But similar views were voiced by many others, including Catholics and conservative figures, for whom the American practice of democracy represented the worst excesses of an individualist mass politics.[199]

196. T. Mann, *Goethe und die Demokratie* (Oxford, 1949); D. Dennis, *Beethoven in German Politics, 1870–1989* (New Haven, CT, 1996), 175–97.

197. Raymond Aron, "Institutions politiques de l'occident," 41–42.

198. Quoted in Ventresca, *From Fascism to Democracy*, 150.

199. C. H. Müller, *West Germans against the West: Anti-Americanism in Media and Public Opinion in the Federal Republic of Germany, 1949–68* (Basingstoke, UK, 2010), esp.

These views were not universal: Jacques Maritain, who spent the 1950s at Princeton, repeatedly praised American democracy as "a living reality," characterized by associational pluralism and local participation.[200] He, however, was an isolated voice, whose praise of American democracy served primarily as a means of deploring the preoccupation with popular sovereignty that he identified in European democracies.[201] Much more commonplace were what Irwin Wall termed the "prejudicial stereotypes" of municipal corruption, racial divisions, and an unstable demagogic political culture, which Western Europeans associated with American democracy.[202] In part, this was simply a product of ignorance. Even among European intellectuals there was little knowledge of the institutional structures and practices of American democracy, and still less of its historical development. But it was also the consequence of European claims to ownership of democracy. No matter that the modern European model of democracy might have initially been forged by the American revolutionaries in the 1770s; for most Western European political figures, the copyright of democracy resided in Europe. Western Europeans might be dependent on the United States for military protection and economic aid, but they could act, in the prevalent British cliché of the time, as the Athens to the new Rome, directing the power of the USA and more generally of the free world in ways that compensated for the decline of European global ascendancy.[203]

This attempt to claim democracy for Europe did, however, inevitably raise the question of *which* Europe. The smaller and more exclusive Western Europe forged by the events of the Second World War, the Cold War, and subsequent decolonization was separated by military and political boundaries from the newly de-Europeanized lands of the southern and eastern Mediterranean as well as from what Jacques Rupnik termed the

63–89; L. Bruti Liberati, "Witch-Hunts and *Corriere della Sera*: A Conservative Perception of American Political Values in Cold War Italy—the 1950s," *Cold War History* 11 (2011): 73–81.

200. J. Maritain, *Reflections on America* (New York, 1958), 161–88.

201. See p. 119.

202. I. Wall, *The United States and the Making of Post-War France, 1945–1954* (Cambridge, UK, 1991), 303–6.

203. I. Hall, *Dilemmas of Decline: British Intellectuals and World Politics, 1945–1975* (Cambridge, UK, 2012); Brogi, *Confronting America*, 191–93; A. Schildt, *Zwischen Abendland und Amerika: Studien zur westdeutschen Ideenlandschaft der 50er Jahre* (Munich, 1999), 36. Attitudes to American democracy would evolve during the 1960s: see p. 266.

"other Europe" of Soviet-controlled central and eastern Europe.[204] These diminished horizons encouraged an essentializing of Western Europe as the "true" Europe. Unsurprisingly, definitions of this identity varied according to the national or political viewpoint of the commentator. For some, such as Georges Bernanos, this was a French-oriented definition of Europe, focused on the heritage of the Revolution of 1789.[205] But for others, and more especially many Catholic West German intellectuals and politicians, it lay in the idea of Europe as a cultural *Abendland*, or evening land. This concept was much deployed by Konrad Adenauer in his time as German chancellor, providing a usefully flexible (and denazified) vision of what he termed a "christlich-abenländischen Weltanschauung": a Christian evening-land conception of the world. This was focused around the banks of the Rhine, where a millennial Christian heritage, traditions of local self-government, and strong bonds of associationism had supposedly fostered a stable and human political culture.[206] Democracy too formed part of this imaginary landscape. This was, however, a depoliticized democracy of communities and shared values, rather than of elections and party structures—what the Cologne historian Peter Rassow described as "ein altes abendländisches Kulturgut", or an old Christian evening-land cultural value.[207]

A sense of place was central to these invocations of Western Europe's democratic heritage. What Salvador de Madariaga termed "the mural fresco of European life" was characterized by the intricate interplay of influences and historical experiences within the tessellated landscape of Western Europe, from the North Sea and Baltic to the western Mediterranean and the Adriatic.[208] This post-war evocation of Western Europe served various purposes, of which perhaps the most explicit was to reinforce the solidarity of the Western European states (including, crucially, West Germany, shorn of its Communist and Prussian territories) within the Atlantic alliance of the 1950s.[209] But, whatever its instrumental uses, the idea of Western Europe—as a place where successive layers of history, language, social development, religion, and even landscape and climate

204. J. Rupnik, *The Other Europe* (London, 1988), 3–23.

205. Bernanos, *Tradition of Freedom*, 11, 20, 28–34, 59–63.

206. Quoted in P. T. Jackson, *Civilizing the Enemy*, 129. Re. the usage of the *Abendland* concept in the post-1945 period, see notably Schildt, *Zwischen Abendland und Amerika*, 21–38; Forlenza, "Politics of the *Abendland*," 261–86.

207. P. Rassow, "Die geschichtliche Einheit des Abendlandes," in *Die geschichtliche Einheit des Abendlandes* (Cologne, 1960), 3.

208. S. de Madariaga, *Portrait of Europe* (London, 1952), esp. 6 (quotation), 9–11.

209. P. T. Jackson, *Civilizing the Enemy*.

had forged a distinctive model of society—formed an important element of how post-war Western Europeans thought about their past and their political identity. Democracy became the regime natural to what Raymond Aron in his anti-Communist polemic *Le grand schisme* of 1948 termed this "terre modérée, de climat et de dimensions."[210]

It was unsurprising that this western democracy was juxtaposed against the "oriental" nature of the Soviet Union, which was repeatedly portrayed as the product of a fundamentally non-European culture, as reflected in Willy Brandt's declaration that "Berlin belongs to Europe, not to Siberia."[211] More remarkable, however, was the apparent ease with which central Europe was effaced from these accounts. With the exception of West Berlin and Vienna (which remained under partial Soviet occupation until 1955), all of the principal cultural centres of European modernity—Warsaw, Prague, and Budapest, in particular—were effectively exiled from these post-war definitions of Western Europe. Instead, Europe acquired a new and more exclusive geographical definition; one which was tilted away from the contested landscapes of central Europe that had been so important in European life over the preceding decades, and towards what appeared to be the more peaceful landscapes of western Germany, the Low Countries, northern Italy, and France.[212] In this way, the indisputably artificial division of Europe imposed by the limits of the military advance of the Soviet, British, and American armies in 1945 became normalized as a wider fault line. It juxtaposed the freedom and intellectual energy of the western half of the continent against the oppressive regimes and conformism of the east.[213] The west of Europe, it seemed, did not miss what it had lost.

This territorial demarcation of democracy within Europe also had more long-standing origins. As Jacques Rupnik observed, although the heart of Europe might be difficult to locate, the continent certainly had several peripheries.[214] Thus, regions such as the Balkans became part of a second-zone Europe: lands of ancestral and incorrigible conflict that had missed out on the long-term processes of institutional and

210. Raymond Aron, *Grand schisme*, 58.

211. S. Labin, *Stalin's Russia* (London, 1949), 31; Marshall, *Willy Brandt*, 34. In very similar terms, the National Socialists in post-war Czechoslovakia criticized the pro-Communist tone of the Košice governmental declaration of 1945, stating that it was "an Eastern programme and therefore unsuitable for our conditions"; quoted in Myant, *Socialism and Democracy*, 120–23.

212. See notably O. Dhand, *The Idea of Central Europe* (London, 2018).

213. Mosse, *Culture of Western Europe*, 3.

214. Rupnik, *Other Europe*, 22.

cultural maturation that had created the distinctive civilization of Western Europe.[215] The South of Italy, or Mezzogiorno, constituted an even more marked case of such peripheralization. The concept of a "Southern question" was at least as old as the Italian state itself; but it acquired a new prominence and urgency in the post-1945 years, as the pitiless statistics of socio-economic development (measured in terms of income and education, but also by more modern criteria such as ownership of radios, cars, and telephones) demonstrated just how far the South lagged behind other areas of the peninsula. The ambitious infrastructure projects initiated by the government development agency, the Cassa per il Mezzogiorno established in 1950, were therefore intended to open up the South, and to lift its people out of the *ignoranza* and *miseria* in which they had languished for too long.[216] Roads, schools, and electricity were all intended to play their part in this project of socio-economic development; but the greater challenge was to remake the Southern Italians as citizens of a democratic republic.

Cultural and literary explorations of the differentness of the South and, more especially, of its people proliferated in the post-war years. Reinforced by journalism and travel writing, it found its full expression in the remarkable success of Giuseppe di Lampedusa's novel, *Il gattopardo* (*The Leopard*), published posthumously in November 1958—and rapidly made into a very successful film—with its portrayal of a traditional and languorous Sicilian society on the eve of its integration into a united Italy in 1860.[217] Similar ideas pervaded much academic writing. In the influential formulation of an American anthropologist, Edward Banfield, who studied a Southern village in the 1950s, the civilization of the Italian South was less European than Mediterranean and Levantine in character. Thus, rather than joining together to improve the well-being of their community, the villagers pursued an "amoral familism" in which they looked upon the resources provided by the state as opportunities for personal enrichment.[218]

215. M. Todorova, *Imagining the Balkans* (New York, 1997), esp. 184–89.

216. Cassa per il Mezzogiorno, *Cassa per il Mezzogiorno Development Plan: Results of the First Four Years* (Rome, 1955), 1–3; C. Barbagallo, *La questione meridionale* ([Milan], 1948), 261–92; Ginsborg, *History of Contemporary Italy*, 159–62.

217. A. M. Ortese, *Il mare non bagna Napoli* (Turin, 1953), translated and republished as *Evening Descends upon the Hills* (London, 2018); R. Peyrefitte, *South from Naples* (London, 1954), 249–71; G. di Lampedusa, *Il gattopardo* (Milan, 1958). Re. the impact of Lampedusa's novel, see D. Gilmour, *The Last Leopard: A Life of Giuseppe di Lampedusa* (London, 1988), 171–90.

218. E. Banfield, *The Moral Basis of a Backward Society* (Glencoe, IL, 1958), 7–11, 85–104. See also, for a more nuanced version of a similar argument, P. Allum, *Politics and Society in Post-War Naples* (Cambridge, UK, 1973).

This image of the South was at heart a discourse about the borders of Europe, and about the difficulty or even the impossibility of integrating such peripheral territories into the new democratic Europe. Southerners in Italy—along with the inhabitants of the Mediterranean territories of southern Spain, or across the sea in the coastal cities of French-ruled Algeria—had become part of an outer sphere of half-Europeans, defined by their cosmopolitan past.[219] As such, they were unscrupulous profiteers, or people of simple tastes and enthusiasms, who lacked the discernment and education essential to the modern practice of democracy: they cast their votes on the basis of coercion, bribery, or illusory promises, without any comprehension of the larger issues at stake. Writing about the Southern problem in 1958, the year of the enactment of the Treaty of Rome, the Italian Liberal politician Francesco Compagna significantly entitled his study *Mezzogiorno d'Europa*, presenting the South as a test case for the larger project of trying to integrate the "Europe of the South" into the "Europe of the Six."[220]

These exclusive definitions of Europe and of democracy also had obvious implications for how Europeans viewed their colonial territories and populations. The often contested, or straightforwardly violent, resubordination of colonies that occurred in South East Asia, the Middle East, and North Africa in the immediate post-war years accelerated changes in the way in which Europeans justified their continued colonial rule to themselves, to their subject populations, and to the institutions of the nascent global community. Empire was no longer a right derived from conquest, but a custodianship, legitimized by history and by the material and cultural goods which their rule provided. Europeans fulfilled their duty of care to the territories under their stewardship by deploying their particular expertise in social and economic development, education, and health to the benefit of populations who had not had the good fortune to share this European heritage. The consequence was the intensification of a diverse range of programmes, which used the statistical measurements of the age to demonstrate the ways in which the lives of ever larger numbers of individuals and communities were being transformed for the better.

219. Albert Camus was outspoken in his defence of the European population of Algiers, criticizing the scorn with which he felt they were regarded by the population of metropolitan France, while also advocating a political settlement in Algeria that would recognize the rights of all of its populations. See A. Camus, *Actuelles III: Chronique algérienne 1939–1958* (Paris, 1958), esp. 11–29, 144–47. Re. cultural representations of southern Spain, see notably G. Brenan, *South from Granada* (London, 1957).

220. F. Compagna, *Mezzogiorno d'Europa* (Rome, 1958), 84.

How far these benefits included a preparation for democracy was much less apparent. In some of its elements, post-war colonialism implied an intensive education of colonized populations, or more frequently of certain elites among them, in self-rule and the practice of democracy. Thus, for example, one contemporary British report described the provision of extramural education in West Africa as a means of fostering "a democratic habit of mind."[221] But in other ways the mindsets of colonial development replicated, in a much more authoritarian form, the bureaucratic culture of welfare provision in post-war Europe. The increased resources made available to colonial administrations in the post-war era gave a new energy and scale to policies of development; but reinforced a culture of enlightened but irresponsible government, whereby a colonial elite implemented policies, embedded in the scientific logic of disciplines such as tropical medicine, that they imposed on the populations over whom they ruled.[222]

This ethos of activist government and modernization did contain components of a new culture of citizenship, as expressed in the various statements issued by the colonial administrations, notably at the Brazzaville conference held by the Free French authorities in January and February 1944, with its promises to grant different levels of citizenship to the colonial populations.[223] To democracy and self-government there was, however, much less reference. The nature of colonial rule—be it the "decentralized despotisms" created by structures of indirect colonial rule,[224] or the more centralized state administrations established by the imperial powers during the 1940s—provided little space for mass enfranchisement and still less for popular sovereignty. Instead, colonial rule remained, in its state and police structures, essentially authoritarian in inspiration and practice. In the words of Aimé Césaire, in his timely polemic of the 1950s, colonial rule was an essentially indefensible regime founded on the threat and the application of force.[225] Its logics rested, above all, on the conviction that colonial administration existed to benefit its subject peoples rather than to empower them, behind which lay

221. K. Skinner, "Agency and Analogy in African History: The Contribution of Extra-Mural Studies in Ghana," *History in Africa* 34 (2007): 277.

222. D. A. Low and J. M. Lonsdale, "Introduction: Towards the New Order, 1945–1963," in *History of East Africa*, vol. 3, ed. Low and A. Smith (Oxford, 1976), 12–16; O. Le Cour Grandmaison, *L'empire des hygiénistes: Vivre aux colonies* (Paris, 2014).

223. M. Thomas, *The French Empire at War 1940–45* (Manchester, 1998), 249–54.

224. M. Mamdani, *Citizen and Subject* (Princeton, NJ, 1996), 37–61.

225. A. Césaire, *Discours sur le colonialisme*, 3rd ed. (Paris, 1955), 8.

the assumption, as expressed by one Belgian writer, that "not all peoples possess the same capacity for democracy"—tous les peuples ne possèdent pas au même degré la capacité démocratique.[226] Resistance was therefore all too easily dismissed as a demonstration of the lack of appreciation by colonized populations of the benefits brought by the enlightened rule of the colonial administration. This was especially so in Algeria during the 1950s. As the FLN-led revolt gathered pace, the modernizing discourse of the French administration denied self-government to the Algerian people in the name of bringing them a higher freedom. Thus, it justified the forcible resettlement of populations, intended to separate them from the corrupting influence of the nationalist rebels, in terms of the liberation it would bring the populations within an eventual trans-Mediterranean French Republic.[227]

This was also true of decolonization. The decision to retreat from empire was composed in each instance of varying degrees of institutional panic, pragmatic calculations, and nationalist pressures; but, in its aftermath, it required above all justification. As Todd Shepard has argued with reference to the French withdrawal from Algeria, the very concept of decolonization was a retrospective construction. Having insisted for almost a century that Algeria was an integral part of France, the decision to withdraw was hurriedly presented as the logical culmination to colonial rule over a territory that had never been truly French.[228] Democracy formed an integral part of this process of rationalization. The democratic rights of colonized peoples had attracted only limited support in European political debate, ahead of the decision to decolonize.[229] But, once it had been done, the granting of self-government to former colonial subjects could be justified as a generous action, one that reflected the democratic values of the European powers. The manner in which it was enacted conveyed much too about the underlying ethos of that democracy. In much the same manner as the enfranchisement of women had been decreed

226. Hoyois, "Réponse des peuples," 233.

227. M. Feichtinger and S. Malinowski, "'Eine Million Algerier lernen im 20. Jahrhundert zu leben': Umsiedlungslager und Zwangsmodernisierung im Algerienkrieg 1954–1962," *Journal of Modern European History* 8 (2010): 107–33; J. McDougall, "The Impossible Republic: The Reconquest of Algeria and the Decolonization of France, 1945–1962," *Journal of Modern History* 89 (2017): 772–811.

228. T. Shepard, *The Invention of Decolonization: The Algerian War and the Remaking of France* (Ithaca, NY, 2006), esp. 1–15.

229. P. C. Sorum, *Intellectuals and decolonization in France* (Chapel Hill, NC, 1977), 239–41.

after the war, self-government was presented as a grant rather than a right. It was implemented without seeking through a democratic vote the opinions of the peoples concerned, or the European populations, be they in the colonies or the metropole.

Decolonization was therefore a decision about democracy undertaken with only limited reference to democratic principles or procedures. Much as in Europe at the end of the Second World War, the institutions of democracy in the newly independent states were fashioned from above, and implemented through a carefully managed process of transition, in which the representatives of the subject peoples played their invited roles—often as members of a consultative council—but were not sovereign. Above all, it concerned the transfer of power, rather than its redistribution. Through the rituals of decolonization—of flags lowered and raised, cities renamed, and new constitutions granted—the power of the state was handed carefully from colonial officials to new elites. Unsurprisingly, the democratic cultures of the post-colonial states reflected the circumstances of their birth. In some cases, practices of democracy flourished, whilst in others they gave way to forms of authoritarianism that replicated the practices of later colonial rule.[230]

Decolonization was post-war European democracy reflected in the colonial mirror. The stark dichotomy suggested by the establishment of universal suffrage in liberated Europe at the same time as its denial to the populations of Europe's colonial empires should not disguise the extent to which state policies within and outside Europe were directed by similar assumptions about the preconditions necessary for effective democracy. In the colonies, as in Europe, democracy would flourish only where the right structures of state administration were in place, and the necessary levels of social capital present within the population. These attitudes were projected from the European states to the colonies through the European-staffed bureaucracies of colonial rule. But the direction of traffic was not one-way; the practices and mentalities of colonial administration influenced state governance within Europe. This interpenetration was the consequence of the particular nature of the Second World War. For the Allied powers, the war effort after the defeats of 1939–40 had been by necessity located primarily outside continental Europe. They had drawn to an unprecedented degree on the human and material resources of empire; indeed, Free France was, it should be remembered, an empire before it

230. Mamdani, *Citizen and Subject*, 25–27; F. Cooper, *Africa since 1940: The Past of the Present* (Cambridge, UK, 2002), esp. 1–19, 156–83.

was a nation-state.[231] Consequently, notwithstanding the role played both by Britain and by Resistance groups within occupied Europe, the subsequent liberation of Europe was conducted in large part from the territories of empire, notably the southern shores of the Mediterranean, presenting Europeans with liberators who were in significant numbers far from European. Moreover, the structures of military rule established in the liberated territories of Europe owed much to colonial practices. Occupying powers, be they British, French, or American, fell back on their personal or institutional experiences of colonial rule, drawing on what Robert Gerwarth and Stefan Malinowski have aptly termed "the colonial archive" of state and police practices to ensure peace and order within liberated Europe.[232]

Empire and Europe remained closely intertwined after the war. The democratic states of post-war Europe used their scarce resources of men, equipment, and finance to fight wars to re-establish and maintain their colonial rule in Africa, the Middle East, and Asia long after the Second World War had ended. But the practices of colonialism also influenced the actions of states within Europe. Programmes of educational provision, public health, and social welfare initially developed in colonial contexts provided models for the policies deployed in rebuilding communities and addressing social ills within post-war Europe. Nor did these interconnections disappear after decolonization. The "return" of European settler populations from the lands of empire, followed by the arrival of non-European immigrant populations—often from the same former territories of empire—presented substantial logistical and material challenges to the governments of Western Europe during the 1950s and 1960s. Housing, education, and welfare were mobilized to meet the needs of these new populations, as well as enabling them to adapt to the norms of the "host" society.[233] The integration of these immigrants from beyond Europe—and more especially their families—in the values of democracy therefore became a priority for European states. But so too, from the 1970s onwards did the transfer of those values to the territories from where they had arrived. The shift in development aid from infrastructure provision and countering humanitarian crises to the durable development of societies of the Third World made democracy once again a product for export. European states, international agencies, and non-governmental

231. Thomas, *French Empire at War*.

232. R. Gerwarth and S. Malinowski, "Hannah Arendt's Ghosts: Reflections on the Disputable Path from Windhoek to Auschwitz," *Central European History* 42 (2009): 287–88.

233. A. Lyons, *The Civilizing Mission in the Metropole: Algerian Families and the French Welfare State during Decolonization* (Stanford, CA, 2013).

organizations (NGOs) collaborated in a new ethos of development that focused on building the social attitudes, associational structures, and civil society that would foster the values of democracy.

{⚊⚊⚊⚊⚊}

As these interrelationships between European states and their former colonies well illustrate, attitudes to democracy oscillated in the post-war era between a rhetorical universalism and a much more restricted sense of the ability of societies to adopt the practices of democracy. Democracy was difficult, and it therefore needed the right "sub-soil"—as one study of democracy in Scandinavia in the 1950s put it—in which to flourish.[234] This sense that democracy was a matter of fine judgement, which could easily tip over, through naivety or a lack of collective intelligence, into the various ills of demagogic chaos, executive impotence, or totalitarian dictatorship was well conveyed by the repeated use in post-war discourse of the concept of "true" democracy. The phrase "true" or "real" democracy was deployed by a wide range of political and intellectual figures during the post-war years, ranging from Pius XII to the Austrian Socialist Karl Renner and the French Republican Pierre Mendès France.[235] In some cases, the purposes of this linguistic formula were emphatically partisan: by invoking the concept of a true democracy, Pius was seeking all too obviously to delegitimize those secular political forces that, in his words, advocated merely the "outward semblance of democracy."[236] But the notion of "true" democracy also had a wider significance. It expressed the widely shared sense that the version of democracy that Europe had chosen after the war was the right one; and that it needed to be distinguished from those other democracies, past and present, that explicitly or implicitly were judged to be "false."

Foremost among these were of course the Communist regimes of the east. The great partition—geographical, political, and intellectual—that took place in Europe in the later 1940s meant that inevitably much discussion of democracy was defined in relation to the opposing camp. The polarization between the people's democracies of the east and the parliamentary and legal democracies of the west obliged the one to assert its

234. Lauwerys, *Scandinavian Democracy*, 281–82.

235. Pius XII, "Democracy and Peace," 303; Renner, "Was ist Demokratie?" 195; P. Mendès France, "La crise de la démocratie," in *Oeuvres complètes*, vol. 4 (Paris, 1987), 82.

236. Pius XII, "Democracy and Peace," 307. Re. Pius XII's conception of democracy, see p. 175.

democratic character by denying the democratic credentials of the other. This was evident in the ever greater insistence with which the regimes of the east asserted their democratic credentials even as their authoritarian actions ended any meaningful dialogue with the societies they ruled.[237] But the same was also true in Western Europe, where the propaganda initiatives of organizations such as NATO to emphasize their defence of freedom formed just one component of how Western Europeans came to define their societies as free and democratic in opposition to the fake democracies of the east.[238]

One way in which this took place was through the realization of how oppressive and undemocratic were the Communist regimes. This might seem, in retrospect, to be a rather obvious point; but many Western Europeans initially knew little about the reality of the Communist-directed regimes, and not all of what they believed they knew was negative. The legacies of a certain positive representation of the Soviet Union during the 1930s and the war years remained visible in the immediate post-war years, and was reinforced by the people's democracies—"democracies of a new type," as the Hungarian-born Soviet economist Eugen Varga termed them in 1946—that appeared to be coming into existence in the eastern half of Europe.[239] Moreover, despite the evident harshness of the Soviet invasion of central Europe—as evinced by the displacement of large numbers of destitute ethnic Germans towards the western zones of occupation in Germany[240]—an awareness that what was happening in the east was fundamentally undemocratic developed only incrementally. The collapse of multiparty coalitionism in Hungary, Poland, and, most tangibly, in Czechoslovakia served to reveal with what the Danish political philosopher Alf Ross termed "dreadful clarity" the reality "that East and West attach different meanings to the word democracy."[241] The concept of the people's democracies had tangibly become by the end of the 1940s a façade, controlled by Soviet dictates, and rooted in the wooden rhetoric of late Stalinist socialism.[242] The spectacle of manipulated displays of

237. M. Pittaway, "The Reproduction of Hierarchy: Skill, Working-Class Culture and the State in Early Socialist Hungary," *Journal of Modern History* 74 (2002): 737–69.

238. L. Risso, "Propaganda on Wheels: The NATO Travelling Exhibitions in the 1950s and 1960s," *Cold War History* 11 (2011): 9–25.

239. Skilling, "People's Democracy," 18, 21 (quotation).

240. M. Frank, *Expelling the Germans: British Opinion and Post-1945 Population Transfer in Context* (Oxford, 2008).

241. A. Ross "What is Democracy?" in Lauwerys, *Scandinavian Democracy*, 48. Ross's article was first published in 1949.

242. Skilling, "People's Democracy," 16–33, 131–49.

mass support, combined with the show trials of alleged foreign agents, led western populations to form a much more negative image of the east, where the appearances of democratic participation disguised the reality of the power of the Soviet Union, and those who acted as its "puppets."[243]

This was reinforced by the accounts provided by those who had experienced life in the east and had come to the west. First-hand testimonies such as the widely read *I Chose Freedom* (1947) by the former Soviet official Victor Kravchenko, or the more complex analysis of the double-think of Communist societies presented by the Polish writer and former cultural diplomat of the Polish Communist regime Czeslaw Milosz in his *The Captive Mind* (1953), created a new genre of refugee literature about the totalitarian world of the east. However far they were packaged to respond to the expectations of their western audience, these accounts nevertheless gave a new immediacy to the realities of life on the other side of the Iron Curtain.[244] While David Rousset's *L'univers concentrationnaire* had aroused much controversy when it was first published in 1946,[245] a few years later his description of the Soviet camp system had become widely accepted. This was reinforced by personal accounts of experiences in the Soviet Gulag, notably Gustav Herling's *A World Apart* of 1951, in his preface to which Bertrand Russell presented as an established fact "the almost unbelievable horrors being inflicted upon millions of wretched men and women, slowly done to death by hard labour and starvation in the Arctic cold."[246] All of this preconditioned the response in Western Europe to the Soviet repression of attempts to create a more independent regime in Hungary in 1956. The spectacle of Soviet troops firing on crowds in the streets of Budapest seemed to crystallize all that Western Europeans had learned about the Communist half of Europe over the previous years. Rather than a rival democracy, it constituted its antithesis.[247] This was especially so after the abrupt construction of the Berlin Wall in August 1961. The symbolism of a Communist regime on German soil creating a barrier of concrete, barbed wire, and trip wires to imprison its people prompted

---

243. F. Fejtö, *Le coup de Prague 1948* (Paris, 1976), 221–27; M. Feinberg, "Fantastic Truths, Compelling Lies: Radio Free Europe and the Response to the Slánský Trial in Czechoslovakia," *Contemporary European History* 22 (2013): 107–25. See also the characteristic collection of essays: T. Hammond, ed., *The Anatomy of Communist Takeovers* (New Haven, CT, 1975).

244. V. Kravchenko, *I Chose Freedom* (London, 1947); C. Milosz, *The Captive Mind* (London, 1953).

245. D. Rousset, *L'univers concentrationnaire* (Paris, 1946).

246. B. Russell, preface to *A World Apart*, by G. Herling (London, 1951), ix–x.

247. See p. 108; Hacohen, *Karl Popper*, 524–25.

immediate outrage, as well as inevitable comparisons with the concentration camps of the Nazi era, which was sustained over the subsequent years by the very public deaths of East Germans trying to cross to West Berlin.[248]

By that point, Communism, in its Soviet-directed form, no longer constituted a major political challenge to Western European democracy. The rather tortuous efforts of Western European Communists to defend the Soviet model of socialism after 1956 were never going to convince many; and, as Aron commented, the conservative-minded rulers of the Soviet bloc had effectively abandoned their revolutionary purpose in favour of repressing their captive populations, while seeking, largely vainly, to match the economic achievements of the states of Western Europe.[249] What had been a civil war within European politics had become something much larger but also much less European. It was to the newly independent states of post-colonial Africa and Asia that the conflict between a politics of freedom and of revolutionary progress had been transferred.[250]

But Communism had never been simply a political alternative. The mystique that surrounded Communism, both for many of its supporters but more especially for its opponents, made it something much broader: an almost existential challenge to the values of individual freedom and intellectual pluralism that western democracy claimed to embody. Books such as the collective volume *The God that Failed* presented the personal accounts of Western European former Communists and fellow travellers, such as Arthur Koestler, according to what soon became a familiar format. Their authors had been drawn into the Communist world through the political and social struggles of the 1930s, before gradually coming to realize that they had become pawns of an all-powerful and malevolent Soviet Union.[251] The religious metaphors contained in such accounts were not accidental. They served to emphasize that Communism was very different from a normal political movement. It was a cult that—in the manner of a new religion—demanded an unquestioning obedience on the part of the "Communist convert."[252]

248. Ahonen, *Death at the Berlin Wall*, 25–29, 41–42.

249. M. Schumann, *Le vrai malaise des intellectuels de gauche* (Paris, 1957), 1–6; Raymond Aron, *Démocratie et totalitarisme*, 15–17.

250. W. Lippmann, *The Communist World and Ours* (London, 1959), 53–56.

251. Koestler et al., *God that Failed*.

252. Crossman, introduction to Koestler et al., *God that Failed*, 7. For an influential example of this psychological and anthropological approach to Communism, see A. Kriegel, *Les communistes français: Essai d'ethnographie politique* (Paris, 1968). See also Morin, *Autocritique*.

This was an idea energetically propagated by Raymond Aron, who in an essay published in 1944, entitled "L'avenir des religions séculières," had anticipated much of the subsequent analysis of the phenomenon of totalitarianism by presenting Nazism and Communism as secular religions that had filled the void left in the lives of many intellectuals by the death of God.[253] This somewhat crude thesis, which Aron recycled untiringly in his publications over the subsequent fifteen years, analysed Communism as a latter-day *trahison des clercs*, or betrayal by the intelligentsia. Western intellectuals who had espoused Communism had in effect renounced their duty of independent thought in favour of the comfort provided by unthinking adherence to the texts and articles of faith of Soviet Marxism.[254] This perception of Communism as a disease primarily of the intellectuals became a persistent theme of western anti-Communist rhetoric. Ordinary people, so it was argued, were rarely so gullible as to fall for the promises of Communism; and, if they did vote for Communist parties out of a misplaced loyalty to their class identity or memories of wartime resistance, they could nevertheless be coaxed back to democratic politics. Intellectuals were, however, a different matter. As the privileged beneficiaries of western intellectual freedom, their adoption of the orthodoxies of Communism was a betrayal of the values from which they derived their oxygen.

For most Western Europeans, therefore, the freedom of the west became less a democratic rallying cry than an established fact.[255] The mentality of anti-Communism consequently also changed. The challenge to a democratic society did not come from the tanks of the Soviet Union or from the waning electorates of the Western European Communist parties of the later 1950s and 1960s, but from the model of ideologically defined politics that Communism represented. In contrast, "true" democracy resided not in particular beliefs, but in the attitudes of scepticism and objectivity suited to a world that had lived through, and barely survived, the clash of political faiths over the preceding decades.[256] Democracy became in this way the political badge of the new European society being brought into existence by the economic and social changes of the post-war decades. As the shadows cast by the war receded in the later 1950s

253. B. Anderson, *Raymond Aron*, 64–71. See also Oppermann, *Raymond Aron und Deutschland*, 351–55.

254. See, for example, Raymond Aron, *L'opium des intellectuels* (Paris, 1955), 328; A. Koestler in Koestler et al., *God that Failed*, 26.

255. P. Rassow, "Deutschland in Europa" (1956), in *Die geschichtliche Einheit des Abendlandes* (Cologne, 1960), 46–56.

256. E. Weil, "Philosophical and Political Thought in Europe Today," *Daedalus* 93 (1964): 493–513.

and 1960s, European democracy acquired a much more consciously modern character. Its achievements were measured by its results: the material prosperity created by technological innovation, but also the welfare systems, and the new homes, schools, and urban environments that had been made possible by the combination of rapid economic growth and intelligent government.[257] Judged by these achievements, democracy had vanquished its opponents, both present and past. But, in doing so, it had ceased to be a specific form of politics. Instead, it had become the organizing principle of modern society.

257. See, for characteristic examples, F. Lauwers, J. Stalmans. M. Schuermans and V. Verbruggen, *België, een levende democratie* (Antwerp, 1964); M. Childs, *Sweden: The Middle Way*, 3rd ed. (New Haven, CT, 1961); SPÖ Wien, *Bericht 1959* (Vienna, 1960).

CHAPTER THREE

Debating Democracy

THE DIALECTIC OF CHRISTIAN DEMOCRAT
AND SOCIALIST VARIANTS OF DEMOCRACY

THE DEMOCRACIES OF THE POST-WAR ERA looked more similar from the outside than they felt from the inside. Though in retrospect the most striking feature of the era from 1945 to the end of the 1960s was the similarity of democratic structures, as well as the broad basis of institutional and political support for them, democracy in Western Europe was more consensual in its practices than in its heritage or its inspiration. Quite apart from the fundamental question—which politicians were generally reluctant to pose—as to how the sovereign will of the people should be respected and implemented, there remained strong differences of principle and purpose behind the shared façade of support for parliamentary democracy after 1945. Democracy in that sense was initially a point of convergence between the major political parties, and subsequently a shared space; but this did not efface the very different heritages of the political and intellectual traditions that populated it. Moreover, none of those traditions regarded democracy as a neutral formula: for each of them, there were good and bad variants of democracy, and support for any regime of democracy was conditional on how far it accorded with what each political movement held to be the attributes of a good democracy, as well as its particular interests.

This was hardly surprising. Democracy came with considerable historical baggage, inherited from the political and ideological disputes of the previous century. Ever since European history had taken a decisive tilt towards mass politics in the mid-nineteenth century, each of the major political traditions had developed its own particular understanding, and more especially its critique, of democracy. Contrary to what they were understandably keen to claim after 1945, neither of the two major political traditions of the post-war years—Christian Democracy and Socialism—had hitherto been enthusiastic supporters of parliamentary democracy. On the contrary, Socialist and Catholic political movements had long defined their political principles not only in opposition to each other but also to the "false" freedom offered by what they variously regarded as the secular and bourgeois regimes of parliamentary rule that had developed in Europe during the nineteenth century. This hostility, it is true, had often been more rhetorical than practical, and had rarely prevented Socialist and Catholic parties from participating energetically in the electoral combats of municipal and parliamentary politics during the latter decades of the nineteenth century. Nevertheless, Catholics and Socialists alike retained a sense that these representative structures were not their own, encouraging a mentality whereby their willingness to engage in electoral politics, and even more so in the coalitions and compromises inherent to the process of government, depended more on seizing the opportunities that these offered to advance their sectional interests than on any wider commitment to representative democracy.[1]

The democratic settlement of 1918–19 had, at first, appeared to draw both Catholics and Socialists more firmly into the practice of parliamentary politics, most strikingly through the decisive role that German and Austrian Socialist and, to a lesser extent, Catholic political parties played in bringing the new republican regimes into existence, as well as in defeating their alternatives on the radical right and left. However, this convergence towards a multiparty republicanism, based on mass electoral suffrage, proved to be short-lived. Over the course of the 1920s and 1930s, antipathy to the institutions and more especially the practices of parliamentary politics regained momentum in Socialist and Catholic ranks, driven in part by the electoral pressure exerted by more explicitly revolutionary movements at both extremes of the political spectrum but also by the perceived failure of the parliamentary regimes to respond effectively to the intense economic crisis from the end of the 1920s onwards.

Initially, these forces appeared to force Catholic and Socialist political movements in divergent directions. Catholic parties tilted towards the authoritarian right, and engagement with the extra-parliamentary

1. Such ideas were especially evident in the Second International prior to 1914: see J. Joll, *The Second International 1889–1914*, rev. ed. (London, 1968), 77–105. See also Eley, *Forging Democracy*, 86–93.

leagues, uniformed groups, and protest movements that flourished during the 1930s. In contrast, and partly in response to this surge in right-wing politics, Socialist parties found common ground with liberal and Communist parties in the defence of republican democracy under the banner of the anti-fascist Popular Fronts that came to power in Spain and France in 1936. Their ascendancy was, however, short-lived, as the Popular-Front governments were challenged by the Nationalist military uprising in Spain and by the dissolution of Republican unity in France. By the later 1930s, parliamentary democracy seemed to belong more to the past than to the future. With the collapse or overthrow of parliamentary regimes in many states of central and southern Europe, the future appeared to belong to more hierarchical and authoritarian political regimes, which to many Europeans—including Socialists and Catholics—seemed to offer a more effective means of ensuring political and social stability. Unsurprisingly, therefore, the German military victories in 1939 and 1940, and the consequent establishment of a New Order across much of continental Europe, seemed to mark the terminus of the model of parliamentary politics inherited from the nineteenth century.

The period between 1940 and 1942 was, in much of Axis-occupied Europe, one of decisive transition in Catholic and Socialist movements. The enthusiasm that had been evident within sections of both movements in 1940 for some form of New Order model of authoritarian politics dissipated rapidly under the impact of German occupation policies and the establishment of local pro-German collaborationist regimes. Instead, within the Catholic and Socialist parties, as well as their broader affiliated organizations, there was a reorientation towards language of patriotism, freedom, and political liberty. This was not only a political and ideological change, but also one of leaders and of mentality. An older generation of figures, rooted in the political landscapes of the first decades of the twentieth century retreated, discredited in some cases by their engagement with projects of authoritarian government. In their place there emerged new cadres—middle-aged and often middle class—who were less rooted in the conflicts of the past. This change of personnel reinforced the momentum of ideological and organizational change generated during the latter war years by ever more intense political expectations of what would follow the eventual collapse of the Third Reich. In Socialist and Catholic movements, the final months of the German occupation and the often tumultuous period following liberation were times of almost frantic activity, as both hastened to issue manifestos giving voice to their ideas and restructured their political parties in expectation of the anticipated return to a regime of electoral democracy.

Everywhere the emphasis was understandably on the new. Catholic and Socialist movements vied with each other after 1945 to present themselves as fundamentally new in their intellectual inspiration, their organizational structures, their leadership, and their programmes. In truth, of course, not everything was quite as novel as it was presented. Party names, especially in Catholic ranks, were indeed often changed, as the confessional political groupings of the interwar years were dissolved in favour of new political parties—such as the MRP in France or the Christian Democrat Union that emerged in western Germany—that were committed in name and doctrine to the inclusive ideas of Christian Democracy that had come to the fore during the war years. Not everything, however, had changed. Manifestos and party programmes were easy to produce, but the Catholic and Socialist movements that emerged from the war operated within pre-existing milieux and mentalities. The war did not destroy the political frontiers of confession and of social class; indeed, in many ways the suspension of normal political life during the war years in much of Europe had strengthened the social power of institutions such as the Catholic Church, and its considerable array of confessional social and cultural groupings. Thus, whatever the ambitions of reformers in the relaunched Catholic and Socialist parties to forge new forms of politics, the Socialist and Christian Democratic parties that contested the immediate post-war elections in liberated Europe were built on compromises, both ideological and organizational, between innovative ideas and more long-standing political mentalities.[2]

One undisputed element of their newness was, however, their clear orientation towards democratic politics. In truth, the practice generally came more easily than the principle. While the adjectival addition of "democratic" to their policies and goals was easy, and indeed seemed unavoidable as a badge of their membership of the new political world, Socialist and Christian Democratic parties were more circumspect in their identification with a regime of political democracy. Circumstance, however, dictated the urgent need to plunge into the new democratic politics. Socialists and Christian Democrats alike were fearful of the electoral challenge

2. Studies of Socialist and Catholic political reconstruction in liberated Europe include B. D. Graham, *Choice and Democratic Order: The French Socialist Party, 1937–1950* (Cambridge, UK, 1994); P. Letamendia, *Mouvement républicain populaire*; Conway, *Sorrows of Belgium*; and M. Mitchell, *The Origins of Christian Democracy: Politics and Confession in Modern Germany* (Ann Arbor, MI, 2012).

presented by the Communists and by entirely new political groupings—such as the Partito d'Azione in northern Italy or the Union démocratique belge in Belgium—that presented themselves as the heirs of wartime resistance groups.[3] They therefore mobilized quickly in the aftermath of liberation, reforging links with affiliated social organizations such as the Socialist and Christian trade unions, and imposing, often quite ruthlessly, their order on local dissident groups.[4] Power now derived from the ballot box, and nobody could have any certainty as to how the millions of first-time voters—the newly enfranchised women in France and Italy, but also many voters under the age of thirty-five or forty in states such as Austria, Germany, and Italy who had not previously had the opportunity to vote in free elections—would cast their votes. Socialists and Catholics were therefore intensely aware that they needed to establish their party structures and more especially their political visibility ahead of the first local and national elections. Lists of candidates were hastily drawn up, congresses held, and the rudiments of a national political hierarchy established. In all of this, they were largely successful. Though the Communists increased their pre-war share of the vote in many of the immediate post-war elections, it was the Socialist and Christian Democratic parties that in the core territories of the nascent Western Europe, from northern Germany to central Italy, proved to be the more durable political victors of the new democratic politics. This success owed much to the efforts of these party elites; but it was also a demonstration of the wider resilience of social and confessional frontiers in post-war Europe. Whatever else had changed in their lives, in terms of their political affiliations most voters opted for parties that appeared to reflect their social background, family identities, and local communities.

What remained to be determined was the nature of the commitment of these parties to democratic politics. Given the haste with which they had been re-established after the war, the Socialist and Christian Democratic parties were often uneasy coalitions, composed of younger radicals and more established figures, some of whom had been in exile in Britain, Switzerland, or Sweden during the war years, as well as of regional power groupings, and of specific organizations, such as trade unions and farmers' leagues, each of which was ambitious to bend the new party structures towards its specific agenda. In this fluid political situation, democracy was

3. De Luna, *Storia del Partito d'Azione*; J. C. Willame, "L'Union démocratique belge: Essai de création 'travailliste,'" *Courrier hebdomadaire du CRISP* 743–44 (1976).

4. See, for example, Conway, *Sorrows of Belgium*, 177–224.

often more a tool to be manipulated, or a symbol to be invoked, than an established principle. There was, moreover, much for both camps to be apprehensive about in a new regime of post-war democracy. Nervousness in Catholic ranks that an anti-clerical alliance of Liberals, Socialists, and Communists would dismantle the hard-won regimes of protection for the Church's educational and welfare institutions were matched by Socialist fears that the discipline of Catholic social organizations would enable the Christian Democratic parties to rally a mass electorate—now expanded to include the supposedly devout ranks of women—behind their confessional goals. Above all, there were the Communists. The degree to which the Communist parties would be able to profit from the patriotic legitimation they had gained through their Resistance actions, and subsequently from the material hardships created by the disruptions of the transition to peace, dominated the political calculations of the era. Only if democracy proved to be an effective means of countering the demagogic appeal of the Communists would it be able to retain the support of the Christian Democrats and of most Socialists.[5]

There was therefore a significant degree of hidden conditionality to the espousal of democracy by Christian Democrats and Socialists in the politics of liberation Europe. In common with many other political groupings, they initially made little use of the term, deflecting discussions of political regime by emphasizing their commitment to the wide-ranging socio-economic reforms that would bring about a democratic society. It was only after the immediate material problems left behind by the war had been addressed, and the first post-war elections had been held, that Socialist and Christian Democratic parties came to engage more substantially with the construction of regimes of democracy. During the prolonged genesis of the Fourth Republic in France, and the emergence of a quasi-national constitutional framework in West Germany, all parties were obliged to engage with the specifics of the institutional design of the new regimes. In doing so, once again, issues of ideological principle were influenced, albeit often sotto voce, by calculations of self-interest. The electoral success of Socialist and Christian Democratic parties had put them in positions of decision-making power in many states, which in turn enabled them to have an impact on the wording of constitutional texts and, perhaps more importantly, on the technical details—the systems of proportional representation used, the distribution of powers between different parliamentary chambers, and the use of qualified majorities for decisions on certain

5. See pp. 56–57.

matters—that would determine how the new democracies would operate and, more especially, in whose interests.[6]

This engagement in government and in constitution-making worked both ways. If it ensured that the structures of the new political system often reflected their interests, it also bonded Socialists and Christian Democrats to the new democratic order. They were to a large extent "their" regimes; and, even though attitudes among the rank and file of both movements to the workings of the new democratic institutions were often somewhat circumspect, their leadership cadres were committed to their operation and, in most cases, to participation in government. This bonding with the institutions of democracy was reinforced too by the events of the early Cold War. Democracy—the "true" democracy of the west European states, as opposed to the people's democracies of the Soviet-controlled east—became for Socialists and Christian Democrats alike a cause to be defended against external invasion and internal subversion, as well as a badge of their allegiance to the politics of anti-communism. There was, consequently, diminishing space within Socialist and Christian Democratic ranks for voicing fundamental criticisms of the political status quo. Democracy had become a regime and a principle to be celebrated and defended, as well as the defining political identity of a new place: Western Europe.

The surprising rapidity with which the politics of post-war Western Europe settled into this democratic shape blunted the strength of former antipathies, transforming erstwhile rivals into fellow participants in the coalition politics that tended to be the rule at both the national and more local levels of government. It also eroded national boundaries, drawing Socialists and Christian Democrats into European federations of like-minded parties,[7] as well as enabling members of both movements to collaborate in the construction of the many transnational institutions—the Council of Europe, NATO, the ECSC, and subsequently the EEC—that became the agents of the new mood of post-war European cooperation. These forms of collaboration did not, however, efface the historic and often deeply felt divisions of heritage between Socialists and Christian Democrats. Most strikingly, in Italy, the majority Socialist tendency led by Nenni

6. This was very much in evidence during the lengthy debates about the constitutional structures of the new Italian and French republics: see U. Terracini, *Come nacque la Costituzione* (Rome, 1978), 3–42; Elgey, *République des illusions*, 205–29.

7. See, notably, Kaiser, *Christian Democracy*, 191–252; T. Imlay, *The Practice of Socialist Internationalism: European Socialists and International Politics, 1914–1960* (Oxford, 2018), 263–462.

eschewed alliance with the Christian Democrats in favour of an alliance with the Communists until 1956.[8] More generally too, the two political traditions remained at the local level distinct milieux, each characterized by a strong sense of its historic identity. Within Socialist and Christian Democratic ranks, political choice was rarely an individual matter, but one inherited and structured by family background, education, employment, and community. Moreover, far from being undermined by economic and social change, this sense of difference was deepened by the way in which in many areas of Western Europe the Socialist and Christian Democratic parties were able to ensure that their respective "pillarized" institutions— school systems, social-insurance leagues, and professional organizations— reinforced their position within the modernizing structures of post-war European society.[9]

Convergence came from the top down, rather than the bottom up, and owed much to the pragmatic dictates of electoral competition and coalition-making. This was reinforced by the preoccupation with the political centre ground that developed from the 1950s onwards. It was in the centre of the political spectrum that the new votes appeared to be available, and where electoral and governmental deals could be struck. Both Socialist and Christian Democratic parties, and, more especially, their leaders, therefore came to perceive themselves as engaged in a contest to stake their claim to this new centre ground. The more intransigent voices within Socialist and Christian Democratic ranks alike were marginalized; instead, policies and strategies were framed with a view to occupying the centre ground, a key element of which was an emphatic commitment to the existing regime of democracy.

This chapter explores how the Socialist and Christian Democratic movements competed and collaborated in the process of democracy-building. Much of the historical writing about both Christian Democracy and Socialism in the post-1945 era has had a somewhat teleological (and occasionally self-congratulatory) character, dominated by self-contained narratives of the path that each political movement followed into democracy, and the ways that these movements in turn enriched the content of that democracy.[10] This approach reflects the way in which these accounts have often been written from within their respective political traditions,

---

8. De Grand, *Italian Left*, 103–8, 121–23; Di Scala, *Renewing Italian Socialism*, 73–77.

9. See p. 218.

10. Characteristic examples include S. Berman, *The Primacy of Politics: Social Democracy and the Making of Europe's Twentieth Century* (Cambridge, 2006), esp. 6–8; M. Gehler and W. Kaiser, eds., *Christian Democracy in Europe since 1945* (London, 2004).

with the consequence that they have been primarily concerned with reconstructing the trajectories of their political traditions, rather than the democracy that they made together.[11] In contrast, this chapter will explore the understandings of democracy advanced by Socialists and Christian Democrats through the prisms of their past history, their ideological declarations, and—perhaps most importantly—their programmes for the future construction of democracy. These threefold claims regarding past, present, and future could at times be convergent and complementary, especially when directed against Communism, but they were more frequently dialectical as Socialists and Christian Democrats defined their positions against each other, and thereby advanced their claims to ownership of democracy.[12]

⟨⟫⟫⟩⟩⟆⟆⟆⟩

Debates about past history were unsurprisingly key to the politics of legitimacy in liberation Europe. For Socialists and Christian Democrats—as indeed for the advocates of other political traditions, including Communism—it was politically and emotionally essential to locate themselves within historical narratives that privileged their own role in the past struggles and present victory of democracy. This was not, however, a straightforward process for Catholics or Socialists. For both, it required treading carefully across the previous half-century of history, linking together rather disparate elements to construct a narrative that could be presented as leading to their espousal of democracy.

This was perhaps most obviously so in the case of the Christian Democrats. For many of the Catholic activists and intellectuals of the 1940s, the origins of a Catholic engagement with modern democracy appeared to lie in the 1890s, when a range of social Catholic movements had taken up the lead provided by Pope Leo XIII in the encyclical *Rerum Novarum* of 1891 and by national ecclesiastical elites in challenging the injustices and anti-Christian spirit of the capitalist (dis)order.[13] Their rhetoric was at times

11. See the critical comments of W. Kaiser in "From Siege Mentality to Mainstreaming?: Researching Twentieth-Century Christian Democracy," in *Christian Democracy across the Iron Curtain: Europe Redefined*, ed. P. Kosicki and S. Lukasiewicz (n.p., 2018), 3–23.

12. This is the principal thesis of P. Corduwener, *The Problem of Democracy in Postwar Europe: Political Actors and the Formation of the Postwar Model of Democracy in France, West Germany and Italy* (New York, 2017), notably pp. 1–10.

13. S. Kalyvas, *The Rise of Christian Democracy in Europe* (Ithaca, NY, 1996); P. Misner, *Social Catholicism in Europe: From the Onset of Industrialization to the First World War* (London, 1991).

radical, presenting Catholicism as the only agent of a truly democratic transformation of society.[14] But the focus of these Christian Democratic groups remained more social than political, reflecting the way in which the notion of the sovereignty of the people—and more especially the mechanism of representative government—remained anathema to Catholic ways of thinking. Moreover, these groups were only one, and generally a minority, element of the more conservative and clerical Catholic politics in the pre-1914 era. They operated within Catholic political movements, such as the Centre Party in Wilhelmine Germany or the Catholic Party in Belgium, that essentially served as federating structures for the defence of the interests of the Catholic Church and of the Catholic faithful. As such, their participation in parliamentary politics was more pragmatic than principled, and remained constrained within the disciplined mentality of the Catholic Church, which sought to build a closed and almost ghetto-like Catholic community, protected against the heresies of the modern era.[15]

This instinctive antipathy to the social and political pluralism of democracy was demonstrated by the engagement of large numbers of Catholic militants in authoritarian and explicitly anti-democratic movements and campaigns during the interwar years. The principal Catholic political parties, such as the Centre Party in Germany, the People's Party in Austria and the Catholic Party in Belgium, lost momentum during the 1920s, as Catholic energies were absorbed by a wide range of more militant Catholic movements that defined themselves against pluralist structures of parliamentary democracy and liberal freedom in favour of the construction of a new order based on Catholic values of order and authority.[16] The Catholic youth movements, student groups, and the burgeoning world of Catholic periodicals and spiritual organizations that formed the initial basis of this anti-democratic turn within European Catholicism acquired a new urgency, and a broader social basis, during the economic depression of the early 1930s, when Catholic denunciations of the failures of governments and parliaments were allied with the material grievances of middle-class and rural populations. This upsurge in Catholic militancy provided much of the energy behind the replacement of the parliamentary

14. See, for example, S. Apruzzese, "Modernismo e mito nazionale a Milano nel primo Novecento," *Storia Contemporanea* second series, 3 (2018): 93–106.

15. M. L. Anderson, *Windthorst: A Political Biography* (Oxford, 1981); U. Altermatt, *Der Weg der Schweizer Katholiken ins Ghetto* (Zurich, 1972); M. Conway, "Belgium," in *Political Catholicism in Europe 1918–1965*, ed. T. Buchanan and Conway (Oxford, 1996), 190–92.

16. E. Gerard, *De Katholieke Partij in crisis: Partijpolitiek leven in België (1918–1940)* (Leuven, 1985).

regimes of Austria and Portugal by new corporatist and authoritarian constitutions, and also gave momentum to the extreme-right movements of the mid-1930s in France and Belgium, as well as to the authoritarian regimes that were established in France, Slovakia, and Croatia in the wake of German military victories in 1939–41. Though Catholic militants distanced themselves from the statist forms of extreme-right politics that they associated with fascism, the dominant trend of Catholic political engagement in the 1930s stood emphatically against democratic pluralism, and in favour of a united national community and a corporatist social order in which the contests of electoral politics had been replaced by the natural units of family, workplace, and locality.[17]

Any attempt by the Christian Democratic parties that emerged after 1945 to claim to be the heirs to a long-standing tradition of Catholic democratic politics would therefore have entailed what John Hellman has termed too much "historical editing" to carry conviction.[18] At the same time, however, the events of the 1930s and the war years brought about significant changes in Catholic attitudes. The emergence of new forms of dominant state power in the Soviet Union, Nazi Germany, and Fascist Italy had prompted intellectuals—and, more hesitantly, the papacy—to voice their hostility to such state totalitarianism, especially when it was wedded, as in the case of the Third Reich, to the heresies of a scientific racism.[19] This was reinforced by the experiences of the war. The policies of oppression and exploitation implemented by the German authorities in much of Europe during the early 1940s, most notably the deportation of civilian workers to the Third Reich and the large-scale persecution of Jewish populations, thrust many Catholic institutions and individuals to the fore in the improvised actions of protection and charity that developed in many areas of Occupied Europe into significant networks of resistance against the illegitimate use of military and state power.[20] These forms of engagement forged a new political language in Catholic ranks. The familiar Catholic emphases on social justice, concern for the sufferings of the

17. M. Conway, *Catholic Politics in Europe, 1918–1945* (London, 1997), 47–72.

18. J. Hellman, *Emmanuel Mounier and the New Catholic Left 1930–1950* (Toronto, 1981), 208.

19. Chappel, "Catholic Origins of Totalitarianism," 561–87; G. Chamedes, *A Twentieth-Century Crusade: The Vatican's Battle to Remake Christian Europe* (Cambridge, MA, 2019), 167–96; Greenberg, *Weimar Century*, 120–68.

20. J. McMillan, "France," in *Political Catholicism in Europe, 1918–1965*, ed. T. Buchanan and M. Conway (Oxford, 1996), 57–59; R. Bédarida, *Armes de l'esprit*, esp. 341–45.

poor, and the necessary autonomy of Church institutions from state power were combined with new concepts of individual rights and collective freedoms. The consequence was a spirit of urgent debate, especially within Catholic worker groups and among intellectual circles, in which calls for wide-ranging social reforms—what some even began to term a Catholic-inspired revolution—was accompanied by a new willingness to work with those beyond Catholic ranks who shared their radical ambitions.[21]

This also implied a new openness to democracy. Emblematic of this evolution were the writings of Jacques Maritain, who in France in the 1930s and during his subsequent wartime exile in North America emerged as a prominent exponent of a more positive Catholic vision of democracy and of what he termed a personalist social order. Maritain's starting point had been a conventional Catholic hostility to the liberal principles of the Enlightenment, which had led him in the 1920s to share the sympathy for right-wing authoritarian ideas so prevalent in Catholic politics. But, over the subsequent years, his hostility to both the totalitarian ambitions of fascism and communism and the chaotic individualism of liberalism led him to advocate a new Christian-inspired regime of democratic rights and liberties.[22] It would be too simplistic to think of Maritain's evolution—and that of a number of other Catholic thinkers, such as Emmanuel Mounier and Augusto Del Noce—as a conversion to democracy. Rather, it reflected their wish to invest democracy with a new meaning: what Maritain termed "the genuine vital principle of a new Democracy, and at the same time of a new Christian civilization."[23] Nevertheless, for Maritain and like-minded figures, this did mark a break from the counter-revolutionary reflexes that had prevailed for so long within Catholicism. Instead of adopting a hostile opposition to the modern world, or somehow seeking to overthrow it to restore a neo-medieval social and spiritual order, their ambition was to create a modern-facing Catholicism. This was a Catholicism that consciously sought to return to the radical, even revolutionary, traditions within Christian teachings by developing a model of Catholic politics that was willing to engage with others, and above all with democracy. By accepting a pluralist political and social structure, Catholic movements

21. G.-R. Horn and E. Gerard, eds., *Left Catholicism, 1943–1955: Catholics and Society in Western Europe at the Point of Liberation* (Leuven, 2001); Horn, *Western European Liberation Theology*, esp. 110–74.

22. Doering, *Jacques Maritain*, 178–90. The influence of Maritain's wider values during the post-war years is detailed in S. Moyn, *Christian Human Rights* (Philadelphia, 2015).

23. Maritain, *Scholasticism and Authority*, vii–viii.

would make their values one of the ingredients of the more human order that they intended should emerge from the war.[24]

This more positive vision of the purposes of Catholic political action had an influence that spread beyond the intellectual circles where it initially developed. The latter war years, and the subsequent liberation, were a period of considerable debate in Catholic ranks. The aspiration to create a new and more open Catholic politics was widely shared among those lay activists, notably in the considerable subculture of Catholic social and spiritual organizations across Europe, who during the war had collaborated with people from a wide range of backgrounds.[25] But this new spirit did not imply a waning of more familiar Catholic attitudes. The confessional mindset that prioritized the interests of the Catholic community, and more especially its constituent institutions, and looked with distrust on other forces—in particular atheistic liberalism and socialism—remained tangible in Catholic ranks. Above all, fears of Communism continued to be stoked, by the actions of the Soviet forces in the east of Europe and what they might presage for the actions of the Communist parties and their allies within Western Europe. This led some Catholic conservatives towards an acceptance of democracy, in the hope that a robust regime of democratic freedoms constituted the best means of forestalling Communist subversion.[26] But this cautious engagement with democracy was accompanied too by a surge in loyalty to Church and faith. In 1945 Catholicism seemed to be more necessary than ever. In Germany, but also in many other areas of Europe, the Catholic Church and its welfare and social organizations were among the few institutions that remained standing at the end of the war. Thus, rather than posing awkward questions about the choices made by Church leaders during the war years, most Catholics preferred to rally to the reassuring authority represented by the Church.[27] For many intellectuals and activists the experiences of the war years appeared to have been a vindication of Catholic teachings: Europe had been brought to its nadir by the errors of anarchic individualism and

24. E. Mounier, *The Spoil of the Violent* (London, 1955), 4; Chappel, *Catholic Modern*, 59–143; Hellman, *Emmanuel Mounier*, 202–25; B. Thomassen and R. Forlenza, "Christianity and Political Thought: Augusto Del Noce and the Ideology of Christian Democracy in Post-War Italy," *Journal of Political Ideologies* 21 (2016): 186–89; P. Sauvage, *La cité chrétienne (1926–1940): Une revue autour de Jacques Leclercq* (Brussels, 1987), 222–31.

25. P. Misner, *Catholic Labor Movements in Europe: Social Thought and Action, 1914–1965* (Washington, DC, 2015).

26. Greenberg, *Weimar Century*, 120–68.

27. T. Brodie, *German Catholicism at War, 1939–1945* (Oxford, 2018), 224–41.

an atheistic cult of the state, from which the only remedy lay in a return to the values of Catholicism.[28]

Thus, Christian Democracy was from the outset a complex amalgam of the new and the old. For some Catholics, Christian Democracy represented an ambition to engage in a new pluralist politics, while for others it was a new means of articulating the distinctiveness of Catholic values.[29] The combination of the two was evident in the stance of Pope Pius XII, who in his Christmas message in December 1944 expressed his support for what he termed "a true and healthy democracy." This unexpected statement, and the break that it appeared to represent from the anti-democratic and anti-liberal tone that the papacy had adopted over the preceding years, was in almost every element more circumspect than emphatic, reflecting the careful calculations of interests that lay behind its genesis within the Vatican wartime bureaucracy.[30] Indeed, rather like the Lateran Accords that his predecessor, Pius XI, had signed fifteen years earlier with the Italian Fascist regime in 1929, Pius's Christmas message took the form of an implied contract, suggesting that the Church would look with favour on the new regime of democracy, so long as that regime proved respectful of the interests of the Church, and provided a context conducive to the dissemination of Catholic teachings.

Yet, that an authoritarian figure such as Pius—who had played such an influential role in the construction of the anti-liberal alliances of the Church after the First World War—should have felt it necessary to make this statement was an emphatic indication of how dramatically the political context within which the papacy operated had altered.[31] For all of the careful presentation of the text as a considered statement of doctrine, the Christmas message was a rather hasty attempt by the Vatican to catch up with how the world had changed. At the time that it was issued, Catholic activists in many areas of Europe were already active in democratic politics, or were preparing to become so. The Church therefore had little choice but to follow on behind these initiatives, while seeking to encourage the new political groupings to remain loyal to a clear Catholic identity and, perhaps more especially, to act as the defenders of the interests

28. M. Mitchell, "Materialism and Secularism: CDU Politicians and National Socialism, 1945–1949," *Journal of Modern History* 67 (1995): 278–308.

29. Conway, "Age of Christian Democracy," 52–54.

30. Pius XII, "Democracy and Peace," 303. See also Chamedes, *Twentieth-Century Crusade*, 238–39.

31. Re. Pius XII, see R. Ventresca, *Soldier of Christ: The Life of Pius XII* (Cambridge, MA, 2013); M. Walsh, "Pius XII," in *Modern Catholicism: Vatican II and After*, ed. A. Hastings (London, 1991), 20–26.

of the Church. However much Pius might regret it, the time when the Church could direct the political activism of the laity had clearly passed. The flowering of political and social movements, as well as of intellectual debate, that had occurred over the previous decades, and the powerful impetus provided by events during the war, had created a much more self-confident and articulate Catholic world. This too was a form of democracy. The predominantly younger generations of Catholic militants who played such a prominent role in the Christian Democratic movements during the immediate post-war years accepted the authority of the papacy and of the Church without being constrained by it.[32] They had developed their own understandings of Catholic teachings, which they were eager to put into action, through discussion, organization, and activism with fellow Catholics, but also with the wider society. Thus, while there was much that remained undefined about the content of Christian Democracy, its more immediate importance lay in the way it brought democracy into the Catholic world.

For Socialists, the adoption of a democratic heritage was, superficially, a more straightforward task. The aspiration to build a more democratic—namely, equal—society had, after all, always been a central purpose of the Socialist parties that emerged as a powerful presence in much of Europe in the second half of the nineteenth century. Moreover, the term "democracy" formed part of the intellectual and emotional heritage of many European Socialists, stretching back to the era of the French Revolution of 1789. The project of socialism, as developed by the *fin de siècle* generation of Socialist leaders such as Jaurès in France or Vandervelde in Belgium, was democracy writ large. Rejecting the constraints of liberalism, it combined a language of Marxist progress with the achievement of collective and individual economic freedom, the victory of secular values of tolerance, and the establishment of a political system based on the full representation of working people. This pre-1914 understanding of socialism and democracy as inherently interconnected projects had, however, been substantially disrupted by subsequent events. The First World War had divided Socialist ranks along national lines, while simultaneously bringing Socialist politicians and trade unionists into wartime government within a number of the combatant states. The tensions that the war generated were further complicated by the Bolshevik seizure of power in Russia in October 1917, as well as the more short-lived revolutions that occurred across

32. Kreichbaumer, *Parteiprogramme*, 63–65; I. Woloch, "Left, Right and Centre: The MRP and the Post-War Moment," *French History* 21 (2007): 93–96.

central Europe at the end of the war, all of which raised urgent questions for Socialists about the relationship between revolution, legality, and the exercise of governmental power.

The consequent divisions destroyed the unity of the Socialist movement, and more especially rendered the relationship between democracy and socialism considerably more problematic. Its more revolutionary tendencies—somewhat precariously unified by the mid-1920s within a nascent Communist movement led from Moscow—rejected participation in parliamentary politics, in favour of the direct democracy of soviets or communes, and, ultimately, the establishment of a single-party regime on the Leninist model. Many European Socialists eschewed the Communist path, but this did not mean that they were ready to adopt parliamentary reformism. They remained for the most part suspicious of anything that might smack of the abandonment of their revolutionary heritage. Yet, at the same time, the changes of political regime that occurred in central Europe in 1918–19—in which the Socialists and the choices they had made often played a significant role—as well as the expansions of the suffrage that took place in a number of other European states, transformed the Socialists from outsiders to partners in governmental coalitions and municipal administration. Representative democracy, it appeared, had arrived as the default template of modern politics at the national and local levels, thereby posing with greater acuity than had previously been the case the question as to how far Socialist parties should subordinate their sectional loyalties to ideology and class to the common or national interest. Moreover, where Socialists did participate in government in the 1920s, notably in Britain, Weimar Germany, and Belgium, it was rarely a positive experience. The achievement of limited reforms in fields such as welfare was offset by the pervasive hostility with which they were confronted by parties of the right, and by the accusations of betrayal voiced by the revolutionary left.[33]

As a consequence, for many Socialists, democracy—in the somewhat rigid parliamentary form that it assumed in almost all European states during the 1920s—came to seem almost like a trap. Especially during the intense economic depression of the early 1930s, participation in government required them to sacrifice progress towards socialism to the defence of the existing capitalist order, while the language of revolutionary change was increasingly appropriated by the Communists, and by the leagues and parties of the radical right. In response, a number of Socialist parties, such

33. Berman, *Primacy of Politics*, 97–102.

as the SPD in Germany, withdrew from national government, even if they often remained an influential presence in local and regional administrations.[34] More radically, in the volatile politics of the new Second Republic in Spain, the Socialist Party (PSOE) initiated a general strike that in the mining region of the Asturias became an outright uprising against the right-wing republican government.[35] A similar frustration at the limits of parliamentarism was evident in the attitudes of a range of socialist intellectuals, such as the neo-socialists in France and the president of the Belgian Socialist Party, Hendrik De Man, who advocated the implementation of an economic plan that would use the tools of state power to transform the economic base of society.[36] These ideas had obvious affinities with the projects of authoritarian reform being advanced on the political right at the same time.[37] Ideas of economic planning tended to marginalize, or indeed reject entirely, parliamentary democracy in favour of a revolution implemented from above, supplemented by the disciplined engagement of mass movements, notably the trade unions. Only in Sweden did it prove easier to combine such projects of economic and social reform with parliamentary government. The success of the Swedish Socialist Party (SAP) in the elections of 1932 enabled it to build a coalition government with the Agrarians, constructed around a programme of active measures to combat the economic depression combined with protectionist measures for small farmers. Reinforced by a further increase in the vote for the SAP at the subsequent elections in 1936, this led to a durable regime of social democracy, enacted through parliament but extending well beyond it to incorporate corporatist agreements with economic interest groups.[38]

Elsewhere, however, the relationship between socialism and parliamentary democracy remained much more contested. The ruthless

34. S. Miller and H. Potthoff, *A History of German Social Democracy: From 1848 to the Present* (Leamington Spa, UK, 1986), 91–103, 111–19; Saage, *Erste Präsident*, 155–82.

35. P. Preston, *Coming of the Spanish Civil War: Reform, Reaction and Revolution in the Second Republic*, 2nd ed. (London, 1994), 161–79; M. Kerry, "Radicalisation, Community and the Politics of Protest in the Spanish Second Republic, 1931–34," *English Historical Review* 132 (2017): 318–43.

36. A. Bergounioux, "Le néo-socialisme—Marcel Déat: Réformisme traditionnel ou esprit des années trente," *Revue historique* 260 (1978): 389–412; P. Dodge, *Beyond Marxism: The Faith and Works of Hendrik De Man* (The Hague, 1966); G.-R. Horn, *European Socialists Respond to Fascism: Ideology, Activism and Contingency in the 1930s* (New York, 1996), esp. 3–16.

37. Sternhell, *Neither Right nor Left*.

38. S. Berman, *The Social Democratic Moment: Ideas and Politics in the Making of Interwar Europe* (Cambridge, MA, 1998), 150–75. The classic contemporary statement of Socialist progress in Sweden during the 1930s is Childs, *Sweden*.

consolidation of power by the NSDAP in Germany during 1933, combined with right-wing demonstrations in Paris in February 1934 and large-scale violent confrontations in the same month between the Austrian Socialists and the authoritarian regime of Dollfuss in Vienna and other major Austrian cities, created a strong momentum, particularly in France and Spain, towards a broadly based alliance of progressive forces incorporating Socialists, left republicans, and Communists. The defence of democracy against the fascist threat was a key element of the rhetoric of the Popular Fronts that emerged as the strongest bloc from the national elections in both France and Spain in 1936.[39] But converting this vague language of democracy into concrete practice proved difficult. In Spain, the Socialists chose not to join the Popular Front government, but then found themselves forced back on an alliance with the Spanish Communist Party, the PCE, after the military uprising against the Republic had plunged Spain into civil war.[40] In France, the Socialist leader Léon Blum became the prime minister of a coalition government of Radicals and Socialists (with external Communist support) in France in May 1936, but the government soon lost momentum in the face of Radical hesitations, social tensions, and the increasing threat of war. Blum resigned from office in 1937 and the Popular Front was effectively dissolved in 1938.[41]

The failure of the popular-front politics of the 1930s left unresolved the stance of Socialist parties towards democracy. Neither the practice of the existing forms of democratic power nor the attempts to construct an alternative socialist form of democracy had proved fruitful. Instead, by the end of the 1930s the Socialists in the few remaining democratic states of Europe seemed to have lost any clear sense of political purpose or hope for the future. Indeed, with the Francoist victory in Spain in 1939, and the subsequent German military victories in Scandinavia, the Low Countries, and France in the spring and summer of 1940, the very survival of socialism as a force in Europe appeared to be threatened. With the rare exceptions of Sweden and the British Labour Party's participation in the wartime national government in Britain, Socialists had become prisoners,

39. T. Buchanan, "Antifascism and Democracy in the 1930s," *European History Quarterly* 32 (2002): 39–57.

40. H. Graham, *Socialism and War: The Spanish Socialist Party in Power and Crisis, 1936–1939* (Cambridge, UK, 1991), 34–103; "Spain 1936—Resistance and Revolution: The Flaws in the Front," in *Opposing Fascism: Community, Authority and Resistance in Europe*, ed. T. Kirk and A. McElligott (Cambridge, UK, 1999), 63–79.

41. J. Jackson, *The Popular Front in France: Defending Democracy, 1934–38* (Cambridge, UK, 1988). See also M. Alexander and H. Graham, eds., *The French and Spanish Popular Fronts: Comparative Perspectives* (Cambridge, UK, 1989).

exiles, or at best an entirely marginal political force. During the war years, they were therefore obliged to rethink the purposes of their action, essentially from the bottom up. Some Socialists were in exile in London or elsewhere, while others were working within the bureaucracies of state administrations or military forces, or had thrown their energies into the burgeoning range of Resistance groups and clandestine newspapers. But, despite these variations of context, their ideas were broadly convergent: Socialism needed to move beyond the doctrinal disputes of the past, and construct forward-looking and ambitious programmes of reform of state institutions and socio-economic structures, which would create a new model of activist government, economic modernization, and expanded systems of social welfare.[42]

Quite what place democracy would occupy within the nascent project of a post-war socialism remained largely unclear. Unsurprisingly, few Socialists in liberation Europe were inclined to dwell on their past experiences of participation in government. References to the interwar years risked revivifying still strongly felt divisions, especially in Austria where the alliance from 1945 of the Socialists of the SPÖ with the former Christian Socials, who had supported Dollfuss's authoritarian regime, obliged them to abstain, a few somewhat guarded comments aside, from referring to the violent conflicts of the 1930s.[43] Much the same was true in Germany, though the leader of the SPD, Kurt Schumacher, recently released from a Nazi camp, did allow himself to point out that "all the other parties needed the war potential, and the supremacy of anglo-saxon supremacy in order to discover that their hearts were set on democracy. But we did not need this. We would be democratic even if the English and the Americans were fascists."[44] Such partisan point scoring was, however, relatively rare. Instead, European Socialists preferred to link together past, present, and future in a somewhat unconvincing chain of continuity, by adopting the familiar rhetoric of a "road" or "transition" to socialism. Thus, the Belgian Socialists declared blandly at their victory congress in June 1945 that "la victoire de la démocratie sera celle du socialisme" (the victory of democracy will be that of socialism), while the Czechoslovak and

42. A. Shennan, *Rethinking France: Plans for Renewal, 1940–1946* (Oxford, 1989), 58–61, 85–92, 121–24; Bailey, *Between Yesterday and Tomorrow*, 130–34.

43. Renner, "Gesellschaft, Staat und Demokratie," 137; Herz, "Compendium of Austrian Politics," 586; Saage, *Erste Präsident*, 333. Very different, and much more polemical, was the work of a scholar based in the United States, who had no hesitation in presenting the Austrian Socialists as the defenders of democracy in the face of the fascist authoritarianism of the Christian Socials: C. A. Gulick, *Austria from Habsburg to Hitler* (Berkeley, CA, 1948).

44. Quoted in P. T. Jackson, *Civilizing the Enemy*, 125–26.

Austrian Socialist parties both adopted the almost identical formulation that "democracy is our road, socialism is our aim."[45] Quite how the one would lead to the other remained, however, more an article of rhetorical faith than a concerted plan.

✦

How Socialists and Christian Democrats related their past struggles to their present situation mattered to both leaders and militants, as it invested their post-war activities with a sense of the historical rectitude of their cause. But of more immediate importance were the nature and internal content of the democracy that they chose to espouse. Much, in this respect, remained to be defined. Democracy was an unbounded territory in 1945, upon which all of the political parties sought to imprint their particular emphases: the radicalism of popular sovereignty on the one hand, or the controlling hand of law on the other; effective authority on the part of the state, or the protection of the rights of the individual. These were not simply divisions that defined one party from the other, or the political left from the right; they were also visible within the newly launched political forces at the liberation, and more especially the Socialists and the Christian Democrats. Both lacked a settled political programme seeking to pick their way between the dictates of the moment, pressures from their militants and potential electors, the initiatives of their opponents, and the logics of their own convictions. Unsurprisingly, therefore, the path towards self-definition, and especially towards their understanding of democracy, was slow. It was only once the politics of post-war Europe had acquired a recognizable shape in much of Western Europe, around 1947–48, that Socialists and Christian Democrats arrived at a clear sense of their relationship to democracy.

This was especially so among the European Socialists. There was no common starting point for the various Socialist parties in Europe at the end of the war. The complex legacies of the recent past were further complicated by the different political contexts in which—in the west and particularly in the east—they operated.[46] Not surprisingly, therefore,

45. Conway, *Sorrows of Belgium*, 183–84 (Belgian Socialists' quotation); Myant, *Socialism and Democracy*, 122 (Czechoslovak Socialists' quotation); Herz, "Compendium of Austrian Politics," 588 (Austrian Socialists' quotation); De Graaf, "European Socialism," 346.

46. This is the principal thesis of J. De Graaf, *Socialism across the Iron Curtain: Socialist Parties in East and West and the Reconstruction of Europe after 1945* (Cambridge, UK, 2019).

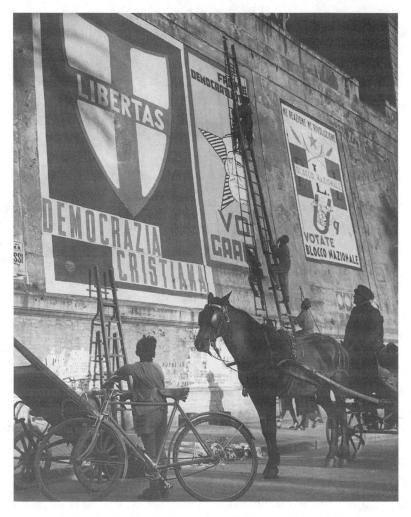

FIGURE 6. The visual universe of democracy: election posters on wall in Rome in 1948. Hulton Deutsch/Corbis Historical via Getty Images

the various attempts made by the Socialist parties to arrive at a redefinition of their purpose on the whole resulted in them falling back on reaffirming past statements—as in the case of the decision of the Austrian Socialists to readopt the Linz programme of 1926—or adopting anodyne compromise formulae that offered little by way of programmatic content, as in the case of the French Socialist Party, the SFIO.[47] For all of their repeated statements that the future did indeed belong to them,

47. Kreichbaumer, *Parteiprogramme*, 61–62; Saage, *Erste Präsident*, 330–32; B. D. Graham, *Choice and Democratic Order*, 271–302; P. Lösche and F. Walter, *Die SPD:*

the Socialist parties had considerable difficulty in articulating a vision of their purpose that went beyond somewhat empty statements of the need for a more just and democratic social order. This hesitation owed much to their nervousness as to the actions of others. Outside of Scandinavia, Socialist parties felt threatened from the right by the Christian Democrats, behind whom they detected a coalition of various reactionary forces, and from the left by the Communists, who appeared to be better placed than the Socialists in appealing to the patriotic legacies of the Resistance and posing as the defenders of the working class. Consequently, socialism tended to define itself less in terms of what it was, than in contradistinction to what it was not.

The most urgent priority for the Socialists in most countries was to respond to the Communists, and more especially the pressing overtures from Communist parties to participate in common electoral lists, popular-front coalitions, or indeed to fuse in a single party. In some cases, the Socialists did opt to work with the Communists, most notably in Italy, where the majority Socialist grouping led by Nenni concluded a Popular Front with the PCI.[48] But elsewhere Socialist parties chose to distance themselves very consciously from the Communists. This was a choice pushed forward by the urgent pressure of international events, but above all by the determination on the part of Socialist party leaders and trade unionists to drive the Communists and their allies out of the positions of local and institutional power that they had acquired, or, in their minds, usurped, during the war years and the liberation.[49]

This organizational struggle came to define the ways in which most European Socialists thought. Hostility to Communism provided a short cut towards the definition of a socialism that was democratic and western, by juxtaposing it against a communism that they defined, conversely, as totalitarian and eastern.[50] In this way, European Socialists came to see themselves as the embodiment of a particular democratic tradition, which they insisted was inseparable from socialism. In the words of Giuseppe Saragat—the leader of the anti-Nenni Socialists who broke away to form the PSLI, the Partito Socialista dei Lavoratori Italiani, in 1947—socialism

---

Klassenpartei-Volkspartei-Quotenpartei—Zur Entwicklung der Sozialdemokratie von Weimar bis zur deutschen Vereinigung (Darmstadt, 1992), 107–10.

48. Di Scala, *Renewing Italian Socialism*, 73–77.

49. Roseman, *Recasting the Ruhr*, 284–86; Conway, *Sorrows of Belgium*, 215–23; De Graaf, "European Socialism," 337–38, 341.

50. Faravelli, *Autonomia del Partito Socialista*, 12–13; Steege, *Black Market, Cold War*, 102; K. Shell, *The Transformation of Austrian Socialism* (New York, 1962), 141–44.

was "the highest form of political democracy"—la forma più alta della democrazia politica.[51] This rhetorical elision of socialism and democracy was an omnipresent feature of Socialist discourse in the post-war era, and formed the basis of the founding declaration of the new (anti-Communist) Socialist International in 1951: "Without freedom there can be no socialism. Socialism can be achieved only through democracy."[52] This formula contained considerable scope for nuance, between those who emphasized the transformative force of socialism and those who defended the legality of democracy; but, for most, it served as a substitute for any more complex definition of their attitude to democracy. In language that echoed the rhetoric of the pre-1914 years, the Austrian SPÖ in its new programme published in 1958 presented socialism as the fullest expression of democracy: "Sozialismus ist vollendete Demokratie." Their goal was the achievement of an "uneingeschränkte politische, wirtschaftliche und soziale Demokratie"—a comprehensive political, economic, and social democracy.[53] The economic and social components of this definition of a socialist democracy were relatively easy to define: the introduction of Keynesian measures of economic management, combined with the establishment of more extensive structures of social welfare, rapidly became part of the standard agenda of European Socialist parties after 1945.[54] But what was much less clear was its political form. Especially in the immediate post-liberation period, there was a clear ambition among Socialist activists and intellectuals to rethink the nature of a democratic politics, and to move, as one Berlin SPD figure put it in 1946, from a passive democracy to an active one.[55] Power needed to be returned to the people, through the achievement of an open and participatory democracy—what one Italian Socialist termed a *democrazia integrale*—that would value human and spiritual freedom as much as material living standards.[56]

The difficulty with such aspirations was that they conflicted with the top-down restructuring of European states that took place after the liberation. That process allowed for universal adult enfranchisement, but

51. Saragat, *Socialismo democratico*, 3. Re. Saragat, see De Grand, *Italian Left*, 106–8.

52. Socialist International, "Aims and Tasks of Democratic Socialism," 30 June–3 July 1951, http://www.socialistinternational.org/viewArticle.cfm?ArticleID=39.

53. [SPÖ], "Das Neue Parteiprogramm der Sozialistischen Partei Österreichs, 1958," in *Österreichische Parteiprogramme 1868–1966*, ed. K. Berchtold (Munich, 1967), 288. See also P. T. Jackson, *Civilizing the Enemy*, 124–27.

54. Bank, "Theorie van de vernieuwing," 109–20; Lidegaard, *Short History of Denmark*, 199–200.

55. Steege, *Black Market, Cold War*, 102–3.

56. Weber, "Freier Sozialismus," 39–94; Faravelli, *Autonomia del Partito Socialista*, 28.

not much more by way of "the creative tasks of citizenship."[57] In practice, therefore, the Socialists very rapidly became a party of the political status quo and of the governing system, rather than of a democratic revolution.[58] Thus, for example, in its new programme, the SPÖ made much of the party's commitment to the defence of democracy against the dictatorship represented by both fascism and communism, but offered little beyond modest measures of workplace participation in terms of citizenship.[59] This absence of a substantive vision of a new democratic order reflected the power structures within the European Socialist parties. For all their ambition that the new or renovated structures of the Socialist parties would be democratic organizations based on a mass membership, the power of policy-making and of patronage was emphatically focused in small elites of officials and political leaders, who ensured that the regional and local federations operated under their firm control.[60]

The difficulties that the Socialists encountered in giving expression to a new democratic definition of their purpose contrasted with the much more emphatic and confident tone of the Christian Democratic parties in the post-war years. As predominantly new political formations eager to distance themselves from the conservative and clerical Catholic parties of the past, the Christian Democratic parties of the 1940s used the statements of party ideology that they drew up in the immediate aftermath of liberation to present the outlines of a democracy that would be new in spirit and content.[61] Newness in this context was, however, something of a double-edged tool. It enabled the Christian Democrats to pose as the advocates of an inclusive spirit of democracy that would move beyond the political realm to incorporate the wide-ranging social reforms that had long formed a staple element of social Catholic rhetoric.[62] But newness was also a means of advocating an exclusively Catholic definition of democracy, one that differed from those long espoused by liberals, Socialists, and Communists. Thus, in contrast to the "démocratie illusoire" of

57. Socialist Union, *New Statement of Principles*, 60.

58. M. Sadoun, *Les socialistes sous l'occupation: Résistance et collaboration* (Paris, 1982), 268–76.

59. [SPÖ], "Neue Parteiprogramm," 287–88. See also the very similar language of the same year in G. Mollet, *Bilan et perspectives socialistes* (Paris, 1958).

60. J. Lewis, *Workers and Politics*, 133–36; S. H. Barnes, *Party Democracy*; Lafon, "Des principes du molletisme," 59–91; Lösche and Walter, *SPD*, 178–81.

61. Letamendia, *Mouvement républicain populaire*, 49–66; Van den Wijngaert, *Stichting van de CVP-PSC*.

62. For characteristic examples, see Woloch, "Left, Right and Centre," 96–100; Mitchell, *Origins of Christian Democracy*, 115–19.

these other political traditions, Christian Democracy would build a genuine democracy, defined by Catholic teachings.[63]

Quite what this Catholic democracy would consist of was often left unclear, and the programmatic statements tended to be longer on general rhetoric than on specific commitments. It was easy, however, to detect the caution that often lay under the surface of this new-found democratic language. Some figures, notably those associated with the review *Esprit* in France or around Giuseppe Dossetti in Italy, envisaged Christian Democracy as a radical force that would ally with the Socialist or even, in a few cases, the Communist left to bring about a much wider political and, above all, spiritual refounding of contemporary society.[64] But there were also plenty of more conservative voices, who found in the new language of Christian Democracy what the prominent German theologian Romano Guardini termed rather carefully "a fortunate unity of order and freedom."[65] A concern for order, combined with other code words such as justice and the need to protect law and the rights of property, was a means of signalling, in the uncertain political climate of the immediate post-war years, that Christian Democracy would reject projects of radical change in favour of reinforcing state authority and social order.[66] Taking their cue from Pius XII's Christmas message of 1944, these conservative voices rejected what they regarded as the fallacious liberal notion of the sovereignty of the people. Modern history, such voices argued, had provided ample evidence that the untrammelled expression of the will of the people led only to dictatorship or revolution; instead, Christian Democracy would combine a democratic spirit with respect for the natural units of society and, above all, for the teachings of the Church.[67]

The confident rhetoric of Christian Democrats in the mid- and late 1940s therefore served to gloss over many nuances of emphasis.

63. Chanoine Dermine, "Christianisme et démocratie," in *Les lignes de faite de la démocratie: XXVIIIe semaine sociale wallonne 1946* (Courtrai, Belgium, n.d.), 25–32; programme of the Christlich Demokratische Union (CDU) of the British Zone, 1 March 1946, cited in Mitchell, *Origins of Christian Democracy*, 91–92.

64. M. Winock, *Histoire politique de la revue "Esprit" 1930–1950* (Paris, 1975), 248–66; M. Tronti, "Introduzione: Dossetti politico—un problema," in *Scritti politici 1943–1951*, by G. Dossetti (Genoa, 1995), xv–xxviii; Thomassen and Forlenza, "Christianity and Political Thought," 184.

65. Quoted in Krieg, *Catholic Theologians*, 127.

66. Kasamas, *Programm Österreich*, 92–100. See also pp. 122–23.

67. L. Picard, "Synthèse de la pensée pontificale," in *Conditions de la démocratie*, by Pius XII (Brussels, 1945), 7–13; L. Harmel, "Lignes de faite de la démocratie politique," in *Les lignes de faite de la démocratie: XXVIIIe semaine sociale wallonne 1946* (Courtrai, Belgium, n.d.), 185–92.

Differences of generation, social class, and of intellectual formation were all apparent in their attitude to what democracy was, and what it might be. Such diversity was not, however, necessarily a weakness; indeed, one of the strengths of Christian Democracy in the immediate post-war years lay precisely in the way in which it avoided too precise a definition of its ideology and goals. In contrast to the Socialists, whose central ideas and preoccupations were all too familiar to many European electors, Christian Democracy had the advantage of presenting itself as a new political force, in which voters could find what they wished to find. This vagueness—or, perhaps more precisely, its multifaceted character—helps to explain the surges in electoral support for Christian Democratic parties that occurred notably in France, Belgium, and Italy in the immediate post-war years, as they garnered votes from a range of voters left orphaned by the political changes of the previous years. The satirical reformulation by the Communists of the initials of the French MRP in 1945 as the "Machine à ramasser les pétainistes"—Machine for Reuniting the Pétainists—[68] was only ever a partial truth, and disguised the extent to which the party acquired a genuinely cross-class and inclusive character during the first years of the Fourth Republic.[69] But, as the rapid electoral decline of the MRP during the 1950s demonstrates, lack of definition could also become a problem. As the fluidity of the politics of the immediate post-liberation years gave way to the more settled electoral and social frontiers of the 1950s, so Christian Democratic parties were obliged to make clearer choices as to the nature of the democratic order that they advocated.

This change of gear in liberation politics from the potentialities of the post-war moment to the more settled patterns of national and local democratic politics took place at different speeds in the states of post-war Europe. In much of Western Europe, it had largely occurred by the end of 1947, while in West Germany it could only fully take place after the inauguration of the Federal Republic in 1949. Everywhere, however, it was reinforced by the twin forces of economic recovery and the Cold War, which had the combined effect of diminishing the spectrum of political possibilities while also moving the practice of democracy from the languages of

68. Quoted in Buton, *Lendemains qui déchantent*, 206.
69. Vinen, *Bourgeois Politics in France*, 154–58; B. Béthouart, "Entry of the Catholics into the Republic: The Mouvement Républicain Populaire in France," in Gehler and Kaiser, *Christian Democracy in Europe*, 86–89.

constitutional and social change to the incremental and material priorities of the present and the future.

This transition from the exceptional to the (newly) normal changed the terms of political discourse among Christian Democrats and Socialists. With the marginalization of the Western European Communist parties as potential actors and allies, so the available range of political choices narrowed to different variants of the centre-right and the centre-left. Consequently, Catholics and Socialists were primarily concerned to maximize their support among those they thought of as their core social constituencies, as well as among those unaffiliated voters—often perceived to be largely female and lower middle class—who were believed to occupy the centre ground of the political spectrum.[70] The pragmatic priorities of electoral politics did not efface the underlying differences between Socialist and Christian Democratic definitions of democracy, but they made the terms of political debate more material and concrete. Democracy ceased to be a political world to be imagined, and became a project to be built through policies intended to bring about a democratic society. This was rarely straightforward, and led the parties to develop policies on issues such as welfare provision, housing, and taxation that would have divergent impacts on different social groups.

This posed a particular challenge for the Christian Democratic parties. Given their cross-class composition, they were often obliged to arbitrate between the conflicting material interests represented within their own ranks—and their federal institutional structures—by Catholic trade unions, farmers' leagues, and a range of professional and sectional interest groups.[71] Christian democratic parties chose to celebrate this social diversity as a symbol of their inclusivity. As the leader of the ÖVP Julius Raab declared in a speech to the party in 1952, the People's Party was the defender—the *Wellenbrecher*, or wave-breaker—of the interests of the "little man" against economic change and the power of the state.[72] This

70. See p. 169.

71. The Austrian ÖVP provides a good example of this internal negotiation: M. Sully, *A Contemporary History of Austria* (London, 1990), 42–48; R. Kreichbaumer, *Zwischen Land und Bund: Die Salzburger ÖVP in der Ära Lechner* (Salzburg, 1988), 15–76. See also *Un parti dans l'histoire 1945–1995: 50 ans d'action du Parti social chrétien* (Louvain-la-Neuve, Belgium, 1996).

72. J. Raab, "Die Österreichische Volkspartei: Ein Wellenbrecher gegen totalitäre Anspruche" (29 January 1952), in *Julius Raab: Ansichten des Staatsvertragskanzlers*, edited by R. Prantner (Vienna, 1991), 14–15. See also the very similar rhetoric of his fellow ÖVP leader Leopold Figl in L. Figl, "Die ÖVP: Eine Integrationspartei für Österreich" (21

was a language that had a particular appeal to the populations of rural and small-town Europe. Concern for the material interests of farmers was rarely far from the surface of post-war European politics,[73] and the Christian Democratic parties established themselves as the guardians of the social and economic welfare of Western Europe's many small-scale farmers. Protection of agricultural prices against the vagaries of market forces was complemented by favourable taxation regimes and inheritance laws, as well as by the deployment of state resources to bring infrastructural development— roads, electricity, water pipes, and new schools—to rural areas.[74]

This same combination of cultural rhetoric and material support was evident in the way that Christian Democratic parties appealed to the values of a property-owning democracy, contrasted against the supposed collectivizing ambitions of the Socialist and Communist left. "Eigentum macht frei" (Property makes people free), declared arrestingly the Austrian ÖVP in its party programme of 1958, promising to spread the benefits of property ownership to ever larger sections of the population.[75] Central to this vision, and more especially its future-oriented language of democracy, was the issue of housing. The construction of family homes was the material expression of the new, and democratic, society that Christian Democrats were bringing into being.[76] By mobilizing state resources—national and local—to build millions of new homes, Christian Democrats were responding to the aspirations of many voters, but also giving expression to the long-standing preoccupation with the family that had long been a strong element of the cultural and pastoral identity of the Catholic faith. By providing a supportive material framework for family life, through new housing, a panoply of social-security measures, health systems, and schooling, the Christian Democrats were creating a family democracy, focused on the

April 1947), in *Leopold Figl: Ansichten eines grossen Österreichers*, ed. R. Pranter (Vienna, 1992), 112.

73. See pp. 231–32.

74. "Was wir wollen: Das Grundsatzprogramm der Österreichischen Volkspartei, 1958," in Berchtold, *Österreichische Parteiprogramme*, 395; R. Forlenza, "A Party for the Mezzogiorno: The Christian Democratic Party, Agrarian Reform and the Government of Italy," *Contemporary European History* 19 (2010): 343–49.

75. "Was wir wollen: Das Grundsatzprogramm der Österreichischen Volkspartei, 1958," in Berchtold, *Österreichische Parteiprogramme*, 392–93.

76. A. Staub "'Einmal im Leben': Rooting the 'Little Man' to Conservative Values in Postwar West Germany," in *After Fascism: European Case Studies in Politics, Society and Identity since 1945*, ed. M. Berg and M. Mesner (Vienna, 2009), 157–62. See also pp. 246–47.

interests of female voters as the primary custodians of the well-being of children and of the family.[77]

There was much in this preoccupation with provincial Europe, property, housing, and the family that could easily seem backward looking at a time when economic and cultural changes were rapidly transforming the day-to-day realities of European life. But, at its most effective, Christian Democracy served as an effective amalgam of material ambitions with the security of the familiar. It enabled voters to move towards the opportunities of a new future while retaining the social stability that they had regained after the often traumatic disruptions of the war years. "Keine Experimente!" (No experiments!)—the famous slogan chosen by the Christian Democrats, the CDU, for the German federal election campaign of 1957, and often deployed on posters together with a reassuring grandpaternal image of the party leader and federal chancellor Konrad Adenauer—was a message, complete with the injunction provided by the exclamation mark, that had a particular resonance in a Germany still recovering from the trauma of the war years. But it was also typical of the careful combination of imagined conservative values and present- and future-minded effective governance that characterized Christian Democracy.[78]

Much the same was true of the relationship between Christian Democracy and Catholicism. Many of the major Christian Democratic parties in post-war Europe, most notably in West Germany and the Netherlands, were explicitly non-confessional, incorporating Protestant figures into their ranks, and emphasizing the Christian rather than the specifically Catholic inspiration for their policies. Nevertheless, across the broad band of Catholic territories from the Low Countries through western Germany to Austria and northern Italy, the embeddedness of the parties within the social and associational structures of Catholicism was emphatic, reflecting the prominence of the Catholic Church and its affiliated mass organizations in local life in many of these areas in the post-war years.[79] Most Christian Democrat leaders were, however, at pains to express their independence from the Church. They wished to avoid the clerical politics of the

77. J. Raab, "Freiheit, Währungsstabilität, Wirtschaftsexpansion, Sorge um die Familien" (15 April 1953), and "Freiheit und soziale Sicherheit für alle Österreicher!" (30 November 1958) in *Julius Raab: Ansichten des Staatsvertragskanzlers*, edited by R. Prantner (Vienna, 1991), 16–22 and 25–28; Mitchell, *Origins of Christian Democracy*, 107–10.

78. R. G. Moeller, *Protecting Motherhood: Women and the Family in the Politics of Postwar West Germany* (Berkeley, CA, 1993), 211.

79. See, for example, D. Forgacs and S. Gundle, *Mass Culture and Italian Society from Fascism to the Cold War* (Bloomington, IN, 2007), 252–59.

recent past, and were aware of the need to appeal beyond the ranks of the conventionally faithful to the larger swathe of voters for whom an identification with Catholicism formed part of an amalgam of social and cultural values. Christian Democratic parties therefore preferred to avoid explicitly confessional language, in favour of more inclusive references to Christian heritage and beliefs. The models of a specifically Catholic-inspired political system that had proliferated in preceding decades were largely abandoned. Instead, the parties accepted the norms of the new democratic constitutions, while using their presence in national and local government to ensure that the new political regime did not limit the freedom of action of the Church and its institutions, notably schools.[80]

The success of this rhetoric of democracy with its interlinking of the languages of freedom, of Catholic-inflected social values, and of individual opportunity was, thus, a mixture of the ideological and the more simply material. It drew on the considerable heritage of Catholic political and social thought, but more importantly converted those ideas into an evolving set of policies—what Kees van Kersbergen has termed "social capitalism"—calibrated to appeal to a cross-class coalition of supporters.[81] In this way, it also fostered a new relationship between the parties and their electors. The somewhat pejorative sense of clientelism that often characterizes studies of Christian Democracy fails to do justice to the way in which the parties operated in their electoral heartlands as a two-way intermediary between voters and the state. They certainly built electoral loyalty by distributing the resources of the state to their voters, but they also provided a channel for the requests of communities and of specific social constituencies to reach the offices of the local and national state.[82]

This was a model of responsive politics that the Socialist parties struggled to emulate. They were, as we have seen, more rigid institutions, constrained both by a loyalty to their own histories and by the vested interests represented within their institutional structures. The Socialists were certainly conscious of the need to reach out to new social constituencies. The historic languages of class politics, and of secularism, were toned down after 1945 and subsumed in a more inclusive concern for all working people, of both town and country, as well as of the middle classes,

80. Kreichbaumer, *Parteiprogramme*, 93–104; Conway, introduction to *Political Catholicism in Europe 1918–1965*, ed. T. Buchanan and Conway (Oxford, 1996), 30–32, and *Sorrows of Belgium*, 190–92; Mitchell, *Origins of Christian Democracy*, 196–201.

81. Van Kersbergen, *Social Capitalism*, esp. 229–34.

82. Forlenza, "Party for the Mezzogiorno," 331–49.

who would work together in what the former exile from Nazism Ernst Fraenkel termed a "collective democracy."[83] The ambition, as expressed in the decision of the Dutch Socialists to rename their party more inclusively as the Partij van de Arbeid, the Party of Work, in 1946, was to reach beyond the strictly economic sphere to build an all-encompassing democratic society.[84] If the legislation introduced by the British Labour governments between 1945 and 1951 served as a partial inspiration for such ideas, it is nevertheless striking how absent explicit borrowings from British models were from European Socialist statements. Neither the universal principles of the welfare state nor the nationalization of key industries featured prominently in post-war Socialist programmes. Instead, they advocated systems of social insurance, corporatist structures of tripartite negotiation between the representatives of employees, employers, and the state, and above all the benefits of a state-directed framework of economic planning.[85]

Planning, in all its forms, became a key element of post-war Socialist policies. In contrast to the emphasis placed by the Christian Democrats on freedom and autonomy, Socialists looked to the institutions of the state to create "a new democratic order" that would avoid the waste and conflict inherent in an unregulated capitalism.[86] Sweden was a central example, and wider inspiration, of this mentality. The combination of institutionalized corporatist negotiation of wages and employment conditions, comprehensive social-welfare provision, and investment in projects of modernization enacted by the Socialist governments of Sweden came close to providing an ideal model for other Socialist parties, who were often less aware of the domestic opposition provoked by high taxation rates and a substantial state bureaucracy.[87] For Tage Erlander, who served as prime minister of Sweden from 1946 to 1969, the overriding goal was to create what he termed a "strong society," by which he meant,

83. "Aktionsprogramm der Sozialistischen Partei Österreichs, 1947," in Berchtold, *Österreichische Parteiprogramme*, 267; S. Timperman, "1945–1954: Le PSB s'ouvre aux classes moyennes," *Revue belge d'histoire contemporaine* 28 (1998): 445–98. Re. Fraenkel, see Greenberg, *Weimar Century*, 76–119.

84. Bank, "Theorie van de vernieuwing," 102–3; Theien, "Shopping," 141.

85. Nicholls, *Freedom with Responsibility*, 257–59, 303–4; Sassoon, *One Hundred Years*, 137–66; Berman, *Primacy of Politics*, 177–88.

86. Quote from Steege, *Black Market, Cold War*, 292.

87. Hilson, *Nordic Model*, 37–45, 65–75, 99–106. See the critical perspectives in B. Larsson, M. Letell, and H. Thörn, eds., *Transformations of the Swedish Welfare State: From Social Engineering to Governance* (Basingstoke, UK, 2012); J. Strang, "The Other Europe?: Scandinavian Intellectuals and the Fragility of Democracy in the Wake of the Second World War," *Journal of Modern European History* 17 (2019): 500–518.

in fact, a strong state, both national and local, which would be able to provide for the ever increasing range of needs that citizens could not satisfy through their own efforts.[88]

As the Swedish case indicated, this preoccupation with the benefits of planning all too easily subordinated democracy to the priorities of organization and provision. If the state was the best means of identifying and meeting the needs of society, what purpose was served by allowing the people a say in this process, especially if this risked giving voice to sectional interests or reactionary prejudices?[89] In the rather stark formulation of the veteran Austrian Socialist Karl Renner, democracy constituted the "Prinzip der Organisation, der geordneten Zusammengliederung von Millionen Individuen eines modernen Volkes zu der Gemeinschaft Staat."[90] This vision of the people's ordered participation in the state reflected the particular context in which Renner was speaking in 1946, at a time of considerable social chaos in Austria. But it was redolent of the state-oriented mentality of Socialist policies in the post-war decades. Renner emphasized in the same speech the need for a modern bureaucracy to be responsive to the will of its citizens;[91] but for him and many other Socialists the driving force behind the creation of a rationally organized society was the state rather than its citizens. As the Belgian Socialist Party, the PSB, declared in its 1965 programme, "dans le cadre et par les moyens d'une démocratie parlementaire, il est possible, par étapes successives, de réaliser progressivement une véritable démocratie économique et sociale."[92]

What this vision of beneficent state action risked excluding was any larger purpose. Images of happy families, new concrete apartment blocks, and the bridges and underpasses of modern urban transport systems served well as records of the achievement of municipal socialism.[93] But Socialist leaders became increasingly conscious during the 1950s of

88. Ruin, *Tage Erlander*, 214–21; Berman, *Primacy of Politics*, 196.

89. M. Peterson, "Pathways of the Welfare State: Growth and Dependency," in Larsson, Letell, and Thörn, *Transformations*, 27–29. See also the comments of Erlander on referenda: p. 134.

90. "the principle of the organization of the ordered collective participation of the millions of individuals of a modern nation in the collective state": K. Renner, "Demokratie und Bürokratie" (22 February 1946), in *Für Recht und Frieden*, 196.

91. Renner, 199–205.

92. "within the framework and the means of a parliamentary democracy, it is possible to achieve gradually in successive stages a true economic and social democracy": Parti socialiste belge, *Programme pour les élections législatives de 1965* (Liège, [1965]), 3.

93. SPÖ Wien, *Bericht 1959*, 15–26.

the need to articulate a message that responded to the aspirations of a more educated and complex society. There needed to be a more thoroughgoing renewal of socialist ideas, if socialism was not to sink into what one group of dissident French Socialists termed "les sables de la prospérité," the sands of prosperity.[94] The language of renewal was omnipresent in socialism in the late 1950s and early 1960s, prompted by a recognition that, in much of Europe, Socialist parties had become confined within a "30 per cent tower," drawing a large majority of their votes from certain socially and geographically defined constituencies.[95] In response to repeated electoral defeats, the challenge for the left was to lop off what the French group termed the "branches mortes du socialisme" in order to create policies that could mobilize a broader basis of electoral support.[96]

The most striking demonstration of this perceived need for renewal was the adoption by the German SPD of a new party programme at its conference in Bad Godesberg in 1959. In common with the doctrinal restatements issued by a number of other Socialist parties during the 1950s, the Bad Godesberg statement has often been presented as a decisive rupture: the moment when the SPD finally shook itself free from the nineteenth-century Marxist paradigm of revolution in order to adopt a more flexible social democracy that accepted the existing economy and society in order to reform it.[97] In truth, the programme did not entirely support this interpretation. The impulse for its adoption had been the failure of the SPD in the elections of 1953 and 1957 to defeat the Christian Democratic government of Konrad Adenauer. This provided an opportunity for reformist voices within the party, such as Willy Brandt and Ernst Fraenkel, to advocate their idea of a less rigid definition of socialism; but the programme, as it was adopted, was very much a compromise text in which new emphases on social inclusivity and reformist governance coexisted with formulae that reflected the party's Marxist heritage.[98]

94. C. Bruclain, *Le socialisme et l'Europe* (Paris, 1965), 103.

95. Stöss, *Politics against Democracy*, 97; Lösche and Walter, *SPD*, 88–94, 140–46; Castles, *Social Democratic Image*, 5–13.

96. Bruclain, *Socialisme et l'Europe*, 17–55; *Nenni, Bevan, Mendès-France*; E. Depreux, *Renouvellement du socialisme* (Paris, 1960); Shell, *Transformation of Austrian Socialism*, 243–56; Hamon, *De Gaulle*, 165–205.

97. Nicholls, *Freedom with Responsibility*, 367–89; Berman, *Primacy of Politics*, 189–91. On the parallel process of doctrinal change within the Austrian SPÖ, see: [SPÖ], "Neue Parteiprogramm," 286–306; Kreichbaumer, *Parteiprogramme*, 330–34.

98. Lösche and Walter, *SPD*, 110–15; Greenberg, *Weimar Century*, 116–19; K. Fertikh, "Bad-Godesberg dans le langage social-démocrate en 1959," *Cahiers d'histoire. Revue d'histoire critique* 114 (2011): 137–51.

The new language of social democracy adopted at Bad Godesberg was therefore rather less than it seemed. It gestured to the wider German society that the SPD was willing to embrace more technocratic methods of governance and economic management. The objective, however, remained the familiar one of bringing about a new economic and social order.[99] Above all, there was no substantive discussion of democracy. The Bad Godesberg programme repeated the orthodoxy that "Socialism can be realised only through democracy and democracy can only be fulfilled through Socialism";[100] but, apart from vague commitments to human dignity and freedom of thought, the content of this democracy remained vague. Where there was innovation in Socialist ranks throughout Western Europe was in the adoption of a language of freedom. This was partly prompted by events in the Communist east, most notably the brutal suppression of the Hungarian uprising in 1956. This had finally led the PSI in Italy to break its alliance with the Communist Party, and its leader Nenni thereafter became an eloquent advocate of a more participatory democracy, based on the liberty of the individual.[101] But freedom was also a term that conveyed wider cultural and political meanings, indicating the wish of Socialist parties to break away from austerity and collectivism. Thus, for example, the new party programme published by the Dutch Partij van de Arbeid in 1951 was entitled *De Weg naar Vrijheid*—The way to freedom—intended to express a future-oriented vision of socialism.[102] However, as this programme and the one subsequently adopted by the SPD at Bad Godesberg both demonstrated, this ambition continued to be conceived of as a freedom provided by the state—most obviously in terms of material prosperity and comprehensive welfare provision—which was in turn guaranteed by it. Only the actions of what the SPD termed "a truly civilized state"—a *Kulturstaat*—could provide the path to the achievement of socialism, and a full democracy.[103]

---

99. K. Fertikh, "Le 'nouvel ordre' du programme de Bad Godesberg: Sociologie d'une construction sociale de l'économie," *Lien social et politiques* 72 (2014): 39–56.

100. SPD, *Basic Programme of the Social Democratic Party of Germany*, reproduced in Miller and Potthoff, *German Social Democracy*, 275; Buton, *Histoire intellectuelle*, 153–54. The same formula is used in Depreux, *Renouvellement du socialisme*, 32.

101. See, for example, Nenni's speech to the PSI Congress in Naples, 15 January 1959, reproduced in Nenni, *Socialismo nella democrazia*, 49–73, esp. 52–53; *Nenni, Bevan, Mendès-France*, 58; De Grand, *Italian Left*, 126–30.

102. Bank, "Theorie van de vernieuwing," 120–21.

103. T.L.M. Thurlings, "Waar staat het hedendaagse socialisme?" *De Economist* 100 (1952): 641–55; SPD, *Basic Programme*, 276–77 (quotation); Shell, *Transformation of Austrian Socialism*, 256–59.

Socialist thinking about democracy seemed to be caught in an eternal loop, as indicated by François Mitterrand's bland statement, when launching the programme of the new Parti socialiste in France in 1972, that "socialism is the accomplishment of democracy" (le socialisme est l'accomplissement de la démocratie).[104] More innovative ideas circulated outside of policy-making circles; but the wider ambition of the "extension of democracy," often voiced by socialist intellectuals in the post-war years, remained a remote goal, and one hindered by the Socialists' commitment to the frameworks of parliamentary and municipal democracy, and their more immediate goals of the delivery of economic growth and social reforms.[105] This was not, however, a shortcoming specific to the Socialist parties. Christian Democratic programmes too had become by the end of the 1950s digests of policy initiatives and infrastructure programmes, often lacking a wider purpose.[106] In that sense, democracy had become for Socialist and Christian Democrats alike more a method of governance than an objective to be achieved. The complexities inherent to modern government, as well as the technical nature of the economic and social problems that governments sought to address, pushed to the margins of political debate the larger question of what a democracy should be.

Dialectical history is perhaps rightly unfashionable. Nevertheless, the notion that post-war European democracy developed out of the competition between Socialist and Christian Democratic definitions of the term contains a certain truth. The democracy that they made was more than the sum of the two principal parts that composed it. In its inspiration, and more especially in its construction over the roughly twenty years following the Second World War, the Western European conception of democracy melded together ideas and techniques that derived from both of these political ideologies. In doing so, it brought within the

104. F. Mitterrand, "Présentation," in *Changer la vie: Programme de gouvernement du Parti socialiste* (Paris, 1972), 23. See also Mitterrand, *Rose au poing*, 28.

105. See, for example, the somewhat pious hopes expressed in M. Young, "Problems Ahead," in *Socialism: The British Way* (London, 1948), 342–45. See also Socialist Union, *New Statement of Principles*, 24–46.

106. See, for example, PSC, *Documents introductifs XIVe Congrès national du PSC, Ypres 13-14-15 mars 1959* (Brussels, 1959); Kreichbaumer, *Zwischen Land und Bund*, 127.

democratic camp the two principal political traditions that remained standing after the destructive conflicts of the war years. This construction of a common, or shared, democratic space did not make democracy a neutral formula: Western European democracy remained strongly marked both by its anti-communism, and by its distrust of other democratic models. But the Socialist and Christian Democratic contest for ownership of democracy had, by the end of the 1950s, undoubtedly become more akin to a collaboration. While the dictates of electoral rivalry at both the national and more local levels remained, this competition lacked the harder edges of mutual antipathy and ideological disagreement. Democracy, as its critics increasingly complained, was becoming by the late 1950s a self-contained game, in which the new techniques of advertising and opinion polling were deployed by the major political parties to try to gain a marginal electoral advantage over their opponents.[107]

This dissatisfaction with the limits of democracy, and more especially with the perceived absence of a more substantive spirit of democratic debate, became ever more vocal during the 1960s. However, its origins were more profound than simply the actions of the major political parties. Socialists and Christian Democrats did indeed share a vested interest in the democratic process, as it had taken shape in the years since the war, and neither showed any substantive interest in the possibility of radical reform. They were not, however, unique in this regard. Indeed, much of the explanation of the success of democracy as a political system in Western Europe lay in the way in which it drew into its processes a wide range of actors—state officials, technicians, trade unionists, and employers, among many others. In addition, however, there were the people. The focus in this chapter has been largely on the party-political elites. But there is another story, which is that of the gradual population—one might be tempted to say colonization—of the democratic structures by the people. Kept at a careful distance from the process of regime construction after the war, the people were subsequently allowed into the democratic process as voters and as citizens, and as they did so they adapted it to their needs. Like the new blocks of

107. See, for example, J. Habermas, *The Structural Transformation of the Public Sphere: An Inquiry into a Category of Bourgeois Society* (Cambridge, UK, 1989). The wider mood of dissatisfaction with the limits of post-war democracy is discussed in chapter five; see pp. 262–69.

apartments and suburban houses that multiplied on the edges of European towns and cities in the post-war years, so democracy changed its appearance and content once it was populated by the people. It is to this story—that of the consumption of democracy—that we shall turn in the next chapter.

CHAPTER FOUR

Living Democracy

STATE POWER, CLASS, GENDER, AND THE CONSUMPTION OF DEMOCRACY

THE DEMOCRACY OF the post-war era was always about much more than politics. The perceived failures of the interwar years that hung so heavily over the project of democracy-building after 1945 suggested that democracy could not be simply a political system. It also had to be a way of managing social conflicts, of building communities at all levels of society, and of providing employment and housing, as well as of creating new ways of living, and of living together. These goals were ambitious, but not utopian. They rested on the assumption that the construction of a stable democratic politics in Europe would not be achieved overnight, or by the stroke of a legislative pen. It would be a longer-term process, which would take place over a couple of generations and would require the fostering of democracy as a way of life among political leaders and state officials as well as among citizens. Above all, the commitment of the people to democracy could not be assumed; instead, it had to be fostered by encouraging Europeans to un-learn the bad habits of their past, and by encouraging new attitudes to citizenship in the population in general, and more especially among the young. Writing at the end of the war, the Danish university professor Hal Koch captured well the new spirit of a democracy that would be about more than politics, declaring that "the essence of democracy is characterized not by voting, but . . . by developing a sense of respect for the common interests of the community."[1]

---

1. Quoted in Jakobsen, "Inventions and Developments," 320. See also p. 137.

It is this broader conception of democracy that gives the decades after 1945 their wider character. Democracy was not so much a political structure as a project of a new model of society. Thus, the re-establishment of democratic constitutions in Europe at the end of the war was regarded, almost universally, as only a beginning; it had to be supplemented by a more substantial process of democratic transformation, which would bring about what another Danish writer, Alf Ross, termed "the Democratic Way of Life."[2] Especially in retrospect, this wider goal has tended to be seen in tacitly radical terms: expectations that the war would lead to a more egalitarian society through reforms to systems of education, health, and welfare were frustrated by the resurgence of more conservative forces as well as by the Cold War.[3] This, however, was only one aspect of the project of democracy-building after 1945. Moreover, equality was on the whole less important than universalization. Through the creation of a democratic citizenry, all of whom possessed the same rights and a common mentality, the states of Europe would achieve what Ross termed "psychological democracy."[4]

The building of this democratic culture was a longer and more complex process than the political changes that followed the Second World War. Many Europeans had, of course, long regarded themselves as democratic, albeit not always in ways that accorded with the preferences of their rulers. For many others, however, especially those who had experienced only the fascist and authoritarian regimes of the recent past, democracy was initially less a matter of conviction than a new form of conformism, imposed by military defeat and foreign conquest. For these Europeans, there was no sudden conversion to democracy. Instead, what happened in the roughly twenty-five-year period from the end of the war to the late 1960s is perhaps best regarded as a process of gradual acculturation. At different speeds and by different paths, a large majority of Western Europeans came to feel at home in democracy, and began to practise democracy for themselves.

This evolution was based on a gradual but nonetheless real change in values. The Allied victory in 1945 marked not only the demise of a certain authoritarian politics, but also of forms of thought and of behaviour that had remained prevalent in many areas of European society over the previous decades. In particular, the society that emerged in Europe after the

2. A. Ross, "What Is Democracy?" 55–57.
3. Eley, *Forging Democracy*, 287–91.
4. A. Ross, "What Is Democracy?" 55.

Second World War was less formal and hierarchical in its social mores. Notions of the natural hierarchies of race, class, age, and gender that had long formed part of the way in which many Europeans interacted with the world around them did not disappear, but they did recede. Authority and deference were replaced by new forms of social interaction, ways of living, and by a new emphasis on democratic forms of social behaviour and language, often associated rather superficially with American values.[5] Europeans behaved towards one another in a newly democratic way. At the same time, however, these ideas of civic universalism—expressed most obviously in the acceptance of female suffrage in those societies where it had not formerly prevailed—were accompanied by a need for restraint and respect for the rule of law. The new spirit of liberty in 1945 was always rather carefully and firmly limited. The constitutions, legal systems, and other reforms of the post-war era brought new freedoms for many Europeans, but they were also more tangibly constrained by a wider culture of governance and education that prioritized values of obedience and social responsibility. Europeans might be freer, but they were also required to be better behaved.

This was most evident in the centrality assumed by the state in the lives of its citizens. The post-war reassertion of the modern hierarchy of government, by which directives descended forcefully from the centre while the petitions of communities and of individuals ascended rather less readily in the opposite direction, did much to define the character of post-war democracy. The states of Western Europe were primarily governed democracies, in which the rapid expansion in the financial, technical, and human resources of the state and the assertion of its privileged status above the other institutions of society limited the collective and individual independence of citizens. Thus, while the state was the provider and facilitator of many new benefits to the population, it was also emphatically their ruler.

Nor did the constraints on freedom come only from the managerial ambitions of the state. There was a conservative, even conformist, character to daily life in the 1950s, as reflected in the definition of gendered social roles, the primacy accorded to the family, and to explicit and implicit codes of moral rectitude. This narrowing of the permitted margins of behaviour owed much to the actions of the state and of those social institutions, such as the churches, that regarded themselves as the arbiters of social norms;

5. R. J. Pulju, *Women and Mass Consumer Society in Postwar France* (Cambridge, UK, 2011), 155–57; B. Bonomo, "Dwelling Space and Social Identities: The Roman Bourgeoisie, c. 1950–80," *Urban History* 38 (2011): 285–98.

but they came also from within European society. Whether as a result
of the pervasive trauma of the war years, or of wider trends inherent to
modern societies, Europeans appeared eager to retreat into the cultivation
of the private, the domestic, and the personal.[6] The frequently stated
desire after the war to return lives and the fabric of society to "normal" was
always somewhat double-edged.[7] Normality meant an end to the exceptionalism of wartime and the manifold forms of state duress, large and
small, caused by the mobilization of citizens in the service of the nation, as
well as the rediscovery of forms of private freedom symbolized by the emotional importance attached to the return to the home and the reunification
of families. But it also implied an end to the anarchic freedoms and forms
of licence that had developed as a consequence of the disruptions of wartime. There was a wish to rein in the perceived permissiveness of the war
years, which manifested itself through the reassertion of norms of behaviour, and of the hierarchies of generation and of gender. But it continued
too into the post-war decades. Unmarried mothers, disruptive teenagers,
homosexual men and women, the mentally ill, and immigrants with different social customs were all groups for whom the freedom of the post-war
years was often constrained by a lack of wider societal tolerance.[8]

The new democracies were therefore more equal in their formal structures than in their social reality. The reassertion of boundaries of race, gender, sexuality, and age, after the more fluid and often chaotic experiences
of the war years, was reinforced by the evolving but persistent inequalities of social class. Western Europe emphatically remained a class society
after 1945. The rapid economic growth that occurred during the post-war
years generated new forms of affluence, but these were distributed in ways
that reinforced pre-existing class divisions. In particular, the post-war
years witnessed a resurgence in the fortunes of the middle class. Whether
assessed in terms of its material prosperity, its influence within and over
government, or its wider social and cultural ascendancy, the middle class
was the dominant social class of the post-war era. The economy, political
life, and the resources of the state were all aligned in ways that served
the interests of the middle class, which itself was expanding and changing as a consequence of processes of economic and social modernization.
Other groups, too, benefited from these changes. In particular, in much

---

6. Judt, *Postwar*, 256, 275–77.

7. Chapman, *France's Long Reconstruction*, 2; Pulju, *Women*, 3.

8. This constraint and the closing down of acceptable forms of behaviour was especially
apparent in West Germany. See, for example, D. Herzog, *Sex after Fascism: Memory and
Morality in Twentieth-Century Germany* (Princeton, NJ, 2005), 101–40.

of Western Europe the reform of agricultural production after 1945 led to a rapid fall in rural populations and to the creation of a more prosperous farming class, protected by national and subsequently European forms of financial assistance and trade barriers. Conversely, the workers of Europe bore the brunt of the far-reaching technological and economic transformations of the post-war decades. Some proved able to take advantage of these changes, while many others found their skills to be redundant or their working conditions to have been eroded. The much-expanded social-welfare structures of the post-war era mitigated to some extent the impact of these swings in fortune for individuals and families. But the welfare system, too, reflected the inequalities of post-war Europe by reinforcing particular models of family organization and tying certain benefits, such as pensions, to income. Thus, welfare was always more about security than equality, acting as a shock absorber against misfortune while respecting the structural inequalities of the wider society.

Democracy in post-war Europe therefore always had a defined social shape, which constrained participation in it. Nevertheless, the decades after 1945 do stand out as the period when millions of Western Europeans felt that they were freer than they had ever been. This sentiment had much to do with the wider demobilization that accompanied the arrival of peace; but it also reflected the way that many Europeans felt more able to make choices about their lives, in the private and public spheres. In doing so, they became accustomed to the new democratic norms, and to adapt them within their own lives. This sense of "being democratic" was far from entirely new. Ever since the nineteenth century, many Europeans had been exposed to democracy, sometimes as enfranchised citizens, but more tangibly through their membership of trade unions, economic organizations, and the other associations of civil society.[9] This gathered pace during the interwar years, initially through the inauguration of new democratic constitutions but also through the rapid expansion in mass movements. Coupled with the development of new forms of economic consumerism, this created new spaces for the social practice of democracy. As a consequence, Europeans—especially the majority who were also women—were becoming democrats in their daily lives even as in national politics parliamentary regimes were being replaced (often through democratic votes)

9. R. Price, *People and Politics in France, 1848–70* (Cambridge, UK, 2004); P. Nord, *The Republican Moment: Struggles for Democracy in Nineteenth-Century France* (Cambridge, MA, 1995), esp. 5–14; G. Morton, B. de Vries, and R. J. Morris, eds., *Civil Society, Associations and Urban Places: Class, Nation and Culture in Nineteenth-Century Europe* (Aldershot, UK, 2006).

by authoritarian and fascist regimes.[10] The dichotomy that this created between state authoritarianism and the daily habits of democracy was an underlying feature of the dictatorships of the 1930s and the war years. Europeans—as in the case of Nazi Germany—often seemed disconcertingly willing to abandon the freedom to engage in democratic politics, but they were much less willing to surrender more personal and immediate freedoms: to dress how they wanted, to listen to the music they liked, and to choose how (and with whom) they lived their lives. This almost instinctual reluctance to surrender individual freedoms and preferences for the sake of state-defined goals was generally unpolitical, and could indeed coexist with sympathy for some variant of authoritarian politics. But it reflected the way in which Europeans had become accustomed to making decisions for themselves, and among themselves.[11]

This gap between the social practice and the political reality of democracy narrowed after 1945, but it did not disappear. For most Europeans, it was the former—the democracy of their daily lives—that was more immediately important to them. The denial of individual choices during the state controls of wartime gave way to a somewhat anarchic mood of hedonism as Europeans caught up with the opportunity to be free.[12] More durably, however, the determination of many Europeans to live their own lives—a phenomenon often referred to by the somewhat problematic term of "individualism"—contributed powerfully to the way in which democratic norms embedded themselves in Western European societies during the subsequent decades. Europeans had not, for the most part, chosen democracy in any meaningful sense after the war, except in the way in which many central Europeans voted with their feet by leaving territories under Soviet control. But the somewhat formal character of post-war democracy matched the disabused mood of populations who were for the most part less concerned with serving the state or influencing its political projects than with ensuring that the state was willing to address their needs and otherwise leave them alone.

10. S. Reynolds, *France between the wars: Gender and Politics* (London, 1996), 204–21; B. Lieberman, *From Recovery to Catastrophe: Municipal Stabilization and Political Crisis in Weimar Germany* (New York, 1998), 76–79; J. Sneeringer, *Winning Women's Votes: Propaganda and Politics in Weimar Germany* (Chapel Hill, NC, 2002).

11. I. Kershaw, *Popular Opinion and Political Dissent in the Third Reich: Bavaria 1933–1945*, 2nd ed. (Oxford, 2002), esp. x–xiv; D. Peukert, *Inside Nazi Germany: Conformity, Opposition and Racism in Everyday Life* (London, 1987), 49–174; P. Fritzsche, *Life and Death in the Third Reich* (Cambridge, MA, 2008), 19–75.

12. P. Schrijvers, *Liberators: The Allies and Belgian Society, 1944–1945* (Cambridge, UK, 2009), 42–68.

The truce in relations between rulers and ruled was often fragile. The rulers rarely listened very attentively to their electorates, and in many cases chose to ignore them in the belief that they knew best. Moreover, the momentum of modern state administration caused governments to engage more closely in the regulation of the lives of their citizens than many Europeans would have wished. In domains as diverse as tax administration, public health, building regulations, and employment practices, the expanding resources of local and central government enabled much closer administration of citizens than had previously been the case. In the longer term, this sense of an enduring gap between Europeans and their rulers—the language of "us" and "them" that recurred in popular discourse and attitudes[13]—contributed to the political tensions that came to the fore during the 1960s, as well as to the language of hostility to politics and to the political class that emerged from the 1970s onwards.[14] But little of this was apparent in the immediate post-war years. Europeans did not welcome state interference in their lives, and often exploited informal means of circumventing it. In an ideal world, many would probably have preferred to be left alone by government, but they also recognized the material benefits that the state brought to them, their families, and their communities. Especially in the years of post-war reconstruction, the state appeared to provide more than it took, blunting popular resentment of state control, and encouraging a temporary armistice in the long-running conflicts between public institutions and their citizens. Each, it seemed, had come to accept the existence of the other, and this too contributed to the democratic stabilization identified by Aron.[15]

<hr/>

At the outset, however, democracy was emphatically about government. As de Gaulle put it with characteristic forcefulness on his arrival in newly liberated Paris in 1944, his task was to ensure "Republican order under the control of the only valid authority, that of the state"—l'ordre républicain sous la seule autorité valable, celle de l'Etat.[16] Few other post-war rulers would have put it so bluntly, but their actions suggested they believed de Gaulle to be correct. Legitimized from below by the democratic

13. L. Wylie, *Village in the Vaucluse*, 3rd ed. (Cambridge, MA, 1974), 206–10; Allum, *Politics and Society*, 93–100.

14. Chiarini, "Antipolitica in Italia," 13–16. See also pp. 302–3.

15. Raymond Aron, "Institutions politiques de l'occident," 11–15.

16. Quoted in Andrieu, "CNR," 73.

mandate of its citizens and from above by its responsibility for the defence of the nation, the state was an institution quite literally in a class of its own. It was the provider of security, welfare, and education, the agent of economic prosperity, the constructor of transport networks and public buildings, the arbiter of social conflicts, and the indefatigable administrator of many aspects of daily life from the collection of taxes and the regulation of commercial businesses to the registration of cars, and people. So much of this activity might now appear natural that it is worth emphasizing that much of it was also novel. States had done much hitherto, but never on such a scale and with such thoroughness. Indeed, compared with the well-ordered and at times almost invisible authority of the state in post-war Europe, the often chaotic and overstretched structures of power that characterized the communist and fascist states of the preceding decades appear to have had something of the character of an improvisation.[17]

The rapid expansion in state power was the dominant fact of the post-war age. Between 1950 and 1973, government spending rose from 27.6 to 38.8 per cent of the gross domestic product in France, and from 30.4 to 42 per cent in West Germany.[18] Exceptionally for a period without major wars, the share of national income taken by the state in the form of taxation rose steadily in Western Europe across the post-1945 decades, generating a new culture of state prosperity. There were still rich people and institutions in Europe, but the wealthiest of them all was the state.[19] This enabled the state to do more—most obviously in the field of welfare—but also to employ more people. The state became the dominant employer, generating millions of manual and administrative posts and drawing in a large proportion of the new generations of skilled graduates emerging from higher education.[20]

This conquest of European society, in the west and—it should be remembered—even more dramatically in the east, was all the more remarkable given the weakness of state authority in many areas of Europe around the point of liberation. The de facto collapse of the power of state institutions to control what took place on their territory in the mid-1940s

17. See, for example, Y. Gorlizki and H. Mommsen, "The Political (Dis)Orders of Stalinism and National Socialism," in *Beyond Totalitarianism: Stalinism and Nazism Compared*, ed. M. Geyer and S. Fitzpatrick (Cambridge, UK, 2009), 41–86.

18. Judt, *Postwar*, 361.

19. F. Lynch, "Harmonization through Competition?: The Evolution of Taxation in Post-War Europe," in *Global Debates about Taxation*, ed. H. Nehring and F. Schui (Basingstoke, UK, 2007), 116, 126.

20. Judt, *Postwar*, 360–62; Finer, *Major Governments*, 1–2.

was, of course, most emphatic in the defeated states; but it extended too to liberated territories from Norway to Greece, where governmental authority and a more generalized culture of obedience to the state had to be restitched into the patterns of daily life.[21] However, the post-war expansion in the resources and reach of the state was also the continuation of trends that stretched back to at least the First World War, and had given rise to the projects of state reform and modernization undertaken during the 1930s. In part, these initiatives had provided the inspiration for the New Order regimes of the war years, notably in Vichy France; and their legacy was all the more apparent in the speed and energy with which a cohort of technically minded bureaucrats set about planning and subsequently implementing projects of reform at the end of the war.[22] A continuity of innovative ideas, derived variously from the New Deal in the United States, wartime campaigns (in both the Allied and Axis camps), and American-led projects of post-war reconstruction, above all the Marshall Plan, created a new confidence among state bureaucrats as well as among a wide range of non-Marxist intellectuals, that the state alone had the capacity and the ideas to act as the comprehensive problem-solver for modern society.[23]

In the immediate post-war years, this dramatic forward march in state power appeared predominantly to be in conflict with democracy.[24] The repressive force of the police (and in extremis the military) in imposing a state-defined order on independently minded populations took power away from people and invested it in a state authority that in its structures and mentality was consciously impervious to popular demands. Nor did this attitude disappear once the immediate circumstances of liberation had receded. Encouraged by the remobilization brought about by the Cold War, state authorities increased and modernized their security resources, supplementing conventional policing with internal intelligence structures intended to identify and neutralize potential sources of subversion. By the 1950s, this reinforcement of the repressive resources of the state had effectively eliminated not only any possibility of a Communist-inspired seizure of power but also ensured that the regular occurrence of industrial conflict in the post-war years did not acquire the wider social momentum

21. See pp. 37–38.

22. Nord, *France's New Deal*, 98–141. See also the contemporary comments in the collective work by the state officials who constituted the Club Jean Moulin: *L'état et le citoyen* (Paris, 1961), 25–26.

23. Scott-Smith, "Parameters of Discourse," 440–44.

24. This is the principal theme of Chapman, *France's Long Reconstruction*, esp. 2–5.

that in the 1920s and 1930s had overwhelmed the forces of order on the streets of many European cities. For the first time in Europe's modern history, the resources of the state had decisively outstripped those of the people, investing Western European states in most circumstances with a routine ability to control their citizens, and defeat direct challenges to their authority.[25]

The state was, moreover, an increasingly autonomous institution. One of the principal ambitions of the democracy-builders of the immediate post-war years was to create a more hierarchical and efficient state structure that would avoid the politicization, corruption, and consequent inefficiency that it was widely believed had hampered governance across the preceding decades.[26] This implied placing the institutions and, particularly, the personnel of the state at a certain distance from, or more exactly above, society. Rather than being close to the people, the state officials of the post-1945 era aspired to be a separate caste, who by virtue of their elitist education, their technical skills, and their professional responsibilities formed a self-contained world.[27] This mentality was not anti-popular, but their methods and instincts were very different from those of democratic government. Rather than being the courtiers or servants of democratically elected politicians, their self-appointed task was to act as the technical agents of effective government. This implied seeing further, and knowing better, than both elected office-holders and the mass of the people. Majorities, as Michel Debré commented dismissively in 1948, were necessarily conservative;[28] while the responsibility of state bureaucrats such as himself was to understand complex problems and to devise solutions that were beyond the comprehension or abilities of the mass of the people. This was a vision that doubly prioritized the state: most immediately as the defender of order, but also as the agent of change, enacting the radical changes that had proved so difficult to bring about by other means.[29]

25. Mencherini, *Guerre froide, grèves rouges*, esp. 81–85; House and Macmaster, *Paris 1961*; H. Reiter and K. Weinhauer, "Police and Political Violence in the 1960s and 1970s: Germany and Italy in a Comparative Perspective," *European Review of History: Revue européenne d'histoire* 14 (2007): 373–95. See also p. 90.

26. See pp. 64–66.

27. Hitchcock, *France Restored*, 2; Kuisel, *Capitalism and the State*, 255–57; E. Suleiman, *Politics, Power and Bureaucracy in France: The Administrative Elite* (Princeton, NJ, 1974).

28. M. Debré, "La véritable faiblesse de la démocratie" (1–2 September 1948), republished in *République et ses problèmes*, 33–34.

29. V. Spini, *I Socialisti e la politica di Plano (1945–1964)* (Florence, 1982), 7–17.

The problem with these attitudes was that they could become an alibi for a rational authoritarianism. As Pierre Mendès France commented in a speech in 1955, it was all too easy for the state to regard the people as the real obstacle to rational government: "L'Etat," he declared with a characteristic touch of rhetorical exaggeration, "dans son comportement, semble redouter le citoyen, le traiter comme un adversaire, un gêneur, un ennemi."[30] State officials had become an enlightened elite, behaving, as Anton Pelinka ironically observed at the end of the 1960s, according to the precept often attributed to Emperor Joseph II: "Alles für das Volk, nichts durch das Volk" (Everything for the people, nothing by the people).[31] This mentality found its expression in the post-war preoccupation with planning. The exigencies of wartime that had, in effect, separated many state officials, both within Europe and outside, from political control fostered an enthusiasm in state circles for visions of state-led projects of change. Initially focused on the immediate goals of national reconstruction, the methods of planning—of looking beyond the immediate and consciously seeking to shape the future—were subsequently extended to economic policy-making as well as to a wide range of social problems. The urgent needs of housing, the modernization of the transport infrastructure and of energy resources, and the reconversion of sectors of heavy industry—most notably coal and iron—were all domains where in the immediate post-war years state officials found fertile territory for planning the future. They also possessed new skills to do so. The rapid adoption and imitation, throughout Western Europe, of techniques of assembling and analysing data on a wide range of subjects, as well as of predicting future challenges and needs, meant that almost for the first time, the bureaucrats of the post-war years knew what they were doing. These new managerial tools of sophisticated financial management of the economy, statistical analysis, and methods of urban planning were tools that worked. But they all served to distance the planners from the people. They spoke their own language, devised complex budgetary plans, and moved and acted in ministerial bureaucracies and parastatal organizations that were remote from democratic, or still less popular, control.[32]

30. "The state seems in its behaviour to fear the citizen, treating him as an opponent, an obstruction, or an enemy": Mendès France, "Crise de la démocratie," 82.

31. Pelinka and Welan, *Demokratie und Verfassung*, 55. Regarding the origins of the phrase, see notably I. Plattner, "Josephinismus und Bürokratie," in *Josephinismus als Aufgeklärter Absolutismus*, ed. H. Reinalter (Vienna, 2008), 61.

32. Mioche, *Plan Monnet*; Pulju, *Women*, 3–9; J. Foreman-Peck, "European Industrial Policies in the Post-War Boom: 'Planning the Economic Miracle,'" in *Industrial Policy in Europe after 1945: Wealth, Power and Economic Development in the Cold War*, ed. C.

Planning was therefore part of a wider change in the dominant ethos of government. The legal and organic metaphors of the recent past were replaced by a new fashion for those of engineering, which encouraged a pervasive mindset of functionalism, whereby the people were the somewhat abstract objects of solicitude by a well-intentioned army of technicians who had become the necessary agents of progress.[33] Thus, for example, the vast housing programmes of the post-war years were devised and implemented according to carefully designed calculations of the spatial needs of the people, but with little reference to the preferences of those who would live in them. As one official in the rapidly expanding city of Toulouse was reported to have commented in 1957: "Works of urbanism require firmness—history shows this—and one shouldn't become overly agitated at the opposition between public and private interests."[34] Only once the female official placed in charge of housing policy by de Gaulle decided to organize a consultative referendum in 1959 on the design of apartments did the planners discover that the people in fact wanted larger kitchens, in which families could eat together, and bedrooms with greater privacy.[35]

The methods and mindsets of planning were not just an alternative to the transience of political will or popular preferences; they were also, albeit less explicitly, a means of countering market forces. Economic freedom sat rather awkwardly within the culture of post-war democracy. The liberty accorded to citizens to spend their money as they pleased, and in particular to enjoy secure ownership of their property, formed a prominent element of how Western European democracies defined themselves as free, especially in contrast with the Communist east.[36] But the unpredictable tides of market forces, and the way they subordinated the national interest

Grabas and A. Nützenadel (Basingstoke, UK, 2014), 13–47; Lidegaard, *Short History of Denmark*, 206–9.

33. Monnet, *Mémoires*, 280–89; J. Fourastié, *Le grand espoir du XXe siècle: Progrès technique, progrès économique, progrès social* (Paris, 1949), 219–20; L. Frohman, "Population Registration, Social Planning and the Discourse on Privacy Protection in West Germany," *Journal of Modern History* 87 (2015): 316–56.

34. Wakeman, *Modernizing the Provincial City*, 69–110, quotation at 87; S. Fishman, *From Vichy to the Sexual Revolution: Gender and Family Life in Postwar France* (Oxford, 2017), 39–40.

35. W. B. Newsome, "The 'Apartment Referendum' of 1959: Toward Participatory Architectural and Urban Planning in Postwar France," *French Historical Studies* 28 (2005): 329–58.

36. This was perhaps most especially so in West Germany. See E. Carter, *How German Is She?: Postwar West German Reconstruction and the Consuming Woman* (Ann Arbor, MI, 1997), 4–6, 46.

to factors beyond state control, or indeed to an irresponsible and increasingly international cohort of business corporations, provoked widespread unease. The neoliberal belief that became dominant in western societies from the 1970s onwards that market forces provide the most effective and, indeed, the most just means of allocating scarce resources within a free society was almost entirely unvoiced in intellectual circles or, more especially, within the corridors of government during the post-1945 decades. Even among those neoliberal figures, such as Friedrich von Hayek, who in the immediate post-war years asserted the rights to private property and individual freedom in the face of what they regarded as the pervasive notions of socialism and planning, there was a general acceptance that the classical liberalism of the past was dead: competition could operate only within a framework established and guaranteed by an effective but self-limiting state.[37] Market forces therefore needed to be tamed—much like the many rivers turned to constructive purpose by the hydroelectric schemes of the post-war years.[38] As Herman Finer argued in his response to Hayek's wartime polemic in 1946, no government could abandon the resolution of social and economic problems to "the competitive system . . . irredeemably caught in the dark tangled wood of its own egoisms, hostilities, frictions and rigidities."[39]

Such language, and the emotions it conveyed, was of course a legacy of the Great Depression of the 1930s, responsibility for which was widely believed to have rested with the selfish actions of industrial and financial groups, exacerbated by the inaction of the state authorities and central banks. In response, a new transnational world of experts had appeared, often out of the legacies of the institutions of the League of Nations, possessed of new tools of economic and financial planning, and determined to pre-empt any return to the fatalism of the past.[40] These officials, and the international institutions that they populated after the war, would work with state officials, financial elites, and an increasingly technocratic

37. D. Plehwe, introduction to *The Road from Mont Pèlerin: The Making of the Neoliberal Thought Collective*, ed. P. Mirowski and Plehwe (Cambridge, MA, 2009), 21–26; Forner, *German Intellectuals*, 87–91; B. Jackson, "At the Origins of Neo-Liberalism: The Free Economy and the Strong State, 1930–1947," *Historical Journal* 53 (2010): 129–51.

38. Re. the cult of hydroelectric power in post-war Scandinavia, both as reality and as metaphor, see the perceptive comments in F. Sejersted, *The Age of Social Democracy: Norway and Sweden in the Twentieth Century* (Princeton, NJ, 2011), 217–18.

39. Finer, *Road to Reaction*, 130–31. See also T. Judt, *Ill Fares the Land: A Treatise on Our Present Discontents* (New York, 2010), 55–63.

40. P. Clavin, *Securing the World Economy: The Reinvention of the League of Nations, 1920–1946* (Oxford, 2013), esp. 1–10, 341–59.

cadre of managers of industrial enterprises to direct the engine of economic growth.[41] As a Swedish Social Democrat, Gunnar Adler-Karlsson, put it in 1967: "All the parties of the economic process have realized that the most important economic task is to make the national cake grow bigger and bigger; because then everyone can satisfy his demanding stomach with a greater piece of that common cake."[42] The pursuit of this common economic purpose—what French planners termed an *économie concertée*—certainly did not imply the abolition of free enterprise. Rather, this capitalist freedom would be both essential and relative. It provided the necessary stimulus of business competition and the means by which consumers made choices as to which vacuum cleaner or radio to buy; but it should not dictate how states determined their economic priorities.[43]

As this assertion of the state over market forces indicates, government was, according to the logic of the times, best directed from above: a "Demokratie von oben," to quote Pelinka again,[44] conducted in a sphere that lay above public opinion or the lobbying of particular interest groups. This manifested itself in the energy that political and bureaucratic elites invested in the construction of institutions of European cooperation in the two decades following the Second World War. The rather sudden transformation of Europe from an arena of diplomatic and military rivalry to one of economic cooperation undoubtedly constituted one of the most striking features of the post-war era.[45] In part, this change reflected the exhaustion of national antipathies, and the understandable wish of Europe's post-war leaders to get beyond the narrow nationalism that they believed had been the underlying cause of the successive wars of Europe's recent history. However, this new-found enthusiasm for European collaboration also had other attractions. In particular, it provided a new screen upon which state officials, politicians, and business figures could project their visions of a future of integration and modernization. It was this rather flexible potentiality of Europe that explains the enthusiasm and energy that developed around the multiple plans for European integration in the later 1940s, primarily across the borderlands of

41. Re. the often-overlooked world of private-sector managers, see notably F. Denord, "Les idéologies économiques du patronat français au 20e siècle," *Vingtième Siècle* 114 (April–June 2012): 171–82.

42. Berman, *Primacy of Politics*, 184.

43. Carter, *How German Is She?* 48–50; Nicholls, *Freedom with Responsibility*, 390–92. Re. consumers, see p. 245.

44. Pelinka and Welan, *Demokratie und Verfassung*, 55.

45. W. Kaiser, B. Leucht, and M. Rasmussen, eds., *The History of the European Union: Origins of a Trans- and Supranational Polity 1950–72* (New York, 2009).

north-western Europe.[46] A logjam in transnational cooperation appeared to have been broken after 1945, enabling the implementation of policies that were impossible to bring to fruition within the more-contested structures of national politics. By evacuating complex dossiers of industrial reform and of support for agriculture from the national political arena to a higher level of interstate decision-making, European integration appeared to offer a means of addressing these issues through the rational principles of economic planning, insulated from the pressure of vested interests.

This was especially so for the predominantly Christian Democratic leaders of Western Europe in the 1950s. By temperament and conviction, they saw in the emergent institutions of Europe a model of post-war reconciliation, and of consciously moderate policy-making, which responded to their political aspirations. In that sense, they became—and in retrospect were keen to present themselves as—convinced Europeans. This espousal of Europe was, however, also for them a matter of calculation. In particular, they recognized the advantages, both for their parties and for their nations, in pooling their resources within a new infrastructure of European institutions.[47] Thus, although the emergence of this transnational sphere of decision-making eroded national sovereignty, it also provided a new means of buttressing the practices of the state authorities, by enabling European political elites and state bureaucrats to resolve problems across nation-state boundaries.[48]

What was less clear, as we have already seen in chapter two, was whether such practices of European decision-making were in any sense democratic. European integration served many purposes after 1945, but the sovereignty of the people was not foremost among them. Indeed, by reinforcing a sphere of governance remote from electoral pressure or effective democratic sanction, the EEC and its satellite institutions served to diminish further the powers of national parliaments, and by extension of the voters. But that is not how it tended to be seen at the time. The signing of the Treaty of Rome in 1957 had relied on a rather fragile political conjuncture, in which the ascendancy of a group of like-minded Christian Democratic leaders was an important element.[49] Over the subsequent

46. V. Dujardin and M. Dumoulin, *Jean-Charles Snoy: Homme dans la cité, artisan de l'Europe* (Brussels, 2010), 221–50.

47. P. Pasture, "Catholic and Christian Democratic Views on Europe before and after World War II," in *Christian Democracy across the Iron Curtain: Europe Redefined*, ed. P. Kosicki and S. Lukasiewicz (n.p., 2018), 25–55.

48. A. Milward, *The European Rescue of the Nation-State* (London, 1992).

49. See notably Kaiser, *Christian Democracy*, 191–252.

years, however, European integration gained increasingly broad political support, within and without the frontiers of its founding states. Part of its appeal was pragmatic: as a manifesto of a reform-minded group of French Socialists declared in 1965, the European institutions provided the best means of countering the dictatorship of market forces, and carrying out effective policies of social reform.[50] But it also rested on the conviction widely shared among many political figures of the 1950s and 1960s that the project of European integration was in itself an expression of democracy. As the Austrian Socialists, the SPÖ, commented in a phrase in 1958 that would become a commonplace in European political rhetoric over the subsequent years, they were committed to the "Schaffung der demokratischen Gemeinschaft der Vereinigten Staaten von Europa."[51]

The problem with these optimistic formulations of the democratic character of a unified Europe was that they were, quite literally, adjectival. The newly bonded union of the EEC—which, it must be recalled, comprised only a minority of the democratic states of Western Europe prior to its expansion in the 1970s—was assumed to be democratic simply because its constituent states were democratic. There was therefore no attempt to import democratic practices into the European institutions; on the contrary, they became a focus for the energies of successive generations of reform-minded officials, for whom the partially depoliticized and denationalized culture of government of the European institutions offered the prospect of rational decision-making removed from the distortions generated by national interests and popular pressures. The embodiment of such attitudes was Jean Monnet, who migrated in the 1950s from his work on the French Plan to a larger stage as the head of the new European Coal and Steel Community (ECSC). His speech at the inauguration of the ECSC in Luxembourg in August 1952 well expressed this mentality, declaring that "Nous exercerons nos fonctions, en pleine indépendance, dans l'intérêt général de la Communauté [i.e., the ECSC]. Dans l'accomplissement de nos devoirs, nous ne solliciterons nous n'accepterons d'instruction d'aucun gouvernement ni d'aucun organisme et nous nous abstiendrons de tout acte incompatible avec le caractère supranational de nos fonctions."[52]

50. Bruclain, *Socialisme et l'Europe*, 103–36. Bruclain was a pseudonym for a collective of younger Socialists.

51. "The creation of the democratic community of the United States of Europe": [SPÖ], "Neue Parteiprogramm," 290. See also pp. 143–45.

52. "We will exercise our functions in full independence, and in the general interest of the Community. In undertaking these responsibilities, we will neither seek nor accept instructions from any government or organization, and we will avoid engaging in

Consequently, the European institutions of the 1950s and 1960s tended to replicate, in a more exaggerated form, the patterns of bureaucratic rule evident at the national level. The logics of rationalization, modernization, and integration that dominated European decision-making from the formation of the ECSC onwards rested on a culture of experts who, as a consequence of their vantage point above nation-state boundaries, felt confident in their ability to act independently of vested interests.[53] Like all such legitimizing ideologies, this notion of the technocratic neutrality of European governance was of course largely a myth. National interests retained a powerful influence over European decision-making; and, just as power migrated from the national to the European level, so too did the actions of interest groups, for whom the new transnational institutions often became more reliable conduits for sectional lobbying than did national parliaments. But the image of the European institutions, powerfully expressed through the self-conscious modernity of the concrete buildings built to house them in Brussels, was emphatically of a new culture of government, in which disorderly democratic practices had been replaced by the edifice of rational administration.[54]

Unsurprisingly, therefore, the British Marxist academic Ralph Miliband was able to begin his critique of the role of the state in an advanced capitalist society, published in 1969, with the emphatic statement that "more than ever before, men live in the shadow of the state. . . . It is to an ever greater degree the state which men encounter as they confront other men."[55] As a consequence of this enormous and irreversible growth in state power, Miliband argued that citizens had ceased to be the masters of their own affairs. Except on those exceptional days when they were called upon to vote for their elected representatives, the people were not so much the sovereign body of Rousseauian dreams, as the managed subjects of a state authority that no individual could afford either to ignore or to challenge.[56] The state had become an unavoidable real-

any actions incompatible with the supranational character of our functions": Monnet, *Mémoires*, 438–39. See also K. Schwabe, *Jean Monnet: Frankreich, die Deutschen und die Einigung Europas* (Baden-Baden, 2016), 261–63.

53. W. Kaiser and J. Schot, *Writing the Rules for Europe: Experts, Cartels and International Organizations* (Basingstoke, UK, 2014), 1–19.

54. J. Habermas, *The Lure of Technocracy* (Cambridge, UK, 2015), 3.

55. R. Miliband, *The State in Capitalist Society* (London, 1969), 1. See also the almost contemporary comments of Félix Ponteil in *Les bourgeois et la démocratie sociale 1914–1968* (Paris, 1971), 401.

56. Re. the concept of the managed, see Wegs and Ladrech, *Europe since 1945*, 158–80.

ity in people's lives, assuming efficient responsibility for many tasks that communities had formerly done rather less efficiently by themselves, or which had not been done at all. This functional dynamic by which the modernization of Europe's socio-economic structures generated an ever-increasing need for the administrative and problem-solving capacities of the state changed Europeans' attitudes to the state, and also their understanding of democracy. The executive authority of the state had expanded far beyond effective control by the people's elected representatives, either national or local, creating instead a state-oriented political culture in which individuals, communities, and interest groups clustered around the institutions of the state bureaucracy.[57] This was perhaps most evident in rural areas, where the post-war invasion of state services brought rural communities into a much more direct relationship with the state and its officials. Electricity, new roads, and schools, as well as subsidies for agricultural production, were all resources that rural notables could win for their communities through timely lobbying.[58] But this culture of negotiation with the representatives of the state was effectively universal, as trade unions, industrial organizations, professional bodies, churches, charities, and voluntary associations were all drawn towards the state as a consequence of the resources it possessed, as well as its wider ability through legislation and administrative measures to set the terms of economic and social life.

This gave rise to a widespread sense that the very nature of democracy had changed. The crisis of the Fourth Republic in France, Léo Hamon observed in a perceptive piece of instant history published in 1958, arose from the way in which the political parties had remained wedded to a parliamentary conception of democracy, denying the state the freedom of action demanded in a modern society.[59] Elsewhere, however, the parties had come to recognize the need to subordinate their partisan interests to the wider purpose of a state-led democracy. The adversarial electoral politics of times past, when some parties had been in government and others were in opposition, appeared to have been replaced by what the influential Dutch political scientist of the 1960s Arend Lijphart termed "consociational democracy." According to Lijphart, the modern business of government had in effect become a "grand coalition," whereby everybody had a share of power, and democratic politics consisted of negotiation between

---

57. Habermas, *Structural Transformation*, esp. 179–80. Re. Habermas, see also p. 262.

58. Sarti, *Long Live the Strong*, 238–39; Wylie, *Village in the Vaucluse*, 223–27.

59. Hamon, *De Gaulle*, 22–24.

elites representing the different elements of segmented and plural societies.[60] The danger, however, as Lijphart admitted, was that the very complexity of this machinery of negotiation would result in immobilism, and even disaffection from a democratic process seemingly unresponsive to public opinion. "We vote," as one disabused citizen of Naples commented to an interviewer in 1963, "but nobody ever changed anything with his vote."[61] Many Europeans, one suspects, would have heartily agreed; but voting was only one means by which citizens could make their views felt. The states of post-war Western Europe had become complex entities—and the object of study by a developing discipline of political scientists—composed of overlapping bodies, and susceptible to lobbying by a wide range of interest and pressure groups.[62] Consequently, the practice of democracy became less a matter of counting the votes cast by citizens at elections or by their representatives in parliament than a more opaque process of negotiation and rivalry between corporate bodies, which took place around the perimeter of the state. Politicians, local and national, campaigned for causes and constituents; local councils and communities pressed for the state to channel its resources in their direction; and interest groups of every kind sought to influence the state's powers of legislation and regulation.[63]

State policy-making consequently often took a crooked path. The idea that government had become a "technocracy," whereby power was concentrated in the hands of a caste of professional officials at the expense of the people and their representatives, was often voiced from the end of the 1950s onwards.[64] However, it only ever expressed a partial truth. The shape of government had indeed changed, at the expense notably of parliaments, which increasingly came to be seen as secondary institutions lacking in any real decision-making power.[65] But the state remained per-

60. Lijphart, "Typologies of Democratic Systems," 76–80; A. Lijphart, *Democracy in Plural Societies: A Comparative Explanation* (New Haven, CT, 1977), 25–52.

61. Allum, *Politics and Society*, 94.

62. J. Meynaud, *Les groupes de pression en France* (Paris, 1958), esp. 345–56; Finer, *Major Governments*, 2–3, 9–10; R. Ruffieux, "Quelques approximations sur l'éthique chez Jean Meynaud," in *Jean Meynaud ou l'utopie revisitée: Actes du colloque tenu à l'Université de Lausanne les 25 et 26 septembre 1986* (Lausanne, 1988), 359–69. See also the elaborate and illuminating diagrams of the pressures on state decision-making provided in P. Allum, *State and Society in Western Europe* (Cambridge, 1995), 10–16.

63. M. Fulbrook, *Germany 1918–1990: The Divided Nation* (London, 1991), 254–56; Forlenza, "Party for the Mezzogiorno," 335–43.

64. See, for example, J. Mandrin, *L'énarchie ou les mandarins de la société bourgeoise*, 2nd ed. (Paris, 1980), 103–11.

65. Ponteil, *Bourgeois et la démocratie sociale*, 402.

meable all the same to a wide range of influences and interests. Particular networks of political influence, of mutual self-interest, of personal and social solidarities, and indeed in some cases of straightforward corruption all bent public decision-making in directions that reflected the wider structures of power in European society.[66] Employment in the public sector, the location of infrastructure investments, and the allocation of economic subsidies were all areas of state action where sectional and private interests were able to exert a strong influence.

But larger issues of state policy-making, too, were moulded by these sectional pressures. The structures of welfare provision in post-war European states, with their manifold regimes of contributions, benefits, and exemptions, was one such characteristic example;[67] but so too was industrial policy, where bold projects of modernization were undermined by the influence of particular interest groups.[68] State neutrality was therefore nearly always an illusion. This was most explicitly so in the case of those states where power was consciously shared between the representatives of different political and social traditions. In the "pillarized" societies of the Low Countries, Austria, and, to a lesser extent, areas of western Germany, Switzerland, and northern Italy, state power was not autonomous of society, but consciously designed to reflect the internal diversity of that society. Nomination to state institutions was to a large extent dependent on partisan or confessional labels, while responsibility for the administration of a wide range of state policies, most especially in the fields of education and welfare, was devolved to institutions that formed part of the Socialist, Catholic, and to a lesser degree Liberal, or Protestant worlds.[69] In these areas of Western Europe, the state and its activities were to a considerable degree restrained, or indeed domesticated, by these social institutions. The imposing networks of pillarized interest groups, notably the trade unions, welfare institutions, and farmers' groups, acted as the gatekeepers of the state's relationship with society, by influencing its decisions and acting as the executants of its policies.

These channels of vested influence, official and unofficial, were rarely entirely transparent, but they too formed part of democracy. The permeable membrane of the state as it developed in post-war Western Europe undoubtedly subverted the clarity of electoral democracy and responsible

---

66. J. Meynaud, *La technocratie: Mythe ou réalité?* (Paris, 1964). See also E. Suleiman, *Politics, Power and Bureaucracy*, 381–83; Chapman, *France's Long Reconstruction*, 302–3.

67. See p. 67.

68. Foreman-Peck, "European Industrial Policies," 13–44.

69. See p. 80.

government. It also, however, created the space for forms of informal mediation between state and society, which blunted popular resentments against the rapid growth in state power. It was the relative absence of such conflicts that, until the 1960s, constituted one of the more remarkable features of post-war Western European politics. There was no shortage of points of tension, most notably over issues of taxation, urban planning, and state regulation of the economy. But, in contrast to the way in which specific and local grievances always threatened to escalate into general insurrections against Communist rule in central and eastern Europe,[70] the state authorities of the west largely avoided being drawn into direct confrontations with society. Much the same was also true of the people. Protest campaigns, as in the case of those for nuclear disarmament in Britain and West Germany at the end of the 1950s, drew on a wide repertoire of established and more novel forms of political protest, combining the tools of mass mobilization, high-profile gestures, and the suasion of moral and political rhetoric, in support of their cause.[71] In doing so, these peace campaigners, like many others unhappy with different aspects of state policy-making, accused their rulers of a wide range of sins, including a disregard for the elementary rules of democracy, law, Christian ethics, and individual freedom; but they also for the most part stopped short of challenging directly the authority of the state.

In part, this hesitation may have reflected the shadow effect of the events of previous decades. The legacy of the upheavals of the 1930s and the war years made Europeans conscious of the potential dangers that lurked in trying to pull down the structures of public administration. Protest consequently often had a self-limiting character, whereby those forms of action, such as the use of weapons or violence, that might harm the innocent were widely deemed to be unacceptable, whatever the rectitude of the cause. Levels of political violence declined considerably, especially in France, where the ritualized cultures of violent confrontation between left and right that had characterized the interwar years almost entirely disappeared.[72] Violence, when it did happen, was therefore more often an accident, the consequence of the unpredictable momentum of events,

---

70. See, for example, K. McDermott, "Popular Resistance in Communist Czechoslovakia: The Plzeň Uprising, June 1953," *Contemporary European History* 19 (2010): 287–307.

71. H. Nehring, "The British and West German Protests against Nuclear Weapons and the Culture of the Cold War, 1957–1964," *Contemporary British History* 19 (2005): 224–30.

72. F. Audigier and P. Girard, introduction to *Se battre pour les idées: La violence militante en France des années 1920 aux années 1970*, ed. Audigier and Girard (Paris, 2011), 15–16; Millington, *Fighting for France*.

or a loss of control by the forces of order.[73] The map of political violence changed shape in post-war Europe, moving east to Soviet-ruled areas and south to the Mediterranean littoral, and away from those areas of central and western Europe that over the previous hundred years had been its principal heartland.[74] The Paris Commune of 1870–71, the Spanish Civil War of the 1930s, and above all the Resistance movements of the Second World War were all ways by which political violence was memorialized in post-war Western Europe; but these were presented as moral and political exempla from the past rather than models to be emulated in the present. This was especially striking in the case of wartime resistance. The fact that significant numbers of European citizens had recently engaged in acts of violent protest and unconventional warfare against state authorities and occupying forces was an awkward presence in post-war Europe. It provided both a moral and political lesson of the legitimacy of revolt and a practical demonstration of the means of doing so. Yet, it is striking how emphatically the repertoire of resistance actions was consigned to the past. The dominant commemoration of Resistance groups as volunteer soldiers of the nation who had acted in response to the illegitimate acts of the armies of the Third Reich marginalized the relevance of the Resistance for more peaceful times. Its members were heroes, but also ordinary citizens whose actions could be safely located within the obligations of modern citizenship.[75]

Post-war Europeans, it seemed, had greater difficulty than their ancestors in accepting the legitimacy of political violence.[76] Notions of the disciplined loyalty that Europeans owed to their state authorities had acquired

73. The attack by the police on North African demonstrators in Paris in October 1961 stands out as a clear such case, when the French police adopted violent methods of repression in the French capital that were routine in a colonial context: House and Macmaster, *Paris 1961*; J. House, "Colonial Containment?: Repression of Pro-independence Street Demonstrations in Algiers, Casablanca and Paris, 1945–1962," *War in History* 25 (2018): 172–201.

74. M. Conway and R. Gerwarth, "Revolution and Counter-Revolution," in Bloxham and Gerwarth, *Political Violence*, 162.

75. M. A. Bracke, "From Politics to Nostalgia: The Transformation of War Memories in France during the 1960s–70s," *European History Quarterly* 41 (2011): 9; P. Cooke, *The Legacy of the Italian Resistance* (Basingstoke, UK, 2011), 91–109, 192–93. The exception was of course the Algerian War, which led some French citizens to engage in resistance against their own state, seeing it as a continuation of wartime Resistance: M. Evans, *The Memory of Resistance: French Opposition to the Algerian War (1954–1962)* (Oxford, 1997), esp. 33–41. See also pp. 275–76.

76. See, for example, the opinion-poll findings in D. Sidjanski, C. Roig, H. Kerr, R. Inglehart, and J. Nicola, *Les suisses et la politique: Enquête sur les attitudes d'électeurs suisses 1972* (Frankfurt, 1975), 3.

deep roots in Europe by the 1940s. The demands that the states, on all sides, made of their citizens during the Second World War had tested that loyalty to its limits; but the resolution with which, for example, German soldiers and civilians responded to the demands placed upon them in battle and under the assault of air raids during the latter years of the war indicated how national duty (reinforced by fear of the consequences of disobedience) went hand in hand with the emotional reserves of family and community solidarity.[77] Nor were these concepts of duty discredited by the collapse of the Third Reich. The states of the post-war years also required soldiers, notably the many conscript soldiers, and volunteers, who defended the frontiers of the Cold War and fought in the distant and dangerous wars of European decolonization.[78] Obedience to rules, as reinforced through the institutions of school and workplace, formed part of a wider repertoire of social control, which led most citizens to hold back from criminal acts that broke legal codes and violated social norms. The advantages that this provided in terms of personal security came, however, with the loss of a more elementary sense of personal freedom. Writing during the war years, Erich Fromm warned that the fears and isolation that had led millions of Europeans to embrace the group identities offered by fascism presented a wider threat to modern societies. A mentality of subordination had become too pervasive; rather than accepting the orders given by state authorities, Europeans needed to rediscover a spirit of "positive freedom" and individual self-awareness.[79]

For most citizens, however, conformity to the rules defined by the state rested less on a mentality of obedience than on a more pragmatic and knowing appreciation of the advantages to be derived from the resources of the modern state. The concept of "Eigen-Sinn" (a sense of one's own interests) used by Thomas Lindenberger to explain the way in which many unwilling citizens of the German Democratic Republic nevertheless found

77. N. Stargardt, "Legitimacy through War?" in *Beyond the Racial State: Rethinking Nazi Germany*, ed. D. O. Pendas, M. Roseman, and R. F. Wetzell (Washington, DC, 2017), 402–22.

78. The phenomenon of conscription, and popular attitudes to it in post-1945 Europe, requires much greater historical research. See, for example, Frevert, *Nation in Barracks*, 266–68; R. Vinen, *National Service: Conscription in Britain, 1945–1963* (London, 2014).

79. Fromm, *Fear of Freedom*, 207–37. For similar comments, see Nathan, *Psychology of Fascism*, 27; Bernanos, *Tradition of Freedom*, 54–55; B. Bettelheim, *The Informed Heart: The Human Condition in Modern Mass Society* (Glencoe, IL, 1960), 65–105. These ideas returned in the 1960s as a critique of the post-war democratic regime: see p. 273.

ways of interacting with the regime and adapting it to their interests at the local level can also be applied to societies west of the Iron Curtain.[80] Government had become a largely accepted fact of life, to be exploited for the opportunities that it provided individually or collectively. Thus, for example, when the French state decided in the later 1950s to establish the first French nuclear reactor in the southern French village of Marcoule, the initial reaction of its inhabitants was not—as it undoubtedly would have been in an earlier period, or indeed only twenty years later—to organize campaigns of resistance against this arbitrary action. They resented the compulsory purchase of farmland, as well as the arrival of the consequent army of construction workers and urban technicians; but they also sought to exploit the opportunities provided by the reactor, ensuring that the state provided ample compensation for loss of land and built new facilities for the village.[81]

This acceptance of state authority had been developing, particularly in most areas of northern and western Europe, since the late nineteenth century; but it rested more especially on the pragmatic settlement reached between Europeans and their rulers in the post-war era. The unprecedented demands made of citizens by their rulers during the Second World War (and its aftermath) accustomed Europeans to a more active state authority, but also raised popular expectations of what states should provide for their citizens. After 1945, Europeans appear to have had a largely settled mind as to what they expected of their rulers. In particular, they aspired to the predictability of "competent administration," delivered without the lurches of arbitrary state action that had been evident over the previous decades.[82] But they also wanted it to be a government that provided more than it took. The sleight of hand whereby during the two immediate post-war decades most Western Europeans believed that they were net beneficiaries of the actions of the state rested on a particular conjuncture of circumstances—notably the healthy state of public finances

80. T. Lindenberger, "Die Diktatur der Grenzen: Zur Einleitung," in *Herrschaft und Eigen-Sinn in der Diktatur: Studien zur Gesellschaftsgeschichte der DDR*, ed. Lindenberger (Cologne, 1999), 13–44. See also C. Ross, *The East German Dictatorship: Problems and Perspectives in the Interpretation of the GDR* (London, 2002), 50–51.

81. G. Hecht, "Peasants, Engineers and Atomic Cathedrals: Narrating Modernization in Postwar Provincial France," *French Historical Studies* 20 (1997): 381–418. On subsequent rural resistance to state policies, see A. Tompkins, *Better Active than Radioactive!: Antinuclear Protest in 1970s France and West Germany* (Oxford, 2016); R. Gildea and A. Tompkins, "The Transnational in the Local: The Larzac Plateau as a Site of Transnational Activism since 1970," *Journal of Contemporary History* 50 (2015): 581–605.

82. Weil, "Philosophical and Political Thought," 504.

in a time of steady economic growth and the provision of reliable sup-
plies of international credit to governments. But it also was a matter of
appearances: the benefits of government were immediate and visible, as
displayed in the ambitious infrastructure policies of the post-war years,
while the structures of taxation, both indirect and direct, were less apparent to most citizens. This combination of circumstances proved, of course,
to be finite. As government expanded, so an awareness of its costs and
demands increased, provoking the return of long-standing criticisms of
state extravagance by the populist anti-tax movements that emerged during the early 1970s in a number of states.[83]

But, while it lasted, this image of a beneficent state contributed to a
reshaping of the attitudes of Western Europeans to their rulers. It was
not surprising that a Fabian-minded figure such as Herman Finer should
have declared in 1946 that "the freedom of our time cannot possibly be
an entire freedom from government; it can only be a freedom within
government."[84] What was surprising, however, is that for about twenty
years a large number of Europeans seem to have agreed with him. Government existed, especially in the circumstances of the Cold War, to provide protection from external threats; but it was increasingly perceived
by its citizens in terms of its provision of tangible benefits to individuals,
families, and communities. What Western Europeans, the American Marshall Plan administrators concluded in a report written in 1949, primarily wanted from government was "security." The definition of that security was, however, personal, and also largely non-political. It consisted of
"employment, health and old-age benefits. It means further that a man's
life, when begun, contains the reasonable assurance and expectation of a
rational progress towards a reasonable conclusion."[85]

Measured by those criteria, Western Europeans received much of what
they wanted from their post-war states. Degrees of satisfaction did of
course vary; not only because of differences in the effectiveness of states in
responding to popular aspirations, but also because of enduring national
differences in the attitudes of populations towards the legitimacy of their
rulers, and indeed the very existence of their states.[86] But the overall trend
was towards the acceptance of state authority. Government had become
more predictable and more beneficial to people in ways that broadly
matched the individualist spirit of a time of rapid social and economic

83. Betz, *Radical Right-Wing Populism*, 4–5.
84. Finer, *Road to Reaction*, 128.
85. Quoted in Ellwood, "Message of the Marshall Plan," 12–13.
86. Sidjanski et al., *Suisses et la politique*, 43.

change. Post-war economic growth enabled the state to focus on areas of government action that—once the spike in defence expenditure provoked by the Korean War had passed—brought new benefits to the people. The rapid expansion in state expenditure gave people new educational opportunities, improved housing, new forms of employment—including a large range of new middle-class careers—and state pensions for their old age.[87] The consequence was to embed an acceptance of state power in large areas of Western European society. Legitimacy, as measured in terms of an underlying popular acceptance of the norms and actions of the state, was a more prominent feature of post-war democracy than popularity. No ruler or party in the post-war era came close to achieving a broad consensus of support, or indeed the levels of popularity, enjoyed by certain of their less democratic predecessors. But the gap between the attitudes of rulers and ruled had indisputably narrowed. State officials, politicians, and their electors disagreed on much, but they shared some common assumptions about what government was for.[88]

◦⟨⟩◦

Acceptance of this culture of state governance, if not of all of its consequences, moulded the way in which Europeans experienced and consumed democracy in the post-war years. Democracy was not so much the way by which the people conducted their own affairs, as the way by which they negotiated their relationship with the state and its local institutions. However, not all citizens stood equally in that relationship to the state. While formal democratic rights had become more equal, the degree of influence that individuals had within this culture of state-led democracy continued to be determined by a wide range of factors, the most pervasive of which was social class.

That Western Europe remained a class society after 1945 is, of course, no more than a truism, albeit one that needs to be asserted in the face of assumptions that the rapid economic growth of the post-war years gradually effaced, rather in the manner of the inscriptions of a bygone age, the

87. The West German government's success in reaching its target of building six million new homes was the focus of much celebration in 1961: A. Grünbacher, *Reconstruction and Cold War in Germany: The Kreditanstalt für Wiederaufbau (1948–1961)* (Aldershot, UK, 2004), 261.

88. I have explored this issue with colleagues in the collectively written volume Conway and Romijn, *War for Legitimacy*. See in particular ch. 6 (written by Mark Pittaway and Hans-Fredrik Dahl) on the post-1945 era: 177–209.

class inequalities generated by Europe's modern development. This might have formed part of the expectations of the liberation era, when the possibility of a more equal—and indeed democratic—society appeared to be within reach.[89] In fact, however, the economic and social changes of the post-war decades changed class frontiers more than they abolished them. The composition of the middle class was transformed by new professions and forms of employment, while rural populations rapidly diminished as a consequence of the capitalist transformation of many forms of agriculture as well as the new jobs available within urban centres.[90] Mobility, indeed, was one of the key features of the post-war era, as people moved more frequently, over longer distances, and in greater numbers.[91] Life experiences were, however, more mobile than class identities. Cars, holidays, and employment opportunities enabled people to change environment, as well as diminishing the self-sufficiency of the local communities of neighbourhood and village.[92] In some cases, this also provided opportunities for mobility between the classes, leading many sociologists of the immediate post-war years, such as Seymour Martin Lipset, to regard increases in social mobility as inherent to modern industrial societies.[93] The reality, however, proved to be distinctly less emphatic. There was a long-term increase in social mobility in many Western European societies over the post-war decades, related notably to new forms of employment in the professions and the service sector; but many of the social changes of those years, such as the expansion in university student numbers, served predominantly to reinforce inequalities of social class.[94] Above all, class remained the primary psychological frontier of post-war society. Whether expressed through the new and expensive material symbols of social status, such as car ownership, or the pervasive codes of socialization and personal manners, class was omnipresent. It defined inclusion and exclusion, and was never more tangible than in the case of those whose class identity did change.

89. See the optimism of J. Leclercq in *Société sans classes*.

90. See, for example, E. März, "Die Klassenstruktur der Zweiten Österreichischen Republik," in *Probleme der österreichischen Politik*, vol. 1 (Vienna, 1968), 67–112.

91. A. Pizzorno, "The Individualistic Mobilization of Europe," *Daedalus* 93 (1964): 205–9.

92. Wylie, *Village in the Vaucluse*, 340–48.

93. S. M. Lipset and R. Bendix, *Social Mobility in Industrial Society* (London, 1959), 11–75.

94. H. Kaelble, *Social Mobility in the 19th and 20th Centuries: Europe and America in Comparative Perspective* (Leamington Spa, UK, 1985), 28–30, 131–33; R. Erikson and J. Goldthorpe, *The Constant Flux: A Study of Class Mobility in Industrial Societies* (Oxford, 1993), esp. 101–6.

The phenomenon of the working-class figure—almost always male—who by dint of education or economic success entered a middle class to which he never fully belonged became a frequent reference point of the post-war years, bringing with it a new literature of deracination and social alienation.[95]

Democracy reflected, and respected, the contours of this class society. Above all, it was marked in its structures and ethos by the middle class. The ascendancy that the middle class attained in post-war Western European society was in large part the consequence of the predominantly capitalist trajectory of post-war economic growth, which retained private ownership of property, wealth, and the large majority of industry, while also generating new forms of middle-class employment in the state sector, in the rapidly expanding service industries, and in professions such as engineering that were essential to processes of economic and technological change.[96] But it was reinforced by the loss of social influence by other social classes. Not only the aristocracy—many of whose remaining social bastions in 1945 fell beyond the frontier of the Iron Curtain[97]—but also the hierarchical world of a largely German-speaking notable culture that had formerly characterized so much of central and eastern Europe became no more than a marginal shadow in European post-war society.[98] Moreover, the combined impact of the economic depression of the 1930s and of the war and its aftermath resulted in a working class that, though numerous and often vocal in the expression of its discontents, lacked the ability to assert its social power.

The reverses experienced by workers in Europe during the 1940s were cumulative. The human and material losses experienced by industrial communities during the war years, the dislocation caused by Allied bombing, and the impact of food shortages, of increased working hours, and within the Third Reich of the arrival of large numbers of foreign workers—all were factors that eroded the bonds that had held working-class communities together.[99] It was workers, too, who experienced most directly

95. S. Gunn, "People and the Car: The Expansion of Automobility in Urban Britain, c.1955–70," *Social History* 38 (2013): 220–37; R. J. Cardullo, "Pride and Prejudice, or Class and Character: *Room at the Top* Revisited," *Journal of European Studies* 42 (2012): 158–67.

96. J. Kocka, "The Middle Classes in Europe," in *Industrial Culture and Bourgeois Society: Business, Labour and Bureaucracy in Modern Germany* (New York, 1999), 248–50.

97. See the evocation of this lost, and very undemocratic, world in P. Leigh Fermor, *Between the Woods and the Water* (London, 1986).

98. See D. Gusejnova, *European Elites and Ideas of Empire, 1917–1957* (Cambridge, UK, 2016).

99. Conway, *Sorrows of Belgium*, 285–88; E. R. Beck, *Under the Bombs: The German Home Front 1942–1945* (Lexington, KY, 1986), 120–21, 142. Re. bombing, see the special

the hardships of the immediate post-war years, notably the shortages of the basic commodities of life, such as food, fuel, and clothing, and the difficulties experienced by many demobilized soldiers in regaining stable employment in civilian life. Nor did workers benefit greatly from the support of the state. Over time the welfare reforms introduced in the immediate post-war years brought protection, albeit at the cost of insurance contributions, against the three primary uncertainties of working-class life: unemployment, ill health, and the poverty of old age. But, more immediately, workers felt most directly the weight of the policies of economic austerity pursued by many post-war governments. Controls on wages, coupled with more effective repression of the wartime grey and black markets, ensured that the incomes of most workers lagged behind increases in prices in most countries until the end of the 1940s. The suffering that this generated in working-class communities was reflected in the extensive strike waves that occurred in many areas of liberated Europe during the later 1940s, as workers used the most direct weapon at their disposal to seek to regain their pre-war living standards.[100]

In contrast, the middle class experienced less directly the hardships and disaggregating effects of wartime and of the immediate post-war years. The decimation of the Jewish middle class excepted, middle-class lives and family structures often possessed the means to absorb or to circumvent the material sufferings of the war years, while businesses and self-employed professionals were among the first to profit from the post-war economic recovery. The middle class was not, however, a static phenomenon. Its shape changed quite rapidly, in response to the expansion in public-sector bureaucracies and most dramatically in the ranks of the professions, which made the middle class one based around education and qualifications rather than around property and business.[101] Employers remained powerful, but they were often professional administrators who administered companies on behalf of others, and whose backgrounds and attitudes were more similar to those of their public-sector and professional equivalents than to the authoritarian bosses of the past.[102]

---

issue of *Labour History Review* 77, no. 1 (2012), especially C. Baldoli and M. Perry, "Bombing and Labour in Western Europe, from 1940 to 1945," 3–9.

100. See, for example, Mencherini, *Guerre froide, grèves rouges*; J. Lewis, *Workers and Politics*, 110, 116, 129, 144–47.

101. M. Malatesta, *Professional Men, Professional Women: The European Professions from the Nineteenth Century until Today* (Los Angeles, 2011).

102. H. Joly, "Les dirigeants des grandes entreprises industrielles françaises au 20e siècle," *Vingtième Siècle* 114 (April–June 2012): 17–32.

Moreover, much of the rigidity and conformism that had long characterized a certain bourgeois society evaporated rapidly after the war. The
middle-class world that Simone de Beauvoir evoked so powerfully in the
memoir of her bourgeois upbringing in provincial France after the First
World War had evaporated by the time she had emerged as a member of
the newly assertive intelligentsia who were the subject of her major post-
war novel, *Les mandarins*.[103] This was a future-oriented middle class, the
members of which were less formal in their social conventions and—as
portrayed by Fellini in his satire of the middle class in Rome in *La Dolce
Vita*—more consciously imitative of the fashions and values that they
absorbed from film, magazines, and advertising.[104]

Openness, and indeed a certain democratic social ethos, therefore
became a defining characteristic of the middle class, the frontiers of which
extended to include many of those employees and small businessmen who
had formerly constituted the distinct world of the lower middle class, as
well as the more prosperous farmers who emerged from the post-war
consolidation in patterns of rural landholding. In so doing, the label of
"middle class" became something of a catch-all category, as expressed in
the sociologist Helmut Schelsky's image of the early Federal Republic of
Germany as a *Mittelstand* society.[105] In fact, being middle class was less
a universal than a threshold: education, housing, family structure, leisure
interests, and appearance all became part of a closely linked network of
symbols by which people expressed their membership, or their aspiration
to membership, of the middle class. As a consequence, middle-class identity fused with a wider ethos of social aspiration. In a time of economic
growth and of increased educational and professional opportunities, the
possibility of becoming middle class appealed to many more than simply
those who had been born and socialized into that class. Middle-class identity became associated instead with certain values and repertoires of taste.
Manners books, for example, in Germany provided, in the very particular
context of a post-Nazi society, a means of reconstructing what Paul Betts
has termed "a bourgeois civility."[106] But they constituted only one element
of the much wider dissemination of ways of learning to be middle class,

103. S. de Beauvoir, *Mémoires d'une jeune fille rangée* (Paris, 1958) and *Les mandarins*
(Paris, 1954); H. Lüthy, "The French Intellectuals," *Encounter*, August 1955, 5–15. See also
Leclercq, *Société sans classes*, 10–14.

104. S. Gundle, "La Dolce Vita," in *The Movies as History*, ed. D. Ellwood (Stroud, UK,
2000), 132–40; Pulju, *Women*, 155–61.

105. Roseman, "Restoration and Stability," 145.

106. Betts, "Manners, Morality and Civilization," 196–214.

FIGURE 7. The shop window of democracy: electrical appliances in a shop
window in West Berlin in 1961. Mondadori Portfolio/Mondadori
Portfolio Premium via Getty Images

which incorporated fields as diverse as new forms of emotionally oriented
parenting, fashions in food, and forms of domestic furniture.[107]

It was this intermingling of middle-class values with those of democracy that gave the post-war era its particular character and temper. A
democracy that presented itself as universal and inclusive in fact found
its centre of gravity in the middle class, who in turn emerged as the dominant class of the post-war decades. This sense of post-war societies as
"middle-class societies"[108] rested less on the material structures of class
hegemony than on the more diffuse sense that "modern middle-class values and tastes, the new set of rituals created by cultural and material consumption, became the obligatory model that all social groups ascribed to

107. B. Spock, *Baby and Child Care* (London, 1956); N. Bakker, "The Meaning of Fear.
Emotional Standards for Children in the Netherlands, 1850–1950: Was There a Western
Transformation?" *Journal of Social History* 34 (2000): 376–80; E. David, *A Book of Medi-
terranean Food* (London, 1955); A. Cooper, *Writing at the Kitchen Table: The Authorized
Biography of Elizabeth David* (London, 1999); Bonomo, "Dwelling Space," 276–300.

108. The phrase is that of Percy Allum: *State and Society*, 77.

with varying degrees of gusto."[109] This cultural triumph of the bourgeoisie should not, however, disguise the more tangible contours of class power. Democracy worked in post-war Western Europe in part because it provided a world safe for the middle class. In particular, the fear of social revolution, and more generally of radical policies of social levelling, which had preoccupied many members of that class since at least 1848, effectively disappeared a century later. In the interwar years, fears of revolution had contributed to middle-class alienation from the mass politics inaugurated by regimes of electoral democracy, and had provided the social basis for the movements of bourgeois defence, which had fed the politics of the authoritarian right.[110] In post-war Europe, in contrast, democracy became the means of forestalling the prospect of revolution. The location of democracy in multiparty parliaments elected by forms of proportional representation acted as a bulwark against dictatorial or minority rule. Only by building a coalition with a sufficiently broad basis of social and political support could a government exercise its power.

And that, in practice, meant a government responsive to, and mindful of, middle-class interests. Democracy became tied to a set of freedoms—of belief, of opinion, of movement, and of opportunity—that appealed most directly to the middle class, and which they were best placed to take advantage of.[111] In more direct terms, too, the electoral success of parties of the centre-right in post-war Europe, and more especially of Christian Democracy, made them all but essential components of any durable parliamentary majority in many Western European states in the post-war era.[112] The middle class was embedded in power, in terms of parliamentary arithmetic but also in wider social terms. In contrast to the political alliances of the working class with agrarian groups that had generated the Popular-Front governments in a number of European states during the 1930s,[113] the dominant class alliance in post-war Europe was that of the middle class with rural populations. This did not exclude the participation of the working class, most notably through the role that Catholic

109. Wakeman, *Modernizing the Provincial City*, 267. See also Kocka, "Middle Classes in Europe," 249.

110. For examples of this process, see notably P. Fritzsche, *Rehearsals for Fascism: Populism and Political Mobilization in Weimar Germany* (New York, 1990); Kennedy, *Reconciling France against Democracy*, esp. 85–112.

111. See, for example, the list of inalienable rights that constituted the preamble to the Basic Law of the German Federal Republic in 1949: Collings, *Democracy's Guardians*, xxiv.

112. Kaiser, *Christian Democracy*, 163–90; Gehler and Kaiser, *Christian Democracy in Europe*. See, more generally, Vinen, *Bourgeois Politics in France*, and pp. 188–91.

113. Luebbert, *Liberalism*, 285–95.

workers' organizations played within many Christian Democratic parties. But that working class was, almost always, a minority presence. Indeed, much the same was true even in the ranks of the Socialist parties, where the electoral incentive to reach out to middle-class electors coincided with the increasingly middle-class composition of their leadership structures.[114]

The influence of the middle class over government reflected, almost unconsciously, their proximity to power. Welfare structures, economic subsidies for businesses, the networks of regulations that provided protection for the professions, and the visible and invisible inequalities in the educational system that entrenched the position of social elites while also controlling access to membership of that elite—all were instances of how the actions of the state worked to reinforce middle-class interests.[115] Much the same was also true of rural populations. During the interwar years, the perceived unresponsiveness of states to rural populations, and more especially small-scale commercial farmers, had been central to the energy of movements of the anti-democratic right.[116] After 1945, however, rural protest largely disappeared from Western European politics. In part, this reflected the impact of economic change, as millions of small-scale farmers and agrarian workers left the land during the 1950s and 1960s to seek employment in urban centres.[117] The other side of this coin, however, was the emergence of an emphatically commercial class of rural farmers with larger landholdings. Thus, in Austria, the number of farms of more than twenty hectares increased over the decade 1951–61, as the number of smaller farming units went into a marked decline.[118] These farmers were, moreover, effective at voicing their economic concerns within the processes of government. The strength of farmers' organizations and their ties to political parties, such as the Christian Democrats of Catholic Europe and the Agrarian parties of Scandinavia, ensured that the protection of this commercial-farming class was a priority for governments in the post-war decades.[119] Welfare provision was tailored to rural needs,

114. See pp. 191–92.

115. Mazower, *Dark Continent*, 305; Malatesta, *Professional Men, Professional Women*, esp. 1–9; E. Suleiman, *Elites in French Society: The Politics of Survival* (Princeton, NJ, 1978), 28–30.

116. Paxton, *French Peasant Fascism*; M. Conway, "The Extreme-Right in Inter-war Francophone Belgium: Explanations of a Failure," *European History Quarterly* 26 (1996): 282–83.

117. R. Petri, "Le campagne italiane nello sviluppo economico," in *Sociétés rurales du XXe siècle*, ed. J. Canal, G. Pécout, and M. Ridolfi (Rome, 2004), 75–104.

118. März, "Klassenstruktur," 92–94.

119. Elder, Thomas, and Arter, *Consensual Democracies?* 69–76; Nevakivi, "From the Continuation War," 243–44. Re. Christian Democrat parties, see p. 189.

while the construction of economic assistance and protection to agricultural producers, at the national and subsequently European levels, was built around the perceived social imperative to protect the family farm.[120]

This sensitivity to the interests of a free and independent farming population rested, moreover, on more than skilful lobbying on the part of what by the end of the 1960s had become a relatively small proportion of the overall population.[121] The impact, and durable memory, of wartime food shortages made issues of agricultural productivity and prosperity a much more important component of the business of the state after 1945: to use an anachronistic term, "food security" was now very much part of the political agenda.[122] In a wider sense, too, a consciousness of the needs of rural communities also formed part of the political legacies of the war years and their immediate aftermath. The experiences of the war years had made more visible the dependence of urban populations on their rural fellow citizens, often exacerbating urban-rural tensions.[123] At the same time, the countryside had become, for many, a place of wartime refuge from bombing and persecution, and through the emergence in 1943 and 1944 of rural-based Resistance movements had acquired a prominent role in national narratives of liberation. Thus, notably in France and Italy, rural communities acquired a new centrality in political life, and in the imaginary of the nation. The countryside was no longer a bastion of political and social reaction, but became through the symbolism of the Maquis and its prominence in post-war memory the custodian of liberty.[124]

120. P. V. Dutton, "An Overlooked Source of Social Reform: Family Policy in French Agriculture," *Journal of Modern History* 72 (2000): 375–412; Nicholls, *Bonn Republic*, 107–8; G. Noël, "La solidarité agricole européenne: Des congrès d'agriculture à la politique agricole commune," in *Sociétés rurales du XXe siècle*, ed. J. Canal, G. Pécout, and M. Ridolfi (Rome, 2004), 318–25; K. K. Patel, "The History of European Integration and the Common Agricultural Policy: An Introduction," in *Fertile Ground for Europe?: The History of European Integration and the Common Agricultural Policy since 1945*, ed. Patel (Baden-Baden, 2009), 18–19.

121. Nevakivi, "From the Continuation War," 288.

122. P. Clavin and K. K. Patel, "The Role of International Organizations in Europeanization: The Case of the League of Nations and the European Economic Community," in *Europeanization in the Twentieth Century: Historical Approaches*, ed. M. Conway and Patel (Basingstoke, UK, 2010), 118–21.

123. Conway, *Sorrows of Belgium*, 288–93; Ventresca, *From Fascism to Democracy*, 52–53.

124. Kedward, *In Search of the Maquis*, 285–89; G. Vergnon, "La construction de la mémoire du Maquis de Vercors: Commémoration et historiographie," *Vingtième Siècle* 49 (1996): 82–97. Re. rural society and Resistance, see also the important essay by A. Ventura, "La società rurale veneta dal fascismo alla Resistenza," in *Società rurale e Resistenza nelle Venezie* (Milan, 1978), 11–70.

All of this contrasted markedly with the diminished social and political power of the working class. The pace of industrial change during the years of high economic growth rates in the 1950s and the 1960s brought individual prosperity for some workers, but also a new precariousness for many industrial communities. Processes of economic rationalization and the preoccupation, encouraged by the Marshall Plan, with higher levels of economic productivity eroded pre-existing patterns of work, before leading at the end of the 1950s to the rapid dismantling and closure of many of the coal mines and iron and steel works that had long constituted the locus of the working class.[125] This, however, formed only one element of a wider vulnerability. The impact of the capitalism of the high-growth decades exerted a durable pressure on workers, imposing new "Fordist" working practices and changes in technologies and in hierarchies of skills, as well as bringing in new categories of workers, including female production-line employees and migrant workers from former colonies and the Mediterranean region.[126] These changes imposed a new mobility and unpredictability on the lives of workers and their families. Their living standards rose more slowly in many areas of Europe than did those of other sections of the population; and, though new material possessions such as motor cars did finally come within reach of a significant number of working-class families by the 1960s,[127] the indices of inequality evident in terms of access to many of the key consumer goods of the era demonstrated that there was no generalized regime of affluence in post-war Europe.[128]

The bottlenecks and tensions created in many Western European societies by processes of industrial change contributed to the wide range of strikes and other forms of industrial action that occurred throughout the supposed years of post-war consensus in the 1950s.[129] In the longer term, too, they fed the revival in worker radicalism that generated the strikes of the later 1960s and the wide range of industrial and social protest that

125. N. Crafts and G. Toniolo, "Postwar Growth: An Overview," in *Economic Growth in Europe since 1945*, ed. Crafts and Toniolo (Cambridge, 1996), 22–25; M. Toromanoff, *Le drame des houillères* (Paris, 1969), esp. 90–95; Chapman, *France's Long Reconstruction*, 305–6.

126. A. Pizzorno, *Comunità e razionalizzazione: Ricerca sociologica su un caso di sviluppo industriale* (Turin, 1960).

127. See, for example, the statistics of the rapid revolution in car ownership in West Germany between 1950 and 1970 in T. Zeller, *Driving Germany: The Landscape of the German Autobahn, 1930–1970* (New York, 2007), 183–85.

128. Pizzorno, "Individualistic Mobilization of Europe," 217–21.

129. G. Ross, *Workers and Communists*, 74–75, 87–88; Dhaille-Hervieu, *Communistes au Havre*, 280–88; Nevakivi, "From the Continuation War," 254, 272–73; J. Neuville and J. Yerna, *Le choc de l'hiver '60–'61: Les grèves contre la loi unique* (Brussels, 1990).

occurred during the 1970s.[130] The nature of that industrial working class had, however, also changed profoundly. The workers were no longer a self-defining category in European society. They merged into an expanding range of technicians, white-collar employees, and public-sector officials, but also a fluid underclass of migrant and part-time workers with limited economic and social rights. And yet workers were still very much a reality of European life. Economic growth created new workers, often women and in new places, even as it swept away old structures of employment and communities.[131] The consequence was a working class that was indisputably less homogeneous, more variegated, and also less disciplined. Patterns of protest and of action changed. General strikes, launched and controlled by a structured trade-union leadership, were increasingly rare. Instead, protest took place within particular factories, carried forward by local trade-union officials or improvised worker committees, who experimented with new techniques such as imprisoning managers in the factory, or taking over the running of the factories themselves.[132]

The undertow of industrial conflict during the post-war decades must throw into question any simple belief that 1945 had created a democracy for all. The assumption that the expansion of democracy must, at least over the long term, have been beneficial to working-class communities is written into the narrative of European history of the twentieth century: the struggles for the suffrage that had been so hard won by workers at the beginning of the century, so the argument goes, brought their rewards after 1945 through the development of a broader democracy that encompassed the social rights of the welfare state as well as the representation of employees within workplaces.[133] This account of a progressive democratization of society—as presented by the Swedish Social Democrats in

130. G.-R. Horn, *The Spirit of '68: Rebellion in Western Europe and North America, 1956–1976* (Oxford, 2007), 100–122; N. Pizzolato, "Transnational Radicals: Labour Dissent and Political Activism in Detroit and Turin (1950–1970)," *International Review of Social History* 56 (2011): 1–30; M. Golden, *Labor Divided: Austerity and Working-Class Politics in Contemporary Italy* (Ithaca, NY, 1988).

131. A. Schildt, *Die Sozialgeschichte der Bundesrepublik Deutschland bis 1989–90* (Munich, 2007), 89–90; Lidegaard, *Short History of Denmark*, 271.

132. X. Vigna, *L'insubordination ouvrière dans les années '68: Essai d'histoire politique des usines* (Rennes, 2007); J. Clarke, "Work, Consumption and Subjectivity in Postwar France: Moulinex and the Meanings of Domestic Appliances 1950s–70s," *Journal of Contemporary History* 47 (2012): 850–56; V. Porhel, "Factory Disputes in the French Provinces in the '1968 Years': Brittany as Case Study," in *May 68: Rethinking France's Last Revolution*, ed. J. Jackson, A.-L. Milne, and J. S. Williams (Basingstoke, UK, 2011), 188–201.

133. This is the central thesis of Eley, *Forging Democracy*. See also S. Berger, "European Labour Movements and the European Working Class in Comparative Perspective," in *The*

their election manifestos of the 1940s and 1950s[134]—was, however, more visible from above than it was from below. Workers were enfranchised and, through their trade-union representatives, represented in social negotiations as well as in parliaments and local municipalities. Their rights too were enhanced through labour and welfare reforms, reflecting the priorities of a political era in which improved living standards for all served as one of the primary indices of social progress.[135] But more-tangible forms of empowerment eluded them. Capitalist control of industry remained emphatic, and with the internationalization of many industries during the post-war decades increasingly operated at a level impervious to worker pressure. In these circumstances, the corporatist reforms of the post-war era always appeared to be struggling to keep up with the changing nature of the economic system, drawing trade-union officials into participation in a culture of social negotiation that removed the sting of worker discontent without creating an economic democracy responsive to worker demands.[136]

Democracy, therefore, proved to be something of a half-victory for workers. Its material and social benefits, as well as its structures of negotiation, may have been preferable to the dictatorship of state and employer that had characterized the authoritarian and fascist regimes of the preceding decades, or to the people's democracies of the east that imposed a disempowered austerity on workers while simultaneously glorifying their social role. But the hopes of the immediate post-war years that the new democracy's governing principles of civic equality and social justice would grant working people the dominant say in the decision-making culture of the nation proved to be disappointed.[137] The experience of the post-war decades showed the limits to the power of the working class within a modern democracy. Workers had never been the homogeneous mass that Socialist leaders in particular had liked to evoke, but the internal fault lines—of region, of skill, of gender, and of language and ethnicity—became all the more evident during the post-war decades. Political culture, too, had tilted away from the interests of the working class. The logics of

---

Western European Labour Movement and the Working Class in the Twentieth Century, ed. Berger and D. Broughton (Oxford, 1995), 245–61.

134. SAP, "Till Sveriges folk!" (To the people of Sweden!), manifestos of 1948, 1952, and 1956, https://snd.gu.se/en/vivill/party/s. I am indebted to James Gardner for his analysis and translation of these manifestos.

135. März, "Klassenstruktur," 103.

136. See pp. 139–40.

137. See the disappointed reflections of F. G. Castles in *Social Democratic Image*, ix.

electoral politics based on universal suffrage focused the attention of parties on those supposedly swing voters—notably women, or members of the burgeoning middle class—whose votes supposedly determined elections. Moreover, the more ordered structure of post-war politics removed much of the direct pressure of the masses. Strikes, marches, and demonstrations no longer possessed the same ability to impress or intimidate rulers, buttressed behind the imposing repressive resources of the modern state; while influence over government was exercised not by weight of numbers but through the more discreet tools of lobbying and representation within the bureaucracies of the political parties.

The fault lines of social class were not the only forces that moulded the social character of post-war democracy. Age too played a role, and more especially the way in which the democratic order was built around the ascendancy of the middle-aged. In the aftermath of the war, there was an understandable preference for new people to assume leadership roles in politics and society, replacing the older generation that had been responsible for the failings of the recent past. Consequently, the late 1940s proved to be a moment of substantial generational change in many European states. An older generation departed or was removed, and in its place there emerged for the first time elites composed predominantly of men (and a few women) who had come of age after the First World War. The generational cohort of those born between the turn of the century and 1914 were particularly numerous; and, unlike their elders, had not been greatly affected by the losses in the First World War.

1945 was therefore the moment when those who had been born since the beginning of the twentieth century took control of their century. They assumed leadership roles in many areas of Western European government and society, which they would retain in large part until the end of the 1960s. Aged in their forties and fifties, this cohort of middle-aged leaders lent post-war democracy its pragmatic mentality as well as its priorities of reconstruction, social reform, and effective government. They had been strongly marked by the authoritarian regimes and political conflicts of the interwar years, as well as by the war years, but had little investment in the mentalities of the past. Instead, they were focused primarily on the needs of the present day, and on the goal of building a more durable political, economic, and social stability for the future. The consequence was a society based around the mentalities of this middle-aged cohort, as expressed through welfare legislation, as well as the modern but rather conservative mores of the post-war era. Family, restraint, and decency all formed part of the emotional regime of the post-war years. This manifested itself in the concern to restore a sense of morality among the young, and subsequently the hostility shown by many of those in authority towards the irreverent attitudes and behaviour of the young of the late 1950s and 1960s.[138]

In addition, there was the highly visible factor of gender. In contrast to almost all of the democracies of Europe's recent past, those of the post-war years were no longer indisputably male. Women were enfranchised at the liberation in Italy, France, and, after some delay promoted by considerations of political expediency, in Belgium.[139] As a consequence, the majority of Western Europe's voters were for the first time female; a majority that was enhanced in the immediate post-war years in central Europe by the absence of large numbers of men as prisoners of war. Thus, for example, 64 per cent of the registered voters in Austria's first post-war elections in November 1945 were female.[140] Civic equality, it seemed, had finally reached women, as expressed in the resonant phraseology of the new Italian constitution of 1948, which stated that it was the duty of the Republic to remove all social and economic obstacles to the full and equal participation of women in public life.[141] Nor was this empty rhetoric. The exigencies of wartime had required women to take on new social roles; some of these proved to be short-lived, but the legacy of the war, and more especially the way in which it had caused women to assume responsibility for many forms of welfare provision, was evident in the influential role that women assumed in fields such as education and healthcare in post-war Europe.[142]

And yet the democracies of the post-war decades remained highly gendered, creating a durable assumption that it was the social changes of the 1960s and not the reforms of the immediate post-war years that constituted the more significant turning point in women's participation in

138. See pp. 88–89 and 109–10; B. Bettelheim, "The Problem of Generations," *Daedalus* 91 (1962): 77–81. On the concept of emotional regimes, see J. C. Häberlen and R. A. Spinney, introduction to "Emotions in Protest Movements in Europe since 1917," ed. Häberlen and Spinney, special issue, *Contemporary European History* 23, no. 4 (2014): 492–96.

139. S. Reynolds, "Lateness, Amnesia and Unfinished Business: Gender and Democracy in Twentieth-Century Europe," *European History Quarterly* 32 (2002): 85–109.

140. E. Weinzierl, "The Origins of the Second Republic: A Retrospective View," in *Austria 1945–1995: Fifty Years of the Second Republic*, ed. K. R. Luther and P. Pulzer (Aldershot, UK, 1998), 24.

141. Tambor, "Essential Way of Life," 209–14.

142. E. Heineman, "The Hour of the Woman: Memories of Germany's 'Crisis Years' and West German National Identity," *American Historical Review* 101 (1996): 356.

democracy.[143] Thus, for example, the presence of women in political life in most European states in the post-war years was almost absurdly marginal. There was a striking lack of women in leadership roles in political parties and in the principal ministerial offices. Indeed, with the emergence of a more professional ethos of government, so the exclusion of women politicians (who generally lacked such qualifications) from positions of responsibility became all the more implacable. Only in the highly gendered, and self-limiting, spheres of health, maternity, and childcare could women claim, by their life experience or professional training, an expertise appropriate to their tasks. The absence of a political breakthrough of women after 1945 reflected, moreover, the wider inequalities of post-war society. The blurring of gender hierarchies that had occurred amidst the exceptional circumstances of war did not endure. Instead, across wide areas of economic and social life, women found themselves relegated as the war receded to a secondary position defined by their gender, as housewives, second-class workers, daughters, and mothers.

Explanations of this post-war normalization of gender relations have often focused on male agency, perceived as a reactionary and indeed anti-democratic force. This owed much to the impact of the war. Military mobilization at the end of the 1930s had reasserted the male ideal of the virile soldier, protecting the feminine spheres of home, family, and country from danger. This, however, was a role that few were able to perform during the war, when large numbers of men (on all sides) were taken captive, countries were occupied, and the greatest threat to civilian populations often came from aerial bombing delivered with relative impunity by largely unseen agents.[144] Moreover, the mobilizations and demands of war had unsettled the more private aspects of gender relations. Many men felt disempowered, in and out of uniform, which helps to explain the self-conscious displays of male authority that developed in much of Western Europe during the latter years of the war, and more especially during the lawless period around the moment of liberation. For some men this took the form of crude attempts to reassert their social power, notably by enacting improvised forms of justice against those women accused of having had too great an intimacy with the German occupiers.[145]

143. Eley, *Forging Democracy*, 320–28, 366–83.

144. D. Voldman, "Les bombardements aériens: Une mise à mort du 'guerrier'?" in *De la violence et des femmes*, ed. C. Dauphin and A. Farge (Paris, 1997), 153–57.

145. Virgili, *Shorn Women*; C. Duchen, "Opening Pandora's Box: The Case of the *femmes tondues*," in *Problems in French History*, ed. M. Cornick and C. Crossley (Basingstoke, UK, 2000), 213–32.

This public theatre of the sexualized humiliation of women formed only the visible tip of a much more broad-ranging upsurge in male violence against women that occurred in the 1940s. In the chaotic circumstances of liberation and its aftermath, sex was omnipresent, but was rarely based on an equality of power. The bartering of sex for material benefits, a sudden surge in prostitution engaged in by women without other means of support, and above all the abrupt arrival of large numbers of Allied soldiers in European communities where the conventional structures of policing had largely disappeared created an environment in which male exploitation of women was all too easy.[146] Accusations of rape—often focused unjustly on black American GIs—were the most immediate consequence of the moral panic this generated, but the more durable legacy was the vilification of those women who were perceived to have dishonoured their communities through their sexual behaviour, or through forming relationships and having children with members of the Allied occupying forces.[147] Placed alongside these events, the gendered inequalities evident in the practices of post-war democracy appear to have been only one aspect of a much wider process of male reconquest. In politics, as in the more private spheres of domestic life, men forcefully reasserted an order that subordinated women through the legitimizing language of law and tradition, as well as the coercive power of the state. Thus, in legislation, legal practice, and wider political debate, highly normative notions of virtuous female behaviour were asserted, which confined women to a restricted sphere defined by their roles as wives and mothers.[148]

The "renegotiation" of gender relations that followed the war was, however, more complex than the simple reassertion of male power.[149] Men too had changed as the consequence both of the war and of long-term evolutions in male identities brought about by changes in education, social structures, and patterns of consumption. Men were no longer, if they had ever been, simply the providers and guardians of the family, but were also

146. M.-L. Roberts, *What Soldiers Do: Sex and the American GI in World War II France* (Chicago, 2013). For a lightly fictionalized contemporary representation of this phenomenon, see Hayes, *Girl on the Via Flaminia*.

147. Fehrenbach, "Black Occupation Children," 30–54.

148. See, notably, Moeller, *Protecting Motherhood*, esp. 3–6, 76–108, 180–209; E. Heineman, *What Difference Does a Husband Make?: Women and Marital Status in Nazi and Postwar Germany* (Berkeley, CA, 1999), 137–75.

149. J. Horne, "Masculinity in Politics and War in the Age of Nation-States and World Wars, 1850–1950," in *Masculinities in Politics and War: Gendering Modern History*, ed. S. Dudink, K. Hagemann, and J. Tosh (Manchester, 2004), 33.

consumers, employees, citizens, and fathers and husbands.[150] The consequence was a gradual change in the pattern of male-female relations and in the structure of the family. Whatever the efforts of the post-war state authorities to reassert conventional norms of gender relations and sexual conduct, these were often little more than ineffectual gestures to control changes in social morality and in individual identities that had been gathering pace since the 1920s. Citizens, both male and female, were less willing to conform to prescribed social standards, choosing to regard issues such as sexual behaviour as primarily a matter of personal choice over which the state had no right of control.[151] The consequence was a shift towards less-formal social norms, and a burgeoning culture of heterosexual sexuality within and outside marriage.[152]

The family too was changing. As a consequence of the disruptions brought about by the war, the position of the father as the head of the household had often been displaced. Many households, especially in central Europe, were headed by women, either permanently, or until prisoners of war and deportees returned some years after the war.[153] Moreover, relations within the family changed, as gendered hierarchies were gradually replaced by the collaborative nuclear family, bonded by ties of love between parents and children. Married couples became collaborators in the shared project of establishing and maintaining a home, managing the resources of the domestic economy, and parenting—a term which in itself indicated an important shift from an exclusively female concept of motherhood.[154]

This trend, however incomplete, towards a democracy within family life, and in male-female relations more generally, indicates the need to understand women's experience in post-war Western Europe in a broader context than the specific prism of equality. Men and women were certainly not equal—least of all in terms of their economic power—but the war years had accelerated the more long-term evolution of European society

---

150. See, for example, L. Segal, "Look Back in Anger: Men in the Fifties," in *Male Order: Unwrapping Masculinity*, ed. R. Chapman and J. Rutherford (London, 1988), 68–96.

151. A. Timm, *The Politics of Fertility in Twentieth-Century Berlin* (Cambridge, UK, 2010), 292–318; Fishman, *Vichy to the Sexual Revolution*, 114–32.

152. Re. sex, see notably Herzog, *Sex after Fascism*, 69–72; E. Heineman, "The Economic Miracle in the Bedroom: Big Business and Sexual Consumption in Reconstruction West Germany," *Journal of Modern History* 78 (2006): 846–77.

153. Heineman, *What Difference*, 108–36; Biess, *Homecomings*, 120–25.

154. M. Wildt, "Continuities and Discontinuities of Consumer Mentality in West Germany in the 1950s," in Bessel and Schumann, *Life after Death*, 217–20; Bakker, "Meaning of Fear," 376–80; Fishman, *Vichy to the Sexual Revolution*, 71–79.

FIGURE 8. Family democracy: a Danish family at the polling station in 1953. The City Archive of Odense

towards a model of gender relations that preserved gender differences while also allowing for new forms of female freedom and opportunity. This was reinforced, too, by the rapid modernization brought about by post-war economic growth, which led to increasing numbers of women entering higher levels of education and new forms of employment. In effect, societal discourses about gender and the reality of people's lives had diverged, creating a sense, especially among women—but also many men—who came of age during the boom years of the later 1950s, that the hierarchies of gender had lost much of their former disciplining and defining character in a more mobile post-war society.[155]

These wider cultural changes complicate any simple account of male control of post-war democracy. Women may not have been anything approaching equal to men in almost all areas of daily life, but they were becoming more influential and, at least in numerical terms, a more decisive force in electoral politics. As all of the major political parties recognized, it was only by positively appealing to women that they could hope to win their votes. The fact of the enfranchisement of adult women in France and Italy at the end of the war, and in Belgium in 1948, had effectively

155. U. Frevert, *Women in German History: From Bourgeois Emancipation to Sexual Liberation* (Providence, RI, 1989), 265–86.

brought to a close the long-delayed integration of female citizens within modern democracy. This was, however, a process that right until its dénouement remained framed, and constrained, within highly gendered discourses.[156] This was in part the consequence of the particular circumstances of liberation. The experience of the war encouraged a patronizing and almost charitable definition of female enfranchisement, whereby women were granted the suffrage not as an inalienable right but as a male gift: a "reward" for the responsibilities they had assumed during the war, or more specifically for their actions in protecting, or safeguarding, Resistance militants or the victims of Nazi oppression.[157] Thus, the granting of the vote signalled less a general recognition of the equality of women with men than a particular solidarity of inclusion in the national community earned through the exceptional circumstances of war. Even then, the decision to grant the vote to women came significantly from outside the country. While the Conseil national de la Résistance, composed of the principal political groupings within France, omitted female suffrage from its comprehensive plan for the post-liberation renovation of France, it was the delegates of the assembly of de Gaulle's Provisional Government in Algiers who in April 1944 decided, a little hesitantly, to more than double the size of the French electorate.[158]

This largest change in post-war democracy—which brought millions of women into the electoral process and gave them the opportunity of access to the offices of political power—therefore seems to be the one that had the least dramatic consequences, and one in which most women were little more than passive bystanders.[159] It finally brought women into the community of political citizens in ways that had been prefigured by female engagement in many forms of political and social action over previous decades.[160] But it was less about women as a particular category

156. Reynolds, "Lateness, Amnesia," 93–94.

157. Regarding women's role in the Resistance, see notably C. Goldenstedt, *Les femmes dans la Résistance* (Herbolzheim, Germany, 2006); R. Vandenbussche, ed., *Femmes et résistance en Belgique et zone interdite* (Villeneuve d'Ascq, France, 2007).

158. Andrieu, *Programme commun de la Résistance*, 76; H. Footitt and J. Simmonds, *France 1943–1945* (Leicester, UK, 1988), 42–43.

159. H. Diamond, *Women and the Second World War in France, 1939–48: Choices and Constraints* (Harlow, UK, 1999), 178–203; S. Chaperon, "'Feminism Is Dead. Long Live Feminism!': The Women's Movement in France at the Liberation, 1944–1946," in *When the War Was Over: Women, War and Peace in Europe 1940–1956*, ed. C. Duchen and I. Bandhauer-Schöffmann (London, 2000), 146–60.

160. S. Reynolds, "Le sacre de la citoyenne?: Réflexions sur le retard français," in *Féminismes et identités nationales: Les processus d'intégration des femmes au politique*, ed. Y. Cohen and F. Thébaud (n.p., 1998), 81–82.

than about liquidating the remnants of civic inequality inherited from the nineteenth century. Henceforth, democracy would be based on the new language of civic universalism, by which all adult citizens—a term that remained hedged around with exemptions for those who as a consequence of their ethnic background, criminal record, or psychological weakness were not deemed to be full members of the political nation—had an equal right to vote.

Unsurprisingly, therefore, female enfranchisement proved to be something of an event without consequences. Campaigns for female equality in other areas of citizenship and socio-economic life were not a prominent element of political life in Western Europe until the mid-1960s, thereby creating the impression that, having had the suffrage bestowed upon them, women somehow failed to seize the opportunity it provided to claim those social rights that would have finally brought about their substantive emancipation.[161] This teleology of twentieth-century women's experience as a forward march towards equality does, however, present many difficulties, notably in terms of the assumptions it makes about the emancipatory character of democracy. Just as with histories of the working class, the notion that democracy must somehow have been beneficial to women forms part of the way in which modern European history has long been approached. This association of women and democracy, however, rests on rather fragile foundations. It implies a fundamental female commitment to democracy, which was often far from apparent in women's political choices; but it also assumes that regimes based on a democratic suffrage have provided the most favourable political context for women's emancipation from gendered structures of discrimination. This was far from being the case. The strongest exponents of democracy in the nineteenth century were often those who most strenuously opposed female suffrage as prejudicial to those same democratic freedoms; while those anti-democratic regimes of the interwar years, such as the Third Reich, which espoused an anti-modern and repressive discourse about women's role in society, pursued policies that in practice offered women social opportunities, at the same time that they denied them political freedom.[162]

This complexity remained evident after 1945. Women had been enfranchised, and all of the political forces now shared a commitment to

161. A. Rossi-Doria, "Italian Women Enter Politics," in *When the War was Over: Women, War and Peace in Europe 1940–1956*, ed. C. Duchen and I. Bandhauer-Schöffmann (London, 2000), 95.

162. Frevert, *Women in German History*, 250–52.

democracy; but the rule of the majority did not of itself ensure the dismantling of the inequalities of gender. Not only did political power at the local and national levels remain emphatically in male hands, but many women—a majority of whom had never voted in free elections prior to the war—retained and indeed reinforced a gendered perception of their political citizenship. Many women, it seemed, wanted to remain women, and oriented their political loyalties accordingly; and it was those parties, notably the Christian Democrats, that gave voice to distinctively female concerns—often expressed through a rather conservative language of familism, and of "womanhood"—that were the most successful in winning women's electoral support.[163] In this way, democracy perpetuated and deepened inequalities of gender, by confining women's political participation within a restricted sphere of supposedly female political issues. But this presence of women as voters and as activists and as members of lobby groups also invested the politics of post-war Europe with a new tone. Once the security crises of the early Cold War had passed, the foremost political issues of the 1950s—such as education, housing, health, and welfare—were ones that were inclusive of women, and where women's voices could make themselves heard. Democracy, consequently, acquired a new permeability to women, both through the issues that were discussed and through the presence of women in the expanding public bureaucracies of post-war Western Europe, acting as experts and officials responsible for issues such as housing provision, child welfare, and nursing care.[164]

The democracy of the post-war years was therefore in no sense a democracy of gender equality, but rather a democracy within which gendered identities found expression, and that had to some degree been feminized. Women were emphatically present, not only as voters but also as party propagandists, elected representatives (albeit still largely at the level of local government), trade unionists, and members of a wide variety of women's organizations. Moreover, though explicit demands for gender equality may have been relatively rare, the women who entered public life after the Second World War campaigned, within and without the formal domains of political action, on issues of direct relevance to female lives, such as equal pay, pension rights, legal reforms, and health and

163. Chappel, *Catholic Modern*, 192–200; C. Berthezène, "Un féminisme conservateur?: Genre et politique en Grande-Bretagne (1928–1964)," in *Conservatismes en mouvement: Une approche transnationale au XXe siècle*, ed. Berthezène and J.-C. Vinel (Paris, 2016), 420–23.

164. Newsome, "'Apartment Referendum,'" 329–57; S. Todd, "Family Welfare and Social Work in Post-war England," *English Historical Review* 129 (2014): 362–87.

welfare provision.[165] This reflected the changing character of economic activity. For all of the rhetorical emphasis placed on women as mothers and housewives, many women performed other roles as well. Industrial mechanization and the multiplication of new forms of bureaucratic work, in both the public and private sectors, made women a much more visible presence in the workplace, and often an assertive one.[166] Above all, women were now emphatically consumers. Consumer movements were established in most Western European states in the 1950s, and their membership expanded rapidly as they articulated a new language of consumer rights, and acquired in some states representation in public decision-making structures. In this way, the consumer emerged during the boom years of the 1950s and 1960s as the new definition of the citizen in democracy. Moreover, this citizen-consumer was perceived as almost always female. According to the gendered stereotypes of the age, it was the housewife as the rationally minded citizen-consumer who took charge of family budgets and made well-informed choices regarding an ever-increasing range of technical products for the home.[167]

Consumerism did of course well demonstrate the ambivalent nature of women's experience within post-war democracy. While it provided women with new channels for voicing their demands, the ever more insistent and pervasive impact of the popular culture of the 1950s and 1960s was in many ways belittling and even infantilizing for women. It imposed predominantly male-defined archetypes of beauty, romantic love, motherhood, and domestic contentment that reduced women to the consumers of an ever-increasing range of material products.[168] Most obviously, the transmission of this popular culture through magazines, films, advertising, and ultimately television reinforced notions of a gendered universe, by emphasizing at every turn the differentness of women from men, and thereby also the supposed naturalness of a social and political

---

165. M. Tambor, *The Lost Wave: Women and Democracy in Postwar Italy* (Oxford, 2014); Heineman, *What Difference*, 140–41.

166. H. H. Chenut, *The Fabric of Gender: Working Class Culture in Third Republic France* (University Park, PA, 2005), 400–401; Clarke, "Work, Consumption and Subjectivity," 838–59; M.-T. Coenen, *La grève des femmes de la F.N. en 1966* (Brussels, 1991).

167. Pulju, *Women*, 2–3; M. Hilton, "The Organised Consumer Movement since 1945," and K. Pence, "Shopping for an 'Economic Miracle': Gendered Politics of Consumer Citizenship in Divided Germany," in *The Expert Consumer: Associations and Professionals in Consumer Society*, ed. A. Chatriot, M.-E. Chessel, and M. Hilton (Aldershot, UK, 2006), 188–93 and 106–10.

168. S. Gundle, *Bellissima: Feminine Beauty and the Idea of Italy* (New Haven, CT, 2007), 170–90.

order in which power rested primarily in the hands of men. In particular, the serious responsibilities of elite politics were defined as an inherently male domain, in which the very notion of a female political leader came to appear to be almost a contradiction in terms. But, at a more popular level, the mass culture of the post-war years also encouraged a heightened sense of female individual identity. Women of almost all social classes could design themselves in terms of their tastes, appearance, way of life, and indeed relationships. This was for most women a limited freedom, constrained by the norms imposed by society and by the limits of their economic means; but it too formed part of the democratic ethos of the post-war years. In their role as democratic consumers, women became accustomed to exercising choice, through their appearance and leisure activities, as well as in their ways of living, their choice of partner, and— through the expansion in the knowledge and use of different forms of contraception—the size and shape of their families.[169]

Family was central to the experience of post-war democracy. The re-establishment of family life from the rubble of the war years was the most tangible symbol of the reconstruction of normality, both for individuals and for the nation as a whole.[170] Consequently, the assertion of domestic-ity and most especially of parenthood, even in those circumstances where the events of war had changed irrevocably the nature of home life, formed a key element of projects of social reconstruction and of the aspirations of millions of individual women and men. For them, founding or recon-structing a family was a statement of their survival, and an expression of their optimism for a better future.[171] This was an aspiration that received ample encouragement from the political parties and from local and cen-tral government, all of which vied to demonstrate their commitment to the family and the social stability that it expressed. Support for the family—and implicitly discrimination against alternative ways of living, such as non-heterosexual partnerships—was therefore evident at every

169. Carter, *How German Is She?*, 6–7; Chenut, *Fabric of Gender*, 397–98. Re. post-war fertility, see J. Gillis, L. Tilly, and D. Levine, eds., *The European Experience of Declin-ing Fertility, 1850–1970: The Quiet Revolution* (Cambridge, MA, 1972); Y. Knibiehler, *La révolution maternelle: Femmes, maternité, citoyenneté depuis 1945* (Paris, 1997), 47–57; F. Sweetser and P. Piepponen, "Fertility Trends and Their Consequences in Finland and the United States," *Journal of Social History* 1 (1967): 101–18.

170. Vaizey, "Empowerment or Endurance?" 61, 77–78; Zahra, *Lost Children*, 240–45; Tambor, *Lost Wave*, 15.

171. Knibiehler, *Révolution maternelle*, 21; Grossmann, "Trauma, Memory, and Moth-erhood," 93–127. See also, more generally, P. Ginsborg, *Family Politics: Domestic Life, Dev-astation and Survival 1900–1950* (New Haven, CT, 2014).

level of post-war public policy-making, from the provision of family allowances and the design and allocation of housing to the resources expended on resolving or pre-empting the threat of family breakdown.[172] Once again, the consequences for women of this project of a family democracy were ambivalent. It provided a means for state authorities to constrain women, confining them, both rhetorically and materially, within a narrow range of gendered activities.[173] But the emphasis placed upon the family as the fundamental unit of society also elevated women in the politics of the new democracy, and gave women a new sense of entitlement. Women were present in post-war democratic politics by right, campaigning on issues such as family allowances and paid maternity leave, which directly helped women and at the same time reinforced a sense of female citizenship.[174]

The example of gender therefore demonstrates the ways in which democracy extended well beyond the realm of politics. The constitutional and political refounding of democracy enacted at the end of the war was translated into social life over the subsequent years in ways that blunted its impact but also reinforced its durability. This was reinforced too by the rapid and irreversible changes in lives brought about by the economic growth of the post-war decades and everything that stemmed from it. Prosperity was neither sudden nor miraculous for most Europeans. The austerity of the war years extended well beyond the end of the conflict, giving rise to "hunger strikes" in post-war Germany, and obliging many throughout Europe to rely on a semi-official "economy of connections" in order to overcome the shortages of food and other basic commodities.[175] Salary levels in most countries continued to lag behind increases in prices until the end of the 1940s, and it was only from around 1955 onwards that most Western Europeans could finally feel that they were leaving the material legacies of the war behind.[176] What happened thereafter was an

172. Staub, "'Einmal im Leben,'" 157–62; Timm, *Politics of Fertility*, 305–8.

173. Moeller, *Protecting Motherhood*, 218.

174. Knibiehler, *Révolution maternelle*, 33–47; G. Bock and P. Thane, introduction to *Maternity and Gender Policies: Women and the Rise of the European Welfare States*, ed. Bock and Thane (London, 1991), 15.

175. Steege, *Black Market, Cold War*, 49–63. See also p. 32.

176. Re. salaries, see, for example, I. Cassiers and P. Scholliers, "Le pacte social belge de 1944, les salaires et la croissance économique en perspective internationale," in *Het Sociaal Pact van 1944*, ed. D. Luyten and G. Vanthemsche (Brussels, 1995), 161–90.

unprecedented period of unbroken economic growth until the early 1970s, which increased the GDP per head of the population of Western Europe from $5,346 in 1950 to $11,905 in 1973.[177] Presented as a digest of statistics, the rise in living standards during these post-war decades was indeed remarkable; but the narrative of post-war prosperity has often been written from the perspective of those bureaucrats and economists who regarded themselves as its architects. Aggregate statistics provide only a partial truth, and the *trente glorieuses*—as the thirty years from 1945 to the renewed economic crises of the mid-1970s have often come to be referred to in France—was neither universal nor emphatic. Inequalities between regions, economic sectors, and social classes determined the distribution of the wealth generated by economic growth, creating an enduring sense of winners and losers.[178] Its most significant impact was therefore more psychological than material. As the sufferings of the depression of the 1930s and the war years finally receded into the distance, so the attitude of Europeans to their present circumstances, and their future hopes, changed. There was a sense that a new age of democratic prosperity had begun, in which participation in new habits of meat eating, of holidays and travel, and of the acquisition of domestic commodities such as fridges, washing machines, and ultimately cars and televisions was possible, if not yet within everybody's immediate grasp.

It was an official of the American Marshall Plan, Harlan Cleveland, who apparently coined the phrase "a revolution of rising expectations" to describe the impact of this rapid economic growth on the populations of post-war Western Europe.[179] Seen through the prism of the popular magazines of the era or of films such as Fellini's *La Dolce Vita* and Godard's *A bout de souffle* (both released in 1960), Western Europeans appeared to have become intoxicated by the expanding empires of choice that surrounded them. Music, fashion, film, and travel were all forms of consumerism that had first developed during the interwar years, but which expanded rapidly from the early 1950s onwards, as the increase in disposable incomes brought them within the reach of a much greater proportion

177. N. Crafts, "The Great Boom 1950–1973," in *Western Europe: Economic and Social Change since 1945*, ed. M.-S. Schulze (London, 1999), 46.

178. R. Pawin, "Retour sur les 'Trente glorieuses' et la périodisation du second XXe siècle," *Revue d'histoire moderne et contemporaine* 60 (2013): 155–75; Chapman, *France's Long Reconstruction*, 15–16.

179. D. Ellwood, "The Propaganda of the Marshall Plan in Italy in a Cold War Context," in *The Cultural Cold War in Western Europe 1945–1960*, ed. G. Scott-Smith and H. Krabbendam (London, 2003), 226.

of the population. This democratization of choice was especially marked for the large cohort of young people born in the immediate post-war years, and who entered their teenage years—in itself a stage of life made possible by post-war prosperity—at the end of the 1950s. These emphatically post-war Europeans were in some ways a turbulent presence, rebelling against the conventions of post-war society and—as in the case of the *Halbstarken*, the German imitators of American youth culture—cultivating an image as rebels. But rebellion, too, had become a form of consumerism, as indicated by the way in which the trappings of youth culture, most notably fashion and music, rapidly lost their contestational character and became products of mass consumption.[180]

Much of the freedom generated by economic growth was, of course, no more than illusory. In a tract of 1958, the Belgian Socialist militant André Renard expressed the themes voiced by many on the political left but also by many others who feared that the desires generated by the rampant retail capitalism of the later 1950s were destroying the values of European life: "Conditionnés par les spécialistes de la publicité, les hommes se ruent vers les paradis artificiels que leur offre le monde capitaliste. . . . Des stimulants renouvellent sans cesse l'éternelle soif de jouissance qui les torture. . . . L'abrutissement par les plaisirs matériels faciles et sans effort est d'ailleurs le meilleur moyen d'atrophier l'activité cérébrale."[181] Women, as always, were seen as the particular victims of this new consumer culture: distracted by their preoccupation with fashion and other forms of selfish indulgence, they were supposedly trapped between the impossible goals of perfect beauty and the ideal home.[182]

There was of course nothing new about these rather extravagant fears and the surges of panic that they generated. They were in many ways just the latest manifestation of an anti-modernism that had been current in European cultural life since the late nineteenth century. Intellectuals had long been inclined to regard technological changes—and more especially those that in some way blurred the boundaries between high and mass

180. U. Poiger, *Jazz, Rock and Rebels: Cold War Politics and American Culture in a Divided Germany* (Berkeley, CA, 2000).

181. "Having been conditioned by advertising specialists, men rush towards the artificial paradises offered to them by the capitalist world. . . . Stimulants ceaselessly renew the thirst for pleasure which tortures them. . . . The brutalisation brought about by easy and effortless material pleasures serves, moreover, as the best means of atrophying the activity of the brain": Renard, *Vers le socialisme*, 30.

182. Moeller, *Protecting Motherhood*, 140; A. Haggett, *Desperate Housewives, Neuroses and the Domestic Environment, 1945–1970* (London, 2012).

culture—as destroying a pre-existing golden age, be it a Christian universe, a rational public sphere of Enlightenment debate, or the forward march of revolutionary progress.[183] Its latest manifestation was termed "Americanization," an amorphous danger that through everything from Coca Cola to washing machines and Hollywood films was undermining European civilization.[184] It was, however, the threat that Renard's "paradis artificiels" allegedly posed to democracy that gave these debates a new edge. The healthy operation of democracy had long been associated with a certain austerity: for Rousseau, Marx, and any number of Christian thinkers, democracy was associated with rural or proletarian egalitarianism, the fraternity of equals, and the rejection of selfish pleasure. Thus, as a tide of new-found material consumption appeared to be inundating Western Europe during the latter 1950s and 1960s, it was accompanied by warnings from intellectuals, who feared that it would crush political debate and associationism while reducing the people to acquiescence and individual isolation. Europe, the French Communist poet Louis Aragon declared in apocalyptic terms in 1951, was confronted by the prospect of an American-style "civilization of bathtubs and frigidaires"; while the Catholic writer Emmanuel Mounier fulminated with characteristic ferocity in the same year against "the individualist struggle for place and profit."[185]

For all its evident exaggeration, there is no doubt that such dystopian commentary had a point. The "consumer wonderland," as Erica Carter has termed it, that many northern Europeans rather suddenly discovered that they had come to inhabit at the end of the 1950s did change profoundly the patterns of European politics and society.[186] Everything from family life to social identities and political engagement was impacted by what was, in effect, a mass (though certainly not universal) transition from the politics of austerity and of getting by to one of consumption and of material opportunity. The change was all the more dramatic for its being relatively unexpected. Coming after decades of disrupted lives, material hardships, and personal tragedies, the prosperity of the latter 1950s and 1960s had an inevitable air of personal and social liberation. Lives had been turned

183. Solchany, *Comprendre le nazisme*, 213–56; Poiger, *Jazz, Rock and Rebels*, 13–29.

184. R. Kuisel, *Seducing the French: The Dilemma of Americanization* (Berkeley, CA, 1993).

185. Aragon quoted in Kuisel, *Seducing the French*, 38; Mounier, chapter 19 (untitled) in McKeon and Rokkan, *Democracy*, 231.

186. Carter, *How German Is She?* 51–59. See also J. Ceuleers, "Het geluk komt morgen," in *De stoute jaren 58 68* (Leuven, 1988), 7–19.

around, not only materially but also psychologically, as people's tastes, and their politics, were changed by the sustained increases in prosperity and the rapid spread of forms of new consumer products and media such as television. Western Europe and the United States had become part of what John Kenneth Galbraith termed in his 1958 book—with a greater sense of timing than of empirical accuracy—"the affluent society," in which individuals and families were preoccupied more by issues of personal consumption than the collective well-being of the community.[187]

This change was all the more profound because it appeared to be irreversible. Previous moments of prosperity in European history had always had a sense of the transient and the unstable. This, however, felt different. Once launched, the new modernity was carried forward by a seemingly endless series of technological breakthroughs that, in the form of space exploration, nuclear power, and medical treatments, were changing the world in ways that could not be undone, unless it was to be by the similarly technological tool of nuclear warfare.[188] Scientists were central to this process. They had come out of the laboratory and into the corridors and processes of government, where their knowledge and expertise had made possible the "democratic revolution."[189] Affluence, as popularized by Galbraith and others, rapidly became a key term for this new age, which changed the terms of political debate.[190] In particular, the emergence of a generalized culture of prosperity appeared to render redundant old disputes about redistribution, in favour of a new mentality of the alleviation of the social consequences of inequality.[191] More generally, however, affluence encouraged a more personal definition of freedom. What Michel Foucault—himself very much a figure marked by the character of the post-war era—termed "cultivation of the self" came to be an emblematic expression of a world in which the inherited identities of origins, or the socio-economic badges of community and of employment, no longer seemed to matter as much as the ways in which people chose how to configure themselves. In this highly visual universe,

187. J. K. Galbraith, *The Affluent Society* (London, 1958). For the context of Galbraith's book, and its enormous impact, see R. Parker, *J. K. Galbraith: A Twentieth-Century Life* (London, 2007), 292–310, and M. Berry, *The Affluent Society Revisited* (Oxford, 2013).

188. For characteristic examples of the future-oriented hyperbole of the era, see S. Zuckerman, foreword to *The Next Hundred Years*, by H. Brown, J. Bonner and J. Weir (London, 1957), ix–x.

189. R. A. Buchanan, *Technology and Social Progress* (Oxford, 1965), 123–44.

190. S. Middleton, "Affluence and the Left in Britain c.1958–1974," *English Historical Review* 129 (2014): 107–38.

191. See pp. 194–95.

the reference points provided by film, mass-circulation magazines, and advertising appeared to provide the resources for individuals to design themselves.[192]

The social ethos of this new era was consequently one of individualism. The term defies any easy definition, and certainly did not mean that the inhabitants of the new Western Europe of the 1950s and 1960s had ceased to be defined by the close networks of family, workplace, and community, which remained one of the distinctive characteristics of European society. But what the Italian sociologist Alessandro Pizzorno, writing in 1964, termed "the individualistic mobilisation of Europe" did express the widely felt truth that those Europeans who had come of age since the end of the war had a new attitude to the wider societies of which they formed part.[193] Mass culture homogenized societies—by encouraging consumption of the same music, radio programmes, or fashion among the most diverse communities—but it also acted in a disintegrative manner, creating new social demarcations and spaces within which individuals found opportunities for self-expression, and for the construction of new communities of taste and affinity.[194]

This change in mentality whereby Europeans came to think of themselves as individuals possessed of rights that, however circumscribed they might be by social norms and state authority, were inalienably their own is one of the most difficult to trace across the post-war period. But an increased self-confidence, and with it a willingness to question structures of authority, was apparent throughout the culture of the 1950s and 1960s. The broader hierarchies of deference that had for so long characterized European life—the respect owed to state officials, to teachers and clergy, or more simply to social superiors and parents—retreated quite rapidly during the post-war decades. Some of this was very conscious, as was evident in the carnivalesque mocking of authority that accompanied the events of 1968;[195] but much more of it was simply an unwinding of the mentalities of the past. Among the numerous young of the post-war generations, but also among many of their elders, the former mentalities of quiet obedience, as taught and replicated through educational institutions and the wider fabric of society, were replaced by a new, and liberating,

192. M. Foucault, *The History of Sexuality*, vol. 3, *Care of the Self* (London, 1986), 39–68; Forgacs and Gundle, *Mass Culture*, 63–91; M. Glancy, *Hollywood and the Americanization of Britain from the 1920s to the Present* (London, 2014), 31–41.

193. Pizzorno, "Individualistic Mobilization of Europe," 199–224.

194. See the intelligent reflections in Forgacs and Gundle, *Mass Culture*, 1–4.

195. See p. 287.

sense of self, which reflected the less formal and simply more democratic ethos of post-war society.[196]

Even illusory forms of freedom, therefore, have a historic importance. It mattered less that the consumerism of the post-war decades generated new forms of emulation and conformity than that it reinforced a pervasive ethos of individual choice. Just as Western Europeans increasingly felt free to choose their appearance, their friends, or their lifestyle, so they also chose their politics. As the new science of opinion polling that developed in the post-war decades well indicated, political preferences were no longer, if they had ever been, the simple consequence of class, confession, and community; instead, they emerged from a more complex amalgam of identities, preferences, and choices that in turn reflected the more complex gradations of post-war society.[197] This also implied a changed relationship to the wider whole. Individuals selected their politics as a consequence not of their inheritance but of their personal preferences and perceived material interests. Terms such as "cynical" or "sceptical," which were often deployed by more conservative-minded commentators—of both the left and the right—when describing the disabused attitudes of post-war generations, offered only a somewhat skewed reflection of the wider reality of the changed attitude adopted by many Western Europeans towards the marketplace of political choices. By becoming less ideological in their world views, post-war Europeans had, it seemed, become more tactical in their political loyalties, prioritizing their personal concerns and the security of social stability over the more fundamental struggles of political regime of the recent past.[198]

In this way, citizenship and consumerism undoubtedly came closer together.[199] In a thoughtful and wide-ranging speech entitled (in its published form) "La crise de la démocratie," the French politician and recent prime minister Pierre Mendès France gave voice in July 1955 to the concerns of many within the political elite when he regretted the decline in civic spirit—*civisme*—that he believed had occurred among voters over recent years. Too many citizens, he observed, seemed to think only of their personal interests, besieging him and other parliamentary deputies, for

196. Fishman, *Vichy to the Sexual Revolution*, 114–77.

197. Kruke, *Demoskopie in der Bundesrepublik*.

198. The concept of a sceptical generation was coined by Helmut Schelsky in *The Skeptical Generation: A Sociological Picture of German Youth* (Dusseldorf, 1957). For critical perspectives, see Poiger, *Jazz, Rock and Rebels*, 119; Weil, "Philosophical and Political Thought," 498–513; Stöss, *Politics against Democracy*, 96–97.

199. Carter, *How German Is She?* 6.

example, with requests that their sons should be exempted from military service in Algeria.[200] Such behaviour, and the wider depoliticization that it seemed to betoken, was, however, a reconfiguration of the relationship between citizens and the political process. As the new social protests of the later 1960s would well demonstrate, individuals had in no sense turned their back on political engagement; still less had they abandoned the ambition to improve their personal or collective position within society. But the means of achieving those goals had changed. Frontal challenges had been replaced by more indirect forms of action; outright commitment had been replaced by a more tactical awareness of knowing when to make demands and when to keep quiet, with the consequence that political engagement was located within a wider calculus of personal and family interest. In these ways, democratic politics might have become less turbulent, but it had also become more pervasive.

200. Mendès France, "Crise de la démocratie," 98–100.

CHAPTER FIVE

Contesting Democracy

THE DEMOCRATIC CRITIQUE OF DEMOCRACY

SOMETHING CHANGED IN the culture of Western European democracy in the early 1960s. The model of rather limited and carefully structured democratic government that had provided the states of Western Europe with their route out of the crises of the 1930s and 1940s no longer garnered the same degree of elite, popular, and—more especially—intellectual support. Instead, a wide variety of voices began to be raised, criticizing the shortcomings of the democratic regimes, as well as advancing alternative visions of a democratic society and politics. Much of this discontent remained muted, constrained by the rejection of the authoritarian past of Nazism (and its allies) and the present reality—especially after 1956— of the tangibly oppressive Communist regimes in central and eastern Europe. This was not, therefore, a return to the debates of the 1930s, with their stark juxtaposition of alternative ideological world views. Instead, the dissenting voices of the 1960s focused on the perceived failings of the existing political structures, questioning whether the vertical hierarchies of representation through parliaments, parties, and interest groups were the best means of achieving the goals of individual freedom, social justice, and a participatory democratic culture. But debates about means also became debates about ends. In particular, a radical cultural and political critique emerged that questioned the forms of authority—explicit and implicit—within modern societies. This also challenged the nature of the post-war settlement. Far from creating a new democratic culture, the changes after 1945, these critics argued, had dismantled the authoritarian regimes while retaining the edifice of state power, and a society of regimented and limited freedoms.

None of this was entirely new. There had always been those, on the right and (particularly) the left, who had placed themselves outside the frontiers of post-war democratic convergence. But what changed was that the debate about democracy became, so to speak, a debate within democracy. The division was no longer between what Karl Popper had termed the open society and its enemies,[1] but between the defenders of the political status quo and those who from a wide variety of standpoints sought variously to reform, restructure, or transform the existing model of democracy. To impose too great a clarity on these critical voices would be misleading; indeed, their principal characteristic was that they remained fluid, or even at times incoherent, inclined to reject formal structures and what Raymond Aron nervously termed "the silken thread of legality"—le fil de soie de la légalité—in favour of the emotive pull of dreams of radical change, new forms of community, and the models of participatory democracy coming into being in the post-colonial world.[2] This was also a debate that was much more than political. One of the distinguishing characteristics of the critical debate of the 1960s was that it encompassed an often bewilderingly diverse range of issues, including social justice, representation, and the nature of the state, as well as human solidarity and the emancipation of the individual.

In their different guises, these advocates of change could be in turn reformist and revolutionary, incremental and local, as well as all-encompassing and explicitly global. But what they shared was a sense of dissatisfaction, and at times of frustration. The wars of the recent past (including those with Soviet Communism) appeared to be effectively over, or at a standstill, and this encouraged a sharper focus on the shortcomings of the society and politics that they had created. These critiques highlighted the social injustices that persisted within societies of affluence, the ever more visible inequalities of race and gender, and the structures of repression and social control engrained within modern state power. Rooted within the new methodologies of social science, these ideas circulated initially among the few rather than the many; but through their wider diffusion they soon became part of how many Western Europeans came to see and judge their own democracy.

The events that contributed to this shift in the terms of democratic debate are not difficult to identify. The world changed shape quite rapidly

---

1. K. R. Popper, *The Open Society and Its Enemies* (London, 1945). Re. Popper, see the essential study by Hacohen, *Karl Popper*, esp. 449–520.

2. Raymond Aron, *Démocratie et totalitarisme*, 374.

from the early 1960s onwards, as the demise of European global empires and the emergence of new forms of economic power and state development in Africa, Asia, and the Middle East appeared to suck power away from Europe and towards the global South. These changes gave rise to new liberation campaigns and wars—most notably in Algeria, Cuba, Vietnam, and across the post-colonial Middle East—and also to new forms of democratic practice. As a consequence, the west lost any claim to an exclusive ownership of democracy, as new states and movements emerged that explicitly rejected western norms.[3] In particular, many of the democracies of the global South dispensed with the formal exercises of multiparty electoral politics in favour of more amorphous mass movements and local community politics, based on the melding of the models of the socialist world with more indigenous traditions.[4] The locus and character of the Cold War was also changed by these global shifts. The Cuban Missile Crisis of 1962 was effectively the last direct confrontation between the two rival power blocs generated by the partition of Europe at the end of the Second World War. Significantly, too, it occurred not in Europe but in the Caribbean, in the wake of the overthrow in 1959 of an American-backed dictatorship in Cuba by a constellation of radical anti-imperialist forces headed by Fidel Castro. Henceforth, US-Soviet rivalries manifested themselves not in preparations for war in Europe, but rather through the competitive pursuit of quasi-imperial influence across the post-colonial world. The tools of diplomatic patronage, military sponsorship, financial aid, and economic development were the new means by which the United States and the Soviet Union built coalitions of support and dependence, particularly in the Middle East, South East Asia, and sub-Saharan Africa.

Western Europeans were spectators, or at most secondary participants, in these wider global events. In the words of Reinhard Bendix—one of the band of German refugees from Nazism who had subsequently built an academic career in the United States—they were witnesses to "a waning of the European age."[5] The European powers were frequently implicated in the conflicts that developed in Africa and Asia from the 1960s onwards,

3. Dipesh Chakrabarty reflects on this decentring of Europe, and the influence of this change on his own intellectual formation, in the preface to the 2007 edition of his *Provincializing Europe: Postcolonial Thought and Historical Difference* (Princeton, NJ, 2008), xi–xv.

4. See notably the suggestive analyses in A. Milner, *The Invention of Politics in Colonial Malaya: Contesting Nationalism and the Expansion of the Public Sphere* (Cambridge, UK, 1994); E. Hunter, *Political Thought and the Public Sphere in Tanzania: Freedom, Democracy and Citizenship in the Era of Decolonization* (Cambridge, UK, 2015).

5. Bendix, *Embattled Reason*, 335–37.

notably through the volatile legacies of their imperial rule. But their role was increasingly cast in the past tense. Europe was becoming simply Europe: a region located between the superpowers, in Anton DePorte's influential formula.[6] And this in turn accorded a new independence to Western European political life. While the structures of Soviet military and political control remained explicit in the east, things were tangibly different in the west. During the later 1940s and 1950s, the need to defend the territories and regimes of Western Europe from Communism, as well as the pressing priorities of material reconstruction, had appeared to provide a self-evident justification of democracy, and of alliance with the United States. By the 1960s, however, this no longer seemed to be the case, and the focus of political and intellectual discussion shifted from trench warfare between democracy and its opponents to the different ways of envisaging democracy.

This was a debate focused on the present and the future; but it was also one about the recent past. With the passage of time, many Europeans came to reflect critically on the events of the war years and their aftermath. In particular, many came to feel that the liberation had been a missed opportunity when Europe could and should have enacted a more radical reconfiguration of social and political power.[7] Control of state institutions, so it was argued, had remained in the grasp of a relatively closed ruling elite, many of whom were linked by their past actions, affiliations, or mentalities to the authoritarian regimes of the preceding decades, be they Nazism in central Europe, the Fascist regime in Italy, or the Vichy state in wartime France. The democratic debates of the 1960s were therefore in part an autopsy of the events of the mid-twentieth century, rooted in a perceived need to come to terms with that past through the purging of state institutions, and the prosecution of those responsible for the crimes of the war years—above all the persecution of Europe's Jewish populations.

At the same time, however, attitudes towards democracy were also influenced by the scale of the changes that had taken place in the societies of Western Europe since the war. The sense of living in an era of ever-accelerating change became one of the most pervasive commonplaces of the 1960s.[8] The modern seemed inescapable, through the ubiquity of new technologies and the tangible newness of the physical and social

6. A. DePorte, *Europe between the Superpowers: The Enduring Balance* (New Haven, CT, 1979).

7. Greenberg, *Weimar Century*, 256–57; Forner, *German Intellectuals*, 279–331.

8. Bendix, *Embattled Reason*, 315–48; G. Therborn, *European Modernity and Beyond: The Trajectory of European Societies 1945–2000* (London, 1995), 351.

environment that had emerged since the war. Western Europeans lived in new ways in new buildings, communities, and even towns, which contrasted with the mid-century societies that they used to inhabit, and which for the most part they could still remember. As a consequence, the frontier between past and present had, it seemed, drawn closer to the present, generating a widespread belief that Europeans were inhabiting an era in which the mindsets and institutions of the past were no longer valid. This also applied to democracy. A political structure that had been created so directly out of the struggles of the past needed to be rethought to match the aspirations of an emphatically modern world.

The apparent disjuncture between a rapidly changing present and the rigidities of the political structure that had developed over the preceding decades was central to the debates of the 1960s. What had once been the solution to Europe's problems of governance was in danger of coming to be seen as the source of the problem, prompting multiple projects for reform. Some of these concentrated on institutional change, with the ambition of creating more efficient structures of decision-making. But many others sought to encourage greater participation. The perception that political institutions had become too remote from wider society was voiced with increasing insistence during the 1960s, leading to calls for a broader refounding of democracy. In its more specific forms, this often focused on plans for countering the trend towards oligarchical rule by elites and experts by revitalizing the methods of election and representation within the political system. But it also encompassed more radical ambitions to relocate democracy to the local and community level. By dismantling the hierarchical structures of state power and control, society would be freed to govern itself. Such ideas, and the aspirations that they expressed, reflected a more educated and individualist society, in which people were no longer content simply to be alive and to be experiencing rising living standards. Instead, they wanted to enjoy a greater personal freedom to live their lives as they chose, and to exercise a real influence on how the affairs of their political community, both local and national, were conducted.

These aspirations lacked a unifying ideology. If there was a movement or individual capable of rallying the diverse voices calling for a reform of democracy in the 1960s, it never succeeded in making itself felt. Instead, the debates of the decade remained obstinately plural and diffuse, in both their inspiration and their ambition. It is important, too, not to exaggerate their radicalism. Partly because of the shadow cast retrospectively by the events of 1968, it would be easy to construct an impression of a dominant

mood of discontent, or even of proto-revolutionary revolt. This is indeed
how narratives of the 1960s have often been written, both at the time and
in retrospect. The quasi-revolutionary events that swept across Paris and
other major cities and university campuses in Western Europe in 1968
are presented as the culmination of pressures that had built up over the
preceding years.[9] Statistics of economic growth, numbers of university
students, pop-music sales, and even the use of the contraceptive pill are all
assembled to construct a catch-all account of Europe's last revolution.[10]

Books on origins and causes were indeed part of the intellectual mentality of the 1960s. The genre had been founded, in its modern form, by the
French historian Georges Lefebvre, who wrote, for the 150th anniversary
of the French Revolution of 1789 in 1939, a succinct account of its origins,
presenting it as the emergence of a new society out of the feudal strait-
jacket of the *ancien régime*.[11] Lefebvre's book was banned the following
year by the new rulers of Vichy France, and eight thousand copies of it
destroyed;[12] but the model proved influential, and a whole series of historical works were published across the post-war decades that approached
past events—notably the English Civil War, the First World War, and the
Russian Revolution—in terms of their political and social causes.[13] Generally broadly Marxist or progressive in inspiration, such works conveyed
a sense that history proceeded through a series of stages of modernization, from which there was no retreat, each of which was rooted in the
divorce that developed between a fixed political system and the changing
society over which it sought to rule. Revolutions, and other major historical upheavals, this literature served to underline, occurred for good reason. Thus, despite, or perhaps because of, its failure to overturn the state

9. See, for example, the phraseology of Damir Skenderovic and Christina Späti with
reference to Switzerland: "68 ne serait pas une simple irruption mais bien la suite logique
d'une histoire longtemps enterrée" (*Années 68*, 19).

10. J. Jackson, Milne, and Williams, *May 68*. The classic expression of this approach to
the "long 1960s" is A. Marwick, *The Sixties: Cultural Revolution in Britain, France, Italy,
and the United States, c.1958–c.1974* (Oxford, 1998), esp. 3–20. But see also G. De Groot,
The 60s Unplugged: A Kaleidoscopic History of a Disorderly Decade (London, 2008), and
Horn, *Spirit of '68*.

11. G. Lefebvre, *Quatre-vingt-neuf* (Paris, 1939), translated into English as *The Coming
of the French Revolution, 1789* (Princeton, NJ, 1947), and many subsequent editions.

12. R. R. Palmer, preface to *The Coming of the French Revolution, 1789*, by G. Lefebvre
(Princeton, NJ, 1947), vi.

13. F. Fischer, *Krieg der Illusionen: Die deutsche Politik von 1911 bis 1914* (Dusseldorf,
1969); L. Stone, *The Causes of the English Revolution, 1529–1642* (London, 1972). For a
more ironic description of this preoccupation with causality, see A. Cobban, *Historians and
the Causes of the French Revolution* (London, 1958).

regimes of Western Europe, 1968 rapidly became incorporated into this historical canon—an event, like the revolutions of 1848 or the Paris Commune of 1870–71, to be celebrated not so much for its achievement as for its potentiality.[14]

Perhaps characteristically, Raymond Aron was an immediate critic of this interpretation, which he believed invested the actions of the student activists with an unwarranted legitimacy. In his polemical *La révolution introuvable* (part of which was originally published as a series of articles in *Le figaro* as the events unfolded in 1968) he invoked Tocqueville's hostile perceptions of the revolutionaries of 1848 to present his own, rather dyspeptic, account of the irrationality of the protest movements. For him, 1968 should not be regarded as a true revolution, but as a series of accidents that had demonstrated the continued presence of what he deplored as "le virus révolutionnaire" within French society. Led astray by their lack of political maturity, the self-styled revolutionaries had neglected the essential modest virtues of democratic freedom. Instead, they pursued chimerical dreams of a millennial moment of transition that, if by some mischance they had come to pass, would have ended in disaster.[15]

Aron's voice was an isolated one, and on the whole has remained so. If nothing else, the activists of 1968 have been fortunate in their historians, who have generally taken as their starting point the assumption that the protests of the era were the expression of a wider political and social malaise.[16] This approach has many strengths, especially because of the way in which it focuses attention on the societal tensions generated in France and elsewhere by the imbalance between rapid socio-economic changes and the absence of equivalent political and institutional reforms. But it also risks confining the democratic debates of the 1960s within a teleological framework whereby everything is presented in terms of how it contributed to the making of "the generation '68."[17] This chapter therefore seeks to avoid the rather self-limiting focus on the events of that year. Instead, it explores the different discourses about democracy that developed during the 1960s—some of which contributed to the radicalism of 1968, while others emphatically did not. Indeed, the sheer diversity of views advanced

14. M. Seidman, *The Imaginary Revolution: Parisian Students and Workers in 1968* (New York, 2004), 1–10.

15. Raymond Aron, *La révolution introuvable* (Paris, 1968), esp. 141–53 (quotation at 144); Craiutu, "Thinking Politically," 73–102.

16. This is an approach that remains apparent in Ludivine Bantigny's excellent recent study of France in 1968: *1968: De grands soirs en petits matins* (Paris, 2018).

17. See the intelligent critique by Julie Pagis in *May '68: Shaping Political Generations* (Amsterdam, 2018), 26–28.

during the 1960s demonstrates how democracy had become itself a subject of debate. And that, too, was a demonstration of the political evolution that had taken place in Western Europe since the war.

{≈≈≈≈≈}

This new mood of debate, and increasingly of contestation, developed rather suddenly from the end of the 1950s into the 1960s. When, for example, the young Jürgen Habermas published his *Habilitation* thesis in 1962, rather indigestibly entitled (in its English translation) *The Structural Transformation of the Public Sphere: An Inquiry into a Category of Bourgeois Society*, it may have launched his distinguished intellectual career, but the themes that he espoused echoed preoccupations that were becoming increasingly prominent in European political debates. Published only two years after Raymond Aron's speech in Berlin, Habermas's study belonged to a tangibly different generation. Born in 1929, his intellectual development had been emphatically post-war, albeit one that remained profoundly overshadowed by the legacies of Nazism and of the war years. Habermas's thesis charted what he regarded as the decline of the public sphere of rational debate first created by the Enlightenment. In contemporary society, parliament had been subordinated to the control of political party-machines, social organizations had "re-feudalized" the public sphere with their private interests, and the "industry of political marketing" had turned political leaders into commodities to be sold to the population. These changes had, in turn, robbed the citizen of his or her sense of participating in a larger democratic politics. The citizen was at best a consumer, and at worst a simple spectator in a process that had the superficial appearance, but little of the substance, of democracy.[18]

Habermas's complex academic formulations were hardly the material of political slogans; but the themes that he foregrounded, and more especially the contrasts he drew between the rituals and reality of democracy, were widely voiced in European political and intellectual debate during the early 1960s. Government, it was asserted, had become too impervious to the concerns of ordinary people, creating what a Belgian politician of impeccably moderate views, Arthur Gilson, politely termed a "worrying discrepancy"—inquiétant décalage—between the existing structures

---

18. Habermas, *Structural Transformation*, quotations at 195 (re-feudalization; repeated on p. 231 at greater length) and 216 (industry of political marketing).

of democratic representation and the needs of the contemporary age.[19] For those on the Marxist left, this disjuncture was unsurprising. It was the expression of the structural inequalities inherent in capitalist society, which had distorted the whole project of democratic representation, generating what the outspoken intellectual of the New Left André Gorz termed "a state of profound crisis."[20] But the complaint that the machinery of democratic representation no longer worked to convey the demands of society was also expressed by many others. For some, the problem lay in the way in which the old vices of party corruption and self-interest had once again inserted themselves between the people and their rulers.[21] For others, however, the explanation lay in the way in which the social, economic, and cultural changes that had occurred in Western Europe since the Second World War had encouraged an oligarchic and anti-democratic structure of decision-making. Rather than government by the people, or at least by their representatives assembled in elected chambers, democracy had become, in the words of the secretary general of the Gaullist Party in 1964, Jacques Baumel, a "management democracy"—démocratie de gestion—where the real power lay in the hands of "a regime of technicians, specialists, and decision-makers."[22]

The remedy to this de-democratization—or *Entdemokratisierung*[23]— of the process of governance lay, it was widely asserted, in creating new and more direct forms of communication between rulers and ruled. This was a language that was exploited most dramatically by de Gaulle. He had become increasingly frustrated by the constraints on his freedom of political manoeuvre imposed by the constitution of the Fifth Republic, and in 1962 he abruptly abandoned his former political caution. Buoyed by the Evian Agreement with the Algerian nationalists of the FLN in March 1962, and its overwhelming ratification by the French people in a referendum in April, de Gaulle decided to create the more presidential structure of rule that had long been his personal preference. He dismissed Michel Debré as prime minister without reference to parliament, and replaced him with his personal nominee Georges Pompidou. Then, in September, he abruptly

19. A. Gilson, *Pour une démocratie efficace* (Louvain, 1965), 11. See, for very similar comments, F. Perin, *La démocratie enrayée* (Brussels, 1960).

20. A. Gorz, *Socialism and Revolution* (London, 1975), 73–82, quotation at 73. Gorz's book was written in 1965–66. Re. Gorz, see also A. Little, *The Political Thought of André Gorz* (London, 1996).

21. Dujardin and Dumoulin, *Jean-Charles Snoy*, 327–51.

22. Quoted in Watson, "Internal Dynamics of Gaullism," 189. See, for similar comments, Club Jean Moulin, *Etat et le citoyen*, 188–89.

23. Falla, *Zwischen Integration und Klassenkampf*, 198.

announced a referendum on a constitutional revision that would institute the direct election of the president by universal suffrage.[24]

What effectively amounted to a second founding of the Fifth Republic aroused strong opposition within the French political elite. His actions provoked predictable outrage from parliamentarians outside of the ranks of the new Gaullist party, the UNR, including on the part of those figures such as the Socialist Guy Mollet who had supported de Gaulle in 1958, as well as more private criticisms by state officials who feared that the direct election of the president would open the way to a demagogic politics.[25] Parliament passed a vote of censure in Pompidou's government on 5 October, to which de Gaulle responded by simply reappointing Pompidou, dissolving parliament, and calling new elections. These actions were far from being entirely constitutional, but de Gaulle received retrospective vindication of them through the majorities he won relatively narrowly in the referendum in October on the constitutional revision, and which the UNR obtained by a more convincing margin in the legislative elections held in November.[26]

As always with the rather sudden changes of direction that characterized de Gaulle's long political career, it is difficult to divine whether his actions reflected anything more than an impulsive wish to evade being constrained by the actions of those—notably elected politicians, but also the officials who constituted the Conseil d'état (Council of State)—whose pretentions and autonomy he clearly resented.[27] However, the changes that they brought about in the democratic politics of the Fifth Republic were significant and enduring. The representative politics embodied by the National Assembly was doubly diminished: the prime minister and ministers, it was now clear, were responsible to the president and not to parliament, while the direct election of the president substantially tilted power within the Fifth Republic towards a president whose democratic mandate and seven-year term of office enabled him to act independently of the constraints imposed by politicians and parties.[28]

24. Berstein, *Republic of de Gaulle*, 67–73.

25. Andrieu, "Politiques de Pierre Sudreau," 76–77; D. Mauss, "Guy Mollet et l'élaboration de la Constitution de 1958," in *Guy Mollet: Un camarade en République*, ed. B. Ménager, P. Ratte, J.-L. Thiébault, R. Vandenbussche, and C.-M. Wallon-Leducq (Lille, 1987), 349–63.

26. A. Shennan, *De Gaulle* (London, 1993), 110–13.

27. J. Jackson, *Certain Idea of France*, 558–63; M.-C. Kieffer, "L'impératif des grands corps," in *De Gaulle et les élites*, ed. S. Berstein, P. Birnbaum, and J.-P. Rioux (Paris, 2008), 82–83.

28. Berstein, *Republic of de Gaulle*, 77–78, 84–86; V. Wright, *The Government and Politics of France* (London, 1978).

In practice, de Gaulle's attempt to create what Aron referred to rather ironically in Bonapartist terms as "le troisième Empire"[29] was only a partial success. In the first and only presidential campaign he contested in 1965, he was unexpectedly forced into a second-round run-off against the fiercest critic of his new political regime, François Mitterrand.[30] Moreover, in 1969, it was his defeat in a referendum held to approve his proposals for a new regional structure of government that would prompt his abrupt resignation as president.[31] More generally, too, the personalized and hierarchical model of governance that de Gaulle aspired to achieve sat awkwardly with the underlying culture of French democracy. The elected representatives assembled in the twin houses of the National Assembly and the Senate remained the expression of the irreducibly partisan and territorial characteristics of French political life. Moreover, for all of the emphasis that de Gaulle liked to place on elevating the autonomy of the state, and the corps of elite officials who embodied it,[32] he was obliged to rely on the collective skills of the same state bureaucrats, technicians, and local notables who had carried so much of the weight of France's reconstruction since the Second World War.[33] Thus, the governing culture of the Fifth Republic continued to operate within the mould created by its predecessor. Rule by assembly, and consequently by coalition governments composed of elected political figures had indeed gone, but this had not freed the central state from the constraints imposed by local officials, as well as a broad range of economic interest groups and social organizations. Governance was a complex matter, and the ability of the state to address dossiers of economic modernization and social reform relied to a large degree on its ability to gain the collaboration of these wider societal forces.[34]

De Gaulle never therefore achieved his desired transformation in state power. But it is difficult not to see in de Gaulle's aspiration for an

29. Raymond Aron, *Démocratie et totalitarisme*, 13.

30. F. Mitterrand, *Le coup d'état permanent* (Paris, 1964), esp. 271–79; Berstein, *Republic of de Gaulle*, 193–202.

31. Berstein, *Republic of de Gaulle*, 233–41.

32. M. O. Baruch, "Les élites d'état dans la modernisation," in *De Gaulle et les élites*, ed. S. Berstein, P. Birnbaum, and J.-P. Rioux (Paris, 2008), 95–111. See also the contemporary celebration of this new state culture in J. Ardagh, *The New France* (Harmondsworth, UK, 1970).

33. Watson, "Internal Dynamics of Gaullism," esp. 181–306; Chapman, *France's Long Reconstruction*, 299–312.

34. See the examples provided by Newsome, "'Apartment Referendum,'" 329–58; H. Bonin, "L'action du premier ministre Chaban-Delmas pour rendre la France industrielle plus performante (1969–1972)," *Revue historique* 654 (2010): 397–426.

"accord direct"—a direct bond—between the president and the people the expression of the wider evolution taking place in the assumptions that had underpinned understandings of democracy in Europe since the Second World War.[35] With the development of new forms of communication, there no longer seemed to be the same need to rely on the intermediate institutions of parliament and the political parties. Instead, referenda, the new technologies of political communication, and above all the media of state-controlled radio and television, seemed to offer the possibility of a permanent dialogue between rulers and ruled. Technology was in that sense not only—as Habermas and many on the left alleged—a threat to the values of a plural civil society, but also had the potential to generate alternative forms of democracy. The increased interest in presidentialism reflected this mentality. Especially during the presidency of John F. Kennedy between 1961 and 1963, American democracy—so long regarded with some disdain in Europe[36]—became a more visible and attractive example for many Western Europeans of how a personalized system of rule could combine effective executive authority, informed by modern forms of technical expertise, with the direct engagement of the electorate.[37]

One such advocate for the need to modernize the machinery of democratic government was the French centre-left politician Pierre Mendès France, who in 1962 published a forceful book entitled *République moderne*.[38] Mendès France was no ally of de Gaulle; indeed, he was one of the few figures within the political elite who had consistently opposed de Gaulle's actions since 1958.[39] But, after a brief period as prime minister in 1954–55, he had become one of the most forthright critics of the timidity and conservative instincts of the parliamentary culture of the Fourth Republic. The source of the problem, Mendès France declared, lay not only with specific individuals and parties but also a more general lack of a shared civic spirit among elected representatives and the wider population.[40] There was therefore a need to rethink the principle of representation to achieve "a democratic irrigation"—une irrigation démocratique—of

35. Charles de Gaulle, speech, 8 June 1962, in de Gaulle, *Discours et messages* 3: 422.

36. See pp. 146–47.

37. Andrieu, *Amour de la République*, 422–37.

38. P. Mendès France, *La République moderne* (Paris, 1962).

39. Chatriot, *Pierre Mendès-France*, 170–74; Chapman, *France's Long Reconstruction*, 209–59.

40. See, for example, Mendès France, "Crise de la démocratie," 81–103, and "La République," in *Oeuvres complètes*, vol. 4 (Paris, 1987), 341–47. See also pp. 253–54.

the collective life of the nation.[41] This required re-engaging people with political debate, and supplementing the individual franchise by the collective representation of interest groups. Thus, just as de Gaulle called on occasions for the involvement of those whom he termed the "living forces"—forces vives—of the nation with the process of government,[42] Mendès France advocated the replacement of the Senate—created in the 1870s as a bastion of the political notables of rural and provincial France—with a Conseil économique et social (Economic and Social Council) composed of the representatives of the economic interest groups of the modern economy.[43]

Mendès France's combination of resonant phrases and rather modest suggestions for reform was characteristic of much of the debate that developed around democracy in Western Europe during the early 1960s. There was a widely shared sense that something needed to be changed, but much less agreement as to how, and in what direction, that change should be effected. On one point, however, almost everybody was agreed: democracy must be "modern." A system of parliamentary government initially devised in the age of the stagecoach, one collective volume published by French state officials and political figures in 1961 declared, was not fit for purpose in the second half of the twentieth century.[44] Throughout Western Europe, there was a preoccupation with modernizing the processes of government. The creation in 1962 of the first centre-left government in Italy since the immediate post-war period fostered hopes of a reformist spirit of government, just as the Labour Party in Britain came into power after the 1964 election as a self-proclaimed modernizing party that would use the new tools of planning to transform Britain's economy and society.[45] The term "modern" in this context often meant little more than the aping of a fashionable rhetoric of science and technology, deployed to avoid addressing

41. Mendès France, *République moderne*, 49. Re. Mendès France's ideas, see also the collection of essays in F. Bédarida and J.-P. Rioux, eds., *Pierre Mendès-France et le mendésisme* (Paris, 1985).

42. A. Chatriot, "A la recherche des 'forces vives,'" in S. Berstein, P. Birnbaum, and J.-P. Rioux, eds., *De Gaulle et les élites* (Paris, 2008), 219–37.

43. Mendès France, *République moderne*, 29–49. When he republished the book in 1966, Mendès France toned down the suggestion of replacing the Senate with a *Conseil*, seemingly because in the interim the same reform had been proposed by his nemesis, de Gaulle: Chatriot, *Pierre Mendès-France*, 178.

44. Club Jean Moulin, *Etat et le citoyen*, 9–18. On the club, see also the essential study by C. Andrieu, *Amour de la République*.

45. Ginsborg, *History of Contemporary Italy*, 267–72; G. O'Hara, *From Dreams to Disillusionment: Economic and Social Planning in 1960s Britain* (Basingstoke, UK, 2007), 9–36.

harder questions about political and economic power.[46] But in some cases it also betokened a more substantial aspiration for political reform. More than fifteen years after the end of the war, the shortcomings of the political settlements concluded in 1945 were becoming more apparent. This was particularly so in Austria and Belgium. In both of these states, political change became entangled with a broader reconfiguration of the nation and its institutions. In Belgium, this arose from the perceived failings of the centralized constitutional structure inherited from the nineteenth century, and the pressure for regional devolution generated by increasing tensions between the francophone south and the Dutch-speaking north.[47] In Austria, the debate surrounding the so-called *Demokratiereform* in the early 1960s reflected similar frustrations at the absence of any substantial constitutional reform after the recovery of national independence in 1945. Instead, the two dominant political forces—the SPÖ and the ÖVP—had effectively divided up power within a grand coalition, denying the electors any significant sense of democratic choice.[48]

The desire to create a more participatory political system and democratic culture became a consistent theme of the 1960s. This was above all a debate conducted among political and intellectual elites. The idea that the somewhat divergent priorities of effective authority and democratic control could be reconciled within a system of government that would be both more efficient and more modern formed part of the mood of the age.[49] But it also reflected a change in generation among the political elites. The new figures who came to the fore in most European states at this time—more self-consciously modern, pragmatic, and in their own minds less ideological—were concerned to differentiate themselves from the more conservative ambitions of their predecessors.[50] Democracy, however, proved easier to rethink or to reimagine—especially within the culture of think tanks and political clubs that proliferated during the 1960s[51]—than to reform. The sheer complexity of the mechanisms of modern government acted as an obstacle to substantial change. State bureaucracies both central and local, parliamentary assemblies and their committees, institutions of social and

46. See the spirited polemic: P. Foot, *The Politics of Harold Wilson* (Harmondsworth, UK, 1968).

47. Conway, *Sorrows of Belgium*, 374–86.

48. Pelinka and Welan, *Demokratie und Verfassung*, 53–54; Kreichbaumer, *Zwischen Land und Bund*, 15–76.

49. Chatriot, *Pierre Mendès-France*, 177; Watson, "Internal Dynamics of Gaullism," 105–6.

50. Aerts et al., *Land van kleine gebaren*, 269.

51. Andrieu, *Amour de la République*, 449–50.

economic negotiation, and the wider world of pressure groups and associations all formed part of the institutional machinery of Western European democracy, which was both its most imposing achievement and also the principal explanation of its immobility.[52] Once it had come into being, this way of conducting and managing democracy obeyed its own internal logic, and cultures of decision-making, which tended to blunt the impact of any reform. The furniture could be moved around, in terms of the particular responsibilities of institutions or the procedures for the taking of decisions, but the wider shape of the democratic political process had reached a level of maturity that seemed to render impossible any more fundamental change.

This lack of significant change encouraged the radicalization of the critiques voiced against the existing order. Rather than simply the failings of particular constitutional structures, or methods of representation, the whole emancipatory pretention of modern democracy was increasingly called into question. The ideal of democratic self-government was the creation of Europe's modern ideologies of liberalism and of revolution, but had been negated by the exploitative mechanics of capitalism and the authoritarianism of state power. The most prominent exponent of this critical discourse was Herbert Marcuse, who had initially been a member of the Frankfurt School until he was forced out of Germany in the Nazi era and had pursued a post-war academic career in the United States. Marcuse was already an established figure, but he acquired a much wider public profile in Western Europe and North America through the publication of his *One Dimensional Man* in 1964.[53]

One Dimensional Man was a consciously polemical work that contained little that had not already been said by others (and, indeed, by Marcuse in his earlier writings), but it brought those themes together in a manner that, rather like Simone de Beauvoir's *The Second Sex* at the end of the 1940s, succeeded in encapsulating certain of the key ideas, and more especially the emotions, of the era. Marcuse's principal target was the new apparatus of "totalitarian" state control generated in the western world by technical advance. This had created a rational universe that excluded the

52. See pp. 205–16.
53. H. Marcuse, *One Dimensional Man: Studies in the Ideology of Advanced Industrial Society* (London, 1964). On Marcuse's ideas and their impact, see also D. Kellner, *Herbert Marcuse and the Crisis of Marxism* (Basingstoke, UK, 1984), 229–319; T. B. Müller, *Krieger und Gelehrte*, 627–49.

means or even the very possibility of imagining a different political system, with the consequence that a "comfortable, smooth, reasonable democratic unfreedom prevails in advanced industrial civilization, a token of technical progress."[54] The fact that the large majority of the population accepted this civilization—and the compensatory benefits that it provided, such as the welfare state—did not make it, in Marcuse's eyes, any more legitimate. Political change, if it was to happen at all, would need to come from the outside. The impetus would not be provided by the rusting institutions of state socialism in the Communist east, but through a revolt from the global South that would demonstrate to the populations of the west the possibility of embracing a true, and human, freedom, liberated from the institutional and ideological structures of state control.[55]

Marcuse's preoccupations, rooted in the tradition of critical social analysis developed by the Frankfurt School, and supplemented with a certain anti-modern romanticism, constituted an unlikely basis for rethinking the basis of a democratic politics.[56] But the pervasive pessimism of Marcuse's text, and his rejection of any easily accessible political alternative, was a major component of its appeal. It reflected the spirit of an age that had moved beyond the ideological battlefields of the early and mid-twentieth century, and had turned instead—as indeed had Habermas, who worked briefly as an assistant to Marcuse—to the analysis of the structures that underpinned, and imprisoned, the project of modern western society. This shift from the visible and the tangible to the invisible and the difficult to grasp was perhaps the most important change that took place in intellectual fashion during the post-war decades. Some of these critiques remained rooted in the intellectual traditions of western Marxism, albeit now increasingly emancipated from the socialist east and, indeed, from the political projects of European Communism.[57] But many drew on other intellectual traditions such as the critical anthropology of Claude Levi-Strauss, the schools of post-Freudian psychology, and the new languages of resistance and critique provided by post-colonial writers and by studies of gendered inequalities.[58] Common to all of these somewhat amorphous bodies of ideas was a preoccupation with the deep structures of language,

54. Marcuse, *One Dimensional Man*, 1.

55. Marcuse, *One Dimensional Man*, 50–51. On Marcuse's ideas, see also J. Abromeit and W. M. Cobb, eds., *Herbert Marcuse: A Critical Reader* (New York, 2004).

56. S. Jeffries, *Grand Hotel Abyss: The Lives of the Frankfurt School* (London, 2016), 303–24.

57. J. G. Merquior, *Western Marxism* (London, 1986), 110–85.

58. For a spirited overview of the intellectual landscape of the 1960s, see F. Dosse, *La saga des intellectuels français*, vol. 1, *A l'épreuve de l'histoire (1944–68)* (Paris, 2018).

of social organization, and of the construction of the psychological self, which explained the conflicts inherent to modern societies but also, simultaneously, the difficulty of imagining, and still more accomplishing, any radical change.

This was therefore a post-political language of social critique, which decoupled the critical analysis of western society from political action. Some of the key thinkers of the 1960s engaged in political militancy—above all, of course, John-Paul Sartre, who in the 1960s threw himself into a wide range of revolutionary causes, spread out across the globe.[59] But others such as Marcuse and Habermas remained primarily in the academic sphere—"tenured radicals," as one right-wing critic of their influence termed them—examining critically contemporary social and intellectual structures without thereby investing in the seemingly illusory possibilities of political or institutional change.[60] This lack of an explicit interconnectedness between intellectual critique and the politics of the age explains also why the primary audience for many of these ideas during the 1960s lay in the expanding ranks of the intelligentsia.

Here too the laws of supply and demand applied. The proportion of young people aged between twenty and twenty-four attending higher education in Western Europe increased quite rapidly during the post-war decades from 3.63 per cent in 1950, to 6.93 per cent in 1960, and to 14.51 per cent in 1970.[61] This expansion in numbers did not imply a democratic revolution: access to higher education remained more limited than in the United States, and most especially very unequally distributed between different social groups. But this inequality increased its short-term impact. It reshaped the younger generations of the European middle class, who shared a common educational background, and a more mobile sociability focused on the new university campuses and the networks of connection that developed around student life.[62] Much as an "excess of educated men" had contributed to the revolutionary fervour of 1848,[63] this new intelligentsia emerged as the principal social constituency of hostility to the democratic status quo. They provided the audience, and indeed the market, for an intellectual culture of political and social critique that was conveyed by the media of print, radio, and television. These were

---

59. R. Hayman, *Writing Against: A Biography of Sartre* (London, 1986), 340–62.
60. J. Abromeit and W. M. Cobb, introduction to *Herbert Marcuse*, 3–4.
61. Kaelble, *Social Mobility*, 42–43.
62. Seidman, *Imaginary Revolution*, 17–47; Jobs, *Backpack Ambassadors*.
63. L. O'Boyle, "The Problem of an Excess of Educated Men in Western Europe, 1800–1850," *Journal of Modern History* 42 (1970): 471–95.

consciously difficult ideas, the comprehension of which demanded not only a wider cultural literacy but also the intellectual training most readily derived from higher education. The consequent merger of audience and ideas generated a socially inverted pyramid of political dissent. The existing structures of democracy were attacked not by the socially disadvantaged or marginalized, but by those who, on the basis of their education and qualifications, were the most obvious beneficiaries of a more urbanized and professional society.[64]

The demands voiced within this milieu reflected their specific grievances against a university system that in many European states lacked the material resources to cope with the substantial increases in student numbers, and remained dominated by outmoded syllabuses and archaic hierarchical structures of internal governance.[65] These institutional grievances provided a focus for their wider spirit of alienation from a society that seemed resistant to their needs and personal freedom. This found expression through the cultural rebellions of fashion, music, and popular culture. But it also became a debate about democracy, and its limits. Both inside and outside their educational institutions, many students wished to have the opportunity to act as democratic citizens, and yet found themselves circumscribed by the rigidities of institutional structures, and by a system of political representation that accorded little space to youth. Hierarchies of age and the organizational structures of political parties and assemblies marginalized voices from below, especially when they were couched in the radical languages and rebellious actions of the young.[66]

In this way, the specific became the general, as the sectional grievances voiced within a more assertive young intelligentsia became part of an amorphous movement of dissent, which denounced the absence of fundamental political debate within Western European societies. The existing "formal democracy" claimed its legitimation from the periodic consultation of the people through elections, while the daily practice of state and institutional power excluded popular participation through the rational logics of bureaucratic procedure and a repressive tolerance, which allowed the expression of alternative ideas while excluding the possibility

64. See, for example, the statistics presented in N. Pereira and R. Schär, "Soixante-huitards helvétiques: Etude prosopographique," *Mouvement social* 239 (April–June 2012): 13–16.

65. E. Morin, "La commune étudiante," in *Mai 1968: La brèche—premières réflexions sur les événements,* by Morin, C. Lefort, and J.-M. Coudray (Paris, 1968), 13; Marwick, *Sixties,* 586–602; Horn, *Spirit of '68,* 54–85.

66. Bettelheim, "Problem of Generations," 77–81.

of any radical change.[67] In common with Marcuse's *One Dimensional Man*, many of these ideas were emphatically anti-modern in tone. Echoing long-established discourses of hostility to modern mass society,[68] they denounced how technology and capitalism constrained citizens within "an oppressive mass state" that offered only the simulated freedoms of material products and welfare provision. Western societies had acquired the means to generate nuclear power, build motorways, and even send spacecraft towards the moon, but human freedom, creativity, and self-expression had been stifled by omnipresent structures of repression—political, economic, and psychological.[69]

Such voices—including that of Marcuse—could easily be dismissed as marginal figures on the intellectual fringes, who lacked a significant audience, or indeed any coherent vision of a political alternative. But what gave their writings a broader impact was the way in which they contributed to the shift that took place during the 1960s in the terms of democratic debate. This did not signify—a few radical voices aside—the wholesale rejection of the concept of democracy; but, rather than focusing on its achievements and benefits, attention turned to the limits, constraints, and failings of democratic politics. This was a perspective that owed much to an enhanced awareness of the inequalities of social class, gender, and race within Western European society; but it was powerfully reinforced by the impact of forces external to Europe. A series of events across the world during the late 1950s and early 1960s served both to emphasize the diminution of European power and to encourage a more critical appraisal of its purposes. The wars of retreat engaged in by European imperial powers and the emergence of new voices of liberation in Africa, Asia, and Latin America, as well as the civil-rights movement in the United States, and even the Eichmann trial held in Jerusalem in 1961 after the kidnapping by Israeli forces of the former Third Reich official from his post-war exile in Argentina—all raised awkward questions about the past and present of European democracy.

Nothing encapsulated these issues more profoundly than the undeclared war conducted by the French army and state from 1954 to 1962

67. J.-W. Müller, "What Did They Think They Were Doing?: The Political Thought of (the West European) 1968 Revisited," in *Promises of 1968: Crisis, Illusion, and Utopia*, ed. V. Tismaneanu (Budapest, 2011), 77–79; Abromeit and Cobb, introduction to *Herbert Marcuse*, 12–13.

68. See pp. 249–50.

69. Bettelheim, *Informed Heart*, 103; H. Lefebvre, *Position: Contre les technocrates* (Paris, 1967); J. Myrdal, *Confessions of a Disloyal European* (London, 1968); Pulju, *Women*, 215–16.

against the nationalists of the FLN and its affiliated organizations in Algeria. The institutional crisis generated by the deployment of a predominantly conscripted army of French citizen soldiers to defend republican legality against the rebels of the FLN brought about the effective collapse of French state authority in May 1958, and the replacement of the Fourth by the Fifth Republic through the agency of the providential figure of de Gaulle.[70] But its political and social impact was far more wide-ranging. More emphatically than any of the many colonial wars engaged in by European powers in the post-war years in Malaya, Vietnam, the Dutch East Indies, Palestine, Kenya, and elsewhere, the Algerian War undermined the historic association of democracy with the languages of freedom and progress.[71] Rather than a conventional war against a formal enemy, the military actions in Algeria were couched in the language of legal exceptionalism. It was a pacification campaign conducted within the frontiers of the French Republic, the successful prosecution of which came to depend on the forcible occupation and control of rural and urban space, and large-scale police actions against an unfortunate civilian population, the true political opinions of which remained almost impossible to divine. There was rarely a defined front line; while the attacks on the French authorities were conducted by an elusive enemy who resorted to all of the unconventional tactics of guerrilla warfare, including assassinations and bomb explosions. This drew the French forces into a cycle of reprisal actions and the institutionalized use of torture in the vain hope of breaking the organizational structures and morale of their opponents.[72]

What was striking about the conflict, as it escalated inexorably during the late 1950s without either side acquiring a decisive advantage, was the way in which it inverted the narratives of the Second World War in France. The French became in effect a conscript army of occupation (assisted by a considerable number of Algerian auxiliaries, perceived in turn as collaborators by the Algerian nationalists of the FLN), seeking to get to grips with an enemy who claimed the higher legitimacy of nationalism to justify its violent resistance to French rule. For its advocates, however, the campaign to defeat the FLN was one conducted in the name of democratic legality and freedom. Algeria was not a colony. It had long been part of

---

70. See pp. 74–77.

71. J.-P. Rioux, "La guerre d'Algérie dans l'histoire des intellectuels français," in *La guerre d'Algérie et les intellectuels français*, Cahiers de l'Institut d'histoire du temps présent no. 10 (Paris, 1988), 21–35.

72. M. Evans, *Algeria: France's Undeclared War* (Oxford, 2012), 148–257; R. Branche, *La torture et l'armée pendant la guerre d'Algérie, 1954–1962* (Paris, 2001).

metropolitan France, and its representatives (albeit elected only by the minority of the population who qualified for French citizenship) sat in the French parliament. The military actions in Algeria were therefore conducted by the democratically elected governments of the French republic, in the name of the defence of republican order. In the language of the propaganda tracts published by the army and distributed to conscripts sent to serve in Algeria, the French soliders were defending "the very values of our civilization" against the "regime of terror" conducted by the FLN and their Communist allies.[73]

French actions in Algeria—much like those by the British state in Northern Ireland over subsequent decades—were therefore conducted through the institutions and language of democracy, but raised ever more pressing questions about the legality of the democratic state and the obedience owed to it by its citizens. The military operations in Algeria initially served to polarize French political and intellectual elites along lines familiar since the Dreyfus Affair, between the defenders of the honour of the French army and nation, and those—including Raymond Aron—who regarded the conflict as a doomed attempt to uphold colonial methods of rule that threatened to undermine the legitimacy of the French Republic.[74] But, as the war continued without any prospect of a resolution, it also prompted more active resistance among sections of French society— some of whom explicitly linked the legitimacy of their actions of resistance against the state to French resistance against German occupation between 1940 and 1944.[75] This entanglement of past and present was reinforced by revelations of the torture conducted by the army in Algeria. Conveyed initially by the first-hand testimony of a Communist in Algeria, Henri Alleg, in *La question* published in 1958, these reached a much larger audience through Sartre's powerful presentation of Alleg's account in *L'express*. The undeniable reality of the brutal actions being carried out in their name could not fail to present awkward comparisons for French citizens with the crimes committed by the German authorities in wartime occupied France.[76] This was especially so for the more than one million French conscripts who were obliged to serve in Algeria. Most of these accepted

73. Quoted in McDougall, "Impossible Republic," 791–92.

74. Raymond Aron, *Tragédie algérienne*, esp. 5. See also Judt, *Burden of Responsibility*, 165–67.

75. M. Evans, *Memory of Resistance*, esp. 31–44, 73–84.

76. H. Alleg, *The Question* (London, 1958). This English translation also includes Sartre's article. See also D. Reid, "The Question of Henri Alleg," *International History Review* 29 (2007): 573–86; and C. Jeanson and F. Jeanson, *L'Algérie hors la loi*, 2nd ed. (Paris, 1955), 16.

their service, no doubt regarding their involvement in the military operations as the legal consequence of their democratic (male) citizenship, but a minority refused to do so, claiming a higher obedience to their political convictions or to their Christian-inspired conscience.[77]

Thus, in much the same way as the civil-rights campaigns taking place at the same time in the United States, the French military operations in Algeria complicated the relationships between democracy, universal citizenship, and legal and human rights. If the state, constituted by the democratically elected representatives of the people, could not be relied upon to act in accordance with the dictates of morality or indeed the simple rule of law, then this legitimized not merely the withholding of consent but also engagement in those actions—even violent ones—that stepped outside of the legal obligations of citizenship. As Aron wrote at the time, Algeria gave the French a bad conscience, not because—as he claimed— their actions were so terrible or so indefensible, but because the conflict was destructive of any confident sense of moral superiority.[78] Nor was it the only such dilemma. Instances of the complex conflicts that could arise between democratic citizenship and obedience to moral conscience, political conviction, or group identity proliferated across Europe during the 1960s. Campaigns of protest conducted in the name of democracy and human rights against, variously, nuclear weapons, the denial of minority language rights, and laws banning homosexual acts, drug consumption, or abortion all emerged as elements of a new agenda of contentious issues in Western Europe in which the personal, the legal, and the political were inextricably intertwined.[79]

Some of these forms of "rights-based activism" concerned primarily questions of individual freedom, while others—such as the civil-rights movement that developed in Northern Ireland at the end of the 1960s—acquired a much more collective and explicitly political character.[80] All, however, worked to unbalance the operation of democracy, caus-

77. R. Johnston-White, "A New Primacy of Conscience?: Conscientious Objection, French Catholicism and the State during the Algerian War," *Journal of Contemporary History* 54 (2019): 112–38.

78. Raymond Aron, *Tragédie algérienne*, 9–10.

79. Judt, *Postwar*, 486–94; D. Herzog, *Sexuality in Europe: A Twentieth-Century History* (Cambridge, UK, 2011), 156–60. See also the examples provided by J. Jackson, *Living in Arcadia: Homosexuality, Politics and Morality in France from the Liberation to AIDS* (Chicago, 2009), 170–94, and the essays in P. G. Cerny, ed., *Social Movements and Protest in France* (London, 1982).

80. C. Moores, *Civil Liberties and Human Rights in Twentieth-Century Britain* (Cambridge, UK, 2017), 16–17.

ing individuals to hesitate before obeying the orders of the state, and also prompting those same state authorities to pause before making demands of their citizens. In response, a new repertoire of forms of collective action emerged that were more questioning of established assumptions and more challenging of hierarchies. These acts of dissidence were generally sectional, and stopped short of a categorical rejection of the legitimacy of the existing state structures; but they were all indications of a less disciplined society in which the absence of explicit revolt could not be mistaken for a broader political consent. Above all, they indicated the way in which democracy was, in effect, changing sides within European politics. Rather than the defining characteristic of the established order, it was becoming the legitimation of the new politics of protest.[81]

One tangible indication of this new social mood was the radical changes that took place within Catholicism in Western Europe during the 1960s. Little that had occurred in Europe since the war had weakened the presence and influence of the Church in the Catholic areas of non-Communist Europe. Indeed, assisted by the presence of Christian Democratic politicians in positions of governmental authority in a number of states, the Church had been able to reinforce its social role in the provision of education and welfare.[82] But much was also changing within Catholic ranks. Despite the efforts of Pope Pius XII to assert the hierarchical discipline of the Church, new doctrines of personal theology encouraged both clergy and laity to adopt a more individual definition of their faith. A new generation of theologians such as Henri de Lubac, Yves Congar, and Gustave Thils came to the fore during the post-war years, who rejected the papal image of the Church as an immutable bastion of truth. Instead, religion was a phenomenon that evolved and interacted with what Thils termed "réalités terrestres." This required the Church to develop a theology of the temporal; but it also empowered the Catholic laity to explore their understanding of their faith, and its social and spiritual implications, rather than simply obeying clerical (and, more especially, papal) authority.[83]

This too was a democratic mentality, and one that transferred easily from the spiritual realm to more political concerns. The successful

81. S. Tarrow, *Democracy and Disorder: Protest and Politics in Italy 1965–1975* (Oxford, 1989), esp. 325–48.

82. K.-E. Lönne, "Germany," in *Political Catholicism in Europe, 1918–1965*, ed. T. Buchanan and M. Conway (Oxford, 1996), 185; Conway, "Belgium," 206–13.

83. G. Thils, *Théologie des réalités terrestres*, vol. 1 ([Bruges], 1946), esp. 7–12, 132–49; Y. Congar, *Jalons pour une théologie du laïcat* (Paris, 1953), esp. 7–18; H. de Lubac, *Sur les chemins de dieu* (Paris, 1956).

establishment of Christian Democracy as the principal vehicle of Catholic politics in post-war Europe had relied on a rather careful ambivalence between different definitions of its purposes.[84] With time, however, the predominantly centre-right and governmental orientation of the Christian Democratic parties led more radical voices within Catholic ranks to explore alternative means of giving expression to their political aspirations. Among many Catholic activists who had participated in the various experiments of collaboration with the political left in the immediate post-war years, as well as the new generations of Catholics active in youth movements and universities, there was a wish to create a more militant and spiritually driven Catholic politics, independent of the conservative social and political alliances favoured by clerical and secular hierarchies.[85]

This mentality of innovation contributed to the energy that characterized the Second Vatican Council (held from October 1962 to December 1965), which was initiated by Pope John XXIII when he succeeded Pius XII in 1958. The major doctrinal and ecclesiastical changes decided upon at the Council were far from being the product of a democratic process. The discussions were conducted within the cloistered institutions of the Vatican, and excluded any role for the Catholic laity. Nevertheless, the changes that emerged from these often intense discussions marked a major victory in terms of doctrine and organization for the new ways of thinking that had been maturing in Catholic ranks over the preceding decades.[86] The reforms served moreover as the inspiration for the spirit of democratization that swept through almost all areas of Catholic life in Western Europe during the 1960s. Catholic women's groups, farmers' leagues, and, above all, youth movements and political parties all underwent an almost continuous process of innovation as they cast off their confessional identity in favour of more open and democratic definitions of their purposes. This process of change was not uncontested, especially when it provoked heavy-handed attempts at reasserting clerical and institutional control. But, especially when the reformers were able to win the support of reform-minded Church figures, it led to a surge in new forms

84. See pp. 186–87.

85. Mounier, *Spoil of the Violent*, 4, 36, 84; Horn and Gerard, *Left Catholicism*; Horn, *Western European Liberation Theology*.

86. J. W. O'Malley, *What Happened at Vatican II* (Cambridge, MA, 2008), esp. 15–52; J. Connelly, *From Enemy to Brother: The Revolution in Catholic Teaching on the Jews, 1933–1965* (Cambridge, MA, 2012); D. Donnelly, J. Famerée, M. Lamberigts, and K. Schelkens, *The Belgian Contribution to the Second Vatican Council: International Research Conference at Mechelen, Leuven and Louvain-la-Neuve (September 12–16, 2005)* (Leuven, 2008), esp. 685–99.

of Catholic-inspired social and political engagement.[87] Much of this took a radical form, motivated by a concern for social injustices in Europe and, more especially, in the developing world, which became a major focus of Catholic activism in the 1960s.[88] It also reflected the ascendancy of a new democratic spirit in Catholic ranks. Rejecting the defensive preoccupations that had often dominated in Catholic organizations, these new Catholic movements sought to build alliances with those from outside Catholic ranks who shared their ideals. For some groups and individuals, this led them over time to loosen their Catholic affiliation in favour of a non-denominational identity; but it also encouraged others to adopt more militant forms of Catholic engagement focused on the assertion of a Catholic presence in the contemporary world.[89]

The trends evident within Catholic movements—less deference and discipline, more assertiveness and outspokenness—were replicated across many other areas of European life during the 1960s. The new spirit of workplace militancy reflected much the same spirit of activism. Rather than relying on corporatist negotiations between trade-union leaders, employers' representatives, and government, workers' committees within factories focused on changing the local reality of workers' lives.[90] A similar radicalization was evident in women's movements and farmers' groups, as well as in a wide range of new movements, which campaigned on local community matters or on more global issues, such as protection of the environment or Third World development. Some of these groups espoused an explicit political agenda; but what mattered more was their democratic spirit of activism. Rather than calling on their national leaders or government—local or national—to act, they took action themselves, by launching forms of direct protest or by instigating local initiatives that operated outside of official structures.[91]

These changes in the forms and spirit of political and social action were democratic; but they also changed democracy. The conscious attempts made during the immediate post-war years to contain political participation and debate within the rational logics of institutions were challenged

87. M. Busani, *Gioventù Studentesca: Storia di un movimento cattolico dalla ricostruzione alla contestazione* (Rome, 2016), 11–26; G.-R. Horn, *The Spirit of Vatican II: Western European Progressive Catholicism in the Long Sixties* (Oxford, 2015).

88. A. Santagata, *La contestazione cattolica: Movimenti, cultura e politica dal Vaticano II al '68* (Rome, 2016); "Les catholiques italiens et la guerre du Vietnam (1965–1968): L'antichambre de la contestation," *Revue d'histoire ecclésiastique* 110 (2015): 215–32.

89. Busani, *Gioventù Studentesca*, 481–84.

90. Vigna, *Insubordination ouvrière*, esp. 131–38; Bantigny, *1968*, 73–99.

91. Horn, *Spirit of '68*, 194–220.

by a younger generation who rediscovered the languages and methods of protest.[92] This forged a less structured and disciplined political culture, which incorporated a range of new cultural and social issues, as well as participants—such as housewives and students—who had previously been on the margins of political debate. The Hungarian political philosopher Agnes Heller once remarked that the greatest shift that took place during the 1960s was from the formal to the informal. Hierarchies of institutions, practices of action, and codes of political behaviour, dress, and language were all challenged or subverted as the terms of European political debate adapted to this wider culture of informality.[93]

This shift in the practices and mentality of democracy took place within Europe, but often drew its inspiration from elsewhere in the world. Models of political and social action poured into Europe in the 1960s—carried by the new direct media of film and television—from the campuses and streets of North America as well as from a wide range of locations and struggles across the post-colonial world. Some of these, such as the Indian subcontinent or the cities of francophone West Africa, were places that had long participated from afar in European intellectual and political debates, but others were emphatically new locations. As a consequence, politics became more direct but also more virtual; Europeans took up causes that did not directly concern them in lands that they did not know, but which seemed to present a vivid contrast to their relatively pale democratic politics. Cuba and Latin America, Vietnam and subsequently Cambodia, and Mao's China, among many others, all served, sometimes in very approximate ways, as exempla of what seemed to be a more vital and participatory politics where people fought—and died—for rights that Europeans took for granted.[94]

The origins of these new forms of politics were often close to home. Western European cities in the post-1945 era were the metropoles of imperial power, but also major sites of anti-colonial resistance. The presence in post-war Europe—as exiles, as students, or simply as migrant workers—of

92. Strote, *Lions and Lambs*, 268–74.

93. Cited in J. Bourg, "The Moral History of 1968," in J. Jackson, Milne, and Williams, *May 68*, 30.

94. T. S. Brown, *West Germany and the Global Sixties: The Antiauthoritarian Revolt, 1962–1978* (Cambridge, UK, 2013); D. Gordon, *Immigrants and Intellectuals: May '68 and the Rise of Anti-Racism in France* (Pontypool, UK, 2012), 19–35; K. S. Bjerregaard, "Guerrillas and Grassroots: Danish Solidarity with the Third World in the 1960s and 1970s," in *Between Prague Spring and French May: Opposition and Revolt in Europe, 1960–1980*, ed. M. Klimke, J. Pekelder, and J. Scharloth (New York, 2011), 213–32.

FIGURE 9. The democracy of protest: a march against the Vietnam War in Odense in Denmark in 1969. The City Archive of Odense

many of those individuals and groups who would emerge over the subsequent decades as the most influential nationalist leaders in former colonial territories also had more local consequences. Many were simultaneously members of European intellectual and political groups of different hues, including particularly Communist and Catholic parties, trade unions, and affiliated organizations. Some were high-profile intellectuals who gave a voice in Europe to the mentalities and opinions of the Third World—as it came to be termed in the early 1960s—most notably Frantz Fanon and Aimé Césaire within French intellectual culture.[95] But others were a more local presence, who helped to create a greater awareness among European populations of the injustices of colonialism, and thereby also a more critical perception of the racial hierarchies within the universalist discourses and structures of European democracy.[96]

This was reinforced, but also complicated, by the mass immigration into the states of Western Europe that occurred during the 1950s and 1960s.[97]

95. The first use of the term "Third World" in a book title appears to have been: P. Worsley, *The Third World* (London, 1964). Re. Fanon and Césaire, see D. Macey, *Frantz Fanon: A Biography* (London, 2000); Césaire, *Discours sur le colonialisme*.

96. Gordon, *Immigrants and Intellectuals*, 37–54.

97. Chin, *Crisis of Multiculturalism*, 23–79.

This most profound of post-war Europe's social transformations was at first almost invisible to the majority of Europeans. The diverse communities of migrant workers, immigrants, refugees, and European populations returning from the lost lands of empire (notably the so-called *pieds noirs* from Algeria) lived, often quite literally, on the margins of society, occupying shanty towns, densely populated public-sector housing, or company accommodation, which expressed their transient position in European societies. Quite rapidly, however, this changed, as these populations entered mainstream employment, and the families they established became a visible presence in wider society. As a consequence, Europe discovered rather abruptly that it had become in effect a society of racial differences. This was nothing new: Europe had long been more diverse in terms of ethnicity and religion than its inhabitants were inclined to think. But the new migrations, and their irreversible nature, had a greater impact because of the way in which Western Europeans had become accustomed over the course of the twentieth century to define themselves as a homogeneous and white society.[98]

Some of these ethnic communities, such as the Portuguese, Spanish, and southern Italian migrants, were the continuation of established routes of passage from areas that had long served as a source of cheap labour for Europe's more northerly industrial regions; but much more novel was the visible presence of African and Asian populations drawn in large numbers from former or current imperial territories, as well as so-called "guest workers" from Turkey and the North African Maghreb. The racial prejudice, and manifold forms of social and economic discrimination, that these populations encountered was accompanied too by a defensive reflex that defined European societies in contradistinction to these minority communities. Democratic practices and values became part of how Europeans defined their social norms, the adoption of which became the price of admission for minority groups into that wider society. But the presence of a cosmopolitan range of minority populations in many of Western Europe's major cities and smaller communities steadily changed the textures of European society, as individuals from these groups became fellow workers, consumers of social and educational services, neighbours, parents and, often rather belatedly, citizens and voters. Western Europe had become multicultural, a term that originated in North America, but which became by the 1970s not only a description of Western European

98. See pp. 86–87.

reality but also a focus of governmental initiatives and, in some quarters, a source of pride.[99]

This change in the make-up of society altered how Europeans viewed their politics. The migrant populations brought with them new political languages, including traditions of communally or religiously defined politics. European democracy as a consequence became more diversified and global, as it incorporated ways of doing democracy that originated in the cities and villages of the global South. The impact of these new influences contributed, too, to the emergence of what became known during the 1960s as the New Left. The decline since 1956 in the political plausibility of pro-Soviet Communism created space for new forms of radical politics, which sought to rescue the emancipatory dynamics of Marxism from the statist and centralizing priorities of the European Communist parties.[100] The New Left had no single political definition, and it drew on a number of alternative left traditions that had become marginalized during the mid-century ascendancy of pro-Soviet Communism.[101] But the appeal exerted during the 1960s by the revolutionary movements of the post-colonial world also encouraged emulation of movements, such as Maoism, that derived their inspiration from outside of Europe.[102] For a generation of student radicals—supported also by more established figures of the left, such as Sartre—the model of neighbourhood mobilization and workplace militancy that they perceived in the Chinese Cultural Revolution seemed to offer an intransigent politics of revolt, freed from the compromises inherent to more conventional politics.[103] While efforts to translate these aspirations into a mass movement were on the whole an emphatic failure, their activism and models of grassroots organization

99. Chin, *Crisis of Multiculturalism*, 14–17.

100. M. A. Bracke, "The *Parti Communiste Français* in May 1968: The Impossible Revolution?" in *Between Prague Spring and French May: Opposition and Revolt in Europe, 1960–1980*, ed. M. Klimke, J. Pekelder, and J. Scharloth (New York, 2011), 66–68.

101. P. Gottraux, *Socialisme ou barbarie: Un engagement politique et intellectuel dans la France de l'après-guerre* (Lausanne, 1997); J.-P. Joubert, *Marceau Pivert et le pivertisme: Révolutionnaires de la SFIO* (Paris, 1977); Little, *André Gorz*, 6; G. Sandoz, "Etre révolutionnaire," in *Ecrits politiques*, by R. Dutschke ([Paris], 1968), 10–11.

102. H. Nehring, "'Out of Apathy': Genealogies of the British 'New Left' in a Transatlantic Context, 1956–1962," in *Between Prague Spring and French May: Opposition and Revolt in Europe, 1960–1980*, ed. M. Klimke, J. Pekelder, and J. Scharloth (New York, 2011), 20; T. Buchanan, *East Wind: China and the British Left, 1925–1976* (Oxford, 2012), 199–204.

103. P. Gavi, J.-P. Sartre, and P. Victor, *It Is Right to Rebel* (London, 2017); D. Reid, "*Etablissement*: Working in the Factory to Make Revolution in France," *Radical History Review* 88 (2004): 83–111; Khilnani, *Arguing Revolution*, 82.

proved to be much more widely influential. The renewed radicalism of workplace committees and environmental and neighbourhood groups, and the direct action engaged in by a broad range of campaigning organizations from the late 1960s onwards, all reflected the way in which the practices of democratic political action in Europe came to be durably inflected by models derived from elsewhere. European democracy had become less distinctively European.

{⊱⋙⟩ꞨＷꞘ⟨⋘⟨}

It is tempting to see these changes in European democracy as a rising tide of discontent, to which the natural conclusion was the outpouring of radical politics that occurred in 1968 and over the subsequent years. But it should of course be remembered that not all of the energy in European politics was located on the extreme left. Right-wing groups, too, were part of the 1960s, generating new languages of economic freedom and the defence of cultural values that would lead over the course of the 1970s to a powerful resurgence of centre-right, and more emphatically right-wing, forms of politics.[104] Moreover, none of these trends substantially destabilized the rhythms of the established political process. If one excepts the intervention by the colonels in Greece and the establishment of their military dictatorship in 1967, the stability of Western European politics continued through the 1960s. At most, what changed was a modest electoral shift to the left, with the establishment of a Labour government in Britain from 1964, and more especially the entry of the SPD into a coalition government with the Christian Democrats in Germany in 1966, and from 1969 their leadership of a coalition government with the Liberals headed by Willy Brandt, and subsequently Helmut Schmidt. This ascendancy, which would last until the 1980s, made the SPD emphatically a party of reformist government, enabling it to increase its overall share of the vote from 31.8 per cent in the 1957 federal elections to 42.7 per cent in the 1969 elections.[105]

The continuity of this electoral politics, and the consequent incremental rebalancing of Western Europe's many coalition governments, indicated that there was much that continued to work well in Europe's

104. See notably the essays in A. von der Goltz and B. Waldschmidt-Nelson, eds., *Inventing the Silent Majority in Western Europe and the United States: Conservatism in the 1960s and 1970s* (Washington, DC, 2017).

105. M. Roseman, "Division and Stability: The Federal Republic of Germany, 1949–1989," in *Twentieth-Century Germany: Politics, Culture and Society 1918–1990*, ed. M. Fulbrook (London, 2001), 197–98. See also pp. 194–95.

FIGURE 10. The world of industrial protest: strikers outside a factory in Frankfurt in 1958, protesting against salary cuts. Ullstein Bild Dtl./Ullstein Bild via Getty Images

democratic politics. The virtuous cycle of democratic participation, stable parliamentary politics, and the expansion in state provision made possible by relatively high taxation rates at a time of consistent economic growth ensured that the democratic model established after the Second World War remained essentially in place. At the same time, as the diverse calls for political and institutional reform voiced during the 1960s indicated, this model was beginning to show its age. Some of these points of tension had a long heritage in modern European politics. This was most obviously so in the case of the strike waves that occurred in a number of industrial sectors in Western Europe during the 1960s, especially those, such as iron and steel production and mining, that were most directly exposed to policies of rationalization and closure.[106] This worker discontent had its independent dynamics; and, even when strike waves coincided with wider forms of social protest, as was the case in France and Italy at the end of the 1960s, they always retained their distinctive forms of action, and sectional goals, which reflected how the often brutal and closed world of the factory

106. Neuville and Yerna, *Choc de l'hiver 60–61*. See also p. 233.

remained at a certain distance—political and, often, geographical—from the broader political culture of the era.[107]

Other sources of conflict had much more recent origins. The women's movements, student groups, and the new forms of single-issue campaigning that emerged during the 1960s were manifestations of discontent generated by rapid material and cultural change. Writing at the time, Reinhard Bendix described it as a "crisis of legitimacy in the midst of affluence."[108] The phrase is an arresting one, which emphasizes the disjuncture between the prosperity of the era and the radicalism of much of the rhetoric of the later 1960s. For those, notably on the political left, who had despaired of achieving radical political change, the events of 1968 therefore came as something of a divine surprise. As the radical French sociologist Edgar Morin commented with an understandable sense of euphoria, the way in which a sudden crisis had overwhelmed "une belle société de consommation"—a beautiful society of consumption— demonstrated the capacity for revolution that still lurked within prosperous western societies.[109]

The recourse to the template of revolution to describe May 1968 was an understandable response to the unexpectedness of those events, and their substantial aftershocks, which would continue into the 1970s. But it sits rather awkwardly with the sheer diversity of the politics of the era. The whole point of 1968 was that it lacked the defined objective that had characterized the upheavals of the Revolutionary age of the eighteenth and nineteenth centuries.[110] When de Gaulle reportedly complained that it was impossible to respond to the demands of the demonstrators in May because their ambitions were so ill-defined—*insaisissable*—he was demonstrating his lack of comprehension of the upheavals that had swept across Paris, as well as much of provincial France and Western Europe.[111] But he also had a point. The goal of the demonstrations, but also of the

---

107. Horn, *Spirit of '68*, 93–122; Reid, "*Etablissement*," 96–100.

108. Bendix, *Embattled Reason*, 338.

109. E. Morin, "Une révolution sans visage," in *Mai 1968: La brèche—premières réflexions sur les événements,* by Morin et al. (Paris, 1968), 66. See also M. Atack, "Edgar Morin and the Sociology of May 1968," *French Cultural Studies* 8 (1997): 295–307. For very similar comments, see E. Hobsbawm, "May 1968," in *Revolutionaries: Contemporary Essays* (London, 1973), 234.

110. Hobsbawm, "May 1968," 239. See also R. J. Evans, *Eric Hobsbawm: A Life in History* (London, 2019), 462–67.

111. J. Jackson, "Rethinking May 68," in J. Jackson, Milne, and Williams, *May 68*, 7. On de Gaulle's wider disorientation amidst the events of 1968, see the vivid description in J. Jackson, *Certain Idea of France*, 717–37.

much wider social mobilization of the era, was not the achievement of a list of reforms—a *cahier* of grievances updated from 1788–89 to reflect the nature of an advanced industrial society—but a much broader set of aspirations about the power relations that should determine democracy and social relations more generally. There was no attempt at a seizure of power, other than the ubiquitous occupations of buildings associated with certain forms of institutional authority; while attempts at federation or central direction contradicted the spontaneity and freedoms of action and of speech that were essential qualities of the radicalism of the moment.

This lack of a clear focus led many at the time, and especially in retrospect, to question the seriousness of the participants.[112] As Morin recognized, there was always a light-hearted, festival character to the actions of many of the student groups.[113] A new street theatre of protest developed in which the act and the language—and indeed the comedy and the mockery—often appeared to take precedence over the goal. What mattered was not the creating of something durably different but unmasking the essential absurdity of the structures of bureaucratic and institutional power; generating what Alain Touraine termed "a revolutionary movement without revolution."[114] This did of course also go far beyond the conventionally political. Much of the force of the events around 1968 arose from their incorporation of a much wider explosion in social and cultural energies, which focused on music, styles of fashion, and ways of living, as much as it did discussions of political change. This explains why, especially in retrospect, it has become commonplace to refer to 1968 as a cultural revolution: in effect, an assault on bourgeois values in all their forms.[115] Given the way in which cultural norms did indeed change, often radically, during the later 1960s and 1970s, this is not misplaced; but an exclusively cultural reading of the events of the era risks marginalizing the political and the social.[116] Tony Judt's emphatic judgement that the events of May 1968 were "fundamentally apolitical," therefore contains only a partial truth.[117] While the movements of the later 1960s lacked anything that might have amounted to a defined political goal, they did have a very

112. J. Jackson, "Rethinking May 68," 9–10.

113. Morin, "Commune étudiante," 20–21.

114. A. Touraine, "The French Student Movement of May 1968," in *Political Sociology*, ed. A. Pizzorno (Harmondsworth, 1971), 315.

115. Morin, "Commune étudiante," 14.

116. C. Lefort, "Le désordre nouveau," in *Mai 1968: La brèche—premières réflexions sur les événements*, by E. Morin et al. (Paris, 1968), 59; M. A. Bracke, "*Parti Communiste Français*," 64–66.

117. Judt, *Postwar*, 412.

strong sense of what they opposed. This included the repressive structures of the existing ruling order—most notably the Gaullist Fifth Republic in France—and the actions of an increasingly global capitalism, as well as the imperialist actions of the United States in the post-colonial world, above all in Vietnam.[118] This suggests the value of a more political approach to the events of 1968.

Placed in the context of a longer history of democracy, the ideas that were voiced were a mixture of the familiar and the novel. The emphasis placed on the need to liberate society from the oppressive weight of structures that prioritized a rational bureaucratic order over the human needs of people echoed an aspiration that had been voiced in different ways on both right and left over the preceding decades.[119] However, it was accompanied by a much more categorical rejection of the legitimacy of state authority, and dreams of what Aron angrily dismissed as the "anarchist utopia" of a self-governing society.[120] Taking their inspiration variously from the model of the Paris Commune in 1871 and the factory councils that emerged in Germany in the immediate aftermath of the First World War, the exponents of radical ideas, such as the German student leader Rudi Dutschke, envisaged a radical devolution of power from state institutions to self-government in localities and workplaces.[121]

The dismantling of the apparatus of state bureaucracies would be accompanied, too, by a transformation in the structures of power within society, as the managerial dictatorship of modern capitalism would be replaced by workers' power within factories. What became known as *autogestion*—the self-management of economic enterprises—was a key aspiration of the 1968 era, which led over the subsequent decade to a range of attempts to make it a reality, most notably by the workers in the Lip watch factory in Besançon.[122] The inspiration provided by such small-scale initiatives spread, however, far beyond the factory gates. The appeal

118. Dutschke, *Ecrits politiques*, 91–101; K. Ross, *May '68 and Its Afterlives* (Chicago, 2002), 8.

119. See, for characteristic examples of the rhetoric of the age: K. Bednarik, *The Male in Crisis* (London, 1970), 176–83; J.-M. Coudray, "La révolution anticipée," in *Mai 1968: La brèche—premières réflexions sur les événements*, by E. Morin, C. Lefort, and Coudray (Paris, 1968), 89–142.

120. Raymond Aron, *Révolution introuvable*, 152.

121. H. Lefebvre, *La proclamation de la Commune* (Paris, 1965); Dutschke, *Ecrits politiques*.

122. Little, *André Gorz*, 28–49; D. Reid, *Opening the Gates: The Lip Affair 1968–1981* (New York, 2018); M. Černá, J. Davis, R. Gildea, and P. Osęka, "Revolutions," in *Europe's 1968: Voices of Revolt*, ed. Gildea, J. Mark, and A. Warring (Oxford, 2013), 127–28.

of *auto-gestion* formed part of a much wider vision of a society where in all spheres of life—from the factory to the village, and from the university to the school—individuals would work together in a manner that was both democratic and egalitarian.[123]

Once again, there was little fundamentally new about this vision of a devolved and participatory democracy. Much of it indeed recalled the aspirations during the period of liberation at the end of the Second World War.[124] But it did mark a reversal of the logic that had governed the construction of democracy over the intervening decades. In place of the hierarchical structure of sovereign national parliaments presiding over the rational distribution of resources from the central state to local institutions through bureaucratic procedures, the models of self-government that emerged in the late 1960s asserted the primacy of local institutions. They would make their own decisions with the active involvement of those—workers, farmers, students, parents, or simple consumers—who were most directly concerned, and who would thereby participate in the exercise of power. That this was a system that was not well suited to the needs of complex modern societies was both self-evident and also rather beside the point. As Kristin Ross has emphasized, the ambition of those active in radical politics at the end of the 1960s was not to present a programme of institutional change. They used the language and ideas available to them at the time to rethink the nature of power and democracy, while simultaneously seeking to transform society from below through local and small-scale initiatives.[125]

Central to the mentality of the time was the aspiration to bring about a democracy in which everybody would have a voice. The perception that representative regimes of democracy—with their limited space for the participation of "ordinary people" in decision-making—did not foster a pluralist spirit of debate provided the impetus for the creation of alternative arenas for democratic discussion, through general assemblies, workplace meetings, and the student exuberance of communes and sit-ins.[126] Again, the rhetorical excesses and the visual images of such phenomena can all too easily distract from the seriousness of purpose. The arteries of political participation had become thickened throughout Western Europe by the 1960s, through the emergence of a more professional political class,

123. J. Jackson, "Rethinking May 68," 6.
124. See p. 31.
125. K. Ross, *May '68*, 213; Bracke, *"Parti Communiste Français,"* 7.
126. M.-H. Bacqué and Y. Sintomer, eds., *La démocratie participative: Histoire et généalogie* (Paris, 2011).

operating within political parties and drawing increasingly on the tools of advertising and the mass media. More generally, too, the multiple structures of representation, negotiation, and consultation that had developed in European societies since the Second World War often failed to act as a satisfactory means for grievances to be expressed, and opinions voiced. Trade unions, farmers' organizations, and consumer movements were dominated by a cadre of officials who were often reluctant to engage with non-authorized voices, especially when they were those of women, the young, or people from immigrant backgrounds. Representation was not working, or at least not adequately, and that drove the desire to create a more open political culture in which everybody would have the opportunity to speak.[127]

This was a new definition of a democratic society, which took the individual as its starting point. Much of the energy of protest in the later 1960s was focused on self-emancipation, as expressed through campaigns relating to gender rights, race, sexuality, and language use; or more simply the right to live as one wished and say what one wanted, freed from the constraints imposed by state authority, social norms, and family structures. This demand to be free within a society that defined itself as free was the consequence of the generational and cultural strains created by the pace of the social changes that had occurred in Western Europe since the war. But it also had a more political dimension. The democratic model that developed after 1945 had rested on the tacit assumption of social homogeneity: national populations within Europe differed one from the other, but within the borders of each state the people were essentially the same. The principal challenges were therefore ones of inclusion: to ensure that all members of the community were able to participate in that democracy on an equal basis.[128] By the 1960s, however, this democratic universalism was no longer universally accepted. Increasing numbers of individuals and groups defined themselves—or, indeed, were defined by others—against the wider society. Their ambition was not to participate in the majoritarian competition of the democratic process, but to assert their right to be different, as expressed through their life choices and beliefs. This created a new vision of democracy as a differentiated social landscape composed of groups possessed of their own identities, each of which had a right to self-expression and mutual respect that went beyond the regime of "repressive tolerance" so strenuously denounced by Marcuse.

127. Brown, *West Germany*, 328.
128. See pp. 85–86.

This transition to a democracy where citizenship was based on the rights—both human and more collective—that derived from identity was a gradual one, with a subsequent history that, over the following decades, created new democratic norms sensitive to the manifold forms of human difference, and to the need for the positive recognition and promotion of diversity.[129] But, more immediately, the events of the later 1960s provoked a surge in more radical individualism. In place of the disciplined citizenship of the post-war decades, there was now a desire to be free: to live an authentic life without censorship or constraint. This inverted the assumptions of post-war individualism. In place of the pursuit of family life and material acquisitions fostered by what André Gorz described as an all-pervasive "possessive individualism," many of the 1968 generation embraced experiments in collective living, and the conscious rejection of material prosperity.[130]

The more radical manifestations of this individualism were, however, less significant than the way in which they reflected a wider shift in the shape of democracy. The post-war years had seen a huge advance in the role that the state and other public institutions played in people's lives. This boom in state activity had been legitimized by the needs of the moment as well as by the tangible material benefits that it had brought to Europe's populations in the aftermath of war. By the 1960s, these logics had diminished. A more educated and politicized population was no longer so inclined to accept the constraints that a state-oriented democracy placed on the freedom of the individual. Combined with resentment at the influence of the mass media—notably the Springer press empire in Germany—this reluctance to accept the directing authority of the state led to the rediscovery of the appeal of a more personal liberty: individuals, it seemed, wanted to be individuals.

This reassertion of the value of individual freedom was sufficiently flexible to be translated politically in different ways. It provided a focus for the anti-state impulses of many of the New Left and environmentalist groups of the 1970s; but it also contributed to the celebration of the self-reliant individual espoused by those neoliberal advocates of market choice who came to the fore during the final decades of the twentieth century.[131] Its more profound impact, though, was to throw the state on the defensive. The new ideologies of freedom eroded the legitimacy of the state as the central organizing institution in Western European lives. In spheres

129. Eley, *Forging Democracy*, 490.
130. Little, *André Gorz*, 6.
131. See pp. 300–1.

as diverse as economic policy, education, welfare structures, and public broadcasting, the end of the 1960s marked the high-water mark of state direction. Thereafter, these forms of provision gradually receded, as tasks formerly accomplished by public institutions were transferred to private companies, or to semi-public institutions that operated at a distance from state control. This too changed democracy. The turn away from universal provision destabilized a model of democracy that had been designed after 1945 in large part around the directing role of the state. The edifice of parliaments and parties established to bring that state under effective democratic control, and thereby to set the priorities—in particular through control of the budget process—for public policy-making, was in effect diminished by the retreat of central government. Its levers of democratic control no longer had the same efficacity, as the responsibilities of states were assumed by a variety of transnational bodies that operated beyond the sovereignty of parliaments—notably the institutions of European cooperation—or simply by private companies acting according to market forces.

In this way, as in others, the challenges to the existing model of democracy that came to the fore at the end of the 1960s had less the character of an end than of a beginning, providing a preliminary sketch as to how democracy throughout the western world would be reshaped across the final decades of the twentieth century. Yet, the events of the late 1960s were also an ending. More especially, they marked the culmination of the post-war project of democracy that over the preceding twenty-five years had carried the fractured western states of Europe from the chaotic realities of the mid-1940s to a position in which the new entity of Western Europe could present itself with some confidence to the world as the epitome of a modern society that provided its populations with a combination of political stability, social and civic equality, and personal and collective freedom. To describe this as an achievement would be a misnomer, risking replicating the teleologies that have often characterized the writing of Europe's twentieth century.[132] But the scale of the change that had occurred since 1945 was both emphatic and—in marked contrast to the divisions and wars of preceding decades—remarkably unitary. It was also, to all intents and purposes, irreversible. At moments of crisis, notably in 1958 and 1968 in France, Europeans sometimes frightened themselves by imagining the possibility of some form of fascist takeover

---

132. M. Conway, introduction to *Europe's Postwar Periods–1989, 1945, 1918: Writing History Backwards*, ed. Conway, P. Lagrou, and H. Rousso (London, 2019), 1–7.

or military coup. There were, of course, individuals who harboured such ambitions, harking back to the conspiratorial politics or insurrectionary street violence of previous eras. But the unreality of these scenarios was overwhelming. Reversing or overthrowing democracy in Western Europe was as difficult to imagine by the end of the 1960s as it had been easy to achieve in many states of Europe between 1918 and 1945. But this did not mean that democracy had reached some form of stasis. As the contested politics of the 1970s would amply demonstrate, it was easier to denounce the shortcomings in the existing model of democracy than to arrive at a viable alternative. But the underlying reality of the disjunctures that had developed between state institutions, society, and the aspirations of the population were by the end of the 1960s undeniable. Western Europe had reached the end of its post-war democratic age.

Unmaking Democratic Europe

DEMOCRACY AND POST-DEMOCRACY

TWENTY YEARS AFTER the Second World War, it might have appeared that Western Europe had solved the problem of modern democracy. The democratic stabilization proclaimed by Aron in 1960 had become something of a scholarly consensus among political scientists, who insisted that the "advanced" societies of Western Europe and North America (as well as Australia, New Zealand, and Japan) had arrived at a stable form of democratic pluralism, which combined negotiation between different interest groups with effective executive government.[1] The basis of this success, so it was argued, lay in its complexity: by creating multiple vessels of decision-making, which were interconnected both vertically and horizontally, the states of Western Europe ensured that everybody was associated, albeit rather indirectly, to the business of government, but no particular group, individual, or indeed nation was autonomously powerful. This was, also, a model capable of export. Differences of history, of culture, of ethnicity, and of religion were real, but they mattered less than the material indices of socio-economic development. Therefore, as the societies of the non-European world reached particular thresholds of prosperity and education, so they would arrive at the same plateau of political stability as had the democracies of Western Europe. In Soviet-controlled central and eastern Europe, too, the obsolescence of the regimes of state socialism—as manifested by the crude repression of the Prague Spring by the military forces of the Warsaw Pact in the summer of 1968—encouraged a new language of dissidence, as well as the identification of democracy as the ultimate

1. Conway, "Democracy in Western Europe," 231–56. See also pp. 77–78.

destination of these societies.[2] Of course this hegemony of democracy would not be easy. There would be jolts and setbacks along the way: the adventurism of military coups—such as in Greece in 1967—and the disruptive charisma of individual leaders such as de Gaulle, as well as the populism of political movements of social or national liberation. But the direction of travel was clear. Democracy was destined to be the political template of an increasingly integrated and interdependent world.

This optimism did not wear well. Rather suddenly between the end of the 1960s and the 1980s, the west in general, and Western Europe in particular, lost control both of global processes of political development and of this narrative of the spread of democracy. As early as the mid-1970s, Communism had enjoyed new successes, far from its Soviet bastion, in Indochina, as well as in more mitigated forms in the progressive dictatorships and state socialism of the Middle East and of post-colonial Africa. By 1980, it was clear that the challenges to the west lay outside Europe on the emerging battlefields of the so-called Second Cold War in Central America, in sub-Saharan Africa, and—after the twin events in 1979 of the Iranian revolution and the Soviet invasion of Afghanistan—in Central Asia. Fears of the collapse of the west proved to be exaggerated. The military remobilization of the United States during the first term of Reagan's presidency, and the strongly contested efforts to extend that process to America's Western European allies during the early 1980s, abruptly gave way to the staged transformation and subsequent dismemberment of the Soviet Union, and in 1989 brought about the end of the concept of Western Europe with the implosion of the state-socialist regimes of central and eastern Europe.

The Europe of the 1990s was, consequently, for the first time in its history both united and democratic; but the sudden turning point of 1989 lacked something of the global significance of the other European

---

2. Émigré groups were, not surprisingly, the first to embrace democracy. See, for example, V. Ivanovic, *Democratic Yugoslavia: An Outline for Discussion* (London, [1967]), 8–10. Attitudes towards democracy among dissident groups in the USSR were more nuanced. See, for example, the Sakharov manifesto, which preferred "democratization" to "democracy": A. Sakharov, R. Medvedev, and V. Turchin, "Appeal for a Gradual Democratization," in *Samizdat: Voices of the Soviet Opposition*, ed. G. Saunders (New York, 1974), 399–412. Debates among Soviet dissidents tended to focus on ethical issues of justice and rights, rather than ones of political regime: see J. Bergman, *Meeting the Demands of Reason: The Life and Thought of Andrei Sakharov* (Ithaca, NY, 2009), xii–xiii. In central-eastern Europe, democracy became a much clearer basis of the manifestos of dissident groups, notably Charter 77 in Czechoslovakia. See H. G. Skilling, *Charter 77 and Human Rights in Czechoslovakia* (London, 1981), 183–85, 209–12.

post-war moments of the twentieth century in 1918 and 1945.[3] Europe no longer stood at the centre of its own history, as demonstrated by the ineffective response of the European Union to the violent disintegration of Yugoslavia during the 1990s, and by the divisions that emerged among European states during the American-led wars in Iraq and Afghanistan. In economic terms, too, the ascendancy of a new global capitalism obliged Europe to accept the economic weather generated by more distant or universal forces. In addition, however, Europe had lost confidence in the democratic model that it had developed and, to a large degree, patented. From the beginning of the 1970s onwards, the tone of debate about democracy in Western Europe had changed markedly, as expressed somewhat precociously by a journalist of *Le Monde*, Claude Julien, in his *Le suicide des démocraties* published in 1972. In truth, Julien's title was more emphatic than the contents of his now forgotten book; but his half-political and half-moral denunciation of the failings of contemporary democracy was a precursor of many works in a similar vein published over the subsequent years. The electorates of the western democracies, Julien declared, were unhappy. They were frustrated by their lack of effective control over those who ruled them; while the material prosperity achieved since the war had not been matched by equivalent progress towards social justice. The west, he concluded, in a return to the rhetoric that had been so popular in the interwar years, was experiencing a "crise de civilisation" that called into question its entire political and social order.[4]

Julien's anxieties about the future of democracy became commonplace over the course of the 1970s. Against the backdrop of renewed economic crisis, strike waves, and the rekindling of political violence within Europe, as well as renewed geopolitical tensions between the United States and the Soviet Union, political commentators were concerned to explore, in the unambiguous words of Jean-François Revel, "how democracies end"—comment les démocraties finissent.[5] For these predominantly liberal and conservative figures, Europe had abandoned the rationality that had underpinned the democracy of the post-1945 era in favour of reverting to utopian visions of radical change.[6] Political debate had been taken over by a conspiracy of progressive voices, provoking the alienation of

3. Conway, "Democracies," 121–36.

4. C. Julien, *Le suicide des démocraties* (Paris, 1972). See the similar comments in Ponteil, *Bourgeois et la démocratie sociale*, 487–97.

5. J.-F. Revel, *Comment les démocraties finissent* (Paris, 1983).

6. R. Lowenthal, "On the Disaffection of Western Intellectuals" (1977), in *Social Change and Cultural Crisis* (New York, 1984), 25–41.

the "hidden majority"—a term initially developed by Nixon in the United States, but widely adopted in Europe during the 1970s—of sensible and conservative-minded citizens.[7]

Unsurprisingly, this attitude was shared by Raymond Aron, whose *Plaidoyer pour l'Europe décadente* published in 1977 was very different in tone from the optimism of his speech in Berlin in 1960. Democracy, he concluded, was in dark times; and only a forthright defence of the principle of liberty would prevent a return to the ideological wars of the interwar years.[8] That the warnings voiced by Aron and others were distinctly overdrawn mattered less than the way in which they contributed to a resetting of the debate about democracy. What had formerly seemed so inevitable, now appeared to be a broken, or substantially flawed, mechanism, scorned by those who should be its defenders, and unable to respond effectively to the challenges of a new and much less certain age.[9]

The arguments deployed to justify this new-found pessimism were various; but at their core lay the assumption that the triple convergence between society, state, and democracy that had developed after 1945 had collapsed. Instead, each of these elements appeared to be in conflict with the others: a newly rebellious society rejected the tutelage of the state and the values of a democratic order; the state, by arrogating powers to itself, constrained individual freedom and impinged on democratic politics; while democracy failed to give adequate expression to societal discontents, but also undermined the effective operation of the state. The consequence, to borrow again from the phraseology of Carl Schorske but on this occasion also that of Tony Judt,[10] was that democratic politics had modulated into another key. Except that this time, it was undoubtedly a minor key. The resurgence in political violence and direct action engaged in by a number of nationalist and revolutionary movements in Western Europe during the 1970s appeared to presage a return to the more confrontational politics of the interwar years, while the radicalization of labour action during the strikes of the late 1960s and 1970s overwhelmed the corporatist structures of negotiation between employers and employees. The protest marches, strikes, kidnappings, assassinations, and bomb explosions that

7. M. Geyer, "Elisabeth Noelle-Neumann's 'Spiral of Silence,' the Silent Majority and the Conservative Moment of the 1970s," in von der Goltz and Waldschmidt-Nelson, *Inventing the Silent Majority*, 251–74.

8. Raymond Aron, *Plaidoyer pour l'Europe.* See p. 7.

9. C. Lefort, *L'invention démocratique: Les limites de la domination totalitaire* (Paris, 1981), 28–31, 41–42.

10. See p. 72; Judt, *Postwar*, 484–503.

were relayed with a new directness by the ubiquitous medium of television changed Europeans' perceptions of their own societies, and of their political systems. They recognized themselves to be in conflict with one another, and in some cases with their rulers, in ways more profound and more sharp-edged than could be resolved through mechanisms of democratic negotiation. As a consequence, democracy appeared to many Western Europeans to be—depending on their political perspective—besieged, on the retreat, or simply the source of the problem.[11]

There was, in response, no shortage of calls to defend democracy. Especially in West Germany, the turn to violence by the Red Army Faction and other New Left groups in the 1970s prompted a return to the language and methods of "militant democracy" first developed by Karl Loewenstein in the 1930s, whereby the fragile pluralism of the Federal Republic had to be protected by forceful action on the part of the state against those who refused to accept its democratic values.[12] More modestly, the French president, Valéry Giscard d'Estaing, wrote a short but eloquent volume in 1976 entitled simply *Démocratie française*, which sought to present a vision of French democracy that was determinedly forward-facing. Arrestingly, Giscard abandoned the familiar tropes of French political rhetoric rooted in past history. Instead he argued that democracy would survive in France only if it adapted to the modern society that had come into being since the war.[13] Many of the problems of French democracy, the president insisted, lay in the disjuncture between the social trends and movements that had come to the fore in the 1960s and a political system that was determinedly a product of a particular mid-century moment.

For many, therefore, the challenge in the 1970s was to adapt democracy to match the evolution of society. This could of course be conceived of in many ways. For the diverse constellation of social and environmental movements that had emerged from the events of 1968, it required abandoning the formal apparatus of political institutions, and adopting instead

11. Re. the wider history of Europe in the 1970s, see notably T. Buchanan, *Europe's Troubled Peace*, 140–61.

12. A. Rosenfeld, "'Anarchist Amazons': The Gendering of Radicalism in 1970s West Germany," *Contemporary European History* 19 (2010): 365–66; P. Terhoeven, "Hitler's Children?: German Terrorism as Part of the Transnational 'New Left Wave,'" in *Revolutionary Violence and the New Left: Transnational Perspectives*, ed. A. Martín Alzarez and E. Rey Tristán (New York, 2017), 126–44. See also p. 121. For a stimulating overview of the history of the concept of "militant democracy," see J.-W. Müller, "Militant Democracy," in *The Oxford Handbook of Comparative Constitutional Law*, ed. M. Rosenfeld and A. Sajó (Oxford, 2012), 1253–69.

13. V. Giscard d'Estaing, *Démocratie française* (Paris, 1976).

a new localist activism based around "the critical renewal of daily life."[14] The bottom-up politics engaged in by these campaigning groups, NGOs, neighbourhood committees, and workers' organizations developed a new culture of direct democracy that operated largely independently of the more official structures of social representation.[15] But for those on the socialist left who still hoped to use the instruments of the state to bring about radical change, the principal priority remained the need to break the power of capitalist structures. Only by adopting what one Belgian socialist tract optimistically termed a "réformisme révolutionnaire"—a revolutionary reformism—that confronted directly the power of capital could the glaring inequalities within democracy be resolved.[16] Similar policies were advocated, but rarely implemented, by a range of Socialist parties in the 1970s and early 1980s, most notably the newly refounded Parti socialiste in France, which in 1972 agreed a common programme with the Communists, committing it to a far-reaching transformation of the structures of the French economy.[17] In Scandinavia, too, the Social Democrats moved beyond the social and welfare goals of past decades. Instead, they developed ambitious, but ultimately abortive, plans in the 1970s to build an economic democracy, through a phased transition to mass participation in the ownership of the principal industries.[18]

This desire to go beyond the limits of the existing democracy was evident, too, on the political right. One of the more remarkable aspects of the democratic settlement after 1945 had been the way in which the major political traditions of the right had largely accepted the need for the state to play a major role in economic and social life. But this pragmatic acceptance of the managerial role of the state broke down as a consequence of the economic downturn of the 1970s. In response to renewed price

14. Pagis, *May '68*, 285.

15. The literature on the new politics of the 1970s is enormous. For representative examples, see Gildea, Mark, and Warring, *Europe's 1968*; Tompkins, *Better Active than Radioactive!*; S. Milder, *Greening Democracy: The Anti-nuclear Movement and Political Environmentalism in West Germany and Beyond, 1968–1983* (Cambridge, UK, 2017), 1–13; Vigna, *Insubordination ouvrière*.

16. [M.-H. Jannc], *Pour un renouveau du socialisme démocratique* (Brussels, 1972), 101–5.

17. D. S. Bell and B. Criddle, *The French Socialist Party: The Emergence of a Party of Government*, 2nd ed. (Oxford, 1988), 72–74. See also Mitterrand, *Rose au poing*, 28. Re. the SPD, see D. Parness, *The SPD and the Challenge of Mass Politics: The Dilemma of the German Volkspartei* (Boulder, CO, 1991), 81–123.

18. N. Elvander, *Scandinavian Social Democracy: Its Strength and Weakness*, Acta Universitatis Upsaliensis no. 39 (Stockholm, 1979), 25–35; Berman, *Primacy of Politics*, 197–98.

inflation, wage demands, and increasing levels of unemployment, radical voices on the right emerged demanding—as in the case of the Progress Party of Morgens Glistrup, which won 16 per cent in the Danish elections of December 1973—a marked reduction in levels of state expenditure, and thereby of direct and indirect taxation.[19] More profoundly, too, there was a shift in the terms of economic debate. The perceived failure of Keynesian methods of economic management to rebalance the European economies after the twin shocks of the rise in oil prices and the collapse of the Bretton Woods structure of fixed exchange rates in the early 1970s led to insistent demands for the state to allow market forces, and more especially the supply of money, to direct economic life.[20] This rejection of the scaffolding of state-directed financial and price controls, collective bargaining of wages, and industrial planning concerned much more than questions of economic policy-making. For the coalition of think tanks, politicians, and lobbyists who advocated this market-led liberalism, the overriding purpose was to move the locus of democratic power. State bureaucracies and the associated interest groups, notably trade unions and protectionist professional organizations, which had colonized the corporatist structures of post-war democracy, would be replaced by the true democracy of consumers and economic actors exercised through their free-market choices.[21]

How far the ascendancy of these ideas amounted to the delayed victory of the neoliberal ideas that had been initially advocated by Hayck and others in the immediate post-war years is open to question.[22] Especially in its European form, the neoliberalism of the thinkers of the 1940s and 1950s had been concerned primarily to insulate the free play of economic forces from the disruptive impact of state structures and mass democracy: legal protection of economic activity and free trade across national boundaries should take precedence over legislation by nation-states and the sectional pressures generated by a mass democracy.[23] The privatization of public enterprises implemented in a rather ad hoc way in a number

19. Lidegaard, *Short History of Denmark*, 293–95.

20. D. Needham, "Britain's Money Supply Experiment, 1971–73," *English Historical Review* 130 (2015): 89–122.

21. For a characteristic example of such ideas, see T. Torrance, "Catchwords of the Left . . . 'Democracy,'" *Free Nation*, 13 April 1978, 8. I am indebted to Tom Buchanan for this reference. See, more generally, B. Jackson, "The Think-Tank Archipelago: Thatcherism and Neo-liberalism," in *Making Thatcher's Britain*, ed. Jackson and R. Saunders (Cambridge, UK, 2012), 43–61.

22. See p. 211.

23. Q. Slobodian, *Globulists: The End of Empire and the Birth of Neoliberalism* (Cambridge, MA, 2018), 1–25, 263–73.

of European states during the 1980s, as well as the measures taken by the European Union to liberate economic competition across national borders, owed something to this European variant of neoliberalism. But the exponents of the new economic liberalism in the 1970s and 1980s adopted a much more radical spirit of mass participation. They saw themselves as agents of fundamental political change, drawing on Hayek's ideas—or, perhaps more accurately, on slogans derived from a superficial reading of his work—to advocate a new democracy of market choice, based on the decisions of millions of consumer-citizens.[24]

The impact of these ideas—espoused initially by the political right but also adopted in the 1990s by many political forces of the centre-left—never matched the ambitions of their more militant exponents. But they did substantially change the structures and spirit of European democracy. The rather formal post-war hierarchy of state institutions, parliaments, and parties gave way to a more complex matrix of public and semi-public bodies—national but also increasingly European in scope—as well as an enhanced role for private-sector companies and for institutions of legal and paralegal regulation. This changed, too, the nature of citizenship. Post-war conceptions of the individual citizen contributing to the decision-making process of democracy through participating in elections, as well as arguing and lobbying, individually or collectively, for the implementation of particular policies, receded. Instead, citizens were recast as sovereign consumers, choosing on the basis of calculations of their self-interest between different material products, service providers, and political choices.

That these neoliberal reforms could be implemented—or indeed even conceived—owed much to broader changes taking place in the operation of democracy. The erosion of the position of political parties as the intermediaries between voters and the institutions of government was hastened by the impact of new techniques of mass communication and of marketing. Political debate ceased to be conducted primarily through text and speech and migrated instead towards the visual and the symbolic, as conveyed by the ubiquitous media of television and political advertising. This encouraged an increasing personalization of politics, as demonstrated by the carefully crafted presentation of individual leaders, such as François Mitterrand and Margaret Thatcher. What mattered was no

---

24. B. Jackson and R. Saunders, "Introduction: Varieties of Thatcherism," in *Making Thatcher's Britain*, ed. Jackson and Saunders (Cambridge, UK, 2012), 5–8, 12–14. See also the ironic comments on the decline in the powers of the *énarques* within the French state in the 1980 second edition of Mandrin, *Enarchie*, 115–61.

longer primarily what political figures said but the messages that they conveyed through their public images. The consequence was to create what Bernard Manin has termed an "audience democracy": the roles previously performed by local representatives and intermediate institutions were supplanted by a much more direct political culture, whereby voters responded to the messages embodied by leaders, who themselves operated increasingly independently of the formal structures of political life.[25]

The combined impact of these changes was to generate a sense of democratic loss. The waning in the influence of the former institutions of democratic debate and participation—notably parties, parliaments, and the print press—coupled with the irresponsible power exercised by media conglomerates, financial institutions, and private companies made many Europeans newly conscious both of their inability to hold their rulers to account and of the powerlessness of those same rulers to have any impact on a global economic system that operated beyond governmental control. Power and democracy had diverged, generating an impotence common to both rulers and ruled.[26] The consequent "democratic deficit" encouraged a recrudescence in movements of the populist right that presented themselves as the defenders of the interests of citizens and communities against the actions of, variously, national governments, European institutions, and multinational companies.[27] The initial beneficiaries of this angry political mood were movements of the radical right during the 1980s and 1990s, such as the National Front in France and the Freedom Party (FPÖ) in Austria, who repackaged their long-standing anti-establishment rhetoric to attack the new enemies of the people. But it also prompted the emergence of entirely new political movements that were not clearly of right or left. Parties led by charismatic individuals, such as Pim Fortuyn's eponymous list in the Netherlands and Silvio Berlusconi's *Forza Italia*, combined an amorphous language of "anti-politics," and more especially of antipathy to a supposedly self-interested political class, with a range of neo-populist campaigns based on hostility to immigrant groups, economic regulation, and taxes on consumption. The impact of these new groupings had consequences that went beyond their often rather transient electoral success.

25. B. Manin, *The Principles of Representative Government* (Cambridge, UK, 1997), 218–26.

26. Wolfgang Streeck has termed this the crisis of democratic capitalism. See *Buying Time: The Crisis of Democratic Capitalism* (London, 2014), esp. 3–20.

27. The concept of a "democratic deficit" was originally developed in the 1970s to describe the perceived weakness of structures of democratic accountability within the institutions of European integration, but it subsequently acquired a wider currency: A. Moravcsik, "The Myth of Europe's 'Democratic Deficit,'" *Intereconomics* 43 (2008): 331–32.

Most especially, they eroded the electoral base of those "establishment" parties—above all the Socialists and the Christian Democrats—who had long dominated political life in many European states. As a consequence, European electoral politics lost what had hitherto been its most distinctive characteristic: its relative predictability.[28]

{⁂⁂}

The more fractured and fluid politics that had emerged in Europe by the end of the twentieth century might be more appropriately described as post-democracy: a politics still conducted through the language and institutional structures of democracy, but which lacked much of the former substance of democratic politics. In Colin Crouch's formulation of the term, post-democracy was a means of expressing how the democratic decision-making structures of the recent past had given way during the final decades of the twentieth century to a carefully choreographed politics of presentation, behind which many of the most substantive issues were decided by elites whose actions were immune from any meaningful degree of popular accountability.[29] For Crouch, as for many others on the political left, such as Tony Judt, these changes were perceived in emphatically negative terms: the state had been dethroned, and the sovereign body of citizens determining (through their elected representatives) the direction of their society had been supplanted by the debased currency of market choice.[30] This sense of living "after democracy" gathered pace after the events of 1989. With the demise of its antithesis in the state-socialist regimes in central and eastern Europe, democracy seemed to lack a clear direction. As Alain Touraine declared rather grandly in 1996, democracy had lost hope. The progressive narratives that, since the nineteenth century, had integrated the achievement of democracy within the promise of a better collective future had been replaced by an individualized democracy that existed only to facilitate "the free construction of personal life."[31]

Laments for a lost age of democracy—but also for the broader culture of social progress that it incarnated—became, and have remained, a key

28. Betz, *Radical Right-Wing Populism*; Chiarini, "Antipolitica in Italia," 5–29.

29. Crouch, *Post-Democracy*, esp. 4.

30. For a powerful statement of this mentality, see Judt, *Ill Fares the Land*, esp. 150–51. See also, in a similar spirit, E. Hobsbawm, "The Prospects of Democracy," in *Globalisation, Democracy and Terrorism* (London, 2007), 95–114.

31. A. Touraine, *Democracy versus History*, Institute for Advanced Studies, Vienna, Political Science Series no. 34 (Vienna, 1996), 3, 16.

component of the spirit of the age: a means by which a post-war generation of predominantly liberal-minded Europeans look back on their past. Yet, this frame of reference can all too easily ignore the way in which democracy had simply taken on a new shape. As a number of writers in the 1990s recognized, democracy had been reconfigured to meet the needs of a new world, where borders no longer had the same finality, the location of power had become more elusive, and personal and political identities were more flexible.[32] Above all, a shift had taken place from contractual and representative definitions of democratic governance to a democracy based on the interrelated spheres of personal choice, identity, and legal and human rights. This regime—which Bauman, never at a loss for a new formulation, termed "liquid modernity"[33]—inverted the hierarchy of democratic power. Instead of democracy acting as an upward transmission belt by which the aggregated votes of citizens were converted, however imperfectly, into governmental actions, democracy was reoriented downwards towards ensuring a personal sphere of freedom within which citizens could exert real control over their lives and give expression to their identities. As a consequence, democracy ceased to be primarily about citizens choosing their rulers but rather about the ways that the rights of citizens were guaranteed in an increasingly plural society.

This latest reconfiguration of democracy also encouraged its globalization. In the immediate post-1989 world, in which the principal challenge to the west appeared to have disappeared, democracy re-emerged not as a particular political regime but as a universal language of personal freedom, human rights, and good government. Samuel Huntington's thesis—first coined in 1991—of a "third wave of democratization" that had gathered pace since the 1970s as democratic regimes multiplied in Latin America, Asia, and Africa, emulating the previous waves of democratization that had taken place in the west, was expressive of this new optimism.[34] Democracy had become more mobile. It was no longer the product of long-term evolutions within a society, but a set of legal rights, institutional frameworks, and forms of social provision, which could be exported, and adapted, through the application of more intelligent

32. See, for example, D. Held, *Democracy and the Global Order: From the Modern State to Cosmopolitan Governance* (Cambridge, UK, 1995).

33. M. Carleheden, "Bauman on Politics: Stillborn Democracy," in *The Sociology of Zygmunt Bauman: Challenges and Critique*, ed. M. H. Jacobsen and P. Poder (Aldershot, UK, 2008), 177–87.

34. S. P. Huntington, *The Third Wave: Democratization in the Late Twentieth Century* (Norman, OK, 1991). See, for a more recent restatement of the same thesis, B. Weijnert, *Diffusion of Democracy: The Past and Future of Global Democracy* (Cambridge, UK, 2014).

policies of socio-economic development, to meet the needs of any society. This optimism proved, in many cases, to be unjustified. As the resurgence in non-democratic forms of authoritarian rule during the first decades of the twenty-first century amply illustrated, there remain limits to the transferability of democracy. But, more importantly, the durable differentness of many of the democracies in Asia and Africa from any western template has demonstrated that globalization does not imply uniformity. On the contrary, the differentiated cultures of democracy across the contemporary world indicate the emergence of what Ewan Harrison and Sara McLaughlin Mitchell have termed "a post-western democratic order."[35]

Yet, though there is no longer much that is distinctively western, or more especially European, about democracy, the idea that Europe is distinctively democratic has remained a prominent element of European political rhetoric. Democracy, it is frequently asserted, is what unites Europe's nation-states, defines its political institutions, and underpins its social and cultural value structures. The reasons why this should be so owe much to the history of Europe since 1945: democracy became during the second half of the twentieth century something that Europeans told one another about themselves, and thereby about their own collective identity.[36] But this "Europeanization" of democracy also owed much to a series of alternative others against which European societies defined themselves: initially communism and, less explicitly, the mass society of the United States, but subsequently the popular movements and dictatorships of the decolonizing world, and from the 1990s onwards the Islamic world, and its alternative definitions of personal identity and of political community. In this way democracy remains a means by which Europe describes its differentness, as well as enabling it to continue to lay claim to the ownership of democracy.

{⚜}

As this book has sought to argue, there is a need for a more critical understanding of the interrelationship between the history of democracy and the history of Europe. Such an approach has two distinct elements. Firstly, the democratic era that lasted for roughly twenty-five years from the end of the Second World War to the late 1960s needs to be analysed

35. E. Harrison and S. McLaughlin Mitchell, *The Triumph of Democracy and the Eclipse of the West* (Basingstoke, UK, 2013), 5.

36. See pp. 145–46. See also Conway and Depkat, "Towards a European History," 132–56.

as a particular moment in the history of contemporary Europe. Secondly, however, Western Europe's democratic age should be conceptualized as a particular moment in the history of democracy.

The first of these points probably needs little further elaboration. The establishment of a stable regime of democratic nation-state polities in Western Europe in the years following the Second World War was not the ineluctable product of long-term processes or of the outcome of the war. Its origins lay instead in the threefold convergence between the dictates of circumstance, the intentions of rulers, and the aspirations of the ruled. The democracy was not perfect; indeed, in important respects it was deliberately imperfect—or, in the normative language of contemporary political-science analyses, defective[37]—sacrificing popular sovereignty to the more pragmatic goal of the reconstruction of effective state power. Nor was it a once-and-for-all moment of transition. Democracy in post-war Europe was a grand improvisation, which rejected more than it borrowed from previous models of democratic government, and which acquired greater coherence in retrospect than it possessed at the time of its creation. Yet, precisely because it was moulded by the various pressures of its time, the democracy that took shape in Western Europe by the end of the 1940s reflected closely the dominant social realities of the age, most especially through the priority it accorded to state authority and to the representation of different interest groups, as well as its avoidance of majoritarian rule. This also explains its rather consciously unheroic character. The turn to democracy after 1945 was something less than the celebration of the sovereignty of the people. Instead, it provided a pragmatic mechanism by which Western Europeans managed and negotiated their many divisions of ideology, of political and confessional identity, and of material interest.

The process whereby democratic structures became embedded into a Europe that had formerly proved rather resistant to the politics of mass democracy makes it an instructive case for those concerned to understand the nature of democratic transitions. Democratization—the study of the processes by which states and societies move from authoritarian or single-party regimes to ones of pluralist democracy—has become, since the 1970s, a major focus of comparative political science. The collapse of the dictatorships in Greece, Portugal, and Spain in the 1970s, the events of 1989 in central and eastern Europe, and the subsequent attempts at

---

37. C. Rodriguez, A. Avalos, H. Yılmaz, and A. J. Planert, "Democratization Processes in Defective Democracies: The Case of Turkey," in *Turkey's Democratization Process*, ed. Rodriguez, Avalos, Yılmaz, and Planert (Abingdon, UK, 2014), 3–7.

"democracy-building" in south-eastern Europe after the Yugoslav wars, as well as in the Middle East as a consequence of the Arab Spring, have encouraged scholars to seek out the key actors, socio-economic forces, and broader cultural factors that might explain why democracies happen (and persist) in some places and not in others.[38]

Democratization, of course, is not a phenomenon only of recent decades. The Revolutionary era of 1848–49, the transition to universal male suffrage that occurred in many European states in the late nineteenth century, and the collapse of the multinational empires in central and eastern Europe at the end of the First World War and their replacement in many of their territories by democratic parliamentary regimes might all be regarded, in their rather different ways, as instances—albeit not all of them durably successful—of democratic transition. Amidst these case studies, present and past, 1945 has struggled to find its place. Perhaps simply because the transition was so marked and proved to be essentially irreversible, historians have had difficulty in conceptualizing how Europe became democratic after the end of the Second World War. Moreover, there remains an underlying sense that democratic transitions are more surprising when they happen elsewhere—in the words of one influential study of democratization, in "the most remote and improbable of locations"—rather than in Western Europe or North America, where some variant of democratic government is tacitly assumed to be the norm.[39] However, the neglect of 1945 as an instance of democratic transition is to be regretted. As much of the recent literature on democratization has rightly emphasized, the making of democracy is rarely the product of internal revolution or of external intervention. Instead, it is a gradual process that emerges from the actions of a multiplicity of actors, as well as the interaction of political institutions with medium- or long-term processes of social evolution.[40] Many of those conclusions can be applied without great difficulty to Western Europe in the post-1945 era. The durable establishment of democracy after 1945 resulted not from mass mobilization or the injunctions of external powers such as the United States, but from the (often self-interested) choices of a large number of groups, as well as

38. For a useful survey of the substantial political-science literature on democratic transitions, see D. della Porta, *Mobilizing for Democracy: Comparing 1989 and 2011* (Oxford, 2014), 1–26.

39. P. Whitehead, *Democratization: Theory and Experience* (Oxford, 2002), 1.

40. Whitehead, *Democratization*, 27–33; S. Adejumobi, "Democratic Renewal in Africa: Trends and Lessons Learned," in *Democratic Renewal in Africa: Trends and Discourses*, ed. Adejumobi (Basingstoke, UK, 2015), 1–19.

the maturation within Western European society of daily habits of doing democracy.

Democracy, in sum, was the point of confluence where Western Europe found the political regime of its reconstruction. Elsewhere, and most obviously in the state-socialist regimes of central and eastern Europe, this was not the case. The external structures of Soviet control were of course more explicit in these states, marginalizing—and at moments of regime crisis in 1956 and 1968 repressing—attempts at political change.[41] But the forty-year duration of these regimes, and the ways in which they gradually reached a partial modus vivendi with the societies over which they ruled, indicates not only the plurality of paths through Europe's twentieth century, but also the primacy of less visible factors in determining the evolution of political regimes. The internal architecture of rule, the delivery of effective and predictable governance, and the forms of interaction created between the state, the population, and the principal institutions of society were factors common to both the state-socialist and democratic regimes of post-1945 Europe, but also ones that over the long term explain the greater success of the latter, at the expense ultimately of the former.

The second point—that of the history of democracy—is perhaps less evident. Because of its present-day ascendancy, there has been an understandable tendency to assume that democracy has always been essentially the same, or at least to read back into the democratic ideas and regimes of past eras the assumptions of the present. Unlike the communists or fascists of the past, the democrats are assumed to have been "people like us" in terms of their aspirations and their ideological mindsets. And yet, as work on the history of democratic ideas in the Revolutionary era from the late eighteenth century to the mid-nineteenth century has well demonstrated, conceptions of democracy in previous centuries were often very different from those of the present day.[42] What, say, a lawyer in Dijon in the 1840s, a peasant in Bavaria in the 1890s, a worker in Barcelona in the 1930s, and a shopkeeper in Milan in the 1960s—not to mention their female family members—would have understood democracy to be, and indeed what they thought

41. For an excellent analytical account of the regimes of state socialism in central and eastern Europe, see M. Pittaway, *Eastern Europe, 1939–2000* (London, 2004).

42. J. Innes and M. Philp, introduction to *Re-imagining Democracy in the Age of Revolutions: America, France, Britain, Ireland 1750–1850*, ed. Innes and Philp (Oxford, 2013), 2–3. The evolution of conceptual understandings of democracy is the central theme of Kurunmäki, Nevers, and Te Velde, *Democracy in Modern Europe*.

it should be, would have differed substantially. More challenging, however, is to understand the nature of those differences, and the reasons for their evolution. Political ideologies, as studies of fascist ideas have long since demonstrated, tend to be more amenable to coherent summary in retrospect than they were at the time of their formulation.[43] Indeed, a certain incoherence might be regarded as inherent to the success of political ideologies that rely not so much on statements of doctrine as on the way in which they are able to draw on less explicit human and societal emotions and states of mind.[44]

Approached in this way, democracy owes its durability not to its principles but to its flexibility. In the century that followed the French Revolution of 1789, democracy was a vehicle primarily for those who aspired to a liberation: the pulling down of structures of privilege and of social and intellectual repression, and the achievement of a free and open society. But, with the emergence of a more structured mass politics in many areas of Europe in the second half of the nineteenth century, so democracy became associated with the exercise of power: the establishment through universal (male) suffrage of the will of the majority as the basis of political authority, the eradication of regimes of inequality, and the consequent achievement of a more just social and political order. The democratic reforms introduced in Europe in the aftermath of the First World War marked the culmination of this particular constellation of democracy; but, over the subsequent decades, democracy was submerged and instrumentalized in the conflicts of the 1930s and the Second World War. Democracy became part of other wars: between opposing ideologies of right and left, between social groups, and ultimately between states. It was only once those conflicts reached their terminus after 1945 that the new shape of democracy in the western half of Europe became visible. This was focused on the inclusive representation of different social groups, the development of a more effective structure of government focused on the needs of the people (both male and female), and the provision of an unprecedented range of benefits and services. During the final decades of the twentieth century, however, democracy changed again. The erosion of the sovereignty of government at the national, regional, and even European levels by processes of global economic change deprived political life of any substantive choice between different models

---

43. Sternhell, *Neither Right nor Left*; R. Griffin, *The Nature of Fascism* (London, 1994).
44. R. Toye, "Keynes, Liberalism and 'the Emancipation of the Mind,'" *English Historical Review* 130 (2015): 1162–91.

of society. Rulers became managers and voters became consumers, choosing between different brands and individuals, differentiated more by the values they expressed than the policies they proposed. Consequently, democracy shifted from a discourse of representation and of sovereignty to one of choice and of rights. The yardstick by which a democracy was judged was no longer how directly the will of the people was reflected in governmental action, but how effectively the rights of the individual and of groups were protected.

This narrowing of the political universe has led to fears of an "eclipse of politics," whereby any real debate between different models of society has disappeared,[45] as well as a new wave of works announcing the death of democracy. Stimulated by the emergence of populist parties in certain European states, by the Brexit referendum in the United Kingdom, and by the Trump presidency in the United States, this literature tends to repeat (or reheat) themes already familiar from the writings of the past: the decline in public participation, the withering of ideological debate, and the subordination of politics to the tools of propaganda and advertising.[46] Democracy, one might be tempted to conclude with David Runciman, is always in crisis, and yet is always with us.[47] It is simply the direction and the nature of the critique that changes. Thus, the Communist denunciations of neo-fascist and US influence in the 1950s, the attacks on formal democracy in the 1960s, and the neoliberal manifestos of the 1970s and 1980s have now been succeeded by the regrets of a liberal intelligentsia who no longer feel at home in a less structured and coherent democratic politics.

In fact, nothing would suggest that the current model of democratic politics will mark the end point in its evolution. All democracies are incomplete, not in opposition to any arbitrary ideal, but in contradistinction to one another.[48] In Europe's recent history, they have also tended to superimpose themselves on each other, much like geological strata, incorporating something of the legacies of past eras, while reshaping these to meet new fashions and needs. Political leaders, parties, intellectual fashions, and the impulses provided by non-European regimes and movements have all, at different points in the twentieth century, succeeded in

45. G. Agamben, "What Is an Apparatus?" in *What Is an Apparatus and Other Essays* (Stanford, CA, 2009), 22.

46. A. C. Grayling, *Democracy and Its Critics* (London, 2017).

47. D. Runciman, *The Confidence Trap: A History of Democracy in Crisis from World War I to the Present* (Princeton, NJ, 2013).

48. M. L. Anderson, *Practicing Democracy*, 437.

influencing this process of democratic evolution in Europe. But none, it would seem, has had a decisive role; instead, the definition of democracy, as well as the writing of its history, has often proved so elusive simply because it is a process defined by much wider evolutions in state power, in political and social conflict, and in ideological trends. Democracy, as this book has sought to argue, is not the author of its own history, but a means of understanding that wider history.

Primary Sources

Alleg, H. *The Question*. London, 1958.

Allemann, F. R. *Bonn ist nicht Weimar*. Cologne, 1956.

Amodia, J. *Franco's Political Legacy: From Dictatorship to Façade Democracy*. London, 1977.

Ardagh, J. *The New France*. Harmondsworth, UK, 1970.

Arendt, H. *Men in Dark Times*. London, 1970.

Aron, Raymond. *Démocratie et totalitarisme*. Paris, 1965.

———. *Le grand schisme*. Paris, 1948.

———. "Les institutions politiques de l'occident dans le monde du XXe siècle." In *La démocratie à l'épreuve du XXe siècle*, by Aron, A. Schlesinger, G. Arciniegas, A. K. Brohi, M. Berger, and F. Bondy, 11–42. Paris, 1960.

———. *Mémoires: Cinquante ans de réflexion politique*. Paris, 1983.

———. *L'opium des intellectuels*. Paris, 1955.

———. *Plaidoyer pour l'Europe décadente*. Paris, 1977.

———. *La révolution introuvable*. Paris, 1968.

———. "La société industrielle et les dialogues politiques de l'occident." In *Colloques de Rheinfelden*, by Aron, G. Kennan, and R. Oppenheimer, 9–38. Paris, 1960.

———. *La tragédie algérienne*. Paris, 1957.

Aron, Robert. *Histoire de l'épuration*. Vol. 1, *De l'indulgence aux massacres*. Paris, 1967.

Auriol, V. *Journal du septennat, 1947–1954*. Paris, 1970.

Badoglio, P. "Internal Reconstruction." In *Italy in the Second World War: Memories and Documents*, edited by Badoglio, 203–23. London, 1948.

Banfield, E. *The Moral Basis of a Backward Society*. Glencoe, IL, 1958.

Barbagallo, C. *La questione meridionale*. [Milan], 1948.

Bardèche, M. *Qu'est-ce que le fascisme?* Paris, 1961.

Bednarik, K. *The Male in Crisis*. London, 1970.

Bell, D. *The End of Ideology: On the Exhaustion of Political Ideas in the Fifties*. Glencoe, IL, 1960.

———. "The End of Ideology Revisited." *Government and Opposition* 23 (1988): 131–50 and 321–31.

Bendix, R. *Embattled Reason: Essays on Social Knowledge*. New York, 1970.

Berlin, I. *Four Essays on Liberty*. London, 1969.

Bernanos, G. *Tradition of Freedom*. London, 1950.

Bettelheim, B. *The Informed Heart: The Human Condition in Modern Mass Society*. Glencoe, IL, 1960.

———. "The Problem of Generations." *Daedalus* 91 (1962): 68–96.

Bobbio, N. *A Political Life*. Cambridge, UK, 2002.

Brenan, G. *South from Granada*. London, 1957.

Brend, W. A. *Foundations of Human Conflicts: A Study in Group Psychology*. London, 1944.

Bruclain, C. *Le socialisme et l'Europe*. Paris, 1965.

Buchanan, R. A. *Technology and Social Progress*. Oxford, 1965.

Camus, A. *Actuelles III: Chronique algérienne 1939–1958*. Paris, 1958.

———. "Democracy and Modesty" (30 April 1947). In *Camus at Combat: Writing 1944–1947*, edited by J. Lévi-Valensi, 286–88. Princeton, NJ, 2006.

Cassa per il Mezzogiorno. *Cassa per il Mezzogiorno Development Plan: Results of the First Four Years*. Rome, 1955.

Césaire, A. *Discours sur le colonialisme*. 3rd ed. Paris, 1955.

Chabod, F. *L'Italie contemporaine: Conférences données à l'Institut d'études politiques de l'Université de Paris*. Paris, 1950.

Childs, M. *Sweden: The Middle Way*. 3rd ed. New Haven, CT, 1961.

Club Jean Moulin. *L'état et le citoyen*. Paris, 1961.

Compagna, F. *Mezzogiorno d'Europa*. Rome, 1958.

Congar, Y. *Jalons pour une théologie du laïcat*. Paris, 1953.

Coudray, J.-M. "La révolution anticipée." In *Mai 1968: La Brèche—premières réflexions sur les événements*, by E. Morin, C. Lefort, and Coudray, 89–142. Paris, 1968.

Crossman, R.H.S. Introduction to Koestler et al., *God that Failed*, 7–17.

David, E. *A Book of Mediterranean Food*. London, 1955.

De Beauvoir, S. *Les mandarins*. Paris, 1954.

———. *Mémoires d'une jeune fille rangée*. Paris, 1958.

Debré, M. *Refaire une démocratie, un état, un pouvoir*. Paris, 1958.

———. *La République et ses problèmes*. Paris, 1952.

De Gaulle, C. *Discours et messages*. Paris 1970.

De Lubac, H. *Sur les chemins de dieu*. Paris, 1956.

De Madariaga, S. *Portrait of Europe*. London, 1952.

———. *Victors, Beware*. London, 1946.

Depreux, E. *Renouvellement du socialisme*. Paris, 1960.

Dermine, Chanoine. "Christianisme et démocratie." In *Les lignes de faite de la démocratie: XXVIIIe semaine sociale wallonne 1946*, 19–46. Courtrai, Belgium, n.d.

Di Lampedusa, G. *Il gattopardo*. Milan, 1958.

Domenach, J.-M. "Democratic Paralysis in France." *Foreign Affairs* 37 (1958): 31–44.

———. *La propagande politique*. Paris, 1950.

Droz, J. "Travaux récents sur la révolution de 1848 en Allemagne." *Revue d'histoire moderne et contemporaine* 1 (1954): 145–55.

Dupuis, R., and A. Marc. *Jeune Europe*. Paris, 1933.

Dutschke, R. *Ecrits politiques*. [Paris], 1968.

Duverger, M. *Les partis politiques*. Paris, 1951.

Eyskens, G. *De memoires*. Tielt, Belgium, 1993.

Fabian, B. *Alexis de Tocquevilles Amerikabild*. Heidelberg, 1957.

Faravelli, G. *Per l'autonomia del Partito Socialista: Marxismo ed utopismo*. N.p., 1946.

Fejtö, F., ed. *1848 dans le monde: Le printemps des peuples*. Paris, 1948.

Fierlinger, Z. "Programme gouvernemental de reconstruction de l'état." In *La Tchécoslovaquie sur une route nouvelle*, 5–14. Prague, 1947.

Figl, L. "Die ÖVP: Eine Integrationspartei für Österreich" (21 April 1947). In *Leopold Figl: Ansichten eines grossen Österreichers*, edited by R. Pranter, 111–13. Vienna, 1992.

———. "Wer hat wen befreit?" (8 May 1946). In *Leopold Figl: Ansichten eines grossen Österreichers*, edited by R. Pranter, 54–59. Vienna, 1992.

Finer, H. *The Future of Government*. London, 1946.

———. *The Major Governments of Western Europe*. London, 1960.

———. *Road to Reaction*. London, 1946.

Foot, P. *The Politics of Harold Wilson*. Harmondsworth, UK, 1968.

Fourastié, J. *Le grand espoir du XXe siècle: Progrès technique, progrès économique, progrès social*. Paris, 1949.

Friedrich, C., and Z. Brzezinski. *Totalitarian Dictatorship and Autocracy*. Cambridge, MA, 1956.

Fromm, E. *The Fear of Freedom*. London, 2001.

Fukuyama, F. *The End of History and the Last Man*. London, 1992.

Galbraith, J. K. *The Affluent Society*. London, 1958.

Gavi, P., J.-P. Sartre, and P. Victor. *It Is Right to Rebel*. London, 2017.

Gilson, A. *Pour une démocratie efficace*. Louvain, 1965.

Giscard d'Estaing, V. *Démocratie française*. Paris, 1976.

Goguel, F. *La politique des partis sous la IIIe République*. 2 vols. Paris, 1946.

Golding, W. *Lord of the Flies*. London, 1954.

Gorz, A. *Socialism and Revolution*. London, 1975.

Grass, G. *Peeling the Onion*. London, 2008.

Grayling, A. C. *Democracy and Its Critics*. London, 2017.

Habermas, J. *The Lure of Technocracy*. Cambridge, UK, 2015.

———. *The Structural Transformation of the Public Sphere: An Inquiry into a Category of Bourgeois Society*. Cambridge, UK, 1989. Originally published 1962.

Hamon, L. *De Gaulle dans la République*. Paris, 1958.

Harmel, L. "Lignes de faite de la démocratie politique." In *Les lignes de faite de la démocratie: XXVIIIe semaine sociale wallonne, 1946*, 179–92. Courtrai, Belgium, n.d.

Hayes, A. *The Girl on the Via Flaminia*. London, 1949.

Herz, M. "Compendium of Austrian Politics" (2 December 1948). In *Understanding Austria: The Political Reports and Analyses of Martin F. Herz, Political Officer in the US Legation in Vienna, 1945–1948*, edited by R. Wagnleitner, 550–630. Salzburg, 1984.

Histoire du Parti communiste français: Manuel. Paris, 1964.

Hobsbawm, E. *Interesting Times: A Twentieth-Century Life*. London, 2002.

———. "May 1968." In *Revolutionaries: Contemporary Essays*, 234–44. London, 1973.

———. "The Prospects of Democracy." In *Globalisation, Democracy and Terrorism*, 95–114. London, 2007.

Hook, S. "Democracy as a Way of Life." In *Tomorrow in the Making*, edited by J. N. Andrews and C. A. Marsden, 31–46. New York, 1939.

Hoyois, G. "La réponse des peuples à la démocratie." In *Les lignes de faite de la démocratie: XXVIIIe semaine sociale wallonne, 1946*, 215–38. Courtrai, Belgium, n.d.

Huntington, S. P. *The Third Wave: Democratization in the Late Twentieth Century*. Norman, OK, 1991.

Ibrugger, F. *Au fond, qu'est-ce que la démocratie?* Paris, 1941.

Ionescu, G., and E. Gellner, eds. *Populism: Its Meanings and National Characteristics.* London, 1969.

Ivanovic, V. *Democratic Yugoslavia: An Outline for Discussion.* London, [1967].

[Janne, M.-H.]. *Pour un renouveau du socialisme démocratique.* Brussels, 1972.

Jeanson, C., and F. Jeanson. *L'Algérie hors la loi.* 2nd ed. Paris, 1955.

Jeger, S. W., and M. Orbach. *Austria 1946.* London, 1946.

Journal officiel de la République française, débats parlementaires, Assemblée nationale, 1947.

Julien, C. *Le suicide des démocraties.* Paris, 1972.

Kardelj, E. *De la démocratie populaire en Yougoslavie.* Paris, 1949.

Kasamas, A. *Programm Österreich: Die Grundsätze und Ziele der Österreichischen Volkspartei.* Vienna, 1949.

Koch, H. *Hvad er demokrati?* Copenhagen, 1945.

Koeppen, W. *Das Treibhaus.* Stuttgart, 1953.

Koestler, A., I. Silone, A. Gide, R. Wright, L. Fischer, and S. Spender. *The God that Failed: Six Studies in Communism.* London, 1950.

Kongress für kulturelle Freiheit. *Die Bewährung der Demokratie im 20. Jahrhundert: Das Seminar von Berlin.* Zurich, 1961.

Košický vládní program: Program nové československé vlády Národní fronty Čechů a Slováků. Prague, 1974.

KPÖ (Kommunistische Partei Österreichs). "Programmische Leitsätze der Kommunistischen Partei Österreichs, 1946." In *Österreichische Parteiprogramme 1868–1966,* edited by K. Berchtold, 316–23. Munich, 1967.

Kravchenko, V. *I Chose Freedom.* London, 1947.

Kreichbaumer, R. *Parteiprogramme im Widerstreit der Interessen: Die Programmdiskussion und die Programme von ÖVP und SPÖ 1945–1986.* Vienna, 1990.

Kriegel, A. *Les communistes français: Essai d'ethnographie politique.* Paris, 1968.

Labin, S. *Stalin's Russia.* London, 1949.

Lalmand, E. *Bâtir une Belgique nouvelle.* Brussels, 1946.

———. *Notre lutte pour l'indépendance nationale, la démocratie et la paix.* Brussels, 1952.

———. *Reconquérir l'indépendance nationale: Sauver la paix. Rapport présenté au Xe Congrès National du PCB, Bruxelles, 23-24-25-26 mars 1951.* Brussels, 1951.

Lauwers, F., J. Stalmans, M. Schuermans, and V. Verbruggen. *België, een levende democratie.* Antwerp, 1964.

Lauwerys, J. A., ed. *Scandinavian Democracy: The Development of Democratic Thought and Institutions in Denmark, Norway and Sweden.* Copenhagen, 1958.

Leclercq, J. *Allons-nous à une société sans classes?* [Namur, 1946.]

Lefebvre, G. *Quatre-vingt-neuf.* Paris, 1939.

Lefebvre, H. *Position: Contre les technocrates.* Paris, 1967.

———. *La proclamation de la Commune.* Paris, 1965.

Lefort, C. "Le désordre nouveau." In *Mai 1968: La Brèche—premières réflexions sur les événements,* by E. Morin, Lefort, and J.-M. Coudray, 37–62. Paris, 1968.

———. *L'invention démocratique: Les limites de la domination totalitaire.* Paris, 1981.

Leigh Fermor, P. *Between the Woods and the Water.* London, 1986.

Lewis, N. *Naples '44*. London, 1978.

Lijphart, A. *Democracy in Plural Societies: A Comparative Explanation*. New Haven, CT, 1977.

———. *Patterns of Democracy: Government Forms and Performance in Thirty-Six Countries*. 2nd ed. New Haven, CT, 2012.

———. *The Politics of Accommodation: Pluralism and Democracy in the Netherlands*. Berkeley, CA, 1968.

———. "Typologies of Democratic Systems." In *Politics in Europe: Comparisons and Interpretations*, edited by Lijphart, 46–80. Englewood Cliffs, NJ, 1969.

———. "Varieties of Nonmajoritarian Democracy." In Crepaz, Koeble, and Wilsford, *Democracy and Institutions*, 225–45.

Lippmann, W. *The Communist World and Ours*. London, 1959.

Lipset, S. M. Introduction to *Political Parties: A Sociological Study of the Oligarchical Tendencies of Modern Democracy*, by R. Michels, 15–39. New York, 1962.

Lipset, S. M., and R. Bendix. *Social Mobility in Industrial Society*. London, 1959.

Loewenstein, K. "Militant Democracy and Fundamental Rights." *American Political Science Review* 31 (1937): 417–32 and 638–58.

———. *Political Reconstruction*. New York, 1946.

Lowenthal, R. "On the Disaffection of Western Intellectuals" (1977). In *Social Change and Cultural Crisis*, 25–41. New York, 1984.

Lüthy, H. "The French Intellectuals." *Encounter*, August 1955, 5–15.

Luyendijk, A. F. "Ontnuchterd radicalisme." In *Visioen en werkelijkheid*, 38–46.

Lyon-Caen, G. "L'avenir de la démocratie classique." *Cahiers internationaux* 26 (1951): 11–26.

Malagodi, G. *Massa non-massa: Riflessioni sul liberalismo e la democrazia*. Rome, 1962.

Malaparte, C. *The Skin*. New ed. New York, 2013.

Mandrin, J. *L'énarchie ou les mandarins de la société bourgeoise*. 2nd ed. Paris, 1980. Originally published 1967.

Mann, T. *Goethe und die Demokratie*. Oxford, 1949.

Marcuse, H. *One Dimensional Man: Studies in the Ideology of Advanced Industrial Society*. London, 1964.

Maritain, J. *Man and the State*. Chicago, 1951.

———. *Reflections on America*. New York, 1958.

———. *Scholasticism and Authority*. Glasgow, 1940.

Marty, A. *L'affaire Marty*. Paris, 1955.

McKeon, R., and S. Rokkan, eds. *Democracy in a World of Tensions: A Symposium Prepared by UNESCO*. Paris, 1951.

Mendès France, P. "La crise de la démocratie." In *Oeuvres complètes*, vol. 4, 81–103. Paris, 1987.

———. "La République." In *Oeuvres complètes*, vol. 4, 341–47. Paris, 1987.

———. *La République moderne*. Paris, 1962.

Meynaud, J. *Les groupes de pression en France*. Paris, 1958.

———. *La technocratie: Mythe ou réalité?* Paris, 1964.

Michels, R. *Political Parties: A Sociological Study of the Oligarchical Tendencies of Modern Democracy*. New York, 1962.

Middleton Murry, J. *The Free Society*. London, 1948.

Miliband, R. *The State in Capitalist Society*. London, 1969.

Milosz, C. *The Captive Mind*. London, 1953.

Mitterrand, F. *Le coup d'état permanent*. Paris, 1964.

———. "Présentation." In *Changer la vie: Programme de gouvernement du Parti socialiste*, 5–33. Paris, 1972.

———. *La rose au poing*. Paris, 1973.

Mollet, G. *Bilan et perspectives socialistes*. Paris, 1958.

Monnet, J. *Mémoires*. Paris, 1976.

Morante, E. *La storia: Romanzo*. Turin, 1974.

Morin, E. *Autocritique*. Paris, 1959.

———. "La commune étudiante." In *Mai 1968: La Brèche—premières réflexions sur les événements*, by Morin, C. Lefort, and J.-M. Coudray, 13–33. Paris, 1968.

———. "Une révolution sans visage." In *Mai 1968: La Brèche—premières réflexions sur les événements*, by Morin, C. Lefort, and J.-M. Coudray, 63–87. Paris, 1968.

Mosse, G. *The Culture of Western Europe*. London, 1963.

Mounier, E. Chapter 19 (untitled) in McKeon and Rokkan, *Democracy*, 228–37.

———. *The Spoil of the Violent*. London, 1955.

Myrdal, J. *Confessions of a Disloyal European*. London, 1968.

Nathan, P. *The Psychology of Fascism*. London, 1943.

Nenni, P. *Il socialismo nella democrazia*. Florence, 1956.

The Opening of the Prague Parliament: Message of President Dr. Edvard Beneš to the National Assembly of the Czechoslovak Republic. Prague, 1946.

Ortese, A. M. *Il mare non bagna Napoli*. Turin, 1953.

Orwell, G. *Nineteen Eighty-Four: A Novel*. London, 1949.

Ozouf, M. *Composition française: Retour sur une enfance bretonne*. Paris, 2009.

Parliamentary Debates, Commons, 5th series (1947).

PCB (Parti communiste belge). *Démocrates, la loi est pour vous: Faites-la respecter*. Brussels, [early 1950s].

PCF (Parti communiste français). *Au travail pour gagner la bataille de la production*. N.p., [1945].

PSC (Parti social chrétien). *Documents introductifs XIVe Congrès national du PSC, Ypres 13-14-15 mars 1959*. Brussels, 1959.

PSB (Parti socialiste belge). *Programme pour les élections législatives de 1965*. Liège, [1965].

Pasquier, A. *Amérique 44*. Brussels, [1944 or 1945].

Perin, F. *La démocratie enrayée*. Brussels, 1960.

Peyrefitte, R. *South from Naples*. London, 1954.

Picard, L. "Synthèse de la pensée pontificale." In *Conditions de la démocratie*, by Pius XII, 7–15. Brussels, 1945.

Pius XII. "Democracy and Peace." In *Selected Letters and Addresses of Pius XII*, edited by Catholic Truth Society, 299–318. London, 1949.

Pizzorno, A. *Comunità e razionalizzazione: Ricerca sociologica su un caso di sviluppo industriale*. Turin, 1960.

———. "The Individualistic Mobilization of Europe." *Daedalus* 93 (1964): 199–224.

Polcz, A. *One Woman in the War: Hungary 1944-1945*. Budapest, 2002.

Pompe, W.P.J. *Bevrijding: Bezetting—herstel—vernieuwing*. Amsterdam, 1945.

Ponteil, F. *Les bourgeois et la démocratie sociale 1914-1968*. Paris, 1971.

Popper, K. R. *The Open Society and Its Enemies*. London, 1945.

Poujade, P. *J'ai choisi le combat*. Saint-Céré, France, 1955.

Raab, J. "Freiheit, Währungsstabilität, Wirtschaftsexpansion, Sorge um die Familien" (15 April 1953). In *Julius Raab: Ansichten des Staatsvertragskanzlers*, edited by R. Prantner, 16-22. Vienna, 1991.

——. "Freiheit und soziale Sicherheit für alle Österreicher!" (30 November 1958). In *Julius Raab: Ansichten des Staatsvertragskanzlers*, edited by R. Prantner, 25-28. Vienna, 1991.

——."Die Österreichische Volkspartei: Ein Wellenbrecher gegen totalitäre Anspruche" (29 January 1952). In *Julius Raab: Ansichten des Staatsvertragskanzlers*, edited by R. Prantner, 14-15. Vienna, 1991.

——. "Parteiverantwortung für das Staatsganze in der Republik" (1951). In *Julius Raab: Ansichten des Staatsvertragskanzlers*, edited by R. Prantner, 13-14. Vienna, 1991.

Ranulf, S. *On the Survival Chances of Democracy*. Copenhagen, 1948.

Rassow, P. "Deutschland in Europa" (1956). In *Die geschichtliche Einheit des Abendlandes*, 46-56. Cologne, 1960.

——. "Die geschichtliche Einheit des Abendlandes." In *Die geschichtliche Einheit des Abendlandes*, 3-34. Cologne, 1960.

Rémond, R. "Tocqueville et la démocratie en Amérique." In *Alexis de Tocqueville: Livre du centenaire, 1859-1959*, 180-90. Paris, 1960.

Renard, A. *Vers le socialisme par l'action*. Liège, 1958.

Rencontres: Nenni, Bevan, Mendès France (février 1959). Paris, 1959.

Renner, K. "Die Demokratie ist der Friede!" (Christmas 1949). In *Für Recht und Frieden*, 279-82.

——. "Demokratie und Bürokratie" (22 February 1946). In *Für Recht und Frieden*, 196-220.

——. "30 Jahre Republik Österreich" (12 November 1948). In *Für Recht und Frieden*, 75-88.

——. *Für Recht und Frieden: Eine Auswahl der Reden des Bundespräsidenten Dr. Karl Renner*. Vienna, 1950.

——. "Gesellschaft, Staat und Demokratie" (18 November 1948). In *Für Recht und Frieden*, 113-40.

——. "Was ist Demokratie?" (22 October 1949). In *Für Recht und Frieden*, 186-95.

Revel, J.-F. *Comment les démocraties finissent*. Paris, 1983.

Robrieux, P. *Notre génération communiste, 1953-1968: Essai d'autobiographie communiste*. Paris, 1977.

Rokkan, S. "Norway: Numerical Democracy and Corporate Pluralism." In *Political Oppositions in Western Democracies*, edited by R. A. Dahl, 70-115. New Haven, CT, 1966.

Ross, A. "What Is Democracy?" In Lauwerys, *Scandinavian Democracy*, 48-57.

Rousset, D. *L'univers concentrationnaire*. Paris, 1946.

Russell, B. Preface to *A World Apart*, by G. Herling, ix-x. London, 1951.

Sakharov, A., R. Medvedev, and V. Turchin. "Appeal for a Gradual Democratization." In *Samizdat: Voices of the Soviet Opposition*, edited by G. Saunders, 399–412. New York, 1974.

Sandoz, G. "Etre révolutionnaire." In Dutschke, *Ecrits politiques*, 7–35.

SAP (Sveriges socialdemokratiska arbetareparti). "Till Sveriges folk!" (To the people of Sweden!). Manifestos of 1948, 1952, and 1956. https://snd.gu.se/en/vivill/party/s.

Saragat, G. *Socialismo democratico e socialismo totalitario: Per l'autonomia del Partito Socialista*. Milan, 1946.

Schelsky, H. *The Skeptical Generation: A Sociological Picture of German Youth*. Dusseldorf, 1957.

Schlichting, L.G.A. "De eenheid en de herzuiling." In *Visioen en werkelijkheid*, 47–55.

Schumann, M. *Le vrai malaise des intellectuels de gauche*. Paris, 1957.

Socialist International. "Aims and Tasks of Democratic Socialism." 30 June–3 July 1951. http://www.socialistinternational.org/viewArticle.cfm?ArticleID=39.

Socialist Union. *Socialism: A New Statement of Principles*. London, 1952.

Soustelle, J. *La page n'est pas tournée*. Paris, 1965.

SPD (Sozialdemokratische Partei Deutschlands). *Basic Programme of the Social Democratic Party of Germany*. Reproduced in *A History of German Social Democracy: From 1848 to the Present*, by S. Miller, and H. Potthoff, 274–87. Leamington Spa, UK, 1986.

[SPÖ (Sozialdemokratische Partei Österreichs)]. "Das Neue Parteiprogramm der Sozialistischen Partei Österreichs, 1958." In *Österreichische Parteiprogramme 1868–1966*, edited by K. Berchtold, 286–306. Munich, 1967.

SPÖ Wien. *Bericht 1959*. Vienna, 1960.

Spock, B. *Baby and Child Care*. London, 1956.

Steinberg, P. *Speak You Also: A Survivor's Reckoning*. London, 2001.

Struye, P. *L'évolution du sentiment public en Belgique sous l'occupation allemande*. Edited by J. Gotovitch. Brussels, 2002.

Talmon, J. *The Origins of Totalitarian Democracy*. London, 1952.

Tchakhotine, S. *Le viol psychique des masses: Obstacles à une vraie démocratie*. Paris, 1946.

Tersen, E. "Les révolutions de 1848." *Revue historique* 201 (1949): 272–89.

Thils, G. *Théologie des réalités terrestres*. Vol. 1. [Bruges], 1946.

Thurlings, T.L.M. "Waar staat het hedendaagse socialisme?" *De Economist* 100 (1952): 641–55.

Tourainc, A. *Democracy versus History*. Institute for Advanced Studies, Vienna, Political Science Series no. 34. Vienna, 1996.

———. "The French Student Movement of May 1968." In *Political Sociology*, edited by A. Pizzorno. 310–19. Harmondsworth, UK, 1971.

Trevor-Roper, H. Preface to *Invitation to Moscow*, by Z. Stypulkowski, ix–xvi. London, 1951.

Van Rompuy, H. "Europe, Political Democracy and the Flux of Time." In *The Road to Political Democracy*, edited by R. Senelle, E. Clément, and E. Van de Velde, 1007–14. Brussels, 2012.

Vercleyen, J. *Témoignage sur Achille Van Acker*. Brussels, 1967.

Visioen en werkelijkheid: De illegale pers over de toekomst der samenleving. The Hague, 1963.

Wagnleitner, R. ed. *Understanding Austria: The Political Reports and Analyses of Martin F. Herz, Political Officer in the US Legation in Vienna, 1945–1948.* Salzburg, 1984.

Walgrave, V. *Onze Vlaamse Volksbeweging.* Tielt, Belgium, 1949.

Weber, A. "Freier Sozialismus: Ein Aktionsprogramm." In *Freier Sozialismus,* by A. Mitscherlich and Weber, 39–94. Heidelberg, 1946.

Weil, E. "Philosophical and Political Thought in Europe Today." *Daedalus* 93 (1964): 493–513.

Whelan, R., and C. Capa, eds. *Robert Capa Photographs.* London, 1985.

Worsley, P. *The Third World.* London, 1964.

Wylie, L. *Village in the Vaucluse.* 3rd ed. Cambridge, MA, 1974.

Young, K. *A Handbook of Social Psychology.* London, 1946.

Young, M. "Problems Ahead." In *Socialism: The British Way,* 317–45. London, 1948.

Young, M., and P. Wilmott. *Family and Kinship in East London.* Harmondsworth, UK, 1962.

Zuckerman, S. Foreword to *The Next Hundred Years,* by H. Brown, J. Bonner, and J. Weir, ix–x. London, 1957.

Secondary Sources

Abromeit, J., and W. M. Cobb, eds. *Herbert Marcuse: A Critical Reader.* New York, 2004.

———. Introduction to Abromeit and Cobb, *Herbert Marcuse,* 1–39.

Adejumobi, S. "Democratic Renewal in Africa: Trends and Lessons Learned." In *Democratic Renewal in Africa: Trends and Discourses,* edited by Adejumobi, 1–19. Basingstoke, UK, 2015.

Aerts, K., and B. De Wever. "Het verzet in de publieke herinnering in Vlaanderen." *Journal of Belgian History* 42 (2012): 78–107.

Aerts, R., H. De Liagre Böhl, P. De Rooy, and H. Te Velde. *Land van kleine gebaren: Een politieke geschiedenis van Nederland 1780–1990.* Nijmegen, 1999.

Agamben, G. "What Is an Apparatus?" In *What Is an Apparatus and Other Essays,* 1–24. Stanford, CA, 2009.

Agosti, A. *Rodolfo Morandi: Il pensiero e l'azione politica.* Bari, 1971.

Ahonen, P. *Death at the Berlin Wall.* Oxford, 2011.

Alapuro, R. "Conclusion: How History Matters in Putting Nordic Associations into a European Perspective." In *Nordic Associations in a European Perspective,* edited by Alapuro and H. Stenius, 309–17. Baden-Baden, 2010.

Alexander, M., and H. Graham, eds. *The French and Spanish Popular Fronts: Comparative Perspectives.* Cambridge, UK, 1989.

Algazy, J. *La tentation néo-fasciste en France 1944–1965.* Paris, 1984.

Allardt, E., and H. Valen. "Stein Rokkan: An Intellectual Profile." In *Mobilization, Center-Periphery Structures and Nation-Building,* edited by P. Torsvik, 11–38. Bergen, 1981.

Allum, P. *Politics and Society in Post-war Naples.* Cambridge, UK, 1973.

———. *State and Society in Western Europe.* Cambridge, UK, 1995.

Altermatt, U. *Der Weg der Schweizer Katholiken ins Ghetto.* Zurich, 1972.

Amar, T. C. *The Paradox of Ukrainian Lviv: A Borderland City between Stalinists, Nazis, and Nationalists.* Ithaca, NY, 2015.

Amrith, S., and G. Sluga. "New Histories of the United Nations." *Journal of World History* 19 (2008): 251–74.

Anderson, B. *Raymond Aron: The Recovery of the Political.* Lanham, MD, 1997.

Anderson, M. L. *Practicing Democracy: Elections and Political Culture in Imperial Germany.* Princeton, NJ, 2000.

———. *Windthorst: A Political Biography.* Oxford, 1981.

Andrieu, C. "Le CNR et les logiques de l'insurrection résistante." In *De Gaulle et la Libération*, edited by Fondation Charles de Gaulle, 69–125. Brussels, 2004.

———. "Introduction: Politiques de Pierre Sudreau." In *Pierre Sudreau, 1919–2012: Engagé technocrate, homme d'influence*, edited by Andrieu and M. Margairaz, 65–81. Rennes, 2017.

———. *Pour l'amour de la République: Le Club Jean Moulin, 1958–1970.* Paris, 2002.

———. *Le programme commun de la Résistance: Des idées dans la guerre.* Paris, 1984.

Applegate, C. *A Nation of Provincials: The German Idea of Heimat.* Berkeley, CA, 1990.

Apruzzese, S. "Modernismo e mito nazionale a Milano nel primo Novecento." *Storia Contemporanea* second series, 3 (2018): 93–106.

Arieli, Y. "Jacob Talmon: An Intellectual Portrait." In *Totalitarian Democracy and After*, edited by Arieli and N. Rotenstreich, 12–45. London, 1984.

Atack, M. "Edgar Morin and the Sociology of May 1968." *French Cultural Studies* 8 (1997): 295–307.

Atkin, N. *The Fifth French Republic.* Basingstoke, UK, 2005.

Audigier, F., and P. Girard. Introduction to *Se battre pour les idées: La violence militante en France des années 1920 aux années 1970*, edited by Audigier and Girard, 7–20. Paris, 2011.

Bacqué, M.-H., and Y. Sintomer, eds. *La démocratie participative: Histoire et généalogie.* Paris, 2011.

Badcock, S. *Politics and the People in Revolutionary Russia: A Provincial History.* Cambridge, UK, 2007.

Bailey, C. *Between Yesterday and Tomorrow: German Visions of Europe, 1936–1950.* New York, 2013.

Bakker, N. "The Meaning of Fear. Emotional Standards for Children in the Netherlands, 1850–1950: Was There a Western Transformation?" *Journal of Social History* 34 (2000): 369–91.

Baldoli, C., and M. Perry. "Bombing and Labour in Western Europe, from 1940 to 1945." *Labour History Review* 77 (2012): 3–9.

Bank, J. "De theorie van de vernieuwing en de praktijk van de wederopbouw: Het Nederlandse socialisme in de tweede helft van de jaren veertig." In *In dienst van het gehele volk: De West-Europese sociaal-democratie tussen aanpassing en vernieuwing 1945–1950*, by J. Bank, M. Van Haegendoren, and W. Kok, 98–121. Amsterdam, 1987.

Bantigny, L. *1968: De grands soirs en petits matins.* Paris, 2018.

Barnes, S. H. *Party Democracy: Politics in an Italian Socialist Federation*. New Haven, CT, 1967.

Barnes, T. "The Secret Cold War: The CIA and American Foreign Policy in Europe 1946–1956." *Historical Journal* 24 (1981): 399–415, and 25 (1982): 649–70.

Baruch, M. O. "Les élites d'état dans la modernisation." In *De Gaulle et les élites*, edited by S. Berstein, P. Birnbaum, and J.-P. Rioux, 95–111. Paris, 2008.

Bauman, Z. *Memories of Class: The Pre-history and After-Life of Class*. London, 1982.

Beck, E. R. *Under the Bombs: The German Home Front 1942–1945*. Lexington, KY, 1986.

Becker, J.-J. "L'intérêt bien compris du Parti communiste français." In *La guerre d'Algérie et les Français*, edited by J.-P. Rioux, 235–44. Paris, 1990.

Bédarida, F. "Vichy et la crise de la conscience française." In *Le régime de Vichy et les Français*, edited by J.-P. Azéma and Bédardia, 77–96. Paris, 1992.

Bédarida, F., and J.-P. Rioux, eds. *Pierre Mendès-France et le mendésisme*. Paris, 1985.

Bédarida, R. *Les armes de l'esprit: Témoignage chrétien (1941–1944)*. Paris, 1977.

Beerten, W. *Le rêve travailliste en Belgique: Histoire de l'UDB 1944–1947*. Brussels, 1990.

Behan, T. *The Long-Awaited Moment: The Working Class and the Italian Communist Party in Milan, 1943–1948*. New York, 1997.

Bell, D. S., and B. Criddle. *The French Socialist Party: The Emergence of a Party of Government*. 2nd ed. Oxford, 1988.

Berchtold, K., ed. *Österreichische Parteiprogramme 1868–1966*. Munich, 1967.

Berger, S. "European Labour Movements and the European Working Class in Comparative Perspective." In *The Western European Labour Movement and the Working Class in the Twentieth Century*, edited by Berger and D. Broughton, 245–61. Oxford, 1995.

Bergman, J. *The French Revolutionary Tradition in Russian and Soviet Politics, Political Thought, and Culture*. Oxford, 2019.

———. *Meeting the Demands of Reason: The Life and Thought of Andrei Sakharov*. Ithaca, NY, 2009.

Bergounioux, A. "Le néo-socialisme—Marcel Déat: Réformisme traditionnel ou esprit des années trente." *Revue historique* 260 (1978): 389–412.

Berg-Schlosser, D., and J. Mitchell, eds. *Conditions of Democracy in Europe 1919–39: Systematic Case Studies*. Basingstoke, UK, 2000.

Berman, S. *The Primacy of Politics: Social Democracy and the Making of Europe's Twentieth Century*. Cambridge, UK, 2006.

———. *The Social Democratic Moment: Ideas and Politics in the Making of Interwar Europe*. Cambridge, MA, 1998.

Berry, M. *The Affluent Society Revisited*. Oxford, 2013.

Berstein, S. "L'arrivée de de Gaulle à Paris." In *De Gaulle et la Libération*, edited by Fondation Charles de Gaulle, 127–42. Brussels, 2004.

———. *The Republic of de Gaulle*. Cambridge, UK, 1993.

———. "La seconde guerre mondiale et les fondements d'une démocratie libérale rénovée." In *La démocratie libérale*, edited by Berstein, 689–729. Paris, 1998.

Berthezène, C. "Un féminisme conservateur?: Genre et politique en Grande-Bretagne (1928–1964)." In *Conservatismes en mouvement: Une approche transnationale au XXe siècle*, edited by Berthezène and J.-C. Vinel, 409–34. Paris, 2016.

Bessel, R., and D. Schumann, eds. *Life after Death: Approaches to a Cultural and Social History of Europe during the 1940s and 1950s*. Washington, DC, 2003.

Béthouart, B. "Entry of the Catholics into the Republic: The Mouvement Républicain Populaire in France." In Gehler and Kaiser, *Christian Democracy in Europe*, 85–100.

Betts, P. "Humanity's New Heritage: Unesco and the Rewriting of World History." *Past and Present* 228 (2015): 249–85.

———. "Manners, Morality and Civilization: Reflections on Postwar German Etiquette Books." In *Histories of the Aftermath: The Legacies of the Second World War in Europe*, edited by F. Biess and R. G. Moeller, 196–214. New York, 2010.

Betz, H.-G. *Radical Right-Wing Populism in Western Europe*. Basingstoke, UK, 1994.

Biess, F. "Feelings in the Aftermath: Toward a History of Postwar Emotions." In *Histories of the Aftermath: The Legacies of the Second World War in Europe*, edited by Biess and R. G. Moeller, 30–48. New York, 2010.

———. *Homecomings: Returning POWs and the Legacies of Defeat in Postwar Germany*. Princeton, NJ, 2006.

Bjerregaard, K. S. "Guerrillas and Grassroots: Danish Solidarity with the Third World in the 1960s and 1970s." In *Between Prague Spring and French May: Opposition and Revolt in Europe, 1960–1980*, edited by M. Klimke, J. Pekelder, and J. Scharloth, 213–32. New York, 2011.

Blank, R. "Wartime Daily Life and the Air War on the Home Front." In *Germany and the Second World War*, vol. 11, pt. 1, edited by J. Echternkamp, 371–476. Oxford, 2008.

Bloch-Lainé, F., and J. Bouvier. *La France restaurée, 1944–1954: Dialogue sur les choix d'une modernisation*. Paris, 1986.

Bloxham, D., and R. Gerwarth, eds. *Political Violence in Twentieth-Century Europe*. Cambridge, UK, 2011.

Bock, G., and P. Thane. Introduction to *Maternity and Gender Policies: Women and the Rise of the European Welfare States*, edited by Bock and Thane, 1–20. London, 1991.

Boehling, R. *A Question of Priorities: Democratic Reform and Recovery in Postwar Germany*. New York, 1996.

Bonin, H. "L'action du premier ministre Chaban-Delmas pour rendre la France industrielle plus performante (1969–1972)." *Revue historique* 654 (2010): 397–426.

Bonomo, B. "Dwelling Space and Social Identities: The Roman bourgeoisie, c. 1950–80." *Urban History* 38 (2011): 276–300.

Borne, D. *Petits-bourgeois en révolte?: Le mouvement poujade*. Paris, 1977.

Bourg, J. "The Moral History of 1968." In J. Jackson, Milne, and Williams, *May 68*, 17–33.

Boxhoorn, A. *The Cold War and the Rift in the Governments of National Unity: Belgium, France and Italy in the Spring of 1947*. Amsterdam, 1992.

Bracke, M. A. "From Politics to Nostalgia: The Transformation of War Memories in France during the 1960s–70s." *European History Quarterly* 41 (2011): 5–24.

———. "The *Parti Communiste Français* in May 1968: The Impossible Revolution?" In *Between Prague Spring and French May: Opposition and Revolt in Europe, 1960–1980*, edited by M. Klimke, J. Pekelder and J. Scharloth, 64–83. New York, 2011.

Branche, R. *La torture et l'armée pendant la guerre d'Algérie, 1954–1962*. Paris, 2001.

Broadbent, P., and S. Hake, eds. *Berlin: Divided City, 1945–1989*. New York, 2010.

Brockliss, L., and R. Robertson, eds. *Isaiah Berlin and the Enlightenment*. Oxford, 2016.

Brodie, T. *German Catholicism at War, 1939–1945*. Oxford, 2018.

Brogi, A. *Confronting America: The Cold War between the United States and the Communists in France and Italy*. Chapel Hill, NC, 2011.

Brooke, C. "Isaiah Berlin and the Origins of the 'Totalitarian' Rousseau." In Brockliss and Robertson, *Isaiah Berlin*, 89–98.

Brower, D. R. *The New Jacobins: The French Communist Party and the Popular Front*. Ithaca, NY, 1968.

Brown, T. S. *West Germany and the Global Sixties: The Antiauthoritarian Revolt, 1962–1978*. Cambridge, UK, 2013.

Brun, G. *Technocrates et technocratie en France (1914–1945)*. Paris, 1985.

Bruti Liberati, L. "Witch-Hunts and *Corriere della Sera*: A Conservative Perception of American Political Values in Cold War Italy—the 1950s." *Cold War History* 11 (2011): 69–83.

Buchanan, T. "Antifascism and Democracy in the 1930s." *European History Quarterly* 32 (2002): 39–57.

———. *East Wind: China and the British Left, 1925–1976*. Oxford, 2012.

———. *Europe's Troubled Peace: 1945 to the Present*. 2nd ed. Chichester, UK, 2012.

———. "'The Truth Will Set You Free': The Making of Amnesty International." *Journal of Contemporary History* 37 (2002): 575–97.

Busani, M. *Gioventù Studentesca: Storia di un movimento cattolico dalla ricostruzione alla contestazione*. Rome, 2016.

Buton, P. *Une histoire intellectuelle de la démocratie*. Paris, 2000.

———. *Les lendemains qui déchantent: Le Parti communiste français à la Libération*. [Paris], 1993.

Capoccia, G. *Defending Democracy: Reactions to Extremism in Interwar Europe*. Baltimore, MD, 2007.

Cardullo, R. J. "Pride and Prejudice, or Class and Character: *Room at the Top* Revisited." *Journal of European Studies* 42 (2012): 158–67.

Carleheden, M. "Bauman on Politics: Stillborn Democracy." In *The Sociology of Zygmunt Bauman: Challenges and Critique*, edited by M. H. Jacobsen and P. Poder, 175–92. Aldershot, UK, 2008.

Carney, S. *Breiz Atao! Mordrel, Delaporte, Lainé, Fouéré: Une mystique nationale (1901–1948)*. Rennes, 2015.

Carter, E. *How German Is She?: Postwar West German Reconstruction and the Consuming Woman*. Ann Arbor, MI, 1997.

Cassiers, I., and P. Scholliers. "Le pacte social belge de 1944, les salaires et la croissance économique en perspective internationale." In *Het Sociaal Pact van 1944*, edited by D. Luyten and G. Vanthemsche, 161–90. Brussels, 1995.

Castles, F. G. *The Social Democratic Image of Society: A Study of the Achievement and Origins of Scandinavian Social Democracy in Comparative Perspective*. London, 1978.

Černá, M., J. Davis, R. Gildea, and P. Osęka. "Revolutions." In Gildea, Mark, and Warring, *Europe's 1968*, 107–30.

Cerny, P. G., ed. *Social Movements and Protest in France*. London, 1982.

Ceuleers, J. "Het geluk komt morgen." In *De stoute jaren 58 68*, 7–19. Leuven, 1988.

Chakrabarty, D. *Provincializing Europe: Postcolonial Thought and Historical Difference*. Princeton, NJ, 2008.

Chamedes, G. *A Twentieth-Century Crusade: The Vatican's Battle to Remake Christian Europe*. Cambridge, MA, 2019.

Chaperon, S. "'Feminism is Dead. Long Live Feminism!' The Women's Movement in France at the Liberation, 1944–1946." In *When the War was Over: Women, War and Peace in Europe 1940–1956*, edited by C. Duchen and I. Bandhauer-Schöffmann, 146–60. London, 2000.

Chapman, H. *France's Long Reconstruction: In Search of the Modern Republic*. Cambridge, MA, 2018.

Chappel, J. *Catholic Modern: The Challenge of Totalitarianism and the Remaking of the Church*. Cambridge, MA, 2018.

———. "The Catholic Origins of Totalitarianism Theory in Interwar Europe." *Modern Intellectual History* 8 (2011): 561–90.

Chatriot, A. "A la recherche des 'forces vives.'" In *De Gaulle et les élites*, edited by S. Berstein, P. Birnbaum, and J.-P. Rioux, 219–37. Paris, 2008.

———. *Pierre Mendès-France: Pour une république moderne*. Paris, 2015.

Chenut, H. H. *The Fabric of Gender: Working Class Culture in Third Republic France*. University Park, PA, 2005.

Chiarini, R. "L'antipolitica in Italia: Un tentativo di concettualizzazione." *Storia Contemporanea* 19 (2015): 5–29.

Chin, R. *The Crisis of Multiculturalism in Europe: A History*. Princeton, NJ, 2017.

Chin, R., and H. Fehrenbach. "German Democracy and the Question of Difference." In *After the Nazi Racial State. Difference and Democracy in Germany and Europe*, by Chin, A. Grossmann, and G. Eley, 102–36. Ann Arbor, MI, 2009.

Christofferson, M. S. "French Intellectuals and the Repression of the Hungarian Revolution of 1956: The Politics of a Protest Reconsidered." In *After the Deluge: New Perspectives on the Intellectual and Cultural History of Postwar France*, edited by J. Bourg, 253–76. Lanham, MD, 2004.

Clarke, J. *France in the Age of Organization: Factory, Home and Nation from the 1920s to Vichy*. New York, 2011.

———. "Work, Consumption and Subjectivity in Postwar France: Moulinex and the Meanings of Domestic Appliances 1950s–70s." *Journal of Contemporary History* 47 (2012): 838–59.

Clavin, P. *Securing the World Economy: The Reinvention of the League of Nations, 1920–1946*. Oxford, 2013.

Clavin, P., and K. K. Patel. "The Role of International Organizations in Europeanization: The Case of the League of Nations and the European Economic Community." In *Europeanization in the Twentieth Century: Historical Approaches*, edited by M. Conway and Patel, 110–31. Basingstoke, UK, 2010.

Close, D. H. "The Reconstruction of a Right-Wing State." In *The Greek Civil War, 1943–1950: Studies of Polarization*, edited by Close, 156–89. London, 1993.

Cobban, A. *Historians and the Causes of the French Revolution*. London, 1958.

Coenen, M.-T. *La grève des femmes de la F.N. en 1966*. Brussels, 1991.

Coleman, P. *The Liberal Conspiracy: The Congress for Cultural Freedom and the Struggle for the Mind of Postwar Europe*. New York, 1989.

Collings, J. *Democracy's Guardians: A History of the German Federal Constitutional Court 1951–2001*. Oxford, 2015.

Connelly, J. *From Enemy to Brother: The Revolution in Catholic Teaching on the Jews, 1933–1965*. Cambridge, MA, 2012.

Conway, M. "The Age of Christian Democracy." In *European Christian Democracy: Historical Legacies and Comparative Perspectives*, edited by T. Kselman and J. Buttigieg, 43–67. Notre Dame, IN, 2003.

———. "Belgium." In *Political Catholicism in Europe 1918–1965*, edited by T. Buchanan and Conway, 187–218. Oxford, 1996.

———. *Catholic Politics in Europe, 1918–1945*. London, 1997.

———. "Democracies." In *Europe's Postwar Periods—1989, 1945, 1918: Writing History Backwards*, edited by Conway, P. Lagrou, and H. Rousso, 121–36. London, 2019.

———. "Democracy in Western Europe after 1945." In Kurunmäki, Nevers, and Te Velde, *Democracy in Modern Europe*, 231–56.

———. "The Extreme-Right in Inter-war Francophone Belgium: Explanations of a Failure." *European History Quarterly* 26 (1996): 267–92.

———. Introduction to *Europe's Postwar Periods—1989, 1945, 1918: Writing History Backwards*, edited by Conway, P. Lagrou, and H. Rousso, 1–7. London, 2019.

———. Introduction to *Political Catholicism in Europe 1918–1965*, edited by T. Buchanan and Conway, 1–33. Oxford, 1996.

———. "Justice in Post-war Belgium: Popular Pressures and Political Realities." In Deak, Gross, and Judt, *Politics of Retribution*, 133–56.

———. "Legacies of Exile: The Exile Governments in London during the Second World War and the Politics of Post-war Europe." In *Europe in Exile: European Exile Communities in Britain 1940–45*, edited by Conway and J. Gotovitch, 255–74. New York, 2001.

———. "On Fragile Democracy: Contemporary and Historical Perspectives." *Journal of Modern European History* 17 (2019): 422–31.

———. "The Rise and Fall of Western Europe's Democratic Age, 1945–1973." *Contemporary European History* 13 (2004): 67–88.

———. *The Sorrows of Belgium: Liberation and Political Reconstruction 1944–47*. Oxford, 2012.

Conway, M., and V. Depkat. "Towards a European History of the Discourse of Democracy: Discussing Democracy in Western Europe, 1945–60." In *Europeanization in the Twentieth Century: Historical Approaches*, edited by Conway and K. K. Patel, 132–56. Basingstoke, UK, 2010.

Conway, M., and R. Gerwarth. "Revolution and Counter-Revolution." In Bloxham and Gerwarth, *Political Violence*, 140–75.

Conway, M., and P. Romijn, eds. *The War for Legitimacy in Politics and Culture 1936–1946*. Oxford, 2008.

Cooke, P. *The Legacy of the Italian Resistance*. Basingstoke, UK, 2011.

Cooper, A. *Writing at the Kitchen Table: The Authorized Biography of Elizabeth David*. London, 1999.

Cooper, F. *Africa since 1940: The Past of the Present*. Cambridge, UK, 2002.

Corduwener, P. "Challenging Parties and Anti-fascism in the Name of Democracy: The *Fronte dell'Uomo Qualunque* and its Impact on Italy's Republic." *Contemporary European History* 26 (2017): 69–84.

———. *The Problem of Democracy in Postwar Europe: Political Actors and the Formation of the Postwar Model of Democracy in France, West Germany and Italy.* New York, 2017.

Corthals, M. "Welke toekomst voor een bevrijd België?" *Belgisch Tijdschrift voor Eigentijdse Geschiedenis* 48 (2018): 36–63.

Cowans, J. "French Public Opinion and the Founding of the Fourth Republic." *French Historical Studies* 17 (1991): 62–93.

Crafts, N. "The Great Boom 1950–1973." In *Western Europe: Economic and Social Change since 1945*, edited by M.-S. Schulze, 42–62. London, 1999.

Crafts, N., and G. Toniolo. "Postwar Growth: An Overview." In *Economic Growth in Europe since 1945*, edited by Crafts and Toniolo, 1–37. Cambridge, UK, 1996.

Craiutu, A. "Raymond Aron and the Tradition of Political Moderation in France." In *French Liberalism from Montesquieu to the Present Day*, edited by R. Geenens and H. Rosenblatt, 271–90. Cambridge, UK, 2012.

———. "Thinking Politically: Raymond Aron and the Revolution of 1968 in France." In *Promises of 1968: Crisis, Illusion, and Utopia*, edited by V. Tismaneanu, 73–102. Budapest, 2011.

Crepaz, M.M.L., T. A. Koeble, and D. Wilsford, eds. *Democracy and Institutions: The Life Work of Arend Lijphart.* Ann Arbor, MI, 2000.

Crespin, C. "Le poujadisme en Normandie: Un mouvement éphémère." *Annales de Normandie* 67 (2017): 93–115.

Crick, B. "*Nineteen Eighty-Four*: Context and Controversy." In *The Cambridge Companion to George Orwell*, edited by J. Rodden, 146–59. Cambridge, UK, 2007.

Crouch, C. *Post-Democracy.* Cambridge, UK, 2004.

Deak, I., J. Gross, and T. Judt, eds. *The Politics of Retribution in Europe: World War II and Its Aftermath.* Princeton, NJ, 2000.

De Bellefroid, D. "The Commission pour l'Etude des Problèmes d'Après-Guerre (CEPAG) 1941–1944." In *Europe in Exile: European Exile Communities in Britain 1940–45*, edited by M. Conway and J. Gotovitch, 121–33. Oxford, 2001.

De Graaf, J. "European Socialism between Militant and Parliamentary Democracy: A Pan-European Debate, 1945–8." *European Review of History: Revue européenne d'histoire* 26 (2019): 331–52.

———. *Socialism across the Iron Curtain: Socialist Parties in East and West and the Reconstruction of Europe after 1945.* Cambridge, UK, 2019.

De Grand, A. *The Italian Left in the Twentieth Century: A History of the Socialist and Communist Parties.* Bloomington, IN, 1989.

De Grazia, V. *Irresistible Empire: America's Advance through Twentieth-Century Europe.* Cambridge, MA, 2005.

De Groot, G. *The 60s Unplugged: A Kaleidoscopic History of a Disorderly Decade.* London, 2008.

Dekeyser, M. *De amerikaanse droom.* Leuven, 1978.

Della Loggia, G. *La morte della patria.* Rome, 1996.

Della Porta, D. *Mobilizing for Democracy: Comparing 1989 and 2011.* Oxford, 2014.

Del Pero, M. "American Pressures and Their Containment in Italy during the Ambassadorship of Clare Boothe Luce, 1953–1956." *Diplomatic History* 28 (2004): 407–39.

———. "Containing Containment: Rethinking Italy's Experience during the Cold War." *Journal of Modern Italian Studies* 8 (2003): 532–55.

De Luna, G. *Storia del Partito d'Azione 1942–1947*. Rome, 1997.

Dennis, D. *Beethoven in German Politics, 1870–1989*. New Haven, CT, 1996.

Denord, F. "Les idéologies économiques du patronat français au 20e siècle." *Vingtième Siècle* 114 (April–June 2012): 171–82.

Depkat, V. *Lebenswenden und Zeitenwenden: Deutsche Politiker und die Erfahrungen des 20. Jahrhunderts*. Munich, 2007.

DePorte, A. *Europe between the Superpowers: The Enduring Balance*. New Haven, CT, 1979.

De Wever, B. "Het Vlaams-Nationalisme na de tweede wereldoorlog." *Bijdragen tot de eigentijdse geschiedenis* 3 (1997): 277–90.

Dhaille-Hervieu, M.-P. *Communistes au Havre: Histoire sociale, culturelle et politique (1930–1983)*. Mont Saint-Aignan, France, 2009.

Dhand, O. *The Idea of Central Europe*. London, 2018.

Diamond, H. *Women and the Second World War in France, 1939–48: Choices and Constraints*. Harlow, UK, 1999.

———. "Women's Aspirations 1943–47: An Oral Enquiry in Toulouse." In *The Liberation of France: Image and Event*, edited by H.R. Kedward and N. Wood, 91–101. Oxford, 1995.

Diehl, J. *The Thanks of the Fatherland: German Veterans after the Second World War*. Chapel Hill, NC, 1993.

Di Scala, S. M. *Renewing Italian Socialism: Nenni to Craxi*. New York, 1988.

Dodge, P. *Beyond Marxism: The Faith and Works of Hendrik De Man*. The Hague, 1966.

Doering, B. *Jacques Maritain and the French Catholic Intellectuals*. Notre Dame, IN, 1983.

Doering-Manteuffel, A. *Die Bundesrepublik Deutschland in der Ära Adenauer: Aussenpolitik und innere Entwicklung, 1949–1963*. Darmstadt, 1983.

Donnelly, D., J. Famerée, M. Lamberigts, and K. Schelkens. *The Belgian Contribution to the Second Vatican Council: International Research Conference at Mechelen, Leuven and Louvain-la-Neuve (September 12–16, 2005)*. Leuven, 2008.

Donnison, F.S.V. *Civil Affairs and Military Government in North-Western Europe 1944–1946*. London, 1961.

Dosse, F. *La saga des intellectuels français*. Vol. 1, *A l'épreuve de l'histoire (1944–68)*. Paris, 2018.

Duchen, C. "Opening Pandora's Box: The Case of the *Femmes Tondues*." In *Problems in French History*, edited by M. Cornick and C. Crossley, 213–32. Basingstoke, UK, 2000.

Dujardin, V., and M. Dumoulin. *Jean-Charles Snoy: Homme dans la cité, artisan de l'Europe*. Brussels, 2010.

Dutton, P. V. *Origins of the French Welfare State: The Struggle for Social Reform in France, 1914–1947*. Cambridge, UK, 2002.

——. "An Overlooked Source of Social Reform: Family Policy in French Agriculture." *Journal of Modern History* 72 (2000): 375–412.

Elder, N., A. H. Thomas, and D. Arter. *The Consensual Democracies?: The Government and Politics of the Scandinavian States*. Rev. ed. Oxford, 1988.

Eley, G. *Forging Democracy: The History of the Left in Europe, 1850–2000*. New York, 2002.

Elgey, G. *La République des contradictions 1951–1954*. Paris, 1968.

——. *La République des illusions 1945–1951, ou La vie secrète de la IVe République*. Paris, 1965.

Elkins, C. *Britain's Gulag: The Brutal End of Empire in Kenya*. London, 2005.

Ellwood, D. "Italy, Europe and the Cold War: The Politics and Economics of Limited Sovereignty." In *Italy in the Cold War: Politics, Culture and Society 1948–58*, edited by C. Duggan and C. Wagstaff, 25–46. Oxford, 1995.

——. *Italy 1943–1945*. Leicester, UK, 1985.

——. "The Message of the Marshall Plan." In *Selling Democracy, Friendly Persuasion*, edited by R. Rother, 7–15. Berlin, 2006.

——. "The Propaganda of the Marshall Plan in Italy in a Cold War Context." In *The Cultural Cold War in Western Europe 1945–1960*, edited by G. Scott-Smith and H. Krabbendam, 225–36. London, 2003.

——. *The Shock of America: Europe and the Challenge of the Century*. Oxford, 2012.

Elvander, N. *Scandinavian Social Democracy: Its Strength and Weakness*. Acta Universitatis Upsaliensis no. 39. Stockholm, 1979.

Ericsson, K., and E. Simonsen, eds. *Children of World War II: The Hidden Enemy Legacy*. Oxford, 2005.

Erikson, R., and J. Goldthorpe. *The Constant Flux: A Study of Class Mobility in Industrial Societies*. Oxford, 1993.

Erlichman, C., and C. Knowles. "Introduction: Reframing Occupation as a System of Rule." In *Transforming Occupation in the Western Zones of Germany: Politics, Everyday Life and Social Interactions, 1945–55*, edited by Erlichman and Knowles, 3–24. London, 2018.

Estèbe, J. "De l'avant-guerre à la Libération: La stabilité du personnel politique toulousain." In *La Libération dans le midi de la France*, edited by R. Trempé, 283–95. Toulouse, 1986.

Evans, J. *Life among the Ruins: Cityscape and Sexuality in Cold War Berlin*. Basingstoke, UK, 2011.

Evans, M. *Algeria: France's Undeclared War*. Oxford, 2012.

——. *The Memory of Resistance: French Opposition to the Algerian War (1954–1962)*. Oxford, 1997.

Evans, R. J. *Eric Hobsbawm: A Life in History*. London, 2019.

Falla, W. *Zwischen Integration und Klassenkampf: Sozialgeschichte der betrieblichen Mitbestimmung in Österreich*. Vienna, 1981.

Farmer, S. "The Communist Resistance in the Haute Vienne." *French Historical Studies* 14 (1985): 89–116.

Fehrenbach, H. "Black Occupation Children and the Devolution of the Nazi Racial State." In *After the Nazi Racial State: Difference and Democracy in Germany and Europe*, by R. Chin, A. Grossmann, and G. Eley, 30–54. Ann Arbor, MI, 2009.

Feichtinger, M., and S. Malinowski. "'Eine Million Algerier lernen im 20. Jahrhundert zu leben': Umsiedlungslager und Zwangsmodernisierung im Algerienkrieg 1954–1962." *Journal of Modern European History* 8 (2010): 107–35.

Feinberg, M. "Fantastic Truths, Compelling Lies: Radio Free Europe and the Response to the Slánský Trial in Czechoslovakia." *Contemporary European History* 22 (2013): 107–25.

Feinstein, M. M. *Holocaust Survivors in Postwar Germany, 1945–1957.* Cambridge, UK, 2010.

———. *State Symbols: The Quest for Legitimacy in the Federal Republic of Germany and the German Democratic Republic, 1949–1959.* Boston, MA, 2001.

Fejtö, F. *Le coup de Prague 1948.* Paris, 1976.

Fernández Soriano, V. "Las Comunidades Europeas frente al franquismo: Problemas políticos suscitados por la solicitud española de negociaciones de 1962." *Cuadernos de historia contemporánea* 32 (2010): 153–74.

Fertikh, K. "Bad-Godesberg dans le langage social-démocrate en 1959." *Cahiers d'histoire. Revue d'histoire critique* 114 (2011): 137–51.

———. "Le 'nouvel ordre' du programme de Bad Godesberg: Sociologie d'une construction sociale de l'économie." *Lien social et politiques* 72 (2014): 39–56.

Fischer, F. *Krieg der Illusionen: Die deutsche Politik von 1911 bis 1914.* Dusseldorf, 1969.

Fishman, S. *From Vichy to the Sexual Revolution: Gender and Family Life in Postwar France.* Oxford, 2017.

Fogg, S. L. *The Politics of Everyday Life in Vichy France: Foreigners, Undesirables and Strangers.* Cambridge, UK, 2009.

Foot, J. *Italy's Divided Memory.* New York, 2009.

Footitt, H. "American Forces in France: Communist Representations of US Deployment." *Cold War History* 11 (2011): 85–98.

Footitt, H., and J. Simmonds. *France 1943–1945.* Leicester, UK, 1988.

Foreman-Peck, J. "European Industrial Policies in the Post-War Boom: 'Planning the Economic Miracle.'" In *Industrial Policy in Europe after 1945: Wealth, Power and Economic Development in the Cold War*, edited by C. Grabas and A. Nützenadel, 13–47. Basingstoke, UK, 2014.

Forgacs, D., and S. Gundle. *Mass Culture and Italian Society from Fascism to the Cold War.* Bloomington, IN, 2007.

Forlenza, R. "A Party for the Mezzogiorno: The Christian Democratic Party, Agrarian Reform and the Government of Italy." *Contemporary European History* 19 (2010): 331–49.

———. "The Politics of the *Abendland*: Christian Democracy and the Idea of Europe after the Second World War." *Contemporary European History* 26 (2017): 261–86.

Forner, S. A. *German Intellectuals and the Challenge of Democratic Renewal: Culture and Politics after 1945.* Cambridge, UK, 2014.

Foucault, M. *The History of Sexuality.* Vol. 3, *Care of the Self.* London, 1986.

Frank, M. *Expelling the Germans: British Opinion and Post-1945 Population Transfer in Context.* Oxford, 2008.

Freedman, L. "Berlin and the Cold War." In *The Berlin Wall Crisis: Perspectives on Cold War Alliances*, edited by J.P.S. Gearson and K. Schake, 1–9. Basingstoke, UK, 2002.

Frei, N. *Adenauer's Germany and the Nazi Past: The Politics of Amnesty and Integration*. New York, 2002.

Frevert, U. *A Nation in Barracks: Modern Germany, Military Conscription and Civil Society*. Oxford, 2004.

———. *Women in German History: From Bourgeois Emancipation to Sexual Liberation*. Providence, RI, 1989.

Fritzsche, P. *Life and Death in the Third Reich*. Cambridge, MA, 2008.

———. *Rehearsals for Fascism: Populism and Political Mobilization in Weimar Germany*. New York, 1990.

Frohman, L. "Population Registration, Social Planning and the Discourse on Privacy Protection in West Germany." *Journal of Modern History* 87 (2015): 316–56.

Fuchs, A. *Phantoms of War in Contemporary German Literature, Films and Discourse*. Basingstoke, UK, 2010.

Fulbrook, M., ed. *Europe since 1945*. Oxford, 2001.

———. *Germany 1918–1990: The Divided Nation*. London, 1991.

Gault, J.-P. *Histoire d'une fidélité: Témoignage chrétien, 1944–56*. Paris, 1964.

Gehler, M., and W. Kaiser, eds. *Christian Democracy in Europe since 1945*. London, 2004.

Gerard, E. *De Katholieke Partij in crisis: Partijpolitiek leven in België (1918–1940)*. Leuven, 1985.

Gérard, P. "La presse à la Libération dans la région de Toulouse." In *La Libération dans le midi de la France*, edited by R. Trempé, 331–45. Toulouse, 1986.

Gérard-Libois, J., and J. Gotovitch. *L'an 40*. Brussels, 1971.

———. *Léopold III: De l'an 40 à l'effacement*. Brussels, 1991.

Gerwarth, R., and S. Malinowski. "Hannah Arendt's Ghosts: Reflections on the Disputable Path from Windhoek to Auschwitz." *Central European History* 42 (2009): 279–300.

Geyer, M. "Elisabeth Noelle-Neumann's 'Spiral of Silence', the Silent Majority and the Conservative Moment of the 1970s." In Von der Goltz and Waldschmidt-Nelson, *Inventing the Silent Majority*, 251–74.

Geyer, M., and S. Fitzpatrick. Introduction to *Beyond Totalitarianism: Stalinism and Nazism Compared*, edited by Geyer and Fitzpatrick, 1–37. Cambridge, 2009.

Gildea, R. *Fighters in the Shadows: A New History of the French Resistance*. London, 2015.

Gildea, R., J. Mark, and A. Warring, eds. *Europe's 1968: Voices of Revolt*. Oxford, 2013.

Gildea, R., and A. Tompkins. "The Transnational in the Local: The Larzac Plateau as a Site of Transnational Activism since 1970." *Journal of Contemporary History* 50 (2015): 581–605.

Gillis, J., L. Tilly, and D. Levine, eds. *The European Experience of Declining Fertility, 1850–1970: The Quiet Revolution*. Cambridge, MA, 1972.

Gilmour, D. *The Last Leopard: A Life of Giuseppe di Lampedusa*. London, 1988.

Ginsborg, P. *Family Politics: Domestic Life, Devastation and Survival 1900–1950*. New Haven, CT, 2014.

———. *A History of Contemporary Italy: Society and Politics 1943–1988*. London, 1990.

Glancy, M. *Hollywood and the Americanization of Britain from the 1920s to the Present*. London, 2014.

Golden, M. *Labor Divided: Austerity and Working-Class Politics in Contemporary Italy*. Ithaca, NY, 1988.

Goldenstedt, C. *Les femmes dans la Résistance*. Herbolzheim, Germany, 2006.

Gordon, D. *Immigrants and Intellectuals: May '68 and the Rise of Anti-racism in France*. Pontypool, UK, 2012.

Goretti, L. "Truman's Bombs and De Gasperi's Hooked Nose: Images of the Enemy in the Communist Press for Young People after 18 April 1948." *Modern Italy* 16 (2011): 159–77.

Gorlizki, Y., and H. Mommsen. "The Political (Dis)Orders of Stalinism and National Socialism." In *Beyond Totalitarianism: Stalinism and Nazism Compared*, edited by M. Geyer and S. Fitzpatrick, 41–86. Cambridge, UK, 2009.

Gosewinkel, D., ed. *Anti-liberal Europe: A Neglected Story of Europeanization*. New York, 2014.

Gotovitch, J. *Du rouge au tricolore: Les communistes belges de 1939 à 1944*. Brussels, 1992.

Gottraux, P. *Socialisme ou barbarie: Un engagement politique et intellectuel dans la France de l'après-guerre*. Lausanne, 1997.

Graham, B. D. *Choice and Democratic Order: The French Socialist Party, 1937–1950*. Cambridge, UK, 1994.

Graham, H. *Socialism and War: The Spanish Socialist Party in Power and Crisis, 1936–1939*. Cambridge, UK, 1991.

———. "Spain 1936—Resistance and Revolution: The Flaws in the Front." In *Opposing Fascism: Community, Authority and Resistance in Europe*, edited by T. Kirk and A. McElligott, 63–79. Cambridge, UK, 1999.

Gray, J. *Isaiah Berlin*. London, 1995.

Greenberg, U. *The Weimar Century: German Emigrés and the Ideological Foundations of the Cold War*. Princeton, NJ, 2014.

Grémion, P. *Intelligence de l'anticommunisme: Le Congrès pour la liberté de la culture à Paris, 1950–1975*. Paris, 1995.

Gribaudi, G. "Naples 1943: Espaces urbains et insurrection." *Annales. Histoire, Sciences Sociales* 58 (2003): 1079–104.

Griffin, R. *The Nature of Fascism*. London, 1994.

Grob-Fitzgibbon, B. *Imperial Endgame: Britain's Dirty Wars and the End of Empire*. Basingstoke, UK, 2011.

Grosbois, T. "Le renseignement économique et financier en Belgique occupée: L'exemple du Groupement d'études économiques." In *La Résistance et les Européens du Nord*, 183–207. Brussels, 1994.

Grossmann, A. "Trauma, Memory and Motherhood: Germans and Jewish Displaced Persons in Post-Nazi Germany, 1945–1949." In Bessel and Schumann, *Life after Death*, 93–128.

Groth, A. *Democracies against Hitler: Myth, Reality and Prologue*. Aldershot, UK, 1999.

Grugel, J., and T. Rees. *Franco's Spain*. London, 1997.

Grünbacher, A. *Reconstruction and Cold War in Germany: The Kreditanstalt für Wiederaufbau (1948–1961)*. Aldershot, UK, 2004.

Guillon, J.-M. "Administrer une ville ingouvernable: Marseille (1938–1946)." In *Lyon dans la seconde guerre mondiale: Villes et métropoles à l'épreuve du conflit*, edited by I. von Bueltzingsloewen, L. Douzou, J.-D. Durand, H. Joly, and J. Solchany, 61–72. Rennes, 2016.

———. "La Résistance au village." In *La Résistance et les Français*, edited by J. Sainclivier and C. Bougeard, 233–43. Rennes, 1995.

Guirao, F. *Spain and the Reconstruction of Western Europe, 1945–57: Challenge and Response*. Basingstoke, UK, 1998.

Gulick, C. A. *Austria from Habsburg to Hitler*. 2 vols. Berkeley, CA, 1948.

Gundle, S. *Bellissima: Feminine Beauty and the Idea of Italy*. New Haven, CT, 2007.

———. "La Dolce Vita." In *The Movies as History*, edited by D. Ellwood, 132–40. Stroud, UK, 2000.

Gunn, S. "People and the Car: The Expansion of Automobility in Urban Britain, c.1955–70." *Social History* 38 (2013): 220–37.

Gusejnova, D. *European Elites and Ideas of Empire, 1917–1957*. Cambridge, UK, 2016.

Häberlen, J. C., and R. A. Spinney. Introduction to "Emotions in Protest Movements in Europe since 1917," ed. Häberlen and Spinney. Special issue, *Contemporary European History* 23, no. 4 (2014): 489–503.

Hacohen, M. H. *Karl Popper—the Formative Years 1902–1945: Politics and Philosophy in Interwar Vienna*. Cambridge, UK, 2000.

Haggett, A. *Desperate Housewives, Neuroses and the Domestic Environment, 1945–1970*. London, 2012.

Hall, I. *Dilemmas of Decline: British Intellectuals and World Politics, 1945–1975*. Cambridge, UK, 2012.

Hammond, T., ed. *The Anatomy of Communist Takeovers*. New Haven, CT, 1975.

Hanhimäki, J. M. "Europe's Cold War." In *The Oxford Handbook of Postwar European History*, edited by D. Stone, 283–98. Oxford, 2012.

Harrison, E., and S. McLaughlin Mitchell. *The Triumph of Democracy and the Eclipse of the West*. Basingstoke, UK, 2013.

Hayman, R. *Writing Against: A Biography of Sartre*. London, 1986.

Hazareesingh, S. *Le mythe gaullien*. Paris, 2010.

Hecht, G. "Peasants, Engineers and Atomic Cathedrals: Narrating Modernization in Postwar Provincial France." *French Historical Studies* 20 (1997): 381–418.

Heineman, E. "The Economic Miracle in the Bedroom: Big Business and Sexual Consumption in Reconstruction West Germany." *Journal of Modern History* 78 (2006): 846–77.

———. "Gender, Sexuality and Coming to Terms with the Nazi Past." *Central European History* 38 (2005): 41–74.

———. "The Hour of the Woman: Memories of Germany's 'Crisis Years' and West German National Identity." *American Historical Review* 101 (1996): 354–95.

———. *What Difference Does a Husband Make?: Women and Marital Status in Nazi and Postwar Germany*. Berkeley, CA, 1999.

Held, D. *Democracy and the Global Order: From the Modern State to Cosmopolitan Governance*. Cambridge, UK, 1995.

Hellemans, S. *Strijd om de moderniteit*. Leuven, 1990.

Hellman, J. *Emmanuel Mounier and the New Catholic Left 1930–1950*. Toronto, 1981.

Hemmerijckx, R. "The Belgian Communist Party and the Socialist Trade Unions." In *Comrades and Brothers: Communism and Trade Unions in Europe*, edited by M. Waller, S. Courtois, and M. Lazar, 124–42. London, 1991.

——. "Le Mouvement syndical unifié et la naissance du renardisme." *Courrier hebdomadaire du CRISP* 1119–20 (1986).

——. *Van Verzet tot Koude Oorlog*. Brussels, 2003.

Herzog, D. *Sex after Fascism: Memory and Morality in Twentieth-Century Germany*. Princeton, NJ, 2005.

——. *Sexuality in Europe: A Twentieth-Century History*. Cambridge, UK, 2011.

Hilson, M. *The Nordic Model: Scandinavia since 1945*. London, 2008.

Hilton, M. "The Organised Consumer Movement since 1945." In *The Expert Consumer: Associations and Professionals in Consumer Society*, edited by A. Chatriot, M.-E. Chessel, and M. Hilton, 187–203. Aldershot, UK, 2006.

Hitchcock, W. *France Restored: Cold War Diplomacy and the Quest for Leadership in Europe, 1944–1954*. Chapel Hill, NC, 1998.

——. *Liberation: The Bitter Road to Freedom, Europe 1944–1945*. London, 2009.

Hobsbawm, E. J. *Age of Extremes: The Short Twentieth Century 1914–1991*. London, 1994.

Hochgeschwender, M. *Freiheit in der Offensive?: Der Kongress für kulturelle Freiheit und die Deutschen*. Munich, 1998.

Hoffmann, S.-L. "Introduction: Genealogies of Human Rights." In *Human Rights in the Twentieth Century*, edited by Hoffmann, 1–26. Cambridge, UK, 2011.

Hoffmann-Martinot, V. "A Short Biography of Maurice Duverger." *French Politics* 3 (2005): 304–9.

Horn, G.-R. *European Socialists Respond to Fascism: Ideology, Activism and Contingency in the 1930s*. New York, 1996.

——. *The Spirit of '68: Rebellion in Western Europe and North America, 1956–1976*. Oxford, 2007.

——. *The Spirit of Vatican II: Western European Progressive Catholicism in the Long Sixties*. Oxford, 2015.

——. *Western European Liberation Theology, The First Wave (1924–1959)*. Oxford, 2008.

Horn, G.-R., and E. Gerard, eds. *Left Catholicism, 1943–1955: Catholics and Society in Western Europe at the Point of Liberation*. Leuven, 2001.

Horne, J. "Masculinity in Politics and War in the Age of Nation-States and World Wars, 1850–1950." In *Masculinities in Politics and War: Gendering Modern History*, edited by S. Dudink, K. Hagemann and J. Tosh, 22–40. Manchester, 2004.

House, J. "Colonial Containment?: Repression of Pro-independence Street Demonstrations in Algiers, Casablanca and Paris, 1945–1962." *War in History* 25 (2018): 172–201.

House, J., and N. Macmaster. *Paris 1961: Algerians, State Terror and Memory*. Oxford, 2006.

Hunter, E. *Political Thought and the Public Sphere in Tanzania: Freedom, Democracy and Citizenship in the Era of Decolonization*. Cambridge, UK, 2015.

Imlay, T. *The Practice of Socialist Internationalism: European Socialists and International Politics, 1914–1960*. Oxford, 2018.

Innes, J., and M. Philp. Introduction to *Re-imagining Democracy in the Age of Revolutions: America, France, Britain, Ireland 1750–1850*, edited by Innes and Philp, 1–10. Oxford, 2013.

Irvine, W. D. "Fascism in France and the Strange Case of the Croix de Feu." *Journal of Modern History* 63 (1991): 271–95.

Jabbari, E. *Pierre Laroque and the Welfare State in Postwar France*. Oxford, 2012.

Jackson, B. "At the Origins of Neo-liberalism: The Free Economy and the Strong State, 1930–1947." *Historical Journal* 53 (2010): 129–51.

———. "The Think-Tank Archipelago: Thatcherism and Neo-liberalism." In *Making Thatcher's Britain*, edited by Jackson and R. Saunders, 43–61. Cambridge, UK, 2012.

Jackson, B., and R. Saunders. "Introduction: Varieties of Thatcherism." In *Making Thatcher's Britain*, edited by Jackson and Saunders, 1–22. Cambridge, UK, 2012.

Jackson, J. *A Certain Idea of France: The Life of Charles de Gaulle*. London, 2018.

———. *France: The Dark Years 1940–1944*. Oxford, 2001.

———. *Living in Arcadia: Homosexuality, Politics and Morality in France from the Liberation to AIDS*. Chicago, 2009.

———. *The Popular Front in France: Defending Democracy, 1934–38*. Cambridge, UK, 1988.

———. "Rethinking May 68." In Jackson, Milne, and Williams, *May 68*, 3–16.

Jackson, J., A.-L. Milne, and J. S. Williams, eds. *May 68: Rethinking France's Last Revolution*. Basingstoke, UK, 2011.

Jackson, P. T. *Civilizing the Enemy: German Reconstruction and the West*. Ann Arbor, MI, 2006.

Jahr, C. "Fighting Anti-Semitism—Democratizing Society?: Reflections on Germany's Rocky Path towards a Civil Society after the Second World War." In *After Fascism: European Case-Studies in Politics, Society and Identity since 1945*, edited by M. Berg and M. Mesner, 89–107. Vienna, 2009.

Jakobsen, U. "Inventions and Developments of Democracy: The Approach of Conceptual History." *European Political Science* 9 (2010): 316–27.

Jeffries, S. *Grand Hotel Abyss: The Lives of the Frankfurt School*. London, 2016.

Jobs, R. I. *Backpack Ambassadors: How Youth Travel Integrated Europe*. Chicago, 2017.

Johnston-White, R. "A New Primacy of Conscience?: Conscientious Objection, French Catholicism and the State during the Algerian War." *Journal of Contemporary History* 54 (2019): 112–38.

Joll, J. *The Second International 1889–1914*. Rev. ed. London, 1968.

Joly, H. "Les dirigeants des grandes entreprises industrielles françaises au 20e siècle." *Vingtième Siècle* 114 (April–June 2012): 17–32.

Joubert, J.-P. *Marceau Pivert et le pivertisme: Révolutionnaires de la SFIO*. Paris, 1977.

Judt, T. *The Burden of Responsibility: Blum, Camus, Aron and the French Twentieth Century*. Chicago, 1998.

———. *Ill Fares the Land: A Treatise on Our Present Discontents*. New York, 2010.

———. "The Past is Another Country: Myth and Memory in Postwar Europe." In Deak, Gross, and Judt, *Politics of Retribution*, 293–323.

———. *Postwar: A History of Europe since 1945*. London, 2005.

Kaelble, H. *Social Mobility in the 19th and 20th Centuries: Europe and America in Comparative Perspective*. Leamington Spa, UK, 1985.

Kaiser, W. *Christian Democracy and the Origins of European Union*. Cambridge, UK, 2007.

———. "From Siege Mentality to Mainstreaming?: Researching Twentieth-Century Christian Democracy." In *Christian Democracy across the Iron Curtain: Europe Redefined*, edited by P. Kosicki and S. Lukasiewicz, 3–23. N.p., 2018.

Kaiser, W., B. Leucht, and M. Rasmussen, eds. *The History of the European Union: Origins of a Trans- and Supranational Polity 1950–72*. New York, 2009.

Kaiser, W., and J. Schot. *Writing the Rules for Europe: Experts, Cartels and International Organizations*. Basingstoke, UK, 2014.

Kalyvas, S. *The Logic of Violence in Civil War*. Cambridge, UK, 2006.

———. *The Rise of Christian Democracy in Europe*. Ithaca, NY, 1996.

Karamouzi, E. *Greece, the EEC and the Cold War, 1974–1979: The Second Enlargement*. Basingstoke, UK, 2014.

Katzenstein, P. *Policy and Politics in West Germany: The Growth of a Semisovereign State*. Philadelphia, 1987.

Kedward, H. R. *In Search of the Maquis: Rural Resistance in Southern France 1942–1944*. Oxford, 1993.

———. Introduction to *The Liberation of France: Image and Event*, edited by Kedward and N. Wood, 1–11. Oxford, 1995.

Kellner, D. *Herbert Marcuse and the Crisis of Marxism*. Basingstoke, UK, 1984.

Kennedy, S. *Reconciling France against Democracy: The Croix de Feu and the Parti Social Français, 1927–1945*. Montreal, 2007.

Kerry, M. "Radicalisation, Community and the Politics of Protest in the Spanish Second Republic, 1931–34." *English Historical Review* 132 (2017): 318–43.

Kershaw, I. *Popular Opinion and Political Dissent in the Third Reich: Bavaria 1933–1945*. 2nd ed. Oxford, 2002.

Khilnani, S. *Arguing Revolution: The Intellectual Left in Postwar France*. New Haven, CT, 1993.

Kieffer, M.-C. "L'impératif des grands corps." In *De Gaulle et les élites*, edited by S. Berstein, P. Birnbaum, and J.-P. Rioux, 77–94. Paris, 2008.

Klitzing, H. *The Nemesis of Stability: Henry A. Kissinger's Ambivalent Relationship with Germany*. Trier, 2007.

Knibiehler, Y. *La révolution maternelle: Femmes, maternité, citoyenneté depuis 1945*. Paris, 1997.

Knight, R. "Denazification and Integration in the Austrian Province of Carinthia." *Journal of Modern History* 79 (2007): 572–612.

———. "National Construction Work and Hierarchies of Empathy in Postwar Austria." *Journal of Contemporary History* 49 (2014): 491–513.

Kocka, J. "The Middle Classes in Europe." In *Industrial Culture and Bourgeois Society: Business, Labour and Bureaucracy in Modern Germany*, 231–54. New York, 1999.

Koreman, M. *The Expectation of Justice: France 1944–46*. Durham, NC, 1999.

Krause, S. "*Neue Westpolitik*: The Clandestine Campaign to Westernize the SPD in Cold War Berlin, 1948–1958." *Central European History* 48 (2015): 79–99.

Kreichbaumer, R. *Zwischen Land und Bund: Die Salzburger ÖVP in der Ära Lechner*. Salzburg, 1988.

Krieg, R. *Catholic Theologians in Nazi Germany*. New York, 2004.

Krönig, W., and K.-D. Müller, eds. *Nachkriegs-Semester: Studium in Kriegs- und Nachkriegszeit*. Stuttgart, 1990.

Kruke, A. *Demoskopie in der Bundesrepublik Deutschland*. Dusseldorf, 2007.

Kuisel, R. *Capitalism and the State in modern France*. Cambridge, UK, 1981.

———. *Seducing the French: The Dilemma of Americanization*. Berkeley, CA, 1993.

Kupferman, F. *Laval 1883–1945*. Paris, 1987.

Kurunmäki, J., J. Nevers, and H. Te Velde, eds. *Democracy in Modern Europe: A Conceptual History*. New York, 2018.

Kurunmäki, J., and J. Strang. "Introduction: 'Nordic Democracy' in a World of Tensions." In *Rhetorics of Nordic Democracy*, edited by Kurunmäki and Strang, 9–36. Helsinki, 2010.

Kwanten, G. *August-Edmond De Schryver 1898–1991: Politieke biografie van een gentleman-staatsman*. Leuven, 2001.

Laborie, P. "La libération de Toulouse vue par le pouvoir général: Représentations mentales et enjeux de pouvoir." In *La Libération dans le midi de la France*, edited by R. Trempé, 149–73. Toulouse, 1986.

———. *L'opinion française sous Vichy*. Paris, 1990.

Lafon, F. "Des principes du molletisme." In *Guy Mollet: Un camarade en République*, edited by B. Ménager, P. Ratte, J.-L. Thiébault, R. Vandenbussche, and C.-M. Wallon-Leducq, 59–91. Lille, 1987.

Lagrou, P. "De l'histoire du temps présent à l'histoire des autres: Comment une discipline critique devint complaisante." *Vingtième Siècle* 118 (2013): 101–19.

———. *The Legacy of Nazi Occupation: Patriotic Memory and National Recovery in Western Europe, 1945–1965*. Cambridge, UK, 2000.

———. "Victims of Genocide and National Memory: Belgium, France and the Netherlands, 1945–1965." *Past and Present* 154 (1997): 181–222.

Lang, M. *Karl Löwenstein: Transatlantischer Denker der Politik*. Stuttgart, 2007.

Laqueur, W. *Europe since Hitler*. London, 1970.

Larsson, B., M. Letell, and H. Thörn, eds. *Transformations of the Swedish Welfare State: From Social Engineering to Governance*. Basingstoke, UK, 2012.

Laurens, C. "'La femme au turban': Les femmes tondues." In *The Liberation of France: Image and Event*, edited by H. R. Kedward and N. Wood, 155–79. Oxford, 1995.

Lawrence, J. *Electing Our Masters. The Hustings in British Politics from Hogarth to Blair*. Oxford, 2009.

Le Cour Grandmaison, O. *L'empire des hygiénistes: Vivre aux colonies*. Paris, 2014.

Lehmbruch, G. *Proporzdemokratie*. Tübingen, Germany, 1967.

Leleu, C. *Géographie des élections françaises depuis 1936*. Paris, 1971.

Letamendia, P. *Le Mouvement républicain populaire: Histoire d'un grand parti français*. Paris, 1995.

Levsen, S. "Authority and Democracy in Postwar France and West Germany, 1945–1968." *Journal of Modern History* 89 (2017): 812–50.

Lewin, L. *Ideology and Strategy: A Century of Swedish Politics*. Cambridge, UK, 1988.

Lewis, J. *Workers and Politics in Occupied Austria, 1945–55*. Manchester, 2007.

Lidegaard, B. *A Short History of Denmark in the Twentieth Century*. Copenhagen, 2009.

Lieberman, B. *From Recovery to Catastrophe: Municipal Stabilization and Political Crisis in Weimar Germany*. New York, 1998.

Lindenberger, T. "Die Diktatur der Grenzen: Zur Einleitung." In *Herrschaft und Eigen-Sinn in der Diktatur: Studien zur Gesellschaftsgeschichte der DDR*, edited by Lindenberger, 13–44. Cologne, 1999.

Little, A. *The Political Thought of André Gorz*. London, 1996.

Long, R. *Les élections législatives en Côte d'Or depuis 1870*. Paris, 1958.

Lönne, K.-E. "Germany." In *Political Catholicism in Europe, 1918–1965*, edited by T. Buchanan and M. Conway, 156–86. Oxford, 1996.

Lösche, P., and F. Walter. *Die SPD: Klassenpartei-Volkspartei-Quotenpartei—Zur Entwicklung der Sozialdemokratie von Weimar bis zur deutschen Vereinigung*. Darmstadt, 1992.

Low, D. A., and J. M. Lonsdale. "Introduction: Towards the New Order, 1945–1963." In *History of East Africa*, vol. 3, edited by Low and A. Smith, 1–63. Oxford, 1976.

Lucas, W. S. "Beyond Freedom, beyond Control: Approaches to Culture and the State-Private Network in the Cold War." In *The Cultural Cold War in Western Europe 1945–1960*, edited by G. Scott-Smith and H. Krabbendam, 53–72. London, 2003.

Luebbert, G. *Liberalism, Fascism, or Social Democracy: Social Classes and the Political Origins of Regimes in Interwar Europe*. New York, 1991.

Lundestad, G. "Empire by Invitation?: The United States and Western Europe, 1945–1952." *Journal of Peace Research* 23 (1986): 263–77.

Luyten, D. *Sociaal-economisch overleg in België sedert 1918*. Brussels, 1995.

Luyten, D., and P. Magnette. "L'idée du parlementarisme en Belgique." In *Histoire de la Chambre des représentants de Belgique 1830–2002*, edited by E. Gubin, J.-P. Nandrin, E. Gerard and E. Witte, 19–46. Brussels, 2003.

Luyten, D., and X. Rousseaux. "Introduction générale." In "Les professionnels du droit," edited by Luyten and Rousseaux. Special issue, *Cahiers d'histoire du temps présent* 24 (2011): 25–34.

Lynch, F. "Harmonization through Competition?: The Evolution of Taxation in Post-war Europe." In *Global Debates about Taxation*, edited by H. Nehring and F. Schui, 116–33. Basingstoke, UK, 2007.

Lyons, A. *The Civilizing Mission in the Metropole: Algerian Families and the French Welfare State during Decolonization*. Stanford, CA, 2013.

Macey, D. *Frantz Fanon: A Biography*. London, 2000.

Mackenzie, B. A. *Remaking France: Americanization, Public Diplomacy and the Marshall Plan*. New York, 2005.

Magri, L. *The Tailor of Ulm: Communism in the Twentieth Century*. London, 2011.

Maier, C. "Democracy since the French Revolution." In *Democracy: The Unfinished Journey 508 BC to AD 1993*, edited by J. Dunn, 125–53. Oxford, 1993.

Major, P. *The Death of the KPD: Communism and Anti-Communism in West Germany 1945–1956*. Oxford, 1997.

Malatesta, M. *Professional Men, Professional Women: The European Professions from the Nineteenth Century until Today*. Los Angeles, 2011.

Mamdani, M. *Citizen and Subject*. Princeton, NJ, 1996.

Manin, B. *The Principles of Representative Government.* Cambridge, UK, 1997.

Mann, M. *Fascists.* Cambridge, UK, 2004.

Marcot, F. "Voix d'outre-tombe." In *Lettres de fusillés,* edited by G. Krivopissko, 9–25. Paris, 2003.

Mark, J. "Remembering Rape: Divided Social Memory and the Red Army in Hungary, 1944–1945." *Past and Present* 188 (2005): 133–61.

Marshall, B. "The Democratization of Local Politics in the British Zone of Germany: Hanover 1945–47." *Journal of Contemporary History* 21 (1986): 413–51.

———. *Willy Brandt.* London, 1990.

Marwick, A. *The Sixties: Cultural Revolution in Britain, France, Italy, and the United States, c.1958–c.1974.* Oxford, 1998.

März, E. "Die Klassenstruktur der Zweiten Österreichischen Republik." In *Probleme der österreichischen Politik,* vol. 1, 67–112. Vienna, 1968.

Mauss, D. "Guy Mollet et l'élaboration de la Constitution de 1958." In *Guy Mollet: Un camarade en République,* edited by B. Ménager, P. Ratte, J.-L. Thiébault, R. Vandenbussche, and C.-M. Wallon-Leducq, 349–63. Lille, 1987.

Mazower, M. *Dark Continent: Europe's Twentieth Century.* London, 1998.

———. *Hitler's Empire: Nazi Rule in Occupied Europe.* London, 2008.

———. *No Enchanted Palace: The End of Empire and the Ideological Origins of the United Nations.* Princeton, NJ, 2009.

———. "Policing the Anti-Communist State in Greece, 1922–1974." In *The Policing of Politics in the Twentieth Century,* edited by Mazower, 129–50. Providence, RI, 1997.

McDermott, K. "Popular Resistance in Communist Czechoslovakia: The Plzeň Uprising, June 1953." *Contemporary European History* 19 (2010): 287–307.

McDougall, J. "The Impossible Republic: The Reconquest of Algeria and the Decolonization of France, 1945–1962." *Journal of Modern History* 89 (2017): 772–811.

McLaren, M. "'Out of the Huts Emerged a Settled People': Community-Building in West German Refugee Camps." *German History* 28 (2010): 21–43.

McMillan, J. "France." In *Political Catholicism in Europe, 1918–1965,* edited by T. Buchanan and M. Conway, 34–68. Oxford, 1996.

Mehring, F. "Friendly Persuasion, Self-Americanization and the Utopia of a New Europe." In *Selling Democracy, Friendly Persuasion,* edited by R. Rother, 35–45. Berlin, 2006.

Mencherini, R. *Guerre froide, grèves rouges.* Paris, 1998.

Merquior, J. G. *Western Marxism.* London, 1986.

Mesch, C. *Modern Art at the Berlin Wall: Demarcating Culture in the Cold War Germanys.* London, 2008.

Messenger, D. A. "Exporting Republicanism: The French Government's Defence of Political Prisoners in Franco's Spain after France's Liberation." In *After Fascism: European Case-Studies in Politics, Society and Identity since 1945,* edited by M. Berg and M. Mesner, 37–57. Vienna, 2009.

Michel, A. "Guy Mollet en parlement." In *Guy Mollet: Un camarade en République,* edited by B. Ménager, P. Ratte, J.-L. Thiébault, R. Vandenbussche, and C.-M. Wallon-Leducq, 285–97. Lille, 1987.

Michel, F. *La pensée catholique en Amérique du Nord: Réseaux intellectuels et échanges culturels entre l'Europe, le Canada et les Etats-Unis (années 1920–1960).* Paris, 2010.

Middleton, S. "Affluence and the Left in Britain c.1958–1974." *English Historical Review* 129 (2014): 107–38.

Mihelj, S. "Imperial Myths between Nationalism and Communism: Appropriations of Imperial Legacies in the North-Eastern Adriatic during the Early Cold War." *European History Quarterly* 41 (2011): 634–56.

Milder, S. *Greening Democracy: The Anti-nuclear Movement and Political Environmentalism in West Germany and Beyond, 1968–1983*. Cambridge, UK, 2017.

Miller, S., and H. Potthoff. *A History of German Social Democracy: From 1848 to the Present*. Leamington Spa, UK, 1986.

Millington, C. *Fighting for France: Violence in Interwar French Politics*. Oxford, 2018.

Milner, A. *The Invention of Politics in Colonial Malaya: Contesting Nationalism and the Expansion of the Public Sphere*. Cambridge, UK, 1994.

Milward, A. *The European Rescue of the Nation-State*. London, 1992.

Mioche, P. *Le Plan Monnet: Genèse et élaboration, 1941–1947*. Paris, 1987.

Misner, P. *Catholic Labor Movements in Europe: Social Thought and Action, 1914–1965*. Washington, DC, 2015.

———. *Social Catholicism in Europe: From the Onset of Industrialization to the First World War*. London, 1991.

Mistry, K. "Re-thinking American Intervention in the 1948 Italian Election: Beyond a Success-Failure Dichotomy." *Modern Italy* 16 (2011): 179–94.

Mitchell, M. "Materialism and Secularism: CDU Politicians and National Socialism, 1945–1949." *Journal of Modern History* 67 (1995): 278–308.

———. *The Origins of Christian Democracy: Politics and Confession in Modern Germany*. Ann Arbor, MI, 2012.

Moeller, R. G. *Protecting Motherhood: Women and the Family in the Politics of Postwar West Germany*. Berkeley, CA, 1993.

———. "Sinking Ships, the Lost *Heimat* and Broken Taboos: Günter Grass and the Politics of Memory in Contemporary Germany." *Contemporary European History* 12 (2003): 147–81.

———. *War Stories: The Search for a Usable Past in the Federal Republic of Germany*. Berkeley, CA, 2001.

———. "Winning the Peace at the Movies: Suffering Loss and Redemption in Postwar German Cinema." In *Histories of the Aftermath: The Legacies of the Second World War in Europe*, edited by F. Biess and Moeller, 139–55. New York, 2010.

Moores, C. *Civil Liberties and Human Rights in Twentieth-Century Britain*. Cambridge, UK, 2017.

Moravcsik, A. "The Myth of Europe's 'Democratic Deficit.'" *Intereconomics* 43 (2008): 331–40.

Morgan, P. *The Fall of Mussolini: Italy, the Italians and the Second World War*. Oxford, 2007.

Mortimer, E. *The Rise of the French Communist Party 1920–1947*. London, 1984.

Morton, G., B. de Vries, and R. J. Morris, eds. *Civil Society, Associations and Urban Places: Class, Nation and Culture in Nineteenth-Century Europe*. Aldershot, UK, 2006.

Moyn, S. *Christian Human Rights*. Philadelphia, 2015.

———. "Personalism, Community and the Origins of Human Rights." In *Human Rights in the Twentieth Century*, edited by S.-L. Hoffmann, 85–106. Cambridge, UK, 2011.

Müller, C. H. *West Germans against the West: Anti-Americanism in Media and Public Opinion in the Federal Republic of Germany, 1949–68.* Basingstoke, UK, 2010.

Müller, J.-W. *Contesting Democracy: Political Ideas in Twentieth-Century Europe.* New Haven, CT, 2011.

———. "European Intellectual History as Contemporary History." *Journal of Contemporary History* 46 (2011): 574–90.

———. "Militant Democracy." In *The Oxford Handbook of Comparative Constitutional Law,* edited by M. Rosenfeld and A. Sajó, 1253–69. Oxford, 2012.

———. "What Did They Think They Were Doing?: The Political Thought of (the West European) 1968 Revisited." In *Promises of 1968: Crisis, Illusion, and Utopia,* edited by V. Tismaneanu, 73–102. Budapest, 2011.

Müller, T. B. *Krieger und Gelehrte: Herbert Marcuse und die Denksysteme im Kalten Krieg.* Hamburg, 2010.

Müller, T. B., and A. Tooze, eds. *Normalität und Fragilität: Demokratie nach dem Ersten Weltkrieg.* Hamburg, 2015.

Myant, M. *Socialism and Democracy in Czechoslovakia 1945–1948.* Cambridge, UK, 1981.

Needham, D. "Britain's Money Supply Experiment, 1971–73." *English Historical Review* 130 (2015): 89–122.

Nehring, H. "The British and West German Protests against Nuclear Weapons and the Culture of the Cold War, 1957–1964." *Contemporary British History* 19 (2005): 223–41.

———. "'Out of Apathy'. Genealogies of the British 'New Left' in a Transatlantic Context, 1956–1962." In *Between Prague Spring and French May: Opposition and Revolt in Europe, 1960–1980,* edited by M. Klimke, J. Pekelder, and J. Scharloth, 15–31. New York, 2011.

Neri Serneri, S. "Resistenza e insurrezione nel secondo conflitto mondiale: Il Comitato Toscano di Liberazione nazionale verso la 'battaglia di Firenze.'" *Rivista storica Italiana* 131 (2019): 51–92.

Neuville, J., and J. Yerna. *Le choc de l'hiver '60-'61: Les grèves contre la loi unique.* Brussels, 1990.

Nevakivi, J. "From the Continuation War to the Present." In *From Grand Duchy to a Modern State: A Political History of Finland since 1809,* edited by O. Jussila, S. Hentilä, and J. Nevakivi, 215–356. London, 1999.

Newsome, W. B. "The 'Apartment Referendum' of 1959: Toward Participatory Architectural and Urban Planning in Postwar France." *French Historical Studies* 28 (2005): 329–58.

Nicholls, A. J. *The Bonn Republic: West German Democracy, 1945–1990.* London, 1997.

———. *Freedom with Responsibility: The Social Market Economy in Germany 1918–1963.* Oxford, 1994.

Niederacher, S. "Die Entwicklung der Entnazifizierungsgesetzgebung." In *Entnazifizierung zwischen politischem Anspruch, Parteienkonkurrenz und Kaltem Krieg,* edited by M. Mesner, 13–36. Vienna, 2005.

———. "Die öffentliche Rede über Entnazifizierung, 1945–1949." In *Entnazifizierung zwischen politischem Anspruch, Parteienkonkurrenz und Kaltem Krieg,* edited by M. Mesner, 37–58. Vienna, 2005.

Noël, G. "La solidarité agricole européenne: Des congrès d'agriculture à la politique agricole commune." In *Sociétés rurales du XXe siècle*, edited by J. Canal, G. Pécout, and M. Ridolfi, 311–25. Rome, 2004.

Nord, P. *France's New Deal: From the Thirties to the Post-war Era*. Princeton, NJ, 2010.

———. *The Republican Moment: Struggles for Democracy in Nineteenth-Century France*. Cambridge, MA, 1995.

O'Boyle, L. "The Problem of an Excess of Educated Men in Western Europe, 1800–1850." *Journal of Modern History* 42 (1970): 471–95.

O'Hara, G. *From Dreams to Disillusionment: Economic and Social Planning in 1960s Britain*. Basingstoke, UK, 2007.

O'Malley, J. W. *What Happened at Vatican II*. Cambridge, MA, 2008.

Oppermann, M. *Raymond Aron und Deutschland: Die Verteidigung der Freiheit und das Problem des Totalitarismus*. Ostfildern, Germany, 2008.

Orzoff, A. *Battle for the Castle: The Myth of Czechoslovakia in Europe, 1914-1948*. Oxford, 2009.

Osmond, J. *Rural Protest in the Weimar Republic: The Free Peasantry in the Rhineland and Bavaria*. New York, 1993.

Owen, K. *Political Community in Revolutionary Pennsylvania*. Oxford, 2018.

Pagis, J. *May '68: Shaping Political Generations*. Amsterdam, 2018.

Palmer, R. R. Preface to *The Coming of the French Revolution, 1789*, by G. Lefebvre, v–xvii. Princeton, NJ, 1947.

Papastratis, P. *British Policy towards Greece during the Second World War, 1941-1944*. Cambridge, UK, 1984.

Parker, R. *J. K. Galbraith: A Twentieth-Century Life*. London, 2007.

Parness, D. *The SPD and the Challenge of Mass Politics: The Dilemma of the German Volkspartei*. Boulder, CO, 1991.

Un parti dans l'histoire 1945-1995: 50 ans d'action du Parti social chrétien. Louvain-la-Neuve, Belgium, 1996.

Passmore, K. *From Liberalism to Fascism: The Right in a French Province, 1928-1939*. Cambridge, UK, 1997.

Pasture, P. "Catholic and Christian Democratic Views on Europe before and after World War II." In *Christian Democracy across the Iron Curtain: Europe Redefined*, edited by P. Kosicki and S. Lukasicwicz, 25–55. N.p., 2018.

Patel, K. K. "The History of European Integration and the Common Agricultural Policy: An Introduction." In *Fertile Ground for Europe?: The History of European Integration and the Common Agricultural Policy since 1945*, edited by Patel, 7–23. Baden-Baden, 2009.

———. *The New Deal: A Global History*. Princeton, NJ, 2016.

Pawin, R. "Retour sur les 'Trente glorieuses' et la périodisation du second XXe siècle." *Revue d'histoire moderne et contemporaine* 60 (2013): 155–75.

Paxton, R. *French Peasant Fascism: Henry Dorgères's Greenshirts and the Crises of French Agriculture, 1929-1939*. New York, 1997.

Péan, P. *Une jeunesse française*. Paris, 1994.

Peeters, E., and B. Benvindo, eds. *Les décombres de la guerre: Mémoires belges en conflit, 1945-2010*. Waterloo, Belgium, 2012.

Pelinka, A., and M. Welan. *Demokratie und Verfassung in Österreich*. Vienna, 1971.

Pence, K. "Shopping for an 'Economic Miracle': Gendered Politics of Consumer Citizenship in Divided Germany." In *The Expert Consumer: Associations and Professionals in Consumer Society*, edited by A. Chatriot, M.-E. Chessel, and M. Hilton, 105–20. Aldershot, UK, 2006.

Pereira, N., and R. Schär. "Soixante-huitards helvétiques: Etude prosopographique." *Mouvement social* 239 (April–June 2012): 9–23.

Perrier, J. *Michel Debré*. Paris, 2010.

Peterson, M. "Pathways of the Welfare State: Growth and Dependency." In Larsson, Letell, and Thörn, *Transformations*, 23–37.

Petri, R. "Le campagne italiane nello sviluppo economico." In *Sociétés rurales du XXe siècle*, edited by J. Canal, G. Pécout and M. Ridolfi, 75–104. Rome, 2004.

Peukert, D. *Inside Nazi Germany: Conformity, Opposition and Racism in Everyday Life*. London, 1987.

Pittaway, M. *Eastern Europe, 1939–2000*. London, 2004.

———. "The Reproduction of Hierarchy: Skill, Working-Class Culture and the State in Early Socialist Hungary." *Journal of Modern History* 74 (2002): 737–69.

Pizzolato, N. "Transnational Radicals: Labour Dissent and Political Activism in Detroit and Turin (1950–1970)." *International Review of Social History* 56 (2011): 1–30.

Plattner, I. "Josephinismus und Bürokratie." In *Josephinismus als Aufgeklärter Absolutismus*, edited by H. Reinalter, 53–96. Vienna, 2008.

Plehwe, D. Introduction to *The Road from Mont Pèlerin: The Making of the Neoliberal Thought Collective*, edited by P. Mirowski and D. Plehwe, 1–42. Cambridge, MA, 2009.

Poiger, U. *Jazz, Rock and Rebels: Cold War Politics and American Culture in a Divided Germany*. Berkeley, CA, 2000.

Porhel, V. "Factory Disputes in the French Provinces in the '1968 Years': Brittany as Case Study." In J. Jackson, Milne, and Williams, *May 68*, 188–201.

Pradoux, M. *Daniel Mayer, un socialiste dans la Résistance*. Paris, 2002.

Preston, P. *Coming of the Spanish Civil War: Reform, Reaction and Revolution in the Second Republic*. 2nd ed. London, 1994.

Price, R. *People and Politics in France, 1848–70*. Cambridge, UK, 2004.

Pulju, R. J. *Women and Mass Consumer Society in Postwar France*. Cambridge, UK, 2011.

Purtschet, C. *Le rassemblement du peuple français 1947–1953*. Paris, 1965.

Rathkolb, O. *The Paradoxical Republic: Austria, 1945–2005*. New York, 2010.

Rauscher, W. *Karl Renner: Ein österreichischer Mythos*. Vienna, 1995.

Reichold, L. *Geschichte der ÖVP*. Graz, 1975.

Reid, D. "*Etablissement*: Working in the Factory to Make Revolution in France." *Radical History Review* 88 (2004): 83–111.

———. *Opening the Gates: The Lip Affair 1968–1981*. New York, 2018.

———. "The Question of Henri Alleg." *International History Review* 29 (2007): 573–86.

Reiter, H. "Police and Public Order in Italy: The Case of Florence." In *Policing Protest: The Control of Mass Demonstrations in Western Democracies*, edited by D. Della Porta and Reiter, 143–65. Minneapolis, 1998.

Reiter, H., and K. Weinhauer. "Police and Political Violence in the 1960s and 1970s: Germany and Italy in a Comparative Perspective." *European Review of History: Revue européenne d'histoire* 14 (2007): 373–95.

Rémond, R. *1958: Le retour de de Gaulle.* Brussels, 2008.

Reynolds, S. *France between the Wars: Gender and Politics.* London, 1996.

———. "Lateness, Amnesia and Unfinished Business: Gender and Democracy in Twentieth-Century Europe." *European History Quarterly* 32 (2002): 85–109.

———. "Le sacre de la citoyenne?: Réflexions sur le retard français." In *Féminismes et identités nationales: Les processus d'intégration des femmes au politique*, edited by Y. Cohen and F. Thébaud, 71–84. N.p., 1998.

Riall, L. *Garibaldi: Invention of a Hero.* New Haven, CT, 2007.

Rioux, J.-P. *The Fourth Republic.* Cambridge, UK, 1987.

———. "La guerre d'Algérie dans l'histoire des intellectuels français." In *La guerre d'Algérie et les intellectuels français*, 21–35. Cahiers de l'Institut d'histoire du temps présent no. 10. Paris, 1988.

———. "L'héritage difficile ou les contraintes de la Libération." In Bloch-Lainé and Bouvier, *France restaurée*, 15–31.

Risso, L. "Propaganda on Wheels: The NATO Travelling Exhibitions in the 1950s and 1960s." *Cold War History* 11 (2011): 9–25.

Rizi, F. F. *Benedetto Croce and the Birth of the Italian Republic, 1943–1952.* Toronto, 2019.

Roberts, M.-L. *What Soldiers Do: Sex and the American GI in World War II France.* Chicago, 2013.

Robrieux, P. *Histoire intérieure du parti communiste.* Vol. 2. Paris, 1981.

Rodriguez, C., A. Avalos, H. Yılmaz, and A. J. Planert. "Democratization Processes in Defective Democracies: The Case of Turkey." In *Turkey's Democratization Process*, edited by Rodriguez, Avalos, Yılmaz, and Planert, 3–15. Abingdon, UK, 2014.

Rosanvallon, P. *Le sacre du citoyen.* Paris, 1992.

Roseman, M. "Division and Stability: The Federal Republic of Germany, 1949–1989." In *Twentieth-Century Germany: Politics, Culture and Society 1918–1990*, edited by M. Fulbrook, 177–203. London, 2001.

———. *Recasting the Ruhr, 1945–1958: Manpower, Economic Recovery and Labour Relations.* Providence, RI, 1992.

———. "Restoration and Stability: The Creation of a Stable Democracy in the Federal Republic of Germany." In *European Democratization since 1800*, edited by J. Garrard, V. Tollz, and R. White, 141–61. Basingstoke, UK, 2000.

Rosenfeld, A. "'Anarchist Amazons': The Gendering of Radicalism in 1970s West Germany." *Contemporary European History* 19 (2010): 351–74.

Ross, C. *The East German Dictatorship: Problems and Perspectives in the Interpretation of the GDR.* London, 2002.

Ross, G. *Workers and Communists in France: From Popular Front to Eurocommunism.* Berkeley, CA, 1982.

Ross, K. *May '68 and Its Afterlives.* Chicago, 2002.

Rossi-Doria, A. "Italian Women Enter Politics." In *When the War Was Over: Women, War and Peace in Europe 1940–1956*, edited by C. Duchen and I. Bandhauer-Schöffmann, 89–102. London, 2000.

Roussellier, N. "Raymond Aron." In *Dictionnaire des intellectuels français*, edited by J. Julliard and M. Winock, 85–87. Paris, 1996.

Rousso, H. *The Vichy Syndrome: History and Memory in France since 1944*. Cambridge, MA, 1991.

Rubenstein, J. *Soviet Dissidents: Their Struggle for Human Rights*. Boston, MA, 1980.

Rudelle, O. "Gaullisme et crise d'identité républicaine." In *La guerre d'Algérie et les Français*, edited by J.-P. Rioux, 180–201. Paris, 1990.

———. "Le Général de Gaulle et le retour aux sources du constitutionnalisme républicain." In *De Gaulle et la Libération*, edited by Fondation Charles de Gaulle, 11–36. Brussels, 2004.

———. *Mai 58: De Gaulle et la République*. Paris, 1988.

Ruffieux, R. "Quelques approximations sur l'éthique chez Jean Meynaud." In *Jean Meynaud ou l'utopie revisitée: Actes du colloque tenu à l'Université de Lausanne les 25 et 26 septembre 1986*, 359–69. Lausanne, 1988.

Ruin, O. *Tage Erlander: Serving the Welfare State, 1946–1969*. Pittsburgh, PA, 1990.

Runciman, D. *The Confidence Trap: A History of Democracy in Crisis from World War I to the Present*. Princeton, NJ, 2013.

Rupnik, J. *The Other Europe*. London, 1988.

Saage, R. *Der erste Präsident: Karl Renner—eine politische Biografie*. Vienna, 2016.

Sadoun, M. *Les socialistes sous l'occupation: Résistance et collaboration*. Paris, 1982.

Santagata, A. "Les catholiques italiens et la guerre du Vietnam (1965–1968): L'antichambre de la contestation." *Revue d'histoire ecclésiastique* 110 (2015): 215–32.

———. *La contestazione cattolica: Movimenti, cultura e politica dal Vaticano II al '68*. Rome, 2016.

Santarelli, E. *Nenni*. Turin, 1988.

Sarti, R. *Long Live the Strong: A History of Rural Society in the Apennine Mountains*. Amherst, MA, 1985.

Sassoon, D. *One Hundred Years of Socialism: The West European Left in the Twentieth Century*. London, 1996.

Saunders, F. S. *Who Paid the piper?: The CIA and the Cultural Cold War*. London, 1999.

Sauvage, P. *La cité chrétienne (1926–1940): Une revue autour de Jacques Leclercq*. Brussels, 1987.

Schiffers, R. *Elemente direkter Demokratie im Weimarer Regierungssystem*. Dusseldorf, 1971.

Schildt, A. *Die Sozialgeschichte der Bundesrepublik Deutschland bis 1989–90*. Munich, 2007.

———. *Zwischen Abendland und Amerika: Studien zur westdeutschen Ideenlandschaft der 50er Jahre*. Munich, 1999.

Schissler, H., ed. *The Miracle Years: A Cultural History of West Germany, 1949–1968*. Princeton, NJ, 2001.

Schofield, C. *Enoch Powell and the Making of Postcolonial Britain*. Cambridge, UK, 2013.

Schorske, C. "Politics in a New Key: An Austrian Triptych." *Journal of Modern History* 39 (1967): 344–86.

Schrijvers, P. *Liberators: The Allies and Belgian Society, 1944–1945*. Cambridge, UK, 2009.

Schwabe, K. *Jean Monnet: Frankreich, die Deutschen und die Einigung Europas*. Baden-Baden, 2016.

Schwarzenbach, A. *Königliche Traume: Eine Kulturgeschichte der Monarchie von 1789 bis 1997*. Munich, 2012.

Scott-Smith, G. "The Congress for Cultural Freedom: Constructing an Intellectual Atlantic Community." In *Defining the Atlantic Community: Culture, Intellectuals and Politics in the Mid-Twentieth Century*, edited by M. Mariano, 132–45. New York, 2010.

———. "The Congress for Cultural Freedom, the End of Ideology and the 1955 Milan Conference: 'Defining the Parameters of Discourse.'" *Journal of Contemporary History* 37 (2002): 437–55.

———. "The 'Masterpieces of the Twentieth Century' Festival and the Congress for Cultural Freedom: Origins and Consolidation, 1947–52." *Intelligence and National Security* 15 (2000): 121–43.

———. *Networks of Empire: The US State Department's Foreign Leader Program in the Netherlands, France and Britain, 1950–1970*. Brussels, 2008.

Sears, K. *Opposing Hitler: Adam von Trott zu Solz, 1909–1944*. Brighton, UK, 2009.

Segal, L. "Look Back in Anger: Men in the Fifties." In *Male Order: Unwrapping Masculinity*, edited by R. Chapman and J. Rutherford, 68–96. London, 1988.

Seidman, M. *The Imaginary Revolution: Parisian Students and Workers in 1968*. New York, 2004.

Sejersted, F. *The Age of Social Democracy: Norway and Sweden in the Twentieth Century*. Princeton, NJ, 2011.

Setta, S. *L'uomo qualunque 1944/1948*. Rome, 1975.

Shaev, B. "Liberalising Regional Trade: Socialists and European Economic Integration." *Contemporary European History* 27 (2018): 258–79.

Shell, K. *The Transformation of Austrian Socialism*. New York, 1962.

Shennan, A. *De Gaulle*. London, 1993.

———. *Rethinking France: Plans for Renewal, 1940–1946*. Oxford, 1989.

Shepard, T. *The Invention of Decolonization: The Algerian War and the Remaking of France*. Ithaca, NY, 2006.

Sidjanski, D., C. Roig, H. Kerr, R. Inglehart, and J. Nicola. *Les suisses et la politique: Enquête sur les attitudes d'électeurs suisses 1972*. Frankfurt, 1975.

Simmonds, J. C. "Immigrant Fighters for the Liberation of France: A Local Profile of Carmagnole-Liberté in Lyon." In *The Liberation of France: Image and Event*, edited by H. R. Kedward and N. Wood, 29–41. Oxford, 1995.

Skenderovic, D., and C. Späti. *Les années 68: Une rupture politique et culturelle*. Lausanne, 2012.

Skilling, H. G. *Charter 77 and Human Rights in Czechoslovakia*. London, 1981.

———. "'People's Democracy' in Soviet Theory." *Soviet Studies* 3 (1951): 16–33 and 131–49.

Skinner, K. "Agency and Analogy in African History: The Contribution of Extra-mural Studies in Ghana." *History in Africa* 34 (2007): 273–96.

Slobodian, Q. *Globalists: The End of Empire and the Birth of Neoliberalism*. Cambridge, MA, 2018.

Sluga, G. "René Cassin: *Les Droits de l'Homme* and the Universality of Human Rights, 1945–1966." In *Human Rights in the Twentieth Century*, edited by S.-L. Hoffmann, 107–24. Cambridge, UK, 2011.

Sneeringer, J. *Winning Women's Votes: Propaganda and Politics in Weimar Germany*. Chapel Hill, NC, 2002.

Snyder, T. "The Causes of Ukrainian-Polish Ethnic Cleansing 1943." *Past and Present* 179 (2003): 197–234.

Solchany, J. *Comprendre le nazisme dans l'Allemagne des années zéro (1945–1949)*. Paris, 1997.

Sorum, P. C. *Intellectuals and decolonization in France*. Chapel Hill, NC, 1977.

Souillac, R. *Le mouvement Poujade: De la défense professionnelle au populisme nationaliste, 1953–1962*. Paris, 2007.

Specter, M. G. *Habermas: An Intellectual Biography*. Cambridge, UK, 2010.

Spini, V. *I Socialisti e la politica di Plano (1945–1964)*. Florence, 1982.

Stargardt, N. "Legitimacy through War?" In *Beyond the Racial State: Rethinking Nazi Germany*, edited by D. O. Pendas, M. Roseman, and R. F. Wetzell, 402–28. Washington, DC, 2017.

Staub, A. "'Einmal im Leben': Rooting the 'Little Man' to Conservative Values in Postwar West Germany." In *After Fascism: European Case Studies in Politics, Society and Identity since 1945*, edited by M. Berg and M. Mesner, 153–77. Vienna, 2009.

Steege, P. *Black Market, Cold War: Everyday Life in Berlin, 1946–1949*. Cambridge, UK, 2007.

Steinhouse, A. *Workers' Participation in Post-Liberation France*. Lanham, MD, 2001.

Stengers, J. *Léopold III et le gouvernement: Les deux politiques belges de 1940*. Paris, 1980.

Sternhell, Z. *Neither Right nor Left: Fascist Ideology in France*. Berkeley, CA, 1986.

Stone, L. *The Causes of the English Revolution, 1529–1642*. London, 1972.

Stöss, R. *Politics against Democracy: Right-Wing Extremism in West Germany*. Providence, RI, 1991.

Strang, J. "The Other Europe?: Scandinavian Intellectuals and the Fragility of Democracy in the Wake of the Second World War." *Journal of Modern European History* 17 (2019): 500–518.

Streeck, W. *Buying Time: The Crisis of Democratic Capitalism*. London, 2014.

Strote, N. B. *Lions and Lambs: Conflict in Weimar and the Creation of Post-Nazi Germany*. New Haven, CT, 2017.

Suda, Z. *Zealots and Rebels. A History of the Ruling Communist Party of Czechoslovakia*. Stanford, CA, 1980.

Sueur, M. "Approche lexicographique du mot libération dans *La voix du nord* clandestine (avril 1941–août 1944)." *Revue du nord* 57 (1975): 347–64.

Suleiman, E. *Elites in French Society: The Politics of Survival*. Princeton, NJ, 1978.

———. *Politics, Power and Bureaucracy in France: The Administrative Elite*. Princeton, NJ, 1974.

Suleiman, S. R. *Crises of Memory and the Second World War*. Cambridge, MA, 2006.

Sully, M. *A Contemporary History of Austria*. London, 1990.

Suri, J. *Henry Kissinger and the American Century.* Cambridge, MA, 2007.

Sweetser, F., and P. Piepponen. "Fertility Trends and Their Consequences in Finland and the United States." *Journal of Social History* 1 (1967): 101–18.

Tambor, M. "'An Essential Way of Life': Women's Citizenship and the Renewal of Politics in Italy." In *After Fascism: European Case-Studies in Politics, Society and Identity since 1945,* edited by M. Berg and M. Mesner, 205–19. Vienna, 2009.

——. *The Lost Wave: Women and Democracy in Postwar Italy.* Oxford, 2014.

Tarrow, S. *Democracy and Disorder: Protest and Politics in Italy 1965–1975.* Oxford, 1989.

Taylor, L. *Between Resistance and Collaboration: Popular Protest in Northern France, 1940–45.* Basingstoke, UK, 2000.

Terhoeven, P. "Hitler's Children?: German Terrorism as Part of the Transnational 'New Left Wave.'" In *Revolutionary Violence and the New Left: Transnational Perspectives,* edited by A. Martín Alzarez and E. Rey Tristán, 126–44. New York, 2017.

Terracini, U. *Come nacque la Costituzione.* Rome, 1978.

Te Velde, H. *Stijlen van leiderschap: Persoon en politiek van Thorbecke tot Den Uyl.* Amsterdam, 2002.

Theien, I. "Shopping for the 'People's Home': Consumer Planning in Norway and Sweden after the Second World War." In *The Expert Consumer: Associations and Professionals in Consumer Society,* edited by A. Chatriot, M.-E. Chessel, and M. Hilton, 137–49. Aldershot, UK, 2006.

Therborn, G. *European Modernity and Beyond: The Trajectory of European Societies 1945–2000.* London, 1995.

Theunissen, P. *1950, le dénouement de la question royale.* Brussels, 1986.

Thomas, M. *The French Empire at War 1940–45.* Manchester, 1998.

Thomassen, B., and R. Forlenza. "Catholic Modernity and the Italian Constitution." *History Workshop Journal* 81 (2016): 231–51.

——. "Christianity and Political Thought: Augusto Del Noce and the Ideology of Christian Democracy in Post-war Italy." *Journal of Political Ideologies* 21 (2016): 181–99.

Thomson, D. *Democracy in France: The Third and Fourth Republics.* 2nd ed. Oxford, 1952.

Tilly, P. *André Renard: Biographie.* Brussels, 2005.

Timm, A. *The Politics of Fertility in Twentieth-Century Berlin.* Cambridge, UK, 2010.

Timperman, S. "1945–1954: Le PSB s'ouvre aux classes moyennes." *Revue belge d'histoire contemporaine* 28 (1998): 445–98.

Tintori, G. "An Outsider's Vision: Gaetano Salvemini and the 1948 Elections in Italy." *Modern Italy* 16 (2011): 139–57.

Todd, S. "Family Welfare and Social Work in Post-war England." *English Historical Review* 129 (2014): 362–87.

Todorova, M. *Imagining the Balkans.* New York, 1997.

Tompkins, A. *Better Active than Radioactive!: Antinuclear Protest in 1970s France and West Germany.* Oxford, 2016.

Toromanoff, M. *Le drame des houillères.* Paris, 1969.

Torrance, T. "Catchwords of the Left . . . 'Democracy.'" *Free Nation,* 13 April 1978.

Touchard, J. *Le gaullisme 1940–1969.* Paris, 1978.

Toye, R. "Keynes, Liberalism and 'the Emancipation of the Mind.'" *English Historical Review* 130 (2015): 1162–91.

Tronti, M. "Introduzione: Dossetti politico—un problema." In *Scritti politici 1943–1951*, by G. Dossetti, xv–xxviii. Genoa, 1995.

Ullrich, S. *Der Weimar-Komplex: Das Scheitern der ersten deutschen Demokratie und die politische Kultur der frühen Bundesrepublik 1945–1959*. Göttingen, 2009.

Urban, J. B. *Moscow and the Italian Communist Party: From Togliatti to Berlinguer*. London, 1986.

Unger, G. *Gaston Defferre*. Paris, 2011.

Vaizey, H. "Empowerment or Endurance?: War Wives' Experiences of Independence during and after the Second World War in Germany, 1939–1948." *German History* 29 (2011): 57–78.

Vandenbussche, R., ed. *Femmes et résistance en Belgique et zone interdite*. Villeneuve d'Ascq, France, 2007.

Van den Wijngaert, M. *Ontstaan en stichting van de CVP-PSC: De lange weg naar het kerstprogramma*. Brussels, 1976.

Van Doorslaer, R., and E. Verhoeyen. *L'assassinat de Joseph Lahaut: Une histoire de l'anticommunisme en Belgique*. Antwerp, 1987.

Van Kersbergen, K. *Social Capitalism: A Study of Christian Democracy and the Welfare State*. London, 1995.

Van Rahden, T. "Clumsy Democrats: Moral Passions in the Federal Republic." *German History* 29 (2011): 485–504.

Van Schendelen, M.P.C.M. "The Views of Arend Lijphart and Collected Criticisms." *Acta Politica* 19 (1984): 19–55.

Ventresca, R. *From Fascism to Democracy: Culture and Politics in the Italian Election of 1948*. Toronto, 2004.

———. *Soldier of Christ: The Life of Pius XII*. Cambridge, MA, 2013.

Ventura, A. "La società rurale veneta dal fascismo alla Resistenza." In *Società rurale e Resistenza nelle Venezie*, 11–70. Milan, 1978.

Vergnon, G. "La construction de la mémoire du maquis de Vercors: Commémoration et historiographie." *Vingtième Siècle* 49 (1996): 82–97.

Vigna, X. *L'insubordination ouvrière dans les années '68: Essai d'histoire politique des usines*. Rennes, 2007.

Villa, D., ed. *The Cambridge Companion to Hannah Arendt*. Cambridge, UK, 2000.

Vinen, R. *Bourgeois Politics in France, 1945–1951*. Cambridge, UK, 1995.

———. "The End of an Ideology: Right-Wing Antisemitism in France, 1944–1970." *Historical Journal* 37 (1994): 365–88.

———. *National Service: Conscription in Britain, 1945–1963*. London, 2014.

Vion, A. "Town-Twinning in France during the Cold War." *Contemporary European History* 11 (2002): 623–40.

Virgili, F. *Shorn Women: Gender and Punishment in Liberation France*. Oxford, 2002.

Voldman, D. "Les bombardements aériens: Une mise à mort du 'guerrier'?" In *De la violence et des femmes*, edited by C. Dauphin and A. Farge, 146–58. Paris, 1997.

Von der Goltz, A., and B. Waldschmidt-Nelson, eds. *Inventing the Silent Majority in Western Europe and the United States: Conservatism in the 1960s and 1970s*. Washington, DC, 2017.

Von Hirschhausen, U. "From Minority Protection to Border Revisionism: The European Nationality Congress, 1925–38." In *Europeanization in the Twentieth Century: Historical Approaches*, edited by M. Conway and K. K. Patel, 87–109. Basingstoke, UK, 2010.

Wakeman, R. *Modernizing the Provincial City: Toulouse, 1945–1975*. Cambridge, MA, 1997.

Wall, I. *The United States and the Making of Post-War France, 1945–1954*. Cambridge, UK, 1991.

Walsh, M. "Pius XII." In *Modern Catholicism: Vatican II and After*, edited by A. Hastings, 20–26. London, 1991.

Warner, G. "Allies, Government and Resistance: The Belgian Political Crisis of November 1944." *Transactions of the Royal Historical Society* fifth series, 28 (1978): 45–60.

Wasserman, J. *Black Vienna: The Radical Right in the Red City, 1918–1938*. Ithaca, NY, 2014.

Watson, J. "The Internal Dynamics of Gaullism, 1958–1969." DPhil thesis, University of Oxford, 2001.

Waxman, C., ed. *The End of Ideology Debate*. New York, 1968.

Wegs, R., and R. Ladrech. *Europe since 1945*. 4th ed. New York, 1996.

Weijnert, B. *Diffusion of Democracy: The Past and Future of Global Democracy*. Cambridge, UK, 2014.

Weinzierl, E. "The Origins of the Second Republic: A Retrospective View." In *Austria 1945–1995: Fifty Years of the Second Republic*, edited by K. R. Luther and P. Pulzer, 3–27. Aldershot, UK, 1998.

Whitehead, P. *Democratization: Theory and Experience*. Oxford, 2002.

Wierling, D. "Generations as Narrative Communities: Some Private Sources of Public Memory in Postwar Germany." In *Histories of the Aftermath: The Legacies of the Second World War in Europe*, edited by F. Biess and R. G. Moeller, 102–20. New York, 2010.

Wieviorka, O. *Divided Memory: French Recollections of World War II from the Liberation to the Present*. Stanford, CA, 2012.

Wildt, M. "Continuities and Discontinuities of Consumer Mentality in West Germany in the 1950s." In Bessel and Schumann, *Life after Death*, 211–30.

Willame, J. C. "L'Union démocratique belge: Essai de création 'travailliste.'" *Courrier hebdomadaire du CRISP* 743–44 (1976).

Williams, I. *Allies and Italians under Occupation: Sicily and Southern Italy 1943–45*. Basingstoke, UK, 2013.

Wilsford, D. "Studying Democracy and Putting It into Practice: The Contributions of Arend Lijphart to Democratic Theory and to Actual Democracy." In Crepaz, Koeble, and Wilsford, *Democracy and Institutions*, 1–7.

Winock, M. *Histoire politique de la revue "Esprit" 1930–1950*. Paris, 1975.

Woloch, I. "Left, Right and Centre: The MRP and the Post-war Moment." *French History* 21 (2007): 85–106.

Wright, V. *The Government and Politics of France*. London, 1978.

Zahra, T. *The Lost Children: Reconstructing Europe's Families after World War II*. Cambridge, MA, 2011.

Zeller, T. *Driving Germany: The Landscape of the German Autobahn, 1930–1970*. New York, 2007.

A NOTE ON THE TYPE

{≈≈≈w≈≈≈}

THIS BOOK has been composed in Miller, a Scotch Roman typeface designed by Matthew Carter and first released by Font Bureau in 1997. It resembles Monticello, the typeface developed for The Papers of Thomas Jefferson in the 1940s by C. H. Griffith and P. J. Conkwright and reinterpreted in digital form by Carter in 2003.

Pleasant Jefferson ("P. J.") Conkwright (1905–1986) was Typographer at Princeton University Press from 1939 to 1970. He was an acclaimed book designer and AIGA Medalist.

The ornament used throughout this book was designed by Pierre Simon Fournier (1712–1768) and was a favorite of Conkwright's, used in his design of the *Princeton University Library Chronicle*.